Emperor Hirohito and Shōwa Japan

Few historical subjects have aroused as much passionate debate as the Shōwa Emperor, Hirohito. This book, based on extensive research in Japanese and English sources, impartially explores how far Hirohito was responsible for war, why he emerged as a contested 'symbol emperor' in postwar Japan, and his legacy to Japan today.

In reconstructing and evaluating Hirohito's prewar and wartime political role, Dr Large portrays the Emperor's personality, world view and political style while carefully elucidating the Byzantine political context in which he operated, all against the background of momentous crises both within Japan and overseas. The author then examines Hirohito's long career following the defeat of Japan in 1945: his exemption from trial as a war criminal and role during the Occupation; his image-making by the government and the media; his overseas tours, to Europe in 1971 and America in 1975; and contrasting popular reactions to his death in January 1989.

Written for the general reader as well as specialists in Japanese Studies, *Emperor Hirohito and Shōwa Japan* also offers broad insights into the religious and secular nature of imperial authority, power and influence, the political culture of the Japanese aristocracy, the dynamics of the modern Japanese State, and the intricate interplay of nationalism and democracy in Japan since the Pacific War.

THE NISSAN INSTITUTE/ROUTLEDGE JAPANESE STUDIES SERIES

Emperor Hirohito and Shōwa Japan

A political biography

Stephen S. Large

London and New York

First published in 1992
by Routledge
11 New Fetter Lane, London EC4P 4EE

Simultaneously published in the USA and Canada by
Routledge
a division of Routledge, Chapman and Hall, Inc.
29 West 35th Street, New York, NY 10001

© 1992 Stephen S. Large

Typeset in Times by
NWL Editorial Services, Langport, Somerset

Printed and bound in Great Britain by
Biddles Ltd, Guildford and King's Lynn

British Library Cataloguing in Publication Data
A catalogue record for this book is available from the British Library

Library of Congress Cataloging in Publication Data
Large, Stephen S.
Emperor Hirohito and Shōwa Japan: a political biography /
Stephen S. Large.
    p   cm.
Includes bibliographical references and index.
ISBN 0–415–03203–2: £30.00
1. Japan–Politics and government–1926–1989. 2. Hirohito,
Emperor of Japan. 1901–1989. I. Title.
DS888.2.L37   1992
952.03′3–dc20   91–47983
                                                     CIP

ISBN 0-415-03203-2

For Laura and Tim

Contents

Series editor's preface

With growing speed, as we move through the 1990s, Japan in her many aspects is becoming a subject of interest and concern. The successes of the Japanese economy and the resourcefulness of her people have long been appreciated abroad. The increasing impact of Japan on the outside world, with uncertainities about her future direction, also generates suspicion and even hostility in the United States, Western Europe and elsewhere. This is now compounded by the fact that, since 1989, events in the former Soviet Union and in Eastern Europe have begun a revolution in the international system, whose outcome is as yet unclear.

The Nissan Institute/Routledge Japanese Studies Series seeks to foster an informed and balanced – but not uncritical – understanding of Japan. One aim of the series is to show the depth and variety of Japanese institutions, practices and ideas. Another is, by using comparison to see what lessons, positive and negative, can be drawn for other countries. Much contemporary comment on Japan resorts to stereotypes based on outdated or ill-informed ideas. We believe that many aspects of Japan are little known abroad but deserve to be better understood.

If 1989 marks the beginning of a revolution in international politics, it also saw the death of the most controversial and, outside Japan, best known Japanese individual of the twentieth century. Hirohito, the Shōwa Emperor, was a puzzling figure around whom passionate disagreements continue to rage, both outside Japan and in Japan itself. Did he rule Japan in any real sense or was he merely a figurehead? What were his real views on nation, militarism, war and peace? Did he have leadership ability, potential or actual? Could he have prevented Pearl Harbor and thus the Pacific War? How should we evaluate the issue of his war responsibility, and should he have been brought to trial after the war as a war criminal? Did the retention of the Emperor by General MacArthur after the war in any sense open the door to an eventual resurgence of chauvinistic militarism in Japan?

Dr Large addresses these contentious issues soberly and with the multi-faceted approach that they deserve. He has used the available primary sources in Japanese, including those that have become available since the death of the Shōwa Emperor. His book is a crucial landmark in the study of this fascinating subject.

J.A.A. Stockwin
Director, Nissan Institute of Japanese Studies, University of Oxford.

Acknowledgements

I am indebted to too many people for their advice, aid and encouragement to list them all, but in particular I wish to express my appreciation to Arthur Stockwin, Alan Rix, Roger Hackett, the late Louis Allen, John Pritchard, Ian Nish, Michael Cooper, Rikki Kersten and my colleagues in Japanese Studies at the University of Cambridge: Richard Bowring, Carmen Blacker, Mark Morris, Peter Kornicki, Hugh Whittaker and Haruko Laurie. Dr Peter Mathias, Master of Downing College, Cambridge, thoughtfully drew my attention to the excellent article by E.J.H Corner on the Emperor's scientific career. Mrs J. Sheldon graciously permitted me access to the files of her husband, the late Charles D. Sheldon. I received invaluable assistance from Noboru Koyama, curator of the Japanese collection at the University of Cambridge; Frank Shulman, curator of the East Asia Library at the University of Maryland; Mrs H. Murakami, curator of the Gordon W. Prange collection at Maryland; the library staff at the Gerald R. Ford Library in Ann Arbor, Michigan, the School of Oriental and African Studies, and many other collections in Britain, the United States, Japan and Australia.

My research for this book was generously funded by the British Academy and the University of Cambridge. I am very grateful for the help I received all along the way from Peter Sowden and his associates at Routledge. I cannot adequately thank my wife, Kerstin, who patiently endured my scholarly preoccupations and suggested stylistic improvements. The book is dedicated to my children, Laura and Tim, of whom I am very proud.

Any errors of fact and judgment are my responsibility alone.

CONVENTIONS

In this book, except in the case of Westerners of Japanese ancestry, Japanese names are given in the proper Japanese order, with the surname preceding the given name. Long vowels are indicated by the use of macrons but these are omitted in the case of a few well-known place names, e.g. Tōkyō, Ōsaka and Kyōto.

In keeping with the Japanese custom of referring to a deceased emperor according to his reign name and not his personal name, which indeed was rarely used during his lifetime, Hirohito is mostly identified in these pages as the 'Shōwa Emperor', or the 'Emperor'. The same applies to his modern predecessors, the Meiji and Taishō Emperors.

Introduction

The Crown Prince and Regent, Hirohito, became the 124th emperor of Japan at the age of twenty-five, upon the death of his father, the Taishō Emperor, at 1:25 a.m. on 25 December 1926. This historical transition occurred not in Tokyo but at the Hayama detached palace, located on Sagami Bay south of the capital, where Taishō had spent his last days attended by the Crown Prince, other members of the imperial family, and court officials. In a brief accession ceremony (*kenji togyo no gi*), performed at 3:15 a.m., the new sovereign received the imperial seal and replicas of two of the three imperial regalia which always accompanied the Emperor, the sacred sword and jewel.[1]

While this ceremony took place in the cold of the night at Hayama, a Shintō priest at the imperial palace sanctuary in Tokyo reported to the gods the death of Taishō and the accession of the new emperor (Shikama 1980: 439–40). Later that day it was announced in an imperial edict that his reign would be known as 'Shōwa', or 'illustrious peace' (Murakami S. 1983: 255–6).[2] In November 1928, after a period of mourning for Taishō, the Shōwa Emperor would perform the more elaborate ancient rituals of the *daijōsai* ('The Great Feast of Enthronement'),[3] in the former imperial capital of Kyoto.

Thus began the Shōwa era which, lasting slightly more than sixty-two years, from 1926 to 1989, is the longest imperial reign on reliable record in Japanese history and the longest in recent world history. During this period, Japan experienced great upheaval and change wrought by the Depression, a series of wars culminating in the devastation of the country and the destruction of the empire, an unprecedented foreign occupation, recovery from the ruins of war, and the country's rapid development as an economic superpower. It is the purpose of this book, intended for the informed general reader as well as the specialist in modern Japanese studies, to explore, within a concise interpretative narrative, the political role and significance of Emperor Hirohito (1901–1989) throughout these momentous national vicissitudes of Shōwa history.

Although he was not by any means always at the center of events in this history, the Shōwa Emperor was one of the most controversial figures in modern times. In particular, the role he played in the decade of Japanese expansionism leading to the 1941–1945 Asian-Pacific War remains to this day a subject of great debate both within Japan and overseas. But in addition to this question of his 'war responsibility' (*sensō sekinin*), which has dominated most historical accounts, controversy also surrounds the forty-odd years of his reign since Japan's defeat in 1945, as this book, one of the first in Western research to consider his postwar career in some detail, will show.

To illustrate briefly some of the main issues in these debates, on the one hand there are those who portray early Shōwa Japan as virtually the victim of the Emperor (*tennō*) and of the 'emperor system' (*tennōsei*), which 'denotes a framework of power ... including the imperial institution as its keystone, the palace bureaucracy, the legal system anchored in the constitution, the military, the police, the courts, the civil bureaucracy, even the political parties, and so forth' (Bix 1982: 4). As the Japanese historian, Inoue Kiyoshi, states,

> The man Hirohito was no doubt a sympathetic and courteous gentleman to his family and advisers. But Emperor Hirohito reigned at the summit of an atrocious emperor system fascism and continued to direct both aggressive wars and a system which oppressed the people.
>
> (Inoue 1975: 84)

Depicting the Shōwa Emperor as both a willing symbol and active agent of authoritarianism and war, David Bergamini likewise held that Hirohito was instrumental in a ramified 'imperial conspiracy' that led early Shōwa Japan into repression at home and aggression overseas, ending in the Pacific War (Bergamini 1971). A more recent account by the journalist, Edward Behr, is also critical, although unlike Bergamini's, it emphasizes not so much Hirohito's sins of commission as a war leader than his sins of omission, suggesting that he could have done more than he did to prevent war (Behr 1989).[4]

A sequel to these critical perceptions of the Emperor in early Shōwa history is the conviction many share, especially in Japan, that his continuation on the throne and the perpetuation of the Japanese monarchy after the Pacific War meant that the dangers of emperor-centered nationalism and militarism still existed in postwar Shōwa Japan behind the facade of democracy, hence the need to remain vigilant lest Japan be victimized once again by its imperial institution. Irokawa Daikichi typified this concern in 1983 when he wrote, 'To resurrect the Emperor-system in its full power, as some conservative politicians now advocate, is dangerous dallying with illusion. ... There is the real possibility that Japan will turn into a new and monstrous miltary power' (Irokawa 1983: 138).

On the other hand, there are studies which portray the Emperor as a victim of political elites, in particular the military, who manipulated him for their own ulterior purposes leading to aggression and war in early Shōwa. In these works, he emerges as a reluctant symbol and passive agent of dark forces beyond his control. Thus, drawing a distinction between the Emperor and the emperor system, Charles Sheldon writes, what was at fault was not the Emperor but the Emperor system which permitted the abuse by the power-holders of a power greatly enhanced by the general emotional commitment to the myth-laden Imperial institution as a focus for loyalty and patriotism, with its potential for both good and evil.

(Sheldon 1978: 34)

From this perspective, rather than directing a 'fascist' regime which plunged Japan into war, the Emperor personally opposed fascism, militarism, and war, although not the maintenance of the empire he had inherited at the beginning of his reign, but all in vain. 'Hirohito's moderateness and liberal attitudes checked, for a while, the military's attempts to control foreign policy in the 1930s, and brought about the end of the Pacific War in 1945', writes another historian, Ben-Ami Shillony, who also sees him in this more positive light (Shillony 1973: 95). A similar interpretation is found in Leonard Mosley's popular book, the first full-length study of the Emperor in English, and in books by such Japanese writers as Kojima Noboru and Yamamoto Shichihei, to cite but several (Mosley 1966; Kojima 1981; Yamamoto 1989).

The corollary of these assessments of the Emperor in early Shōwa is that his survival and that of the monarchy after Japan's defeat in the Pacific War is not to be deplored, for it enabled him to contribute constructively to Japan's subsequent revival. John Hall emphasizes this theme when, observing that the postwar popularity of the Emperor was no longer widely based on the kind of extremist nationalism which had predominated earlier, he wrote in 1968,

The Emperor today stands as symbol, not of some irrational 'superiority' of the Japanese race, but rather as a projection of their own pride in their own achievement as a modern people; not as a reminder of the terrors of war and humiliation of defeat but rather as symbol of Japan's purity of intent to lead the world in working for peace.

(Hall 1968a: 62)

Unfortunately, all too often in these debates, the Emperor himself is lost in the mists of generalization and inference. But however one interprets his career, the fact is that there is much that will probably never be known about him and for this reason the controversies concerning his political role and place in history may never be resolved to everyone's satisfaction. Although this problem of inadequate information may be somewhat relieved as new written evidence comes to light in the years ahead, the point remains that those documents which are now available will always pose special difficulties to historians.

To begin with, they do not include the personal writings of the Emperor himself: for instance, any diary he may have kept, personal letters, and the like. Either these do not exist or they have been classified, making them unavailable to the historian. Certain records of his conversations are also classified and other materials that might have illuminated different aspects of his political career did not survive the war, owing to their deliberate destruction by Japanese officials or to the effects of Allied bombing. An important exception is a new source, published in 1990, comprising the Emperor's personal account of early Shōwa history: 'Shōwa tennō no doku-haku hachijikan' ('The Shōwa Emperor's Eight-Hour Monologue', hereafter cited as STDH). The circumstances of this document, which was originally recorded in the spring of 1946, are discussed in Chapter 6 of this book.

Because of the dearth of primary materials left behind by the Emperor himself, the historian is forced to rely largely on a core of indirect evidence comprising the memoirs and diaries of court officials, politicians, military men and foreign officials who interacted with the Emperor in one context or another, as well as on Japanese government documents and various secondary sources including biographies, histories, and so forth. Familiar primary sources in this genre include, for example, the memoirs of Harada Kumao, the diaries of General Honjō Shigeru and Kido Kōichi, and the memoranda of General Sugiyama Gen, along with many others. These have been augmented recently by the diaries, published in 1990, of General Nara Takeji, Makino Nobuaki, and two of General Tōjō Hideki's private secretaries. These new materials, and the above-mentioned record of the Emperor's 1946 'Monologue', are especially valuable when used together in researching Shōwa Japanese history (Large 1991a).

In general, these core materials are informative and their authenticity is not in serious question.[5] However, they often omit valuable information at crucial points in Shōwa history, they inevitably reflect the bias of their authors and their contents are often susceptible to different interpretations. Where a given source is the only one available on a particular matter, and hence cannot be cross-checked, these problems are especially formidable.

To compensate, some books on the Shōwa Emperor (in particular Bergamini's) have relied a good deal on oral evidence gleaned from interviews with Japanese who, however, either because they declined to be identified or because the author for whatever reason decided not to identify them, yielded information which cannot be verified by using written evidence. The value of oral history notwithstanding, problems of verification have led to the decision not to undertake interviews, and instead to rely on as wide a range of written primary and secondary sources as possible, in researching this book.

Finally, there is much that is unknown in particular about the Emperor's political career during the long span of Shōwa history since 1945 when, under the new constitutional framework established during the Occupation of Japan, he became a 'symbol of the state' divorced from direct participation in the daily affairs of government. To be sure, the significant and complex role he played as a contested symbol in Japanese politics after 1945 can be detailed. But because he seems to become an increasingly abstract figure in the 'long postwar' of Shōwa history (Gluck 1990: 3), less precision is possible where his specific political activities are concerned. It is in this sense that less is known about his postwar than his prewar and wartime political career.

Yet while, for all of these reasons, he remains something of a 'shadow emperor', it is still possible to clarify his historical role, perhaps with more objectivity than is found in many earlier studies now that the Shōwa period has ended and can be viewed as a whole. In pursuing this objective, the chapters that follow relate the Shōwa Emperor to the political context in which he operated in considering three important questions which apply to his entire reign. First, as the incumbent monarch, how did he perceive his function and role in Japanese political life? Second, how did he act upon his perceptions at critical junctures when he and the nation were tested? And third, without implying that he figured prominently in everything that happened or that he invariably had a decisive impact on events, what were the political consequences of his actions?

The governing assumption here in approaching these questions is that political figures are neither completely free agents nor are they completely determined, in what they think, say, and do, by their environment; 'Not even a man as powerful as Louis XIV was free in any absolute sense of the word. No more was he "absolutely determined" ' (Elias 1983: 30). Therefore, as Steven Lukes suggests, the study of power includes the interplay of 'external' and 'internal constraints' on a political actor. Whereas 'external constraints' in the environment limit or exclude options available to him, thereby limiting what Lukes defines as 'opportunity', the actor's 'internal constraints' limit or exclude options 'which are unacceptable to, beyond the capacity of, or even inconceivable' to the subject. That is, they limit the subject's 'ability' to respond to 'opportunity' (Lukes 1977: 10–13). Accordingly, a given political career may be understood as comprising 'a web of possibilities for agents, whose nature is both active and structured, to make choices and pursue strategies within given limits, which in consequence expand and contract over time' (Lukes 1977: 29).

With these assumptions in mind, it is important now to indicate, in necessarily general terms, how history had shaped the Emperor's political environment by the time he took office, in December 1926, when the Shōwa era began.

THE SHŌWA INHERITANCE: IMPERIAL AUTHORITY, POWER AND INFLUENCE

From ancient times, the Japanese sovereign was held to be an *akitsumikami*, or 'manifest deity', the lineal descendant of the legendary Sun Goddess, Amaterasu Ōmikami, and her divine progeny. According to the myths of Shintō ('the way of the gods'),[6] she gave the sacred sword and jewel, along with the third part of the imperial regalia, the sacred mirror, to her grandson, Ninigi no Mikoto, before he descended to the Japanese archipelago. Ever since then they had been handed down through the generations from one sovereign to the next as symbols of imperial authority deriving from Amaterasu (Bock 1990: 36–7).

But to the extent that this image of 'manifest deity' connoted that the sovereign would truly rule on the basis of his (and in a few early instances, her) essentially religious authority, it was misleading, for in fact few Japanese sovereigns were able to do so. Instead, historians agree that the primary function of the emperors was 'sacerdotal or religious' in character and that it eclipsed their secular political role (Webb 1968: 15). Serving principally as 'chief priests' or 'shaman kings', they were indispensable for their performance of such annual rice-crop rituals as the *kannamesai* and the *niinamesai*, to propitiate the gods in ensuring a good harvest (Mori 1979: 529–30). This ritual association of the emperor, the gods, and the land was one of the distinctive features of Shintō, Japan's indigenous religion.

The sacerdotal functions of the emperor continued to predominate even as, beginning in the seventh century, the monarchy acquired new Chinese dimensions which ostensibly strengthened the political hand of the sovereign. Neither the subsequent development of a Chinese-style capital nor the adaptation of Chinese-style institutions of imperial rule, could obscure the reality that the emperors, with several exceptions, were politically impotent. In the late Heian period (794–1185), the Fujiwara Regents held sway at court and from the Kamakura period (1185–1333) onwards, real secular power remained in the hands of the shōguns, whose political domination reflected the paramount position of the *bushi*, or samurai, class.

As to why the monarchy survived at all in these politically unfavorable circumstances, 'It may well be that the loss of real power by the Emperor and his retention chiefly of ritual sovereignty served in the long run to protect the Imperial House from destruction' (Hall 1965: 154). More precisely, what ensured this survival was the sovereign's 'legitimating function' by which he, through his religious authority, historically conferred legitimacy on elites who ruled Japan in his name (Webb 1968: 64), and for whom he was a 'symbol of elite unity' (Hall 1965: 154). Thus, by the Tokugawa period (1600–1868) the imperial institution had long since been reduced to being 'one of the state's adornments' (Webb 1968: 223). The emperor was esteemed for the most part as a patron of the aristocratic arts at the imperial court in Kyoto and as a 'sacred legitimizer'. Otherwise, politically, he was virtually a captive of the shōgun who governed Japan from Edo.

Despite his political powerlessness, however, during the Tokugawa era the emperor was increasingly seen in Confucian terms as 'a symbol of virtue. He was a physical reminder . . . that society was founded on universal principles of order and morality' (Webb 1968: 182–97). This perception of the emperor drew heavily from precedents in China where historically, at least in theory, the sovereign had personified moral and ethical perfection which was to be emulated in government affairs and social life generally (Webb 1968: 16–18). Significantly, it gave rise to the belief, which continued into modern times as a hallmark of Japanese nationalism, that the 'imperial way' (*kōdō*) was essentially moral in character.

The opening of a secluded Japan and the imposition of the so-called 'unequal treaties' by the Western powers in the mid-nineteenth century dramatically produced new circumstances which were to greatly change the political position of the monarchy. The emperor was politically 'rediscovered' and made the symbolic focus of the armed movement to overthrow the Tokugawa shōgunate so that a new central government capable of saving Japan from foreign exploitation could be established. In this context the rebel slogan, *sonnō jōi* ('revere the emperor and expel the barbarians') signalled the emergence of the imperial court after centuries of political obscurity.[7] Then, once the destruction of the shōgunate was accomplished in the Meiji Restoration of 1868, with the emperor transferred from Kyoto to the shōgun's castle in Tokyo, formerly Edo, there began the modern transformation of the Japanese monarchy through the 'invention of tradition',[8] blending certain elements adapted from Japan's historical legacy and others adapted from the contemporary West. It was these which constituted the Shōwa inheritance with respect to imperial authority, power, and influence.

Their synthesis is most evident in the Meiji constitution, promulgated by Emperor Meiji on 11 February 1889. A hybrid of traditional Japanese and modern Western influences – the latter mostly reflecting Prussian precedents – the constitution ascribed extensive imperial prerogatives, or *taiken*, to the emperor which served notice that he would henceforth rule, as well as reign over, Japan.[9] Article IV began, 'The Emperor is the Head of the Empire, combining in Himself the rights of sovereignty'. Articles V–VIII elaborated his supreme legislative powers, including for example his power to convoke, open, close, and prorogue the imperial Diet, to dissolve the lower house of representatives and to issue imperial ordinances 'in place of law'. In addition, article XI, it should be stressed, gave him 'the supreme command of the Army and Navy'. Article XIII further empowered him to declare war, make peace, and conclude treaties; article XIV stated, 'The Emperor proclaims the law of siege'; and so on.

The point is worth elaborating that these comprehensive powers, which signified an 'absolute monarchy' (*zettai ōsei*), were grounded on the emperor's traditional religious authority, now reclaimed and firmly embedded in the law of the land (Nakano 1987: 133). In promulgating the constitution, the Meiji Emperor declared, 'The rights of sovereignty of State, We have inherited from our Ancestors', in a 'lineal succession unbroken for ages eternal'. This claim to divine lineage was reiterated in article I of the constitution, 'The Empire of Japan shall be reigned over and governed by a line of Emperors unbroken for ages eternal', and in article III, 'The Emperor is sacred and inviolable'. That the sovereign would serve as the spiritual 'pivot' of Japan was intended by the government leaders who were responsible for drafting the constitution, including, above all, Itō Hirobumi (Toriumi 1980: 113). In short, the emperor was the sacred pillar of the *kokutai*, or 'national polity'.

This religious image of the emperor was one of Japan's most potent 'modern myths' (Gluck 1985). For the Meiji leaders, it buttressed 'the German historicist theory of the organic state which they had chosen to be the basis of the first constitution' (Powles 1976–7: 34). In the Meiji period (1868–1912) and thereafter, the idea that the monarch was a 'living god' was expressed in the lofty language of successive imperial rescripts. It was also expressed in the rituals of State Shintō at the Ise Grand Shrine and other imperial shrines, including the palace shrines where, for example, the harvest rites were still performed by the emperor each year, along with many other rites.

These rites, supervised by the board of ceremonies in the imperial household ministry, or Kunaishō, were conducted out of public view, but because 'it is central to its potency as a symbol that it is remote, set apart, omnipresent as the ultimate . . . means of succor' (Edelman 1967: 5–6), the ritual distance of the emperor from the people only deepened their awe of him. The overall result was a fusion of monarchy and nationalism through the 'mythologization of history and the historicization of myth', in what was, in effect, an 'immanental theocracy' (Kitagawa 1974: 226). As John Coleman writes, 'State Shintō was a civil religion of nationalism' in which the deification of the emperor resembled the apotheosis of the Roman emperors (Coleman 1970: 72).

The process, beginning in Meiji Japan, whereby the 'invention of tradition' made the emperor the symbol of the modern Japanese state and of modern Japanese nationalism, emphasized many sub-symbols of imperial authority and power. Yasukuni Shrine, established in Tokyo in 1869 to enshrine the spirits of Japan's war dead in the service of the emperor, is one important example. Others included various national festival days, such as Kigensetsu, celebrated on 11 February to commemorate the accession of the first emperor, Jimmu, and the historic founding of the empire; the national song, 'Kimi ga yo', the words of which praised the eternal nature of imperial rule;[10] the national flag, Hi no maru, which likewise denoted the sacred majesty of the emperor, as brilliant as the sun; the honorific titles, and the decorations and medals (*kunshō*), which he bestowed on officials and dignitaries as blessings of imperial rule; and finally the custom of reign names (*nengō*), which suggested that even a given period of historical time was the emperor's possession.

Of course, not every Japanese citizen believed in the 'modern myths' of imperial supremacy projected by these sub-symbols and more generally by the nationalist ideology of the emperor cult, especially as it was cultivated in the schools and the army (Tsurumi K. 1970: 99–137). But the vast majority of the population came to take these myths very seriously and in any case what counts in the end is that because he theoretically legitimized not only the state but the entire social, political, and moral order as the fountainhead of imperial rule, publicly, 'The Emperor played the role of a god and the people played the role of subjects' (Katō 1974: 211). This was true in Meiji Japan. It was also true in Taishō (1912–1926) and early Shōwa Japan (1926–1945).

Yet, it was equally true that where the emperor's powers were concerned the Meiji constitution contained a profound contradiction, attributable in the first instance to Itō Hirobumi, for it incorporated both the notion of absolute monarchy, discussed above, and that of limited monarchy. Over the years this ambiguous amalgam was to provoke intense controversy among constitutional theorists who interpreted the constitution variously. In fact, so great was the confusion that by Shōwa, 'No authoritative voice or body could have said ... exactly what the Emperor's position was in relation to the major functions and problems of government' (Maxon [1957] 1975: 8).

In his comments on the constitution, Itō held that because the emperor is the ' "pivot" which sustains our country ... the first principle of our constitution is the respect for the sovereign rights of the Emperor'. Significantly, though, Itō added: 'But at the same time, in order to prevent the danger of abuse in the exercise of these sovereign powers, clear checks and limits have been established. The ministers are thus held responsible, so power may not be abused' (Pittau 1967: 177–8).

This principle applied in particular to those administrative imperial prerogatives categorized as *kokumuken*, or 'prerogatives in the duties of state', which required the advice of ministers of state (Shinobu 1967: 666). Specifically, article LV stated, 'The respective Ministers of State shall give their advice to the Emperor and be responsible for it. All laws, Imperial Ordinances and Imperial Rescripts of whatever kind that relate to the affairs of State require the counter-signature of a Minister of State.' Replying to the question, 'Was the Meiji Constitution so formulated that the Emperor could exercise power on a personal basis?', Yasuda Hiroshi points out that this article was deliberately intended 'to prevent the possibility of any arbitrary or personal exercise of will by the Emperor and to make the cabinet a pivotal state organ'. The result was not a system of personal rule by the sovereign but a 'bureaucratic monarchy' in which his principal function was to legitimize bureaucratic rule (Yasuda 1990: 40–1).

Besides the principle that cabinet ministers were responsible for advising the emperor in formulating government policy, there were other major qualifications of imperial power in the constitution. Article IV asserted that the emperor exercises the rights of sovereignty 'according to the provisions of the present Constitution', that is, not in an unlimited, absolute sense, and article V read, 'The Emperor exercises the legislative power with the consent of the Diet', which again qualified his legislative prerogative. Regarding imperial ordinances which he could issue 'in place of law' when the Diet was not sitting, article VIII stipulated, 'Such Imperial Ordinances are to be laid before the Imperial Diet at its next session, and when the Diet does not approve said Ordinances, the Government shall declare them to be invalid for the future'. Article IX added, in part, 'But no Ordinance shall in any way alter any of the existing laws'.

Taken together, these articles reinforced the concept of limited monarchy with respect to the sovereign's *kokumuken*, including his administrative prerogative in military affairs as stipulated in article XII which reads, 'The Emperor determines the organization and peace standing of the Army and

Navy.' In practice, this meant that he would do so upon the advice of the army and navy ministers in the cabinet.

In contrast to the emperor's *kokumuken*, his supreme command prerogative, or *tōsuiken*, provided for in article XI, was distinguished by the fact that it did not depend upon or require the advice of ministers of state and was not part of the cabinet's jurisdiction. Rather, he exercised this prerogative with the advice and assistance of the army and navy chiefs of staff. As in the Prussian military system, which the Japanese adapted to their own circumstances, the chiefs alone were responsible for preparing and acting upon matters of strategy and military operations, as the regulations governing their offices clearly stipulated. Moreover, their independence from the cabinet in this regard was enhanced by their right of 'direct access' (*iaku jōsōken*) to the emperor when reporting to him on their policies, including the strengthening of the armed forces, for which they sought imperial sanction. Once sanction was granted, they then reported to the cabinet through the army or navy minister (Masuda 1990: 78).

In theory, this 'independence of the supreme command' (*tōsuiken no dokuritsu*) greatly accentuated the emperor's 'absolute' powers at the expense of the limitations on his power discussed above. But in practice it was always uncertain as to whether the emperor or the chiefs of staff held the initiative, or had the final say, in exercising the supreme command prerogative. To anticipate a major problem which became especially acute in the Shōwa era, 'there was no clear definition regarding either the scope of the right of supreme command or the person responsible for exercising it' (Masuda 1990: 79).

Because of the tensions it contained between absolute and limited monarchy, the Meiji constitution was a most controversial document. Itō Hirobumi had to defend his qualifications of imperial rule from critics on the privy council before the council finally ratified his draft (Pittau 1967: 179–80). Then, well after these objections were overcome and the constitution was promulgated in 1889, controversies erupted over the nature and scope of the emperor's powers (Banno 1990a). Significantly, though, after an initial period of uncertainty, the Meiji Emperor himself made it a point to fully comply with the concept of limited monarchy, thereby ensuring that his extensive prerogatives were exercised 'only on the advice and consent of the heads of the various state organs and of the elder statemen' who governed Japan in his name (Toriumi 1980: 114). He consistently 'refrained from taking the initiative in handling state affairs', although in private audience he did not hesitate to press ministers to explain specific policies when he was personally unhappy with their advice (Toriumi 1980: 117).

During his reign, from 1912 to 1926, when Japan entered a more democratic phase of political and social development typified by liberal party rule and the proliferation of popular social movements, the Taishō Emperor likewise deferred to his ministers of state, sharing as he did his father's reluctance, as a constitutional monarch, to interfere in state affairs. In his case, however, constant ill health also accounts for Taishō's political self-restraint.

Afflicted with the residual effects of meningitis which he had suffered as a child, he was both mentally and physically unfit for most of his reign.

Nevertheless, however much the Meiji and Taishō Emperors personally complied with the notion of limited monarchy, the people venerated them as absolute monarchs because of their public image as all-powerful rulers possessing sacred authority. The Meiji Emperor, in particular, was idolized. After his extensive tours throughout Japan, many of his subjects 'enshrined places where he rested or venerated things he touched' and offered rice cakes to his image when praying to their own ancestors before the altar at home (Mori 1979: 551). When he died in 1912 he was widely honored as a proud symbol of modernity, including constitutional government as well as the nation's industrial progress and acquisition of empire (Gluck 1985: 215–16). But the outpouring of popular affection in mourning his death also manifested a religious reverence for Meiji which the 'invention of tradition' had cultivated in his era.

The Taishō Emperor was less esteemed. However, notwithstanding his physical and mental debilities, which resulted in his withdrawal from political affairs and the appointment of Crown Prince Hirohito as Regent in 1921, he, too, was generally regarded as an 'animate flag' (Kawai 1960: 74). To illustrate, in a rare national survey of industrial workers carried out by a Tokyo Imperial University team in 1923, of 3,500 replies to the question of who was the 'greatest person' they could think of, 739 recorded Taishō, placing him at the top of the list, ahead of even Emperor Meiji, the Buddha, and many other luminaries (Nakamura M. 1986: 128–9).[11]

Altogether, the contradictory concepts of absolute and limited monarchy in the Meiji constitution contributed to a situation in which the emperor 'was an absolute monarch to the people, but within the ruling class he was treated in terms of the tacit understanding . . . that he was a constitutional monarch' (Kuno 1978: 63). Whatever the perception of his role, however, the reality in practice was that he had little political power in his own right and in this respect, his position resembled that of Japanese sovereigns down through the centuries. For example, he appointed the prime minister, but only on the recommendation of his closest advisers at court. He had virtually no say in the appointment of cabinet ministers and did not attend cabinet meetings. It was unclear whether the emperor could veto cabinet policy but in any event convention dictated that he did not do so in Meiji and Taishō Japan.

The fact was that his prerogatives were delegated, to the cabinet in the case of his executive prerogative and to the Diet in the instance of his legislative prerogative. His power to make treaties was exercised by the foreign ministry and his power to make war and peace was likewise exercised by his government. Furthermore, as explained, his administrative powers with respect to the military were exercised by the army and navy ministers in the cabinet and his prerogative of supreme command, again in practice, was exercised by the army and navy chiefs of Staff. As was true of emperors in the past, therefore, the modern Japanese emperor was to reign, but not rule.

Rather, his chief function in government was still the performance of the monarch's traditional 'legitimating function'. An important theoretical underpinning for this role was the imperial house law (*Kōshitsu tenpan*), promulgated on the same day as the Meiji constitution. This law established succession through the male line to the emperor's oldest son (article I). Its other sections governed virtually every aspect of court affairs, ranging from procedures of accession and 'coronation', honorific styles of address used at court and provisions for a regency should the emperor be gravely incapacitated, to the management of the emperor's hereditary estates and expenditures, which were defrayed from the national budget but administered by the imperial household ministry. However, the law's main effect for the purposes of this discussion was that by it, 'the imperial house was placed in a transcendental but symbiotic relation to political power', giving the emperor autonomy from the government and placing him 'above politics', in a position to bestow legitimacy on his government and its policies through his supreme authority without being responsible for those policies himself (Titus 1974: 46).

In his study of the Japanese monarchy during the Tokugawa period Herschel Webb writes,

> One must be especially on guard against falling into the error, fostered by the surface meaning of contemporary accounts of the matter, of speaking of 'imperial decisions' where one means decisions made by the emperor's ministers. . . . There has been a persistent legal fiction that the court's decisions emanated from the emperor.
>
> (Webb 1968: 122)

Webb's observation applies equally to the emperor's position as sacred legitimizer in the Shōwa inheritance. The emperor formally declared the policies of his government as the 'imperial will' but could not impose his own, personal will, on state affairs; he 'was the transmitter, not the independent judge of the Imperial Will' (Titus 1974: 40). In this sense, he was a 'transcendental prisoner' of the political system (Titus 1974: 16).

To recapitulate, the emperor's situation, by Shōwa, was paradoxical in the extreme: he possessed supreme religious authority but little political power as a reigning, but not a ruling, monarch. To employ different imagery, as symbol of the nation he was the 'pole star' (Titus 1974: 5), or the 'sun' (Bix 1982: 4), of government in Japan but was about as remote from actual power as these celestial metaphors suggest. He was called 'Emperor'.[12] Yet if the term conjures up images of Caesar, the Russian Tsar, or the German Kaiser, it was a misnomer. Perhaps 'Mikado', even with its Gilbert and Sullivan connotations, would have been better, for he was far more the 'exalted gate' of government, a symbol of power, than the wielder of power.

Imperial influence, as distinct from authority and power, is quite another matter, however. It has been suggested elsewhere that while power is the capacity to apply sanctions in exercising authority, influence, based on prestige, relies not on sanctions but on the ability to manipulate perceptions of alternatives in the course of decision-making in order to obtain a desired result (Bell 1975: 21–8, 75–80). By its subtle nature,

> influence appears at once to be more pervasive and potentially more precise than power. Its bases are not *control* of the environment but *knowledge* about the environment and an insight into the decision-making process by which individuals choose how to act . . .
>
> (Bell 1975: 76, italics Bell's)

It is a central task of this book to investigate how, and with what intentions and effects, the Shōwa Emperor endeavored to exert political influence. Here, however, the general question arises, how much influence did the modern Japanese emperor have?

Potentially, he had considerable influence, due to the process of 'working through the court', whereby competing elites jockeyed to obtain ritual sanction for a given policy in declaring it as the imperial will (Imai 1973: 56). This provided him with opportunities to influence decisions before a consensus was reached, which he would duly ratify as 'sacred legitimizer'.

To reiterate, Emperor Meiji frequently endeavored to influence government leaders when he questioned them at court about their policies and in that he was often successful, he was no mere 'puppet' (Toriumi 1980: 115–16). The Taishō Emperor was less influential but during his reign, the greater political pluralism of 'Taishō democracy' and the growing sectarianism of institutions involved in national decision-making made the court an increasingly important clearing house of policy resolution. Therefore, by Shōwa, the emperor, whose political activity was largely confined to the private zone of the court, was in an enhanced position to register informal influence on policies that he would sanction.

It should be appreciated, however, that no emperor could exert imperial influence autonomously. Like any sovereign, he was enmeshed in a 'network of interdependence' (Elias 1983: 230) with others at court whose advice constituted another 'external constraint' on his activity. Of particular importance here were the following: the grand chamberlain, who constantly attended the emperor and scheduled his appointments; the lord keeper of the privy seal, who served as the emperor's chief adviser on political affairs; the imperial household minister, who supervised the palace bureaucracy; and the chief aide-de-camp, supplied by the army, who provided liaison between the emperor and the military. In addition to the holders of these court posts, who changed from time to time, another figure was crucial in advising the emperor in the Taishō and early Shōwa periods. This was the *genrō* ('elder statesman'), Prince Saionji Kinmochi, who will figure prominently in these pages.

It was through these advisers that government officials and foreign envoys were routed to the emperor when they came to court. He especially relied upon them to bridge the court because of the political separation of the emperor and the government and equally, the physical situation of the imperial palace in central Tokyo. Built on the ruins of the Tokugawa shōgun's fortress, and cut off from the city by walls and a moat, the palace compound of 240 acres constituted a closed world unto itself.

At the center of this world stood the main palace complex, the construction of which had begun in 1880. Occupied by Emperor Meiji in 1889, it contained the personal living quarters of the emperor and empress, several grand halls for important ceremonial and formal functions, the emperor's library and other rooms where he held audiences, and many smaller rooms for attendants, ladies-in-waiting, and so forth. Nearby in the spacious palace grounds of gardens and pine trees was located the imperial household ministry building. Elsewhere, a prominent landmark was the Nijūbashi double bridge facing the Marunouchi district. It was here that the emperor greeted the people, who flocked to the imperial palace plaza beyond, on ceremonial occasions and at the New Year.

In sum, the emperor acted politically as part of a collective group at court and, in large measure, his influence was an expression of this group's collective interests. Yet, the will to exert influence, for whatever ends, and the manner in which it would be registered in different situations, also depended fundamentally on the personality, temperament, and political world view of the emperor himself. Since in the case of the Shōwa Emperor these factors, and the resultant 'internal constraints' which he later imposed upon the application of imperial influence, were part and parcel of the Shōwa inheritance, this account now turns to his personal preparation for service on the throne.

1 The making of the Shōwa Emperor

EARLY EDUCATION

Named Michi-no-miya Hirohito after his birth on 29 April 1901, Hirohito was soon separated from his parents, Crown Prince Yoshihito, the future Taishō Emperor, and Sadako, his consort, as was customary at court. They entrusted him to the care of a respected ex-naval officer, Kawamura Sumiyoshi, and his wife (Kawahara 1990: 14). Chichibu-no-miya Yasuhito Shinnō, Hirohito's first brother, born in 1902, likewise was sent to live with the Kawamura family, not far from the imperial palace. After Kawamura died in 1904, however, the young princes rejoined their parents at the Tōgū-gosho, the Crown Prince's palace in Akasaka. In 1905 Hirohito's second brother, Takamatsu-no-miya Nobuhito, was born. A third brother, Mikasa-no-miya Takahito, was born ten years later.

Hirohito and Chichibu attended a special kindergarten in the precincts of the Akasaka detached palace and of the two, Chichibu was the more exuberant child.[1] Hirohito's quieter temperament was apparent in his features: dark in complexion, he 'had a wide, intelligent forehead and limpid, tranquil eyes set below thick eyebrows' (Kanroji 1975: 13). He was a distinctly cautious child. When the boys played tag with other children from aristocratic families who had been chosen to accompany them, 'Prince Hirohito always played strictly according to the rules, never employing any of the little tricks that were possible in this game' (Kanroji 1975: 16). As an adult, he would display the same circumspection in sticking to the 'rules' of political life as he interpreted them.

Under the care of his tutors, Hirohito seldom saw his parents. Nor did he see much of his grandfather, Emperor Meiji, who 'showed his affection only by smiling at the little Prince' on the few occasions when they were together (Kanroji 1975: 23). Meiji later became an important political model for Hirohito but it cannot be said that they were close in a personal sense.

A more immediate model was General Nogi Maresuke, principal of the Peers' School (Gakushū-in), where Hirohito began his formal studies in 1908. A national hero of the Russo-Japanese War of 1904–1905, Nogi personified to Hirohito the virtues of patriotism and the samurai ethic of personal austerity and devotion to duty which constituted part of the legacy of

Tokugawa to Meiji Japan. His guidelines for educating Hirohito emphasized physical fitness, 'the habit of diligence', punishment for misbehavior, no leniency in grading, plain living, and military training (Ōtake 1986: 237). Many years later, in 1975, the Shōwa Emperor told an American reporter, concerning Nogi's influence,

> I particularly recall this episode when I was a small boy: I met him at a certain place and he asked me, 'How do you come to school when it rains?' And I was just a small boy, so I answered off hand, 'I come by horse-drawn carriage'. And Nogi said, 'When it rains you must come here on foot wearing an overcoat'. So he was advocating a very frugal, strenuous, self-disciplined life. That made a profound impression on me.
>
> ('Hirohito: "A Happy Experience" ' 1975: 42)

Under the routine established by Nogi, Hirohito was awakened early in the morning for prayers, to honor the Sun Goddess and Emperor Meiji. Then he and his classmates attended lessons, many of which stressed the imperative of stoicism in the performance of duty and skills in the martial arts (Kojima I 1981: 33–42). Not all the aristocratic students who studied with Hirohito at the Peers' School took Nogi's traditional values very seriously, viewing them as anachronistic in a changing society. This was the impression Nogi made on some Japanese when, after Meiji died in 1912, Nogi and his wife committed ritual suicide, emulating the former samurai practice of loyally following one's lord in death. Others of his countrymen were profoundly moved by Nogi's gesture (Gluck 1985: 221).

For his part, Hirohito took Nogi's spartan samurai example to heart. In later years he abstained from alcohol and tobacco and cultivated physical strength through swimming and other sports, as if to steel himself for performing the manifold duties of his office. Once, in 1928, when reviewing a parade of students in the rain, the Shōwa Emperor was urged by his attendants to take shelter in a tent erected for the occasion. 'His Majesty replied that so long as tens of thousands of students would be standing in the rain, he too would stand in the rain'. When his attendants then gave him a cloak, he 'suddenly flung the cloak down' and stood 'in the pouring rain for over one hour' as the students filed past (Honjō 1975: 248). This austere sense of duty was typical of the Emperor and reflects Nogi's impact on his character.

After he left the Peers' School in 1914 Hirohito entered a special institute established specifically for his further training, the Tōgū-gogakumonsho, which was supervised by another hero of the Russo-Japanese War, Admiral Tōgō Heihachirō. By then, Hirohito held appointments as an officer in the army and navy, and military training was increasingly emphasized in his studies. For example, in 1916, he was entrusted to Prince Fushimi Hiroyasu, a squadron commander in the imperial fleet, for a six-day tour aboard a battleship (Nomura 1988: 55).[2] His formal naval training was similar to, if less extensive than, that received earlier by King George V of Britain when he was a young man (Nicolson 1952: 37–79).

Among his tutors at the Tōgū-gogakumonsho were Sugiura Shigetake (Jūgō) and Shiratori Kurakichi. In a program he characterized as *teiōgaku*, or 'learning for the emperor', Sugiura taught Confucian ethics and such virtues as courage, wisdom, and benevolence, symbolized by the imperial regalia (Yamamoto 1989: 206). He also lectured on Shintō mythology and the history of the Japanese imperial house, underscoring the moral purity of the 'imperial way'. This theme likewise typified Shiratori's lessons in Japanese and Asian history. Both men were ardent loyalists and nationalists who nurtured in Hirohito a deep pride in the imperial institution and Japan's recent rise as a power in Asia. His strong sense of nationalism owed much to their influence and that of Nogi and Tōgō.

For this reason, Sugiura and Shiratori have been roundly criticized as chauvinists. Bergamini calls Sugiura a 'professional jingoist' who was opposed to Western cultural influences (Bergamini 1971: 297). Behr writes dismissively that 'Sugiura's lectures were a hotch-potch of Shintōist superstitions and clichés about Japanese national virtues' (Behr 1989: 38). And Leonard Mosley portrays him as a 'fundamentalist' who 'believed in the Sun Goddess Amaterasu just as fervently as a Plymouth Brethren believes in Adam and Eve . . .' (Mosley 1966: 32).

These assessments are misleading. To be sure, Sugiura and Hirohito's other teachers were influenced by Herbert Spencer's social Darwinism, much in vogue in Meiji Japan, to believe that only the most powerful countries could withstand the intense political, economic, and military competition which prevailed in international relations at the time. For them, Spencer's ideas, which drew parallels between the struggle to survive in nature and the struggle to survive among nations, were authoritative. However, in Sugiura's view, the national power needed for survival was not primarily military or economic power but rather spiritual or moral power. In Japan's case it depended in the first instance on the 'benevolence' of the emperor, the attainment of which, Sugiura thought, required not just ethical training but knowledge in the broadest possible sense (Yamamoto 1989: 49–50).

Accordingly, Sugiura, who had studied agricultural science at Owens College (later, the University of Manchester), and chemistry at London University, helped devise a broad curriculum for *teiōgaku* which exposed Hirohito to a comprehensive range of subjects including mathematics, physics, chemistry, natural history, law, economics, geography, military strategy and tactics, the French language, and world history, as well as Confucian ethics, Japanese history, and the Japanese language (Yamamoto 1989: 52). In addition, he learned about great men in history whose lives illustrated the power of knowledge in one way or another. Rousseau, for his philosophy of education and independence of thought; George Washington, for his sense of justice and fair play; Malthus, for his ideas on demographic and economic change; and so forth (Ōtake 1986: 206–17). The importance of general knowledge prompted Sugiura repeatedly to draw Hirohito's attention to Emperor Meiji's Charter Oath of 1868 which included the statement,

'Knowledge shall be sought throughout the world so as to strengthen the foundation of Imperial rule' (Tsunoda R *et al.* 1960: 644).

Sugiura regarded the Charter Oath as an important document for political reasons, too. He attached special significance to its anticipation that 'Deliberative assemblies shall be widely established and all matters decided by public discussion' and that 'All classes, high and low, shall unite in vigorously carrying out the administration of affairs of state' (Tsunoda R., *et al.* 1960: 644). Interpreting these objectives to mean that imperial rule in modern Japan would be assisted by a measure of popular participation in government, Sugiura stressed that the Meiji constitution had endorsed this vision by providing for an elected lower house of representatives as well as an appointed upper house of peers. Together, the Charter Oath and the constitution signified to him that the Japanese monarchy had reached a new stage in its historical evolution, that of constitutional monarchy (Yamamoto 1989: 251–2). Above all, he wanted Hirohito to respect the principles of constitutional monarchy in emulation of Meiji, whom Sugiura praised as a 'modern' monarch.

Thus, ethically conservative and politically nationalistic he may have been, but Sugiura Shigetake was also a man of Meiji, very open to what the world could offer both to a future monarch and to Japan's continuing national quest for wealth and power generally, as it had unfolded since the Meiji Restoration.

Shiratori had a similarly catholic outlook. A professor of history at Tokyo Imperial University and also responsible for supervising the teaching of history at the Peers' School, Shiratori, like Sugiura, was politically conservative. But he, too, was no obscurantist. Having studied history in the United States and in Germany, where he identified with Leopold von Ranke's school of research, Shiratori introduced Hirohito not only to Western as well as Japanese and Asian history but also to the importance of basing one's interpretations of history on firm evidence.

In particular, he communicated to Hirohito his own scholarly skepticism concerning the validity of myth, which he rigorously distinguished from history. 'Myth is myth and not history', he often insisted (Ōtake 1986: 263). Shiratori's lessons referred to the Sun Goddess and other deities, as was customary in all Japanese history courses at the time and indeed through the Pacific War. But he was always careful to note the difference between what myths said about the Sun Goddess and what a historian might say about her, asserting that although myths were valuable parts of a country's cultural heritage, they did not constitute verifiable evidence for events that happened in the past.

From Shiratori, Hirohito learned to enjoy the study of history with an eye for evidence in reaching his own conclusions about it. That as an adult he would personally reject the myth of his ancestral divinity was due in no small measure to Shiratori's earlier influence, which the authorities of the Tōgū-gogakumonsho debated somewhat uneasily. But they tolerated his ideas as long as he taught Hirohito the content of the myths which were so essential to the tradition of the imperial house (Ōtake 1986: 265). Even so, Hirohito was discouraged from making the study of history his principal interest because the subject was thought to be too controversial.

As it turned out, biological research became Hirohito's greatest lifelong intellectual passion, dating from his studies at the Tōgū-gogakumonsho under the scientist, Dr Hattori Hirotarō, who was seconded from the Peers' School. In 1919 Hirohito made his first scientific discovery, of a new species of prawn (Kanroji 1975: 60). He made a great many other discoveries over the years and wrote many scientific articles and books, mostly on marine life and in particular on hydrozoa, which resulted in an international reputation as a distinguished marine biologist. He carried out his research in a special laboratory, established in the grounds of the imperial palace in 1925 with the assistance of Dr Hattori, who often accompanied him on expeditions to collect marine specimens in Sagami Bay, Tokyo Bay, and elsewhere (Corner 1990). As one account states, he was happiest 'when working with a microscope, absorbed in a factual world quite different from that normally inhabited by a Crown Prince or Emperor' (Kanroji 1975: 58).

Besides encouraging Hirohito's interest in science, Hattori taught him about Darwin's theory of evolution which Hattori had recently encountered in the publications of the zoologist, Oka Asajirō (Saeki 1989: 491). It was natural, therefore, that a bust of Charles Darwin would be found in the library of the Shōwa Emperor, together with busts of Lincoln and Napoleon which reflected Hirohito's interest in history.[3]

Through Hattori, Hirohito shared the widespread belief that nature was governed by the laws of evolution which Darwin had described and which were accessible to human understanding through empirical study of the natural world. Hirohito and his teacher also shared the general assumption that the concept of evolution, and its core notion of progressive development through the adaptive process of natural selection, could be applied to the values and institutions of contemporary society. They accordingly regarded it as given that linked by a common emphasis on empirical evidence to penetrate the 'truths' of the natural world and of human society, the disciplines of biology and history were complementary means of discerning the universal dynamics of rational, evolutionary progress (Saeki 1989: 492). Among thinkers everywhere who were influenced by Darwin, such ideas were commonplace at the time.

In retrospect, this confidence in the efficacy of knowledge, applied to all fields of human endeavor, including politics and government, was the most important legacy of Hirohito's education at the Tōgū-gogakumonsho. For, it was during this phase of his education that he acquired, along with the spirit of nationalism which typified the Meiji leadership, a 'scientific rational spirit' of inquiry, whether from Sugiura's intellectual eclecticism, Shiratori's historical skepticism, or Hattori's lessons on Darwin and scientific methodology (Ōtake 1986: 275). How this legacy influenced his later political career will be considered in the chapters that follow.

A WIDER WORLD

By the time Hirohito concluded his studies at the Tōgū-gogakumonsho in February 1921 he had undergone his investiture as Crown Prince (*Kōtaishi*) on 2 November 1916 and had become engaged to Princess Nagako, the daughter of Prince Kuni-no-miya Kunihiko, in January 1919.

Also by 1921, Japan had emerged as a great power in the new League of Nations, having fought alongside the Western democracies in World War I, and the Japanese empire seemed strong and secure. It now included Taiwan, as a result of victory in the Sino-Japanese War of 1894–1895; Southern Sakhalin island and a sphere of influence in South Manchuria following victory in the 1904–1905 Russo-Japanese War; Korea, after its annexation in 1910; and a number of Pacific islands, wrested from Germany in World War I, which Japan held as mandates under the League. It was in this general context that Hirohito's education, taken in the broadest sense of the term, continued with a long overseas tour to Britain, France, Belgium, Holland, and Italy in 1921. Since the British phase of his journey was the most important in his political development, it is emphasized here.

There were two motives for this tour. First, because the Anglo-Japanese Alliance dating from 1902 had been the cornerstone of Japanese foreign policy, the government of Prime Minister Hara Kei (Takashi) hoped that the tour would contribute to a political atmosphere conducive to the renewal of the Alliance which was due for review at the forthcoming Washington Conference. In this respect, the tour proved inconsequential, for the Alliance was allowed to lapse following the conclusion of the Four-Power Pact involving Britain, Japan, the United States, and France at the Washington Conference in December 1921.

Second, however, Hara and the elder statesman, Prince Saionji Kinmochi, whose advice on court affairs was decisive, had become gravely concerned over Taishō's mental and physical deterioration. They anticipated that a Western tour would enhance the Crown Prince's preparation for the office of Regent, or *Sesshō*, if, as now seemed likely, Taishō could no longer perform his responsibilities at court (Connors 1987: 86).

Notwithstanding opposition to the proposed tour, chiefly on the grounds that it was unprecedented for a member of the Japanese imperial family to go abroad, on 8 February 1921 the government announced the decision to send the Crown Prince overseas (Kojima I 1981: 126). On 3 March, he set sail from Yokohama on board the cruiser *Katori*, which was escorted by the cruiser *Kajima*. He was accompanied by a large entourage which included his cousin, Prince Kan'in Kotohito, his political adviser, Chinda Sutemi, and his aide-de-camp, Nara Takeji, who would later serve in the imperial palace as chief aide-de-camp, from 1922 to 1932.

After a voyage which included stops at the British colonies of Hong Kong, Singapore, Ceylon, Malta, and Gibraltar, on 9 May the two ships reached Portsmouth where the Crown Prince was officially greeted by Edward, Prince of Wales. They then proceeded to Victoria Station in London where the Crown Prince was warmly welcomed by King George V, who conveyed him to Buckingham Palace in an ornate horse-drawn carriage. The next day a formal banquet was held in his honor at the palace, his residence for three nights during the official part of his tour.

The full details of the Crown Prince's three-week stay in Britain need not be repeated since they have been discussed at length elsewhere (Kojima I 1981: 142–207, Mosley 1966: 52–64).[4] In brief, his varied schedule included a visit to the House of Commons; numerous receptions and dinners; visits to banks, schools, and universities, including Cambridge and Edinburgh, where he received honorary degrees, and Oxford; visits to Manchester and Glasgow; a memorable party at Blair Atholl castle in Scotland where 'Kimi ga yo' was played, rather incongruously, by a bagpipe band in an informal atmosphere which impressed the Japanese because local villagers were allowed to mingle casually with aristocracy during the festivities; and a sitting for a portrait by the painter, Augustus John. The Crown Prince was also made an honorary field marshal in the British army and a Knight of the Garter. These honors were later withdrawn when Britain and Japan went to war in 1941.

Of central concern here, however, is the political impact on the Crown Prince of his visit to Britain. In later years, he often recalled how impressed he had been by the King. In 1971, during his second visit to England, he stated at a reception staged in his honor by Queen Elizabeth, that in 1921, 'I was deeply pleased at the time because King George spoke to me as if I were his son' (Yuri and Higashi 1974: 438). Similarly, in 1961, he told reporters that in 1921, 'I had friendly conversations with King George V during my stay of three nights at Buckingham Palace and was able to gain a first-hand knowledge of English politics' (Date 1975: 9).

While it is not known precisely what the King said to him about English political affairs, it is reasonable to assume that the Crown Prince learned a good deal from the King about how constitutional monarchy functioned in Britain. He doubtless learned about it when he attended a lecture at Cambridge by Professor R.J. Tanner, a well-known specialist on constitutional law (Nish 1988: 22). As one account puts it, he 'saw at first hand the operations of constitutional monarchy and learned of its practical routine. . . . This experience left a very strong impression on him' (Shimomura 1949: 54).

One aspect of constitutional monarchy in Britain which was readily apparent to the Crown Prince was the affection with which the British people regarded the King. But another, far more fundamental, feature was the fact that as Lord Erskine stated in the House of Lords in 1807, the King 'can perform no act of government himself. No act of state or government can be the King's; he cannot act but by advice; and he who holds office sanctions what is done from whatsoever source it may proceed' (Nicolson 1952: 160). The royal prerogative of the King was delegated and was always

subject to the overriding principle that such uses or abuses of the

Prerogative are in no sense the personal responsibility of the King in Council, but exercised by him solely on and with the advice of Ministers, who in their turn, are strictly accountable to Parliament.

(Nicolson 1952: 163)

In this context, the King's political function was limited to 'first the right to be consulted, second, the right to encourage, and third the right to warn', as Walter Bagehot had asserted in his influential book, *The English Constitution*, first published in 1867.

When Crown Prince Hirohito met King George V, he encountered a monarch whose 'constant desire was to abide by his Coronation Oath and to act strictly in accordance with his duties and responsibilities as a Constitutional Monarch ...' (Nicolson 1952: 155). Among the many people who had influenced the King in this regard was the above-mentioned Professor Tanner, who in 1894, had been appointed to instruct the future King in the theory and practice of constitutional law. Tanner, indeed, had his student read Bagehot's ideas on the subject (Nicolson 1952: 98–9).

Much the same emphasis was found in the education of the future King George VI, the Shōwa Emperor's contemporary on the English throne. After reading Bagehot, Dicey's *Laws of the Constitution* and similar works at Cambridge, he 'became an expert on the subject and on occasion showed a greater perception of constitutional implications than either his official legal adviser or even Winston Churchill' (Bradford 1989: 86).

Essential to this education of King George V and King George VI was the lesson that, since the time of King Charles I,

the theme of British history has been the long struggle of Parliament to confine the sovereign within Constitutional limits, to remove any real executive power, and to turn him or her into a symbol whose potency derived from the paradox that he could do no wrong because he could actually do nothing at all.

(Bradford 1989: 166)

In short, during his visit to Britain, the Crown Prince came to understand and embrace these concepts of constitutional monarchy, which also coexisted with those of absolute monarchy in the constitution of his own country. That he was receptive to them was due to their resonance with his own earlier education, including especially Sugiura's emphasis on constitutional monarchy and on Emperor Meiji as a model constitutional monarch with limited powers. Moreover, he would soon find that the same ideas were prominent in the thinking of leading democratic figures in Japan, of whom Prime Minister Hara was a major example.

In 1920, Hara wrote in his diary,

It is the role of constitutional government to assume full responsibility without implicating the imperial family, and that, in my view, is best for the Emperor, as well. I believe that the imperial family would be more secure if its members refrain from direct involvement in politics and engage mainly in charitable work, granting awards, and so forth, and my policy is directed toward this.

(Hara K. V 1967: 276)

But Hara went on to complain that 'The military men in the Army General Staff cannot understand this point and tend to meddle in political affairs using a member of the Imperial Family as their figurehead. Nothing could be more mistaken than that' (Hara K. V 1967: 276). Hara regarded the army's political 'meddling' as out of tune with the increasingly democratic atmosphere of Taishō politics which the formation of his own liberal party cabinet in 1918 had epitomized. In another diary entry, he wrote,

It is very thoughtless of the Army General Staff Office to uphold the right of supreme command indiscriminately on the grounds that it is under the direct control of the Emperor, and therefore to act as if it is beyond control by the government.

(Hara K. V 1967: 280)

Hara and the liberal party movement in general therefore sought to check the army's arbitrary exploitation of the right of supreme command. Their inability to do so meant that this problem would severely plague early Shōwa Japan.

Years later, the Shōwa Emperor often remembered his time in Britain as the happiest of his life. He once wrote in a letter to his brother, Prince Chichibu, 'I knew freedom as a man for the first time in England' (Ōtake 1986: 228). And in 1934 he told General Honjō Shigeru, his chief aide-de-camp, 'I enjoyed my freedom when I went on a tour of Europe. The only time I feel happy is when I am able to experience a similar feeling of freedom.' He proceeded to contrast that sense of freedom while on tour in 1921 with the constraints of protocol at the Japanese court, blaming them for his father's deterioration. Of Taishō, he said: 'When he was the Crown Prince he was very cheerful and lively. . . . After he ascended the throne everything became very rigid and restricted. He was weak physically, so he finally became ill' (Honjō 1975: 185).

The sense of freedom which the Emperor recalled from his Western trip mirrored in part his delight with new lifestyles that he retained over the years, such as the pleasures of golf, which he had discovered while in Britain, the habit of wearing Western suits whenever he was not required to dress in military uniform, and the European decor which later graced his private rooms in the palace (Kanroji 1975: 100–5). But as his personal contact with constitutional monarchy in Britain attests, there was also a political dimension, which became more explicit in later years, to the Crown Prince's equation of freedom with his Western tour. Perhaps the growing expectation that one day as emperor he could emulate both Meiji and King George V in promoting a strong constitutional monarchy in Japan explains his buoyancy when conversing with Prime Minister Lloyd George and other dignitaries (Mosley 1966: 60).

His confident demeanor impressed the Japanese who observed him on tour. Yoshida Shigeru, the first secretary in the Japanese embassy in London, described himself in a letter to Count Makino Nobuaki, the imperial household minister, as 'extremely ecstatic' over the Crown Prince's performance (Dower 1979: 52). Similar letters were brought to the attention of Prime Minister Hara, who wrote in his diary on 5 July 1921, 'The trip was a huge success and the Imperial family and Japan will benefit from it in the future' (Hara K.V 1967: 408). To Hara, it was clear that the Crown Prince was ready to serve as Regent, by virtue of a political education which included at least some direct knowledge of the world beyond Japan.

That knowledge, moreover, extended further to military matters. After the Crown Prince arrived in France on 28 May, he was escorted by Marshal Pétain on a tour of Verdun and the Somme. Dressed in military uniform as he surveyed the trenches, he asked detailed questions about the fighting that had occurred there in World War I, for the study of military strategies and tactics had been an important part of his education. But his overwhelming impression upon seeing the physical evidence of war was one of shock. 'When as a youth I saw Europe, I thought how terrible war is', he remembered later, in 1969 (Date 1975: 10–11).

FROM TAISHŌ REGENT TO SHŌWA EMPEROR

The Crown Prince left Naples on board the *Katori* on 19 July 1921, with fresh memories of his recent meetings with King Victor Emmanuel and Pope Benedict XV in Rome, not to mention earlier visits to Paris, Versailles, Amsterdam, and other places on the Continent. Upon his return to Japan on 3 September he was immediately informed that the Taishō Emperor was now too ill to carry out his duties (Hara K. V 1967: 435). Soon, he became involved in the intensive discussions concerning his appointment as Regent, which had preoccupied the Hara government while he was away. On 4 October, Taishō's illness was publicly announced for the first time, although it had long been common knowledge. Plans for establishing a Regency were briefly interrupted by the shock of Hara's assassination, by an ultra-rightist youth on 4 November. However, on 25 November, the Crown Prince was duly installed as Regent (Shikama 1980: 277–81). He was twenty years of age when he embarked on this new phase of his political education.

By assuming the routine duties of his father, the Regent learned what would be required of him one day as Emperor. In addition to signing state papers, hearing reports from government officials, opening the annual sessions of the Diet, and formally authorizing the formation of new cabinets, he represented the Emperor on military maneuvers, and served as head of state in hosting foreign dignitaries. In this last connection, he was especially eager to entertain the Prince of Wales, who visited Japan in 1922, for Edward had treated him kindly during his recent trip to England.

On one occasion during Edward's visit, the Regent suggested a game of golf. Wearing a cap and plus-fours, he managed to hit the ball only after several futile attempts. To prevent his host from losing face, the future King Edward VIII records in his memoirs, 'By design, I developed a disastrous hook'. Edward adds, the next day 'He was as deft as I was clumsy' when the Regent introduced him to the traditional court pastime of catching ducks with long-handled nets (Windsor 1951: 179–80).

This golf vignette, though in itself trivial, is emblematic of the way the Regent wanted to imitate the freer lifestyle of his English guest. But he had already been given notice that this would be difficult. In December 1921, the Regent gave an informal party for friends from the Peers' School. They played records from London and Paris and drank much whisky, a gift from the Duke of Atholl which the Crown Prince had brought back to Japan. Afterwards, he was sharply reprimanded by Prince Saionji for this rowdy lapse of decorum (Mosley 1966: 70–1). He was beginning to learn the constraints of court convention which had imprisoned Taishō and would increasingly restrict him as well.

Another constraint was the religious ritual he was required to perform in Taishō's place, as when he made periodic visits to the great shrines. Soon, he would be fully briefed on how to conduct himself in the arcane rituals of his accession and eventual enthronement. The ceremonies of the *daijōsai* in particular would demand meticulous precision.

To illustrate only in part, on the second evening of this four-day event, he would bathe, put on a white robe, and walk in solemn procession to a hall built only for this occasion, with priests bearing the sacred sword and jewel going ahead of him. There he would offer consecrated food to the invisible gods, for whom a mat was placed next to his, and then eat carefully prescribed amounts of specially-grown rice representing the first fruits of the harvest, and take four sips each of two kinds of *sake*. After bathing once again, he would repeat this ritual at 2 a.m. the next morning in another hall (Blacker 1990: 185–6). Since the *daijōsai* involves a communion meal with the gods, the Regent would perform a ritual which contradicted his personal rejection of the Shintō myth that the emperor was a god. Perhaps he rationalized this conflict with the belief that such rituals were purely symbolic expressions of the monarch's special relationship with the natural world which he himself enjoyed studying. Be that as it may, it was clear that he had to conform to the ritual role expected of the sovereign, regardless of how he interpreted it.

In some areas of court life, however, the Regent found it possible to break with convention, as is apparent in his approval of the selection by the imperial household ministry of Nagako as his future wife. Whereas in the past, imperial consorts had come from the aristocracy, this precedent was partially qualified in her case, for although her father was an offshoot of the imperial family, her mother came from samurai stock, being the daughter of the Lord of Satsuma.

It was mainly on this account that conservatives opposed her selection and plans to set their wedding date after the Regent reached the age of twenty-one, in 1922. However, with his support these objections, based on allegations of Nagako's color-blindness, were overcome and it was announced in April 1923 that the wedding would take place in November that year (Connors 1987: 80–5). In the event, ultimately it occurred on 26 January 1924, having been postponed because of the great earthquake which destroyed much of the Tokyo-Yokohama area on 1 September 1923, leaving more than 100,000 people dead.

The Regent likewise broke with tradition, after he was married, by introducing reforms which did away with the complicated table of ranks for ladies-in-waiting in his wife's service. Commoner women not of aristocratic background could henceforth be considered for these positions as well. These changes created a more democratic atmosphere in his household at the Akasaka detached palace where he and the Crown Princess resided. There, at least, the Regent could manage his domestic life more or less on his own terms (Kawahara 1990: 41).

Otherwise, however, he was bound by the traditional conventions and protocol of court life. And because his role was largely ceremonial, he had little to do with such major events in Taishō as the Washington Conference in the field of foreign policy or, domestically, with the enactment by the Diet in 1925 of two important laws, the universal manhood suffrage law and the peace preservation law.

The former enhanced the popular trends of 'Taishō democracy' by extending the franchise to all males aged twenty-five and over. It thus provided unprecedented opportunities to form new social democratic parties, which soon arose on the political scene as proletarian rivals of the more revolutionary Japanese Communist Party, founded in 1922. In contrast, the peace preservation law revealed the conservative side of Taishō liberalism in reaction to social protest 'from below', for it was enacted to assuage the fears of those who believed that universal manhood suffrage 'would increase the opportunities for radical agitators to spread their subversive ideas among the people' (Duus 1968: 205). Authorizing as it did severe punishment of alleged subversives, it was primarily aimed at the communists. Although by 1925 the communists were a fragmented underground force constantly pursued by the police, they were nonetheless viewed with apprehension by Japan's ruling elites, because of their radical commitment to overthrow the emperor system and Japanese capitalism.

This anxiety towards left-wing radicalism affected the political education of the Crown Prince during his Regency, by creating barriers between him and the people and moulding his lifelong aversion to communism. The sensitivity at court to threats on the lives of the imperial family dated from the High Treason incident, when the anarchist, Kōtoku Shūsui, and eleven others were convicted and hanged in 1911 for having allegedly plotted to assassinate Emperor Meiji. Hence, elaborate security precautions were routine, to protect the life of the Regent, as when he visited Taiwan on military maneuvers in April 1923 amid rumors that a party of Korean terrorists had infiltrated Taiwan with the intention of killing him, to protest against Japanese colonial control of their homeland (Kojima I 1981: 257–8).

No violence occurred on that occasion, but concern for the Regent's safety was heightened all the more by the chaotic circumstances that prevailed immediately after the great Kantō earthquake in 1923. With some of its buildings destroyed by the fires that lashed Tokyo, the palace was in a virtual state of siege. Outside, in the streets, angry mobs massacred Koreans, anarchists, and communists who were (falsely) rumored to have risen up in armed rebellion (Shikama 1980: 394–5).[5] Fearing attacks by radical left-wing elements on the Regent's life, his advisers did not allow him to tour the ravaged city until mid-September. By then, the palace had announced the donation of imperial household funds for public relief to assist the victims of the earthquake. But an opportunity had been lost, owing to considerations of security, for the Regent to publicly display his concern for them earlier.

The imperative of shielding the Regent from threats on his life was dramatically illustrated several months later when a communist sympathizer, one Nanba Daisuke, tried to assassinate him, on 27 December 1923, as the motorcade conveying the Regent to the Diet, where he was officially to open its proceedings, passed through the Toranomon district of Tokyo. Nanba stepped from the crowd lining the street and fired a gun, wounding a chamberlain but missing the Regent, whose car sped on to the Diet (Shikama 1980: 410). Nanba was later executed for treason but the 'Toranomon incident', as it is known, gave credence to the view that police protection for the Regent had to be increased to ensure his safety.

As a consequence, the Regent did not mix with the people in ways reminiscent of the English royal family. Admittedly, the people held him in high esteem. His wedding in January 1924 aroused considerable public enthusiasm, with great crowds shouting 'banzai' outside the imperial palace. Their excitement led the chamberlain, Kanroji Osanaga, to remark, 'There was nothing the police could do to stop this spontaneous outburst'. The people 'saw the marriage as a bright and hopeful event in otherwise gloomy and pessimistic times' after the Kantō earthquake (Kanroji 1975: 105). Then, too, over the years the people took much interest in Nagako's pregnancies, hoping that she would soon produce an heir to the throne. She eventually did, with the birth of Tsugu-no-miya Akihito on 23 December 1933, after giving birth to four daughters, beginning with Princess Teru-no-miya Shigeko on 6 December 1925.[6]

Yet, despite public interest in the Regent and his family, the fact remained that with the Emperor ill and mostly absent from court, and with the Regent separated from the people by his massive police protection, in Taishō, the monarchy became increasingly remote from the people. On the few occasions when the Regent did go out among the people, as when he visited a spinning mill on Awaji Island in Hyōgo Prefecture in November 1924, his activities were tightly circumscribed. At Awaji, in the company of Makino Nobuaki, the imperial household minister, he did not mingle with the workers, most of whom were women from nearby farms. Instead, he stood apart, directing his questions concerning their welfare to the mill owner who took pains to stress that his was an 'exemplary factory' (Kojima I 1981: 252).

This gulf between the monarchy and the people would widen further in early Shōwa Japan as the Emperor became more and more a distant symbol of nationalism. It is well-illustrated by the following scene depicted in Kanroji's memoirs. In the autumn of 1931, when the Emperor's ship on maneuvers passed the coast at night, the local people lit bonfires to signify their respectful greetings from shore, although they could not see the ship in the darkness. On deck to return their salute, the Emperor could see the fires, but not the people. 'It was quite a moving sight ... the Emperor saluting people he could not see and the people hailing an Emperor they could not see' (Kanroji 1975: 120). A moving sight perhaps to the Emperor's attendants, but for the most part, the Emperor and the people viewed each other as abstractions. To them, he was a god incarnate; to him, they were an indistinguishable mass whose daily lives he scarcely knew.

Predictably, therefore, his view of the people was patrician in the extreme. In referring to the calamitous impact of the Great Depression on rural Japan, where many people were on the verge of starvation, he typically stated in 1934, 'It is of course necessary to sympathize with the dire plight of the peasants but peasants in their own way lead happy lives ...' 'They', he said, 'should think about the pleasures of nature that are there for them to enjoy and not dwell on merely the unpleasant aspects of their lives'. (Honjō 1975: 185).

However, for all of these constraints and his elitist attitude toward his future subjects, the Regent acceded to the throne determined to serve as a constitutional monarch. In this, he was significantly influenced by Prince Saionji and a like-minded circle of constitutional monarchists who dominated the court until the mid-1930s. Given the debility of the Taishō Emperor, they saw the Regency as 'a means of protecting the political role of the court and Japan's polity as a constitutional monarchy' (Connors 1987: 88).

Saionji's role as the Regent's chief mentor cannot be overemphasized. Over seventy years of age when the Regency commenced, Saionji was a man of immense political experience, having served as prime minister from January 1908 to December 1912 and as a guiding force in the development of the Seiyūkai party in Japanese politics. In 1918 he had been influential in helping Hara Kei, of the Seiyūkai, to become the first politician to form a majority party cabinet and hold a seat in the house of representatives. That from 1924 to the spring of 1932 either the Seiyūkai or its main liberal rival the Kenseikai (reorganized as the Minseitō in 1927) formed the government was due to Saionji who, in his role as *genrō*, recommended prime ministers for appointment by the Emperor.[7]

Saionji's political liberalism may seem strange for a man whose family was one of the nine prestigious Seiga houses of the old Kyoto aristocracy. However, as his entire career suggests, the liberal party movement was a means whereby the aristocracy could exert political influence after the Meiji Restoration. Accordingly, Saionji was attracted to Western liberal ideas which, reflecting the perceived triumph of liberal democracy over autocracy in World War I, supported the concept of constitutional government in Taishō Japan.

He never accepted the assertion that the emperor was an absolute ruler or a divine personage (Storry 1960: 11). Rather, he was a liberal in the English sense that he wanted the modern Japanese emperor to be 'a monarch who reigned but did not rule and whose powers were limited by the provisions of the Constitution, the exercise of which was subject to the scrutiny of popularly elected representatives' in the Diet (Connors 1987: 213). A boyhood friend of Emperor Meiji, Saionji saw him and his successors, including the Taishō Regent, in precisely these terms. He likewise adhered to an internationalist vision of foreign relations based on cooperation with Britain, and the United States, in promoting Japanese interests overseas.

These same views were held by Makino Nobuaki, imperial household minister from 1921 to 1925 and lord keeper of the privy seal from 1925 to 1935, and Ichiki Kitokurō, imperial household minister from 1925 to 1933 and privy seal in 1936 and 1937. Chinda Sutemi, grand chamberlain from 1927 to 1929, and his successor, Admiral Suzuki Kantarō, who held office from 1929 to 1936, were likewise proponents of constitutional monarchy and international cooperation with Britain and the United States. This was also true of Yuasa Kurahei, imperial household minister from 1933 to 1936; Matsudaira Tsuneo, whose tenure in this post, from 1936 to 1945, outlasted the influence at court of this group; Harada Kumao, Saionji's political secretary; and Admiral Saitō Makoto, the privy seal in 1935 and 1936, who had been prime minister from 1932 to 1934.

All of these men were personally loyal to Saionji and deferred to his political leadership in guiding the Crown Prince during his Regency and later, after he became emperor. However, what especially united the Saionji circle and Hirohito was a common perception of constitutional monarchy as it was interpreted by the leading constitutional scholar of the day, Professor Minobe Tatsukichi, of Tokyo Imperial University.

As mentioned in the Introduction, the dualistic concept of monarchy found in the Meiji constitution had provoked great controversy, including scholarly disputes, in late Meiji, between proponents of absolute monarchy, such as Professor Hozumi Yatsuka and his successor at Tokyo Imperial University, Uesugi Shinkichi, and advocates of limited monarchy, of whom Minobe was foremost. Because political developments in Taishō Japan seemed favorable to liberal democracy, given the ascendancy of cabinets formed by the majority party in the lower house, Minobe's ideas became increasingly popular. His published works were therefore highly respected at court and he was invited to the palace to lecture on his constitutional theories from time to time (Connors 1987: 147).

His interpretative synthesis, which owed much to the theories of the German thinker, Georg Jellinek, was complex but its essence on the issue of limited monarchy may be summarized briefly as follows. In reply to proponents of absolute monarchy who emphasized the sanctity of the 'national polity' in their interpretation of the constitution, Minobe conceded that the *kokutai* was important as a general concept but insisted that it had nothing to do with the constitutional system, which was concerned with the form of the state, or *seitai*. Identifying the state as a juristic personality, he held that 'the state alone is the subject of governmental power and the monarch is an organ [*kikan*, in Japanese] of the state', albeit the highest one (Miller 1965: 27).

This 'emperor–organ theory' (*tennō kikansetsu*) was fundamental to Minobe's interpretation. By stressing the existence, and importance, of other organs of state, it rendered the emperor's constitutional powers conditional. Minobe asserted, 'In fine, the monarch is an organ of the state and whether or not the term "organ" is used this idea is generally endorsed by all but those who insist on closing their eyes to the truth' (Miller 1965: 65).

Minobe contended that under the constitution the prerogatives attributed to the emperor were not unlimited but, rather, were delegated, as Itō Hirobumi had anticipated. Just as the sovereign's legislative prerogative was entrusted to the Diet, Minobe emphasized that the executive prerogative was entrusted to the cabinet and ministers of state who were responsible for it. As Banno Junji remarks, Minobe's 'distinctive theory of the Constitution concentrated upon expanding Itō's interpretation of Article 55', which, it will be recalled, required ministers to advise the emperor and to take responsibility for this advice, 'to allow party cabinets full powers to advise the Emperor, who, Minobe maintained, was quite incapable of directing state affairs without their consent' (Banno 1990a: 74). His main theme was the political supremacy of the cabinet, which came to mean, specifically, the supremacy of party cabinets, and their responsibility to the Diet (Banno 1990a: 75). In this sense, Minobe was a major proponent of liberal democracy in Japan.

Banno likewise points out that, 'Above all, it is important to note that in terms of actual politics Minobe's prime aim was to extend Article 55 to put party cabinets above the military' (Banno 1990a: 75). Minobe acknowledged that the emperor's prerogative of military administration (*gunseiken*), as established in article XII, was delegated to the army and navy ministers in the cabinet. But he argued that the service ministers should not undermine the integrity of the cabinet and that the scope of their powers should be limited and made subject to cabinet approval (Miller 1965: 101).

Similarly, in principle, Minobe agreed that the imperial prerogative of supreme command, *tōsuiken*, as established in article XI of the constitution, was delegated to the army and navy chiefs of staff. However, like Hara Kei earlier, he wished to limit the independence of the supreme command by revising the regulations of the general staffs so that their power to control strategic operations would come into play only after the government had decided to use armed force.

Minobe was aware that the so-called 'independence of the supreme command', which he sought to limit, flowed from various pre-constitutional precedents as much as from the Meiji constitution. A case in point was the 1882 Imperial Rescript to Soldiers and Sailors which, though intended to ensure civilian control of the armed forces, had the opposite effect of encouraging the 'military's privilege-consciousness' as a separate entity beyond the reach of civilian authority (Yamamoto 1976: 75–6). But his primary concern was to reinterpret articles XI and XII to underscore the accountability of the military to civilian authority. Minobe held that the powers of the military 'were subject to parliamentary absorption and to Diet influence through the convention of cabinet responsibility to the Diet' (Miller 1965: 93).

Indeed, in his view, *all* of the emperor's prerogatives were subject to public discussion and criticism, especially in the elected lower house of the Diet. Minobe argued, as Miller summarizes the essence of his constitutional liberalism,

> that the imperial prerogative was limited in scope and in the mediacy of its exercise, that the cabinet's responsibility could and should be extended as nearly as possible to cover the entire prerogative, and that there was no constitutional obstacle to the subjection of the prerogative, in part or in whole, to parliamentary influence and control.
>
> (Miller 1965: 113)

Yet, although Minobe was a 'rationalist' (Banno 1990a: 74), his theoretical attempts to limit the political autonomy of the military were much disputed and the discrepancy between his constitutional interpretation and reality was the most glaring in the gray area of civil–military relations. On this problem and others, he had described how the political system established by the Meiji constitution ought to work, not how it actually worked. Nevertheless, Saionji and other constitutional monarchists who advised the Regent were convinced that Minobe's ideas foreshadowed the future course of Japan's democratic political evolution.

The Regent was no less enthusiastic about these ideas. The 'scientific rational spirit' of inquiry fostered in his world view as a youth made him personally receptive to the rationality of Minobe's constitutional interpretation, which he later would defend at court when Minobe and the 'emperor–organ theory' came under widespread public attack from conservative nationalists in 1935. Matsumoto Seichō comments, 'As the Emperor pursued his special research in biology he was inclined to support the organ theory out of a scientific consciousness, with the result that he scorned the theory that the Emperor was divine', contrary to Minobe's detractors (Matsumoto 1968: 229–30).

Equally, Minobe's constitutional interpretation confirmed the Crown Prince's observations of constitutional monarchy during his tour of England and now, under Minobe's influence, and Saionji's, he 'favoured the idea of a limited monarchy and the theory of the Emperor as an organ of the state that were compatible with the ideals of Taishō democracy' centered on parliamentary politics (Takeda 1990: 7).

But few Japanese 'cherished an utterly whole-hearted, undisillusioned allegiance to parliamentary practice' (Gluck 1985: 246). On the contrary, in early Shōwa, when the nation was perceived to be threatened by a hostile world, 'the drift toward totalitarianism was eased by something which the Japanese desired even more than the conversion of their emperor to a symbol of their own self-government': 'the dream world of the imperial myth', in which Japan was ruled by an absolute monarch who would lead them safely through a time of great peril (Hall 1968a: 59).

This was scarcely the Emperor's dream when, on 28 December 1926, he issued an imperial rescript (*chokugo*) anticipating a bright future for Japan during his reign. Expecting to be a constitutional monarch who would serve in what may be called 'the Minobe way', as an organ of state, he stated in the rescript:

> The world is now in a process of evolution. A new chapter is being opened in the history of civilization. This nation's settled policy always stands for progress and improvement. Simplicity instead of vain display, originality instead of blind imitation, progress in view of this period of evolution, improvement to keep pace with the advancement of civilization, national harmony in purpose and in action, beneficence to all classes of people, and friendship to all the nations of the earth: these are the cardinal aims to which Our most profound and abiding solicitude is directed.
>
> (Murakami S. 1983: 259)

However, this optimistic faith in the nation's evolutionary progress and international goodwill soon would be challenged by the reality of conflict and war, which made early Shōwa anything but a period of 'illustrious peace'.

2 Japanese aggression and the limits of imperial influence, 1926–1933

Economically, Shōwa began with the bank panic of 1927. Arising from long-term financial disorders, this crisis resulted in the closure of thirty-one banks, including the Bank of Taiwan and the Fifteenth Bank, 'the official repository for the imperial household ministry' (Nakamura T. 1987: 56). Then, following the 1929 crash of the stock market on Wall Street in New York, Japan was hit hard by the Depression.

In brief, the collapse of the American market drastically reduced Japanese exports, mainly textiles, and caused the closure of countless Japanese factories, rising unemployment, and associated labor strikes. In village Japan falling prices, especially of silk and rice, plunged many farm households into destitution. As the Depression deepened, the accompanying mood of social and economic crisis that pervaded the country was intensified by subsequent Western protectionist barriers which impeded Japan's economic recovery through renewed exports. The severance of Japan's economic links with the West soon prompted an emphasis on attaining regional economic self-sufficiency in northeast Asia.

The first years of Shōwa were no less turbulent politically. For instance, in 1928, 1929 and again in 1930, the government moved to crush the communist movement in massive police roundups of communists and their sympathizers. But the government did not have a monopoly on violence: during the Depression years, Japan witnessed a stream of terrorist plots and incidents perpetrated by radical ultranationalists whose opposition to the faltering liberal–capitalist order was redolent of European fascism.

For Emperor and nation, however, the greatest tests of early Shōwa arose in the field of foreign relations, beginning with the so-called 'Chang Tso-lin incident' of 1928, the London Naval Treaty controversy of 1930, and the 'Manchurian incident' of 1931. In different ways, these crises posed an increasing problem of control over the Japanese military, and each demanded a political response from the imperial court. Since his position in relation to policy-making was unclear, this required no little improvisation on the part of the young Shōwa Emperor and his advisers amid political circumstances of imposing complexity.

THE CHANG TSO-LIN INCIDENT AND ITS POLITICAL REPERCUSSIONS, 1928–1929

On 4 June 1928, as his train approached Mukden in Manchuria, a bomb exploded on the track killing the Chinese warlord, Chang Tso-lin, who, from his base in the Peking–Tientsin area, had dominated the north China political scene for some years. Given that the South Manchurian Railroad (SMR) zone, in which this incident took place, was a Japanese sphere protected by Japanese forces comprising the Kwantung Army, the immediate question was, did Chang die at the hand of Japanese assassins and if so, who were they?

In the first instance it was up to the Seiyūkai administration of Prime Minister General Tanaka Giichi to deal with this problem. But Chang's death also immediately preoccupied the imperial court, for two reasons. First, for the Emperor, Saionji Kinmochi, and other constitutional monarchists at court, it was crucial that the government determine the identity of Chang's assailants in order to uphold the principle of public accountability under the rule of law, if it were proven that Japanese were responsible for Chang's murder. Second, the Chang Tso-lin incident jeopardized the court's preferred policy of peaceful cooperation with China.

Among the Emperor's advisers, Saionji and Makino Nobuaki were especially well-known as long-standing advocates of cooperative diplomacy. Along with Chinda Sutemi in 1919, they had personally assisted Japan's chief delegate at the Paris Peace Conference, Shidehara Kijūrō, in supporting the establishment of the League of Nations, which they regarded as the harbinger of a new world order based on international harmony (Connors 1987: 67–76). As convinced internationalists, they had similarly welcomed Japan's participation in the new system of multilateral treaties signed during the 1921–1922 Washington Conference, believing that these agreements provided a strong legal framework for the resolution of conflict and the promotion of free trade in Asia.

One of these treaties was the Four-Power Pact, which committed the signatories to respect their mutual rights and interests in the region and to consult should problems arise. Another was the Five-Power Naval Treaty, which promised to stabilize international relations in Asia by limiting the development of capital ships according to a 5 : 5 : 3 ratio for the United States, Britain, and Japan; Japan accepted a lower rate of naval expansion in exchange for an agreement by the United States and Britain not to fortify their naval bases in the western Pacific (Iriye 1965: 19). Finally, there was the Nine-Power Pact. Applying more specifically to China, this agreement pledged respect for the sovereign independence and territorial integrity of China which, at the time, was divided into warlord enclaves.

Shidehara, who as Japan's ambassador in Washington had participated in the Conference, regarded the Washington treaty system as the foundation for cooperative relations with China and the Western powers during his subsequent tenure as foreign minister from 1924 to 1927 in the successive

Kenseikai cabinets of Prime Ministers Katō Takaaki and Wakatsuki Reijirō. In this policy, he again had the full support of the court (Connors 1987: 110). However, after the formation of the Tanaka cabinet in April 1927, which was returned to power in the February 1928 Diet election – the first since the enactment of universal manhood suffrage – the court had reason to view new developments in the government's China policy with apprehension.

Serving concurrently as foreign minister, Prime Minister Tanaka did not wholly repudiate Shidehara's cooperative policy. But when Chiang Kai-shek's Nationalist forces, which had embarked upon the unification of China in 1926, moved north, Tanaka sent Japanese troops in June 1927, and again in the spring of 1928, to protect Japanese nationals in Shantung and, more important, to serve notice that Chiang should not challenge Japan's treaty rights in South Manchuria. These rights included the former Russian lease of the Liaotung Peninsula, military installations at Port Arthur and Dairen, the SMR run by the SMR Company, and the right to encourage Japanese settlement and investment in the railway zone occupied by the Kwantung Army.

Saionji and the Emperor were alarmed by this so-called 'positive policy', for it departed from Shidehara's previous avoidance of force in responding to Chinese protests against Japanese interests in China earlier in the decade. Indeed, when Tanaka had taken office, he was cautioned by the Emperor and Saionji to exercise prudence in dealing with Chiang's unification movement and Chiang's outspoken attack on the treaty rights enjoyed by Japan and the Western powers in China generally (Connors 1987: 113).

Yet, if with reluctance, the Emperor sanctioned Tanaka's military expeditions to north China. Although he shared Saionji's internationalist outlook and emphasis on cooperation with other countries, it should be stated very clearly that neither he nor his chief adviser was prepared to concede Japan's treaty rights in China, especially in Manchuria, to the claims of Chinese nationalism. Both men recognized Chinese sovereignty in Manchuria but, as nationalists, they were committed to defending the legacy of empire inherited from the Meiji and Taishō periods. This was also Shidehara's stance.

The Emperor, Saionji and Shidehara were eager to prevent any further conflict in north China which might spill over into Japan's sphere of influence in south Manchuria. Tanaka, it must be said, fully agreed with this and accordingly urged Chang Tso-lin to evacuate the region and retire to Manchuria, his original power base, lest Chang become embroiled in a military confrontation with Chiang Kai-shek's Nationalist forces in north China. Tanaka believed that Chang's forces and Japanese interests could coexist in Manchuria.

But this was not the view of the Kwantung Army, which pressed Tanaka to authorize at least the disarming of Chang's troops as he moved north. When Tanaka refused, Colonel Kōmoto Daisaku, a staff officer in the Kwantung Army, and several associates, plotted Chang's assassination which they would attribute to Chinese 'bandits'. They hoped that this course of action would stiffen the Japanese government's resolve to render Japan's position in

Manchuria impregnable (McCormack 1977: 248). In this, they were to be disappointed. Nor, ultimately, did killing Chang prevent his son, Chang Hsueh-liang, from eventually entering Manchuria in command of his father's warlord army. After this, Chang Hsueh-liang's political sympathies with Chiang Kai-shek to the south would greatly concern the Kwantung Army.

Against this background, Prime Minister Tanaka immediately pledged himself to ascertain the identity of Chang Tso-lin's assailants. But owing to contradictory reports and attempts by the Kwantung Army to conceal the facts of the case, it was not until October 1928 that he learned from Army Minister General Shirakawa Yoshinori and Army Chief of Staff General Suzuki Sōroku that Kōmoto and his team had killed Chang Tso-lin. Without divulging the names, Tanaka informed Saionji that Japanese forces had killed Chang, whereupon Saionji, speaking for the Emperor, urged him to bring them to justice (Morton 1980: 134).

Tanaka personally wanted Chang's killers to be court-martialed but he immediately ran into strong army opposition. Shirakawa and Suzuki insisted that the case be expedited not through a court-martial, which would involve the release of information prejudicial to the army, but rather as an internal army matter through administrative disciplinary procedures which would permit the army to withold information. William Morton explains, 'The device of administrative punishment, allegedly for having failed to take proper precautionary measures in guarding the crossing point of the two railways [where Chang was killed], would control the release of information embarrassing to the Japanese army and Japanese nationalists' (Morton 1980: 158).

In moving to block Tanaka, the army was aided by the fact that many leading figures in Tanaka's party, the Seiyūkai, and the majority of his cabinet, similarly opposed a court-martial. Trapped between this opposition and the desire of the court to see justice done, and anxious to play for time, on 24 December 1928 Tanaka reported to the Emperor that if, as seemed likely, an army investigation, which he had entrusted to Army Minister Shirakawa, indeed proved that Japanese had killed Chang, they would be punished. The Emperor made it clear that this was precisely his own wish in the matter. He plainly expected Tanaka to ensure that there would be a court-martial (Morton 1980: 150).

During the proceedings of the fifty-sixth Diet in early 1929, Tanaka came under heavy fire from the opposition Minseitō, and from certain members of the house of peers, for failing to solve the Chang Tso-lin case. Yet, Shirakawa repeatedly reported to the Emperor that so far, the army's investigation had been unable to establish the facts surrounding Chang's death. For example, the diary of General Nara Takeji, the chief aide-de-camp, indicates that Shirakawa spoke to this effect in audiences with the Emperor on 27 March and 29 March 1929 (Nara 1990a: 325).

By spring, it was already suspected at court that the army wanted 'to bury' the Chang Tso-lin case, as Saionji's secretary, Harada Kumao, had put it in January (Makino 1990: 328). It was obvious that Tanaka, under pressure from the army, now resisted a court-martial. On 6 May Saionji and Makino learned from Suzuki Kantarō that Tanaka planned to report to the Emperor that the Chang Tso-lin case would be handled by the army through internal administrative procedures (Makino 1990: 359). Otherwise, as Tanaka would explain to Makino three days later, there might be a violent reaction within the army. This warning convinced Makino that Tanaka was less than committed to seeing justice done (Makino 1990: 360–1).

Also on 6 May, Suzuki revealed that the Emperor intended to ask Tanaka to 'take responsibility' for failing to expedite a court-martial (Makino 1990: 359). But should the Emperor intervene in this way?

The extent of the Emperor's powers had long preoccupied his advisers. Well before the Chang Tso-lin case arose, on 3 July 1927, Saionji and Makino had discussed the subject of the 'Emperor's questions', or *gokamon*, which were in fact statements of his wishes when conversing with government leaders. They had concluded that insofar as possible, the Emperor should not be troubled by difficult political issues (Makino 1990: 272). After a similar discussion in April 1928, when the Tanaka cabinet was threatened by a political issue which need not be elaborated here, Makino noted in his diary, 'We are worried that the cabinet may resign as a result of what the Emperor says' (Makino 1990: 299). As constitutional monarchists who subscribed to Minobe Tatsukichi's 'emperor–organ theory', neither Makino nor Saionji wanted the Emperor's words to make this much of a political impact.

Consequently, after the murder of Chang Tso-lin had become a serious public issue, Makino in particular was most unwilling to see the Emperor become involved in it. Nor was he himself prepared to become involved. For example, on 4 January 1929, when the grand chamberlain, Suzuki Kantarō, and the imperial household minister, Ichiki Kitokurō, suggested that Makino, in his capacity as privy seal, should warn Tanaka on behalf of the Emperor to publicize the findings of Shirakawa's inquiry, he 'told them I dislike handling this in such a rough manner. Rather, I responded that it would be better for the grand chamberlain to telephone [Tanaka]' (Makino 1990: 327).

Thus, informed in May 1929 of the Emperor's intention to reprimand Tanaka, Saionji and Makino debated whether this would be appropriate for a constitutional monarch. For his part, Saionji saw no reason to dissuade the Emperor from intervening with Tanaka. However, Makino objected. He was worried that Tanaka would resign, that subsequent cabinets would be weakened if they, too, were subject to the court's intervention, and that the whole affair would redound to the detriment of future relations between the Emperor as commander-in-chief and the armed forces. Upon hearing this, Saionji agreed that the matter of what the Emperor would say to Tanaka indeed required careful study (Makino 1990: 359).

In early June, Makino observed that the Emperor was most anxious to clear up the political and military implications of the unresolved Chang Tso-lin affair (Makino 1990: 372). But whether he should intervene remained a contentious issue for his advisers. By 25 June, as the political crisis of the

Chang Tso-lin case worsened, Makino and Saionji had reversed themselves on the question of what the Emperor should do.

Now Saionji argued that at no time since the reign of Emperor Meiji had the sovereign ever opposed a prime minister and that this should hold true in the present circumstances. Having come to the opposite conclusion that in this instance it would be appropriate for the Emperor to criticize Tanaka for prevaricating over the Chang case, Makino disagreed with Saionji. Ichiki Kitokurō, the imperial household minister, and Grand Chamberlain Suzuki also held this opinion.

Greatly troubled by his clash with Saionji, Makino was determined to resolve the issue and so, on 26 June, experts in constitutional law were consulted. It was finally settled when Saionji accepted their advice that the Emperor should not be prevented from speaking to Tanaka as he wished (Makino 1990: 374–5). The stage was now set for the Emperor's confrontation with Tanaka who, also on 26 June, informed Makino that he would report to the Emperor the next day the army's decision, which the cabinet had endorsed, to discipline Chang's killers through its own administrative procedures (Makino 1990: 376).

The legal advice that he should not be impeded was almost certainly communicated to the Emperor before he saw Tanaka on 27 June. Hence, when Tanaka reported as foreshadowed, the Emperor said, as Makino later noted in his diary, 'This is a change from what you said before', referring to the impression given by Tanaka initially that there would be a court-martial. He then signalled that the audience was over and Tanaka emerged from the room looking very 'anxious', as Suzuki told Makino. Upon seeing Suzuki, Tanaka told him that the Emperor was primarily upset because he was dissatisfied with the inconclusive Shirakawa report (Makino 1990: 377).

Had they been less observant, the Emperor's advisers might have agreed with Tanaka after learning that when Shirakawa saw the Emperor the next day, the army minister had felt 'the imperial wrath', or *gekirin* (Nara 1990a: 330). However, they discerned that the Emperor's censure had been directed not at Shirakawa but at the prime minister, for having strained his patience in failing to bring about the open, and stern, justice which the Emperor had demanded throughout the Chang Tso-lin case. Tanaka, they felt, had simply not understood that the court had held him responsible, as prime minister (Makino 1990: 377–8: Nara 1990a: 330).

Ultimately, Tanaka, who regarded the imperial institution with an almost reverential awe, interpreted the Emperor's words as meaning he should resign. But first he requested another meeting with the Emperor to further explain his part in the Chang Tso-lin case. This request was refused by Suzuki. For, according to Harada Kumao, after seeing Tanaka on 27 June the Emperor had said, 'I simply do not understand what Prime Minister Tanaka says. I do not want to hear him out again' (Harada I 1950: 11). Finally, on 2 July, Tanaka and his cabinet resigned.[1]

The Emperor believed, as he pointed out later, that Tanaka could not satisfy the court's desire for a court-martial mainly because Kōmoto had threatened to expose the full details of the plot against Chang, which would have brought dishonor to the army (STDH 1990: 101). In the event, the punishments were light: Kōmoto was suspended from active duty, Muraoka Chōtarō, the commander-in-chief of the Kwantung Army, who had encouraged Kōmoto, was transferred to another post; and the other officers involved were strongly reprimanded (Morton 1980: 160).

It seems certain that when he saw Tanaka on 27 June, the Emperor, by then thoroughly disgusted by Tanaka's refusal to follow through on the Chang Tso-lin case, wanted the prime minister to resign. Judging from his diary, General Nara evidently believed that this was the Emperor's intention, for he writes that the Emperor wanted to ensure that future cabinets would respect his authority (Nara 1990a: 330). Furthermore, in his own recollections of his meeting with Tanaka, recorded in 1946, the Emperor stated, 'Because what Tanaka told me differed from what he had said before, I spoke to him in a strong manner and said to him, is this not different from what you said before? How about submitting your resignation?' (STDH 1990: 101).

Clearly, the Emperor had sensed that 'The right to be consulted, to encourage, and to warn may give the prudent monarch a degree of influence far greater than a catalogue of "powers" would suggest' (Blake 1969: 26). However, influenced by Saionji, who 'favoured a constitutional monarchy with a politically informed monarch standing outside the practical workings of politics' (Connors 1987: 115), he was surprised and very disturbed to discover that his influence could after all induce a prime minister to resign. He later recalled, inferring that he had acted impetuously, 'My way of speaking [to Tanaka] was due to my youthful vigor' (STDH 1990: 101).

On another occasion he later said, 'At the time, I was still young. . . . As a constitutional monarch I spoke too severely' in admonishing Tanaka (Shimomura 1949: 51). 'Concerning Tanaka' he said, defensively, 'when I asked should he not resign, this was a warning [*chūkoku*], not a "veto" '. He insisted, 'Ever since this incident, whenever the cabinet reported to me, I decided to approve [its policies], even if I disagreed with them myself' (STDH 1990: 101).

In short, the legacy of his confrontation with Tanaka in 1929 was a lasting determination, bred of his constitutional scruples, to maintain a strict neutrality in dealing with the prime minister and his cabinet. Thereafter, his concern not to exceed what he felt were the proper limits of his influence would prevent him, with several notable exceptions, from exerting influence as forcefully as he had in 1929, when reprimanding Tanaka. This form of 'internal constraint', which his advisers encouraged over the years, would not itself prove decisive in enabling the military to have their own way in early Shōwa Japan. Yet there is no doubt that the self-induced neutrality of the court contributed to the weakening of resistance to the military.

In the context of the Chang Tso-lin incident, by obtaining Tanaka's esignation the court was able to uphold the principle of prime ministerial responsibility. But its political cautiousness made the court unwilling to go further and invoke the Emperor's constitutional powers over the military as a possible way of overcoming the army's refusal to punish Chang's killers as the court demanded. This course of action, which was theoretically available to the court, was never seriously considered because it would have departed from Meiji and Taishō precedents while requiring a more activist concept of the Emperor's political role from that which the Emperor and his advisers embraced.

In view of later events in Shōwa history, that these powers were not at least put to the test in attempting to ensure the compliance of the army minister and the army chief of staff with the Emperor's wishes represented a missed opportunity of considerable significance. Had the army been held directly accountable for Chang Tso-lin's murder and had the punishments fitted the crime, it is possible that in future years the army's 'institutional right to declare the Imperial Will in an increasingly wide arena would have been seriously jeopardized' (Titus 1974: 149). Partly because a confrontation with the army was avoided in the Chang Tso-lin incident, the problem of controlling the military became increasingly intractable, as the London Naval Treaty controversy and later, even more so, the Manchurian incident, were to reveal.

THE LONDON NAVAL TREATY CONTROVERSY, 1930

Despite the fact that in 1930 the Minseitō cabinet of Prime Minister Hamaguchi Yūkō (Osachi), Tanaka's successor, was mainly preoccupied with the multiple shocks of the Depression, Hamaguchi and his foreign minister, Shidehara Kijūrō, were determined to maintain cooperative diplomacy in negotiations with Britain and the United States at the London Naval Conference that year. The Conference had been convened to update the Five-Power Treaty, signed at Washington earlier, by extending the limitations on the construction of capital ships to heavy cruisers and auxiliary craft. Quite apart from their instinctive desire to uphold good relations with the Anglo-American powers, Hamaguchi and Shidehara believed it was economically imperative, given the crisis of the Depression, to avoid a naval arms race.

Going into the London meetings, the Japanese navy had wanted a 7 : 10 ratio for cruisers *vis-à-vis* the United States but, at London, the Americans proposed a complex compromise whereby the ratio would be 6 : 10, until 1936 when the treaty would be renegotiated, with a 7 : 10 ratio for auxiliary craft and parity in submarines. When the head of the Japanese delegation, Wakatsuki Reijirō, wired Tokyo for its reaction, Hamaguchi, who had temporarily assumed the portfolio of navy minister while Navy Minister Admiral Takarabe Takeshi was in London, agreed to the proposal and set 22 April as the date for signing the treaty. This concession on heavy cruisers triggered a momentous controversy in Japan on whether to accept the treaty.

In advocating compliance with the American position Hamaguchi and

Shidehara had the complete support of the Emperor, Saionji, Grand Chamberlain Suzuki, Privy Seal Makino, Imperial Household Minister Ichiki, and others at court. As well, they could count on the support of leading officers comprising the 'treaty faction' within the navy, including for example Takarabe, Admiral Okada Keisuke, and Admiral Saitō Makoto.

Opposition to the proposed treaty was formidable and included, above all, Admiral Katō Kanji, the navy chief of staff, who attended part of the Conference; Navy Vice-Chief Suetsugu Nobumasa; the Emperor's relative, Prince Fushimi Hiroyasu, who along with Katō was a member of the supreme war council (Gunji sangi'in); other important figures in the navy's 'fleet faction'; and the president and vice-president of the privy council, Kuratomi Yūzaburō and Hiranuma Kiichirō. Senior officials in both the army ministry and the army general staff and Generals Araki Sadao and Mazaki Jinzaburō, who spoke for radical young officers in the military, likewise opposed the treaty. The main political parties also took sides in the dispute, with the Minseitō for, the opposition Seiyūkai against, the treaty. The press was no less divided (Kobayashi T. 1984: 57–9).

Without question, the treaty's most outspoken critic was Navy Chief Katō Kanji, who, on 31 March, requested an audience with the Emperor to oppose the treaty as detrimental to national security. Katō, though, was politely refused by Suzuki in exercising his control of the Emperor's appointments. Significantly, however, Hamaguchi saw the Emperor that day and received imperial sanction for the proposed treaty (Kobayashi T. 1984: 50).

Katō again sought an audience with the Emperor on 1 April, this time, through the chief aide-de-camp, but again, Suzuki put him off, which Nara thought was 'improper' of the grand chamberlain (Nara 1990a: 330). When Katō finally managed to see the Emperor on 2 April, he insisted that the treaty would gravely weaken the nation's defense. The Emperor only listened silently and the audience came to an abrupt end (Nara 1990a: 331). Despite Katō's protests, Japan ultimately signed the treaty, as scheduled, on 22 April.

Suzuki's rebuffs of the navy chief of staff greatly inflamed opponents of the treaty and led to a fierce public conflict over the right of supreme command (Masuda 1990: 91). Katō firmly believed that article XI of the constitution signified the right and obligation of the navy general staff office to exercise the Emperor's supreme command prerogative in national defense matters and that this principle also applied to determining the peacetime standing of the armed forces, as set out in article XII. As he was to state in a written memorial to the Emperor on 10 June, 'The prerogative embodied in Article 12 is related to that embodied in Article 11. It is always contingent upon the operation of the right of military command and it is not permitted in the slightest degree to function independently' (Kobayashi T. 1984: 67). Katō and his allies charged that in disregarding the navy general staff's opposition to the treaty, the prime minister and his cabinet had violated the right of supreme command.

This constitutional question was heatedly debated in the deliberations of the Diet and the privy council about whether to ratify the treaty once it was signed. In the Diet, Hamaguchi insisted that the navy's views had been considered but that the cabinet had final jurisdiction in deciding the peacetime standing of the navy. His opponents, agreeing with Katō, equally insisted that, as one of them stated,

> If the government's opinion were perfectly right, then the General Staff Office, which was independent of either the government or the Diet, would have to be abolished.... The independent decision-making powers of the General Staff Office and the Naval General Staff Office, those of the important organs of military command which belong directly to the Emperor, would become impotent, and the government would be superior to all of these military organs.
>
> (Shinobu 1967: 673)

Minobe Tatsukichi, however, advised Hamaguchi and the court that the government had not violated the right of supreme command. Minobe contended, 'The Navy General Staff is part of the Emperor's military establishment and by planning assists him in the exercise of his prerogative' but it had 'not the slightest legal right to decide the matter' (Kobayashi T. 1984: 64). With reference to article XII, he declared that the determination of the strength of the armed forces

> strictly belongs to the emperor's prerogative of conducting state affairs (*kokumu taiken*) to be executed with the advice and assistance (*hohitsu*) of the cabinet alone; the General Staff Offices responsible for assisting the Emperor in executing his right of supreme command should not meddle in such matters.
>
> (Masuda 1990: 94)

Furthermore, to Minobe, the so-called 'independence of supreme command' signified the delegated responsibility of the army and navy to advise the Emperor on matters of military strategy and operations but did not mean that the cabinet had to endorse this advice. He concluded that the Emperor had to sanction Hamaguchi's policy, however adamantly Katō had opposed the treaty in exercising his right of 'direct access' to the throne, and whether or not the cabinet had considered Katō's views (Masuda 1990: 94). The whole controversy, Minobe felt, could have been avoided had Suzuki not prevented Katō from seeing the Emperor earlier. That had not been necessary since, in any event, the cabinet was not obligated to heed what Katō said to the Emperor (Masuda 1990: 95).

The Emperor agreed with Minobe's constitutional interpretation. Therefore, although he did not become publicly involved in the supreme command controversy, he assisted Hamaguchi's cause by discouraging Katō whenever the navy chief came to the palace. His final discussion with Katō, on 10 June, was indicative. The details of what was said are unknown but Harada's account, based on what the Emperor revealed later, indicates that Katō threatened to resign his post if the treaty were ratified. He also submitted a written memorial outlining his interpretation of the constitution, as mentioned earlier.

However, as in previous audiences, the Emperor listened to him in silence, which provoked Katō to later complain in distress, 'I have just reported to the Throne but His Majesty had nothing whatsoever to say . . .' After he left the palace, the Emperor, referring to the memorial, told the navy minister, Takarabe: 'Katō brought this to me and spoke to me about it but what he said seems quite improper. As far as his resignation is concerned I leave it to your discretion and I turn this document over to you' (Harada I 1950: 85; Mayer-Oakes 1968: 156).[2] Takarabe soon recommended that Admiral Taniguchi Naozane be posted as the new navy chief and that Katō be transferred to the supreme war council (Harada I 1950: 86).

It appears that the Emperor had anticipated that Katō would carry out his threat to resign, for by the time Katō suddenly resigned the next day, along with his vice-chief, Suetsugu, the Emperor had sent Nara to consult with Admiral Tōgō, whom the Emperor greatly respected, on whether Taniguchi would be a reliable replacement for Katō. Through Nara, Tōgō replied that Katō had been too adamant in his views on the treaty and confirmed that Taniguchi was a strong advocate of treaty ratification (Nara 1990a: 332). Taniguchi was then recognized by the court as the new navy chief; in an audience with the Emperor, he agreed that treaty ratification was absolutely imperative (Nara 1990a: 335).

Taniguchi personally adhered to this view but, on 20 June, he found himself having to concede to the implacable demands of pro-Katō elements in the supreme war council to revise naval regulations concerning the right of supreme command. Thereafter,

> the tradition for navy ministers to be loyal to the cabinet was broken and never resumed; the general attitude in naval circles drew close to the army's view that the right to determine military organization and peace standing was secondary to the right of supreme command.
>
> (Masuda 1990: 97)

This development presaged Japan's abandonment of the London Naval Treaty several years later after the 'fleet faction' prevailed over the 'treaty faction' within the navy on the question of Japanese naval armaments.

Meanwhile Katō, still vehemently opposed to ratification during discussions about it in the supreme war council, made a final attempt to sway the Emperor against ratification, this time through the agency of Prince Fushimi, who saw the Emperor on 3 July, justifying his request for an audience on the pretext that he was a member of the imperial family. Fushimi reportedly began by saying, 'I should like to speak to Your Majesty on the matter of disarmament, if Your Majesty will graciously listen.' But as with Katō, the Emperor said nothing and Fushimi withdrew. Afterwards, the Emperor told Makino he had no intention of discussing the treaty with Fushimi (Harada I 1950: 109). Perhaps because of the Emperor's silent reproach, Fushimi eventually decided to vote for the treaty when it came before the supreme war council, where it was approved. Finally, the London Naval Treaty was ratified by the privy council on 1 October 1930.

It transpired that Hamaguchi's was the last party cabinet to prevail over the military in determining national security policy. But ratification did not mean that the underlying supreme command controversy had been resolved. Opponents of the treaty continued to argue that the navy's right of supreme command had been violated. As Sir Robert Craigie, later Britain's ambassador to Japan, observed, 'Although ... the Emperor had obviously sided with the cabinet against the navy and its supporting extremists, the Imperial prerogative itself was now loudly proclaimed to have been undermined' (Craigie 1946: 16).

In 1933 and 1934 these feelings of betrayal led the 'fleet faction' to renew its attack on the London Naval Treaty while advocating full naval parity with Britain and the United States. Prince Fushimi was a prominent figure in this campaign, having been appointed navy chief in 1932 with the support of Katō Kanji and, in the army, of General Araki Sadao, the then army minister. Aware that the Emperor believed that the levels of Japanese naval development set by the London treaty were adequate for national defense, during an audience with the Emperor, in July 1934, Fushimi demanded imperial approval, at least in principle, of naval parity. How the Emperor responded to him is unknown. But for the navy's purposes it was sufficient for Admiral Ōsumi Mineo, the navy minister at the time, to claim that simply by 'reporting' the navy's objectives to the throne, Fushimi had obtained imperial sanction for parity (Harada IV 1951: 17).

When the government accordingly announced later that year that Japan would abrogate the London Naval Treaty, effective in 1936, the Emperor was powerless but to complain to Fushimi that this decision had been taken precipitously (Honjō 1975: 197). A second naval conference was convened in London in 1935. But its deliberations came to nothing after the Anglo-American powers rejected Japanese demands for naval parity. The lapse of the London Naval Treaty led to a naval arms race between Japan and its maritime rivals which continued with escalating intensity down to the Pacific War (Pelz 1974).

Thus, Hamaguchi's victory, and the court's, in achieving ratification of the London Naval Treaty in 1930 came at the high price of a strong reaction within the navy that led to the treaty's demise by 1936. In reviewing the treaty controversy, it is apparent that although the Emperor, assisted by his advisers, used his influence privately at court to neutralize Katō politically, he refrained from invoking his supreme command prerogative to try and ensure naval compliance with Hamaguchi's determination to decide naval security policy. This restraint sprang from the apprehension that to do so would imply the exercise of absolute powers that neither the Emperor nor Saionji deemed appropriate for a constitutional monarch. One is reminded here of the court's similar cautiousness in dealing with the army over the Chang Tso-lin affair.

Moreover, as in the Chang Tso-lin incident, when the court was worried by Tanaka's allusion to possible violent protest in the army, its reluctance to follow through on the supreme command controversy in 1930 was due to growing fears of violent reprisals from the military if the court publicly supported the right of the prime minister and the cabinet to decide naval policy.

For example, in late 1930 (the exact date is not clear), the court learned of a document criticizing Makino for having allegedly sent his secretary to persuade Katō Kanji to relent over the naval treaty issue. The secretary had visited Katō, it is true, but entirely on his own volition, without Makino's knowledge. Yet the document attributed his mission to Makino's 'machinations' against the anti-treaty forces. Harada Kumao, who relates this matter, blamed Katō for the document and felt it necessary to approach the Metropolitan police out of concern for Makino's safety (Harada I 1950: 117–18).

Nor were these fears at court limited to the navy. Throughout the naval treaty controversy, the army had supported Katō's claim that national security policy fell exclusively within the province of the general staffs, under their delegated right of supreme command (Kobayashi T. 1984: 68–9). On 23 June 1930 the army minister, General Abe Nobuyuki, was on the point of resigning his post to protest Makino's outspoken defense of naval concessions to the Anglo-American powers in London (Nara 1990a: 333). In this context, the court decided upon the necessity of appeasing the army, in hopes that it would support the London Naval Treaty, by capitulating to Abe's demand for the reinstatement of Colonel Kōmoto Daisaku, despite his responsibility for Chang Tso-lin's death.

Nara relates in his diary on 24 June 1930 that the Emperor at first adamantly opposed Kōmoto's reinstatement. Anxious to avoid alienating the army, Nara and Suzuki Kantarō then proceeded to work out a plan whereby Kōmoto would be temporarily reinstated so that he could draw his pension. After Abe accepted this plan, pressure was successfully brought to bear on the Emperor to do likewise and soon, Kōmoto was reinstated (Nara 1990a: 333–4). The same desire to appease the army in future years would also lead to the promotions of men, to be discussed shortly, who defied the court in the Manchurian incident: Ishiwara Kanji was appointed chief of the operations section of the army general staff in August 1935, Itagaki Seishirō became army minister in June 1938, and Honjō Shigeru was appointed as chief aide-de-camp at court in September 1932.[3]

Ultimately, in 1930, the court's strong concern that the government's policy of supporting the naval treaty would spark a violent reaction from one quarter or another, was fully justified when, on 14 November, Prime Minister Hamaguchi was shot by a right-wing assassin and subsequently died of his wounds. In this coercive environment, the Emperor and his circle of advisers shrank further back from confrontation with the military. Consequently, 'After 1930 there was a gradual but steady atrophy of the Emperor's influence in affairs of state' (Maxon [1957] 1975: 49–50).

THE MANCHURIAN INCIDENT AND ITS AFTERMATH, 1931–1933

The Manchurian incident erupted at Mukden on the night of 18 September 1931 with an explosion along the SMR line. Chinese subversives were blamed by the Kwantung Army. However, in truth, this was the work of Lieutenant-Colonel Ishiwara Kanji and Colonel Itagaki Seishirō, both of the Kwantung Army general staff, who precipitated the incident without authorization either from the Kwantung Army commander, General Honjō Shigeru, or the high command in Tokyo, much less the Minseitō cabinet of Prime Minister Wakatsuki Reijirō, who had succeeded Hamaguchi.

Like Kōmoto Daisaku in June 1928, Ishiwara and Itagaki wanted to create a crisis that would compel the Japanese government to incorporate Manchuria into the empire. Thus, after the explosion at Mukden, Kwantung Army units clashed with Chang Hsueh-liang's troops and, securing the area around Mukden, advanced speedily to Kirin, which was taken three days later, and on into other parts of Manchuria. The Nanking government of Chiang Kai-shek was impotent to prevent the complete conquest of Manchuria in the months ahead.

Within Japan, meanwhile, the Manchurian incident ignited a state of emergency and powerful expressions of nationalism in the press and among ordinary people who responded enthusiastically to the crisis by staging large public rallies of patriotic support and by donating money for the construction of new warplanes and the like (Wilson S. 1989). It was in this febrile atmosphere that the Shōwa Emperor, his advisers, and the cabinet labored behind the scenes to bring the conflict under control. However, the task of containing the incident was complicated by uncertainty over the Emperor's command prerogative and by intensified civil–military rivalry in national policy formation as a whole.

Once hostilities were under way, technically it lay within the jurisdiction of the Kwantung Army general staff in the first instance to implement field operations, in accordance with the principle of *dokudan senkō* (Crowley 1966: 115).[4] Still, the problem for the military high command in Tokyo was how to reassert its authority over Japanese forces in Manchuria. The parallel dilemma facing the cabinet was how to restrain the military and re-establish control of foreign policy generally while at the same time ending the Manchurian incident as quickly as possible and with the least damage to Japan's international standing, then under attack not only from China but also from the United States and the League of Nations. From every side, Japan was widely condemned for having violated not only the Washington treaties but also the Kellogg–Briand Pact outlawing war, which Japan had signed in 1928.

This criticism swelled all the more when fighting between Japan and China broke out at the International Settlement in Shanghai in January 1932 and later when, on 15 September 1932, Japan further alienated world opinion by recognizing the Republic of Manchukuo, which had been formed in March by the Kwantung Army (Peattie 1975: 142–68). In 1934, the new Manchurian state, in reality a puppet of Japan's, was transformed into the Empire of Manchukuo with 'Henry' Pu-yi, as he was known to the West, as Emperor.

These problems pressed in heavily on the Shōwa Emperor as the Manchurian incident unfolded. At one point he told a court official, 'I believe that international justice and good faith are important, and I am striving to preserve world peace. . . . But the forces overseas do not heed my commands and are recklessly expanding the incident.' Japan's invasion of Manchuria, he said, 'causes me no end of anguish. This could result in intervention by the major powers and the destruction of our nation and people. . . . When I think of all these problems I cannot sleep at night' (Hane 1982: 63). The Emperor's distress was apparent even to the American ambassador, Joseph Grew, who noted that Saionji, Makino, and others close to the Emperor were equally dismayed (Grew 1944: 118–19). They and the Emperor realized that the crisis of the Manchurian incident had rapidly moved beyond the capacity of the court and the government to influence.

Prior to the incident, rumors of unauthorized military maneuvers in Manchuria had prompted the Emperor on 11 September to elicit a promise from the army minister, General Minami Jirō, to tighten discipline and maintain control over the army (Nara 1990a: 338). Following this audience, Minami told Saionji that it would be difficult to enforce discipline (Harada II 1950: 53).

Indeed it was: on 19 September Minami reported what the court already knew, that war was on in Manchuria. He did not inform the Emperor in detail concerning the widening scope of hostilities but he did reveal that the Kwantung Army had requested the Japanese army in Korea to send reinforcements and that Army Chief of Staff General Kanaya Hanzō would soon request imperial sanction for this deployment. Nara saw immediately that the army intended to dictate developments in Manchuria, which he and the Emperor both found intolerable. They agreed moreover that in any case imperial sanction could not be granted without the approval of the cabinet which, as Prime Minister Wakatsuki had already reported, would not be forthcoming; Wakatsuki was determined to limit, and then end, the incident quickly (Nara 1990a: 339–40). Seeking to bolster Wakatsuki's resolve, the Emperor said to him, 'The government's policy of non-enlargement is most proper. Strive to achieve that goal' (Harada II 1950: 72).

On 22 September the Emperor ordered Nara to instruct Kanaya not to expand the incident in Manchuria under any circumstances whatsoever. But later that day Wakatsuki reported to the Emperor that the cabinet now had no alternative but to approve the transfer of military units from Korea to Manchuria since in fact the transfer was already under way and was a *fait accompli*, the costs of which had to be defrayed. Swayed by Wakatsuki's opinions and out of meticulous respect for the authority of the prime minister's office, the Emperor then reluctantly approved Kanaya's request but warned the army chief to exercise utmost restraint in Manchuria.

Nara, who is an indispensable source on these developments, doubted that the principle of operational discretion on the part of a field army legally applied to the case of reinforcements from Korea, as the Kwantung Army claimed. He wanted an inquiry into this matter, which would also consider whether Kanaya should be held responsible for failing to block their transfer (Nara 1990a: 340–1). The Emperor likewise condemned the reinforcements as 'improper' (Nara 1990a: 343).

Nara's diary reveals that a mood of mounting desperation prevailed at court in October 1931. The Emperor was incensed that General Honjō Shigeru, the commander of the Kwantung Army, had declared his intention to pacify all of Manchuria and Mongolia. Shidehara, who had remained as foreign minister in the Wakatsuki cabinet, was no less upset to see foreign policy being made in the field, as it were. On the other hand, now that Japanese troops were fully engaged in fighting on a wide front, the Emperor worried that Chang Hsueh-liang's forces, which were regrouping in Jehol, would have to be overcome before the incident could be ended. That being the case, he feared that eventually he would be obliged to authorize expansion of hostilities against Chang in Jehol (Nara 1990a: 344). He also worried that this might cause the Western powers to intervene against Japan, for which contingency the military was completely unprepared (Nara 1990a: 345).

This distress over the possibility of conflict with the United States and Britain would grow even more when the so-called 'Shanghai Incident' flared in early 1932. The Emperor urged General Shirakawa Yoshinori, now serving as commander of the Japanese expeditionary force in Shanghai, to bring a swift end to the fighting which had broken out between his forces and those of Chiang Kai-shek in the Shanghai area, lest it provoke the Western powers to intervene against Japan. Fortunately, the fighting in Shanghai was contained in February, although Shirakawa himself was later killed, by a Korean nationalist in Shanghai (Shimada 1984: 305–18).[5]

On 13 December 1931, Wakatsuki resigned after failing to negotiate the formation of a coalition cabinet with the Seiyūkai which he had hoped would help restrain the military. When Saionji then recommended the veteran Seiyūkai politician, Inukai Tsuyoshi (Ki), as the next prime minister, the Emperor instructed him to tell Inukai, 'The indiscipline and violence of the military and their meddling in domestic and foreign affairs is something which, for the welfare of the nation, must be viewed with apprehension. Be mindful of my anxiety' (Harada II 1950: 160). By then, however, the government and the military high command had virtually given up trying to stop the Kwantung Army in Manchuria. Inukai's mandate was to confine the incident to Manchuria, avoid further direct military conflict with China, and repair relations with the Western powers.

To the Emperor, the Manchurian incident signified a deep-seated crisis of political authority. General Honjō, who had not been involved in the plot to precipitate the war in Manchuria, but who had led Japanese forces once it had begun, rather ironically wrote later that throughout the Manchurian incident, the Emperor had consistently wanted to ensure 'that the lines of authority for governance, supreme command, foreign affairs, and so on were clearly distinguished and that the agencies involved did not transgress the proper bounds of their areas of responsibility' (Honjō 1975: 162–3). In the Emperor's view, that was how the state should function, given his concept of constitutional government in which different agencies operated in an orderly, interdependent manner and always responsibly under the rule of law. The incident made a mockery of this perception and of his personal efforts to oppose Japanese aggression in Manchuria. The military simply ignored him.

His continuing determination to uphold the constitutional order during the conflict is illustrated by his confrontation with Prince Chichibu, in late 1931. As subsequently reconstructed by Honjō on the basis of other court accounts, 'The Prince urged His Majesty to take personal charge of the government. He asserted that if necessary the Constitution should be suspended. It appears that a heated argument broke out between His Majesty and the Prince.' Later, the Emperor told the grand chamberlain 'that he would never agree to anything that would besmirch the honor of his ancestors. There is some talk of establishing personal rule, but he was adhering to fundamental principles and overseeing political affairs according to the provisions of the Constitution.' Honjō's recapitulation continues: 'What more could he do? Moreover, suspension of the Constitution means destroying what Emperor Meiji had created. This, he asserted, can never be allowed to happen' (Honjō 1975: 163).

Preserving the constitutional order, by contrast, was irrelevant to radical elements within the military who resented the Emperor's personal opposition to the Manchurian incident which, though registered in private exchanges with leading military and civilian officials at court, was leaked to army circles. Consequently 'the army felt great dissatisfaction concerning the attitude of the Emperor' after he had protested at the unauthorized decision to send Japanese troops from Korea into Manchuria (Ogata 1964: 67). On this account he was condemned as a 'mediocre' sovereign who spent his time playing mahjong instead of attending to his duties as head of state (Shillony 1973: 102). A typical army criticism was that while the army was 'fighting a sacred war in order to expand national power and prestige, the Emperor does not approve and the government has been obstructing every move' (Ogata 1964: 94).

Inevitably, such criticism was also directed at government leaders and the Emperor's advisers, some of whom were listed as targets by radical young officers and right-wing civilians who plotted a coup, to establish a strong regime that would support the Manchurian incident and solve the social problems caused by the Depression, especially the plight of the rural poor whose interests the young officers claimed to represent. This scenario lay behind the aborted 'October incident' of 1931 which involved a plot to kill Prime Minister Wakatsuki, Foreign Minister Shidehara, Grand Chamberlain Suzuki, Privy Seal Makino, and Imperial Household Minister Ichiki. The participants were prepared to force the Emperor to sanction the coup 'even if it means that we shall have to threaten the Emperor with a sword' (Shillony 1973: 106).

It was Inukai, however, who was especially despised by the army for his persistent attempts to restrain it, with the help of the Emperor. Hatred in the army of Inukai soon led to the notorious 15 May 1932 'incident' in which he was assassinated by young officers whose rebel manifesto cynically began, 'In the name of the Emperor, destroy the evil advisers around the throne ...' (Shillony 1973: 67). To the rebel young officers who attacked Inukai, and to their successors who engaged in similar terrorism, 'loyalty to the Emperor meant loyalty to the nation and the imperial institution, rather than obedience to the personal wishes of the man who happened to occupy the throne' (Shillony 1973: 105). Much the same distinction typified the men who had started the Manchurian incident in the first place. Ishiwara Kanji, for instance, merely 'ignored the Emperor, whom he professed to worship' (Etō S. 1974: 264).

The murder of Inukai Tsuyoshi did not lead to the anticipated coup since order was quickly restored. Understandably, the Emperor was very anxious to put an end to terrorism and told Saionji that the new government required a leader who, in opposing 'fascism' and reasserting control over the military, would uphold the constitution and work for peace. Otherwise, he asserted, 'I would not be able to justify and vindicate myself to the Emperor Meiji' (Harada II 1950: 288). As it happened, Inukai was the last prime minister to form a party cabinet in early Shōwa Japan. Saionji recommended, and the Emperor approved, the appointment of a moderate military man, Admiral Saitō Makoto, hoping that he would be able to check the military in Manchuria. But Saitō proved ineffectual. His was also the first of a long string of mainly bureaucratic cabinets which were increasingly responsive to military priorities in national defense planning.

Well before Inukai's assassination, the escalating violence of the period, already apparent in Hamaguchi's assassination and various other plots, had made the court extremely nervous. In early January, the Emperor himself had been threatened from a different source, when a Korean dissident threw a bomb at the imperial car in Tokyo. As with Nanba's attack in 1923, the Emperor was not harmed (Kido I 1966: 127–8). However, this episode highlighted his vulnerability to terrorism and made him tense in audience, prompting Kido Kōichi, then secretary to the lord privy seal, to hope that the Emperor could be composed, like a 'large mountain' (Kido I 1966: 129). Outwardly at least, the Emperor did manage to appear calm. When he received Joseph Grew for the first time in June 1932, the new American ambassdor was struck by the Emperor's steady demeanor. Grew later wrote in his diary, 'The Emperor is young – thirty-one, I believe; he has a small moustache and glasses and smiles pleasantly when talking' (Grew 1944: 16–17).

Behind this appearance of calm at court, the threat of violence drove the Emperor's advisers to protect the Emperor's life and their own by restraining him politically during the Manchurian incident. Kido records that as early as 22 September 1931, he and several other advisers were deeply worried over the army's resentment of the Emperor's opposition to the fighting in Manchuria: 'We agreed that the Emperor had better not say anything further unless necessary'. They also agreed it would be better if Saionji, 'who seems to harbor ill will toward the army', stayed away from the court for the time being: 'if he comes it might make the army's resentment stronger' (Kido I 1966: 101).

However, Saionji, too, wanted to neutralize the Emperor and thereby protect the throne from criticism early in the Manchurian incident. In October 1931, after learning that the Emperor wanted to summon Foreign Minister Shidehara to discuss the implications of the incident for Japan's relations with the League of Nations, Saionji informed Shidehara through Harada Kumao, 'It is not necessary to lie but tell the Emperor things that will please him in order to ease his mind' (Harada II 1950: 115).

Some of his advisers attributed the cleavage between the Emperor and the army over the invasion of Manchuria to the Emperor's 'liberal ideas' concerning the priorities of peace and the progress of constitutional government unimpeded by military usurpation of national policy. For example, at one point Prince Konoe Fumimaro, then a party to conversations at court and later a central figure in Shōwa political history, told Harada Kumao 'The Emperor, holding very liberal ideas, may be the main cause of friction with the army.' Upon hearing this, Saionji remarked disapprovingly, 'It's almost as if Konoe thinks it very bad for the Emperor to hold liberal ideas'. To this Harada responded, 'I do not think that Konoe feels that ... but in view of current army trends, he no doubt fears there will be clashes of opinion' with the army (Harada II 1950: 248).

How to bridge this chasm between the Emperor and the army was a problem that would preoccupy his advisers in future years. During the Manchurian incident, they repeatedly debated, and decided against, the wisdom of having him issue imperial rescripts to oppose Japanese campaigns on the continent, calculating that this would only further antagonize the army and diminish the prestige of the throne if, as appeared likely, the army disregarded the rescripts (Harada II 1950: 420–1).[6] A good illustration of their general cautiousness is the court's response to Japanese military operations in Jehol.

Aware that the army was preparing to invade Jehol, in November 1932 the Emperor asked General Koiso Kuniaki, chief of staff of the Kwantung Army, about the military's intentions in Jehol and expressed his anxiety that any planned operations there would worsen Japan's isolated position in the League of Nations (Nara 1990b: 346). His opposition to a Jehol campaign was shared by Prime Minister Saitō, who, on 5 January 1933, suggested that the Emperor issue an imperial rescript commanding the Kwantung Army not to penetrate Jehol. The Emperor was willing, but the proposal was set aside because his advisers felt that Saitō was trying to deflect criticism from his own weak leadership by shifting responsibility for checking the army in Jehol to the

Emperor. They noted uneasily that Saitō was wondering whether he should resign, to take responsibility for failure to control the situation (Makino 1990: 532).

Four days later, the Emperor suggested that an imperial conference be convened to discuss, in his presence, the Kwantung Army's plans in Jehol, but Saionji, with Makino's agreement, advised against this as well (Makino 1990: 534). They believed it was up to the Saitō cabinet to restrain the Kwantung Army in Jehol and that any directives issuing from an imperial conference would be defied (Makino 1990: 537–8).

On 4 February 1933, the army chief of staff, Prince Kan'in, who had replaced Kanaya in November 1931, requested imperial sanction for strategic Kwantung Army operations against Chang Hsueh-liang's forces in Jehol. Now hoping that would end the Manchurian incident once and for all, the Emperor acquiesced, even though the cabinet had not given its approval. However, he expressly stipulated that Japanese forces should not penetrate further south than the Great Wall. Kan'in appeared to agree to this condition but the Emperor and Nara were still reluctant to see the fighting spread to Jehol; both feared that hostilities there might overflow beyond the Great Wall (Nara 1990b: 347).

But then, after Saitō had expressed his anxiety, on 8 February, that the Jehol campaign would worsen Japan's position in the League, the Emperor at once instructed Nara to tell Kan'in that he wanted to revoke his sanction of the Jehol operation on the grounds that the Saitō cabinet had not approved it (Nara 1990b: 348). However, when the Emperor reiterated his change of heart to Kan'in on 10 February, the army chief replied that most of the cabinet, including in particular the army minister, General Araki Sadao, supported the campaign and that at any rate, the military's right of supreme command was not subject to cabinet approval. He added that for these reasons and because the Emperor had already sanctioned the campaign, it was too late to halt it (Nara 1990b: 348).

Seeing that the Saitō cabinet was incapable of managing the looming crisis in Jehol, on 20 February the Emperor again wanted an imperial conference, to restrain the Kwantung Army. However, since that same day Saitō had reported to the Emperor the government's decision to withdraw from the League in response to the League's censure of Japanese aggression in Manchuria, Makino once again cautiously opposed an imperial conference, arguing this time that it would only be used to ritually endorse Japan's break with the League, which he, Saionji, and the Emperor had resisted all along (Makino 1990: 546). Nara summed up the collective view at court when he wrote in his diary that day that under no circumstances should the 'throne' be held responsible for Japanese policy (Nara 1990b: 350).

Ultimately, on 27 February, the Kwantung Army invaded Jehol from Manchukuo and in April, after units of the Kwantung Army had struck south of the Great Wall against his wishes, the Emperor lamely asked General Honjō, who had replaced Nara as chief aide-de-camp, 'Can the Kwantung

Army be ordered to cease its advances?' (Honjō 1975: 159). On 10 May he again complained helplessly that

> willfully to ignore and take actions that run counter to the conditions to which the Chief of Staff had clearly agreed is not, from the standpoint of the preservation of discipline and authority and the integrity of the supreme command, a trifling matter.
>
> (Honjō 1975: 160)

Three weeks later, with Jehol under Japanese control, the Kwantung Army reached an agreement with Chinese officials known as the Tangku Truce which extended the border of Manchukuo to the Great Wall and established a demilitarized zone in the Peking–Tientsin region of northern China (Crowley 1966: 185). The Tangku Truce notwithstanding, the United States and the League of Nations denounced Japan and refused to recognize the political consequences of its aggression in Manchuria (Ogata 1964: 171–3). By then Japan had broken with the League.

Since the court had emphasized cooperation with the League and the Western powers, from its perspective this rupture represented the greatest casualty of the Manchurian incident, which the Emperor and his advisers had struggled to prevent from occurring. After Britain tabled a censure motion at the League against Japan, Foreign Minister Uchida Kōsai had informed the court on 30 January 1933 that in the opinion of the foreign and army ministries, Japanese public opinion would never tolerate the League's interference in Manchuria. Clutching at illusions, the Emperor had replied that Western disapproval of the Manchurian incident might yet restrain the army in the anticipated Jehol campaign (Makino 1990: 540–1).[7]

Following the League's overwhelming vote of censure and the walk-out staged by Japan's delegation in Geneva on 24 February, he had still instructed Foreign Minister Uchida to emphasize good relations with the Western powers. On 8 March, even as the government discussed an imperial rescript announcing Japan's withdrawal, he had wondered to Makino whether the decision to withdraw could be reconsidered (Makino 1990: 548).

However, it was too late. Even Makino and Saionji now agreed with the Saitō government that Japan had to withdraw as a matter of national honor (Kido I 1966: 224). On 27 March 1933 the Emperor duly promulgated an imperial rescript announcing Japan's exodus from the League. In part, the rescript expressed his personal regret that Japan had withdrawn and his hope that relations with the West might somehow be improved. He stated, 'By quitting the League and embarking on a course of its own, Our Empire does not mean that it will stand aloof in the Extreme Orient nor that it will isolate itself thereby from the fraternity of nations' in striving to 'promote mutual confidence between Our Empire and all the other Powers' (Murakami S. 1983: 276).

He had also wanted to state emphatically that henceforth the civil and military spheres of government in Japan should be strictly separated, to prevent the military from usurping power, as had happened throughout the Manchurian incident. He later explained, referring to the army during the incident, 'I was deeply concerned about the fact that they seemed to be exceeding the limits of their proper responsibility. So I made a special point of mentioning the need to stay within the bounds of their proper areas of responsibility' (Honjō 1975: 186). However, various palace drafts of the rescript to that effect were resisted by Army Minister Araki who resented even this implied criticism of the army.[8] The result was a vague compromise in the rescript which read, 'We command that all public servants, whether civil or military, shall faithfully perform each his appointed duty' (Murakami S. 1983: 276). Beyond this 'command' and the fragile hope that Japan could still cooperate with the League, the Emperor could not go in the rescript.

Looking back at the Emperor's role during the Manchurian crisis, his tendency at times to react indecisively to events caused him to sanction aggression against his better judgment, as when he approved reinforcements from Korea and the Jehol operation. But otherwise, privately at court, he had opposed the incident and its negative domestic and international repercussions, only to find that what he did mattered little given the military's readiness to ignore him when it chose to do so. Had he openly challenged the army's usurpation of his supreme command prerogative, 'any such action might have induced more unrestrained radicalism' within the army (Ogata 1964: 150).

This pervasive threat of violent reprisals, the strength of popular support for a war ostensibly fought in his name, and the *fait accompli* of war itself had made it politically impossible and futile for him to intervene publicly against the military. The Japanese people were therefore completely unaware of his personal opposition to the incident, just as they had been unaware of his stance concerning the Chang Tso-lin affair and the London Naval Treaty controversy earlier. Rejoicing over the success of the 'Emperor's army', they erroneously believed the conquest of Manchuria represented the Emperor's will (Kawahara 1990: 58–9).

Yet, it is also apparent that the Emperor's powerlessness in dealing with the Manchurian crisis was compounded by his own political self-restraint. As he had insisted to Prince Chichibu in 1931, he rejected any attempt to establish 'personal rule' for fear this would violate the principles of constitutional government and his role as a constitutional monarch which he sought to sustain in conscious emulation of Emperor Meiji. Very much the same consideration motivated his advisers to constrain the Emperor and here, Saionji was especially pivotal. To reiterate, 'It was the unswerving conviction of Saionji ... that the function of a constitutional monarch was to act in accordance with the advice of those in responsible posts and not to override their decisions nor to take the initiative in formulating policy' (Ogata 1964: 151). Accordingly, Saionji urged the Emperor to act with restraint in responding to the Manchurian crisis because 'The defeat of constitutional monarchy which Saionji believed would follow any overt interference by the

Emperor in the Manchurian issue, would have undoubtedly resulted in the strengthening of the army and its role in China' (Connors 1987: 132).

Rather, to Saionji and Makino, the best way to preserve constitutional government, and ultimately international peace, was to uphold the principle of a monarch who reigned over, but did not rule, the country. Saionji summed up his position succinctly when he once said, 'My duty to the Emperor is twofold, to avoid damaging the spirit of the Constitution and to honor international treaties' (Harada II 1950: 108), even if, or especially because, others in Japan did neither. This commitment to the constitution and to international cooperation, which the Emperor shared, was already under unprecedented terrorist assault in the early 1930s.

3 The challenge of Shōwa Restoration radicalism, 1931–1937

From the Manchurian incident onward the Japanese people increasingly succumbed to a 'subject mentality' as they projected 'their naive and passionate fantasies toward the Emperor', whom they patriotically viewed as the all-powerful symbol of national greatness (Irokawa 1983: 35). The role of the state in fostering 'the dying monarchist illusions of the masses', which typified this subject mentality, was emphasized in the Comintern's 1932 Theses to guide the Japanese communist movement. The Theses asserted that although 'thinly concealed by pseudo-constitutional forms', the 'absolute' monarchy served the interests of the ruling elite and of Japanese imperialism. Therefore, 'Its destruction must be considered the first of the fundamental tasks of the revolution in Japan' (Beckmann and Okubo 1969: 336).[1]

The Comintern's call to arms in opposing the Japanese monarchy, the bureaucracy, the military and the class system reflected Moscow's own illusions about the prospects of communist revolution in Japan. Nevertheless, it is true that the monarchy was used by the state to ensure public conformity to state authority. Ever since the enactment of the peace preservation law, 'The use of the enigmatic and highly emotional term *kokutai* reflected a continuation of the government drive to indoctrinate its subjects in the way of reverence for the Emperor' (Mitchell 1976: 67). Hence, in the early 1930s, great priority was placed by the Special Higher Police (Tipton 1990), who enforced the law, on eliciting the 'conversion' (*tenkō*) of alleged 'thought criminals' to the ideology of emperor-centered nationalism.

The most dramatic such conversion occurred in 1933 with the widely publicized statement of two prominent communist leaders, Sano Manabu and Nabeyama Sadachika, who had been arrested for plotting the revolutionary overthrow of the state and the emperor system. They proclaimed, 'The imperial system of Japan, unlike tsarism, has never been a system of exploitation and suppression. The imperial household has been an expression of national unity; it has reduced class violence within the country' (Beckmann and Okubo 1969: 246).

Many other communist 'conversions' soon followed but few matched the lyrical hyperbole of Sano's. He later said of the Emperor, 'The essence of the Imperial System lies in the Emperor's position as the Head of the Main

Family of the Japanese people and like the Imperial gods and goddesses, the Creator and Sustainer of heaven and earth.' He continued, 'What supreme bliss it is to be born a Japanese with the privilege of sacrificing oneself for the sake of the noblest and absolute being, the Emperor' (Tsurumi K. 1970: 51).

Believing himself to be a constitutional, not an 'absolute', monarch, the Shōwa Emperor could scarcely have welcomed Sano's effusive character-ization of his position. Still, he was probably as keen as the government to see the communist movement eradicated. After all, a communist sympathizer (Nanba) had once tried to kill him, the communists had called for his overthrow, and with assets at nearly thirty million yen, he would not have looked benignly on communist threats to the capitalist order.[2]

The evidence available does not disclose whether the Emperor was personally involved in the campaign against the communists. But from the government's perspective, it was sufficient that in 1928 his seal appeared on an imperial ordinance desired by Prime Minister Tanaka and the vice-president of the privy council, Hiranuma Kiichirō, to strengthen the peace preservation law by adding the death penalty for enemies of the state. The monarchy was enlisted against the communists in other indirect ways, too. For instance, the imperial household ministry financed the Imperial Rehabilitation Club (Teikoku Kōshinkai), which assisted penitent 'thought criminals' (Mitchell 1976: 129–30).

Thus, whether or not the Emperor himself actively encouraged anti-communism, the monarchy was strongly associated with the suppression of 'dangerous thoughts' the control of which was the responsibility of the police, the home and justice ministries, and the courts. One does not have to accept the notion of 'emperor system fascism' to acknowledge this association; by its very nature, and from the earliest stages of state-formation in Meiji, the monarchy had always been susceptible to manipulation by the government in reacting to left-wing extremism, be it anarchist or communist.

By extension, the imperial institution was also potentially subject to co-optation by the anti-communist extreme right-wing. For this reason, amid the growing nationalistic ethos of the 1930s, controlling the weakened radical left was considerably less important to the court than containing the much greater ideological and political threat to constitutional government posed by the forces of 'Shōwa Restoration' radicalism on the far right. Their persecution of Minobe Tatsukichi in 1935 and their near-success in attempting a coup d'état in 1936 were to have important long-term consequences for the ways in which the Emperor reacted to the crisis of war in future years.

THE IDEOLOGICAL THREAT OF SHŌWA RESTORATIONISM, 1931–1935

The young officers and civilian extremists who engaged in terrorist violence against the established order were persuaded that Japan had reached the point of acute crisis due to the decline of capitalism in the Depression and the failure of liberal party government adequately to ensure national security. In this perception of national crisis, a 'Shōwa Restoration', reminiscent of the Meiji Restoration, was required to save Japan from internal decay and external threats to the empire (Shillony 1973: 56–72). Their accompanying 'revolt against the West' (Najita and Harootunian 1988) rejected such 'foreign' influences as individualism, liberalism, materialism and communism, which in their view had eroded social and political cohesion in Japan. In place of these influences they sought to revive traditional values and myths of an idealized moral, social, and political community united under an absolute sovereign.

The conceptual vocabularly they used to express this vision of a 'Shōwa Restoration' was often contradictory and included, for example, both agrarian utopian and national socialist ideas. Where the translation of these conflicting ideas into radical action is concerned, the picture is complicated by their overlap with different rival factions in the military. Without pressing the correlation too far, the agrarian utopian variety of Shōwa Restoration criticism appealed mostly to the idealistic 'imperial way faction' (Kōdō-ha), while the national socialist variety had greater traction in the more pragmatic and utilitarian 'control faction' (Tōsei-ha), in the army.

More will be said about these factions later. The salient point here is that all advocates of a Shōwa Restoration tended to believe 'that the goals envisaged in the Meiji Restoration that would have maintained national integrity and expansive autonomy . . . and achieved social justice at home for the oppressed people never reached maturity within constitutional government' as it had evolved since the Meiji era (Najita [1974] 1980: 128). This belief made radical restorationism a major ideological and political threat to the Emperor and others at court who respected constitutional government in the 'Minobe way'.

To illustrate briefly the main themes of radical restorationist thought, Gondō Seikei and Tachibana Kōsaburō, two agrarian utopian thinkers, devalued constitutional government by stressing its irrelevance to the central task of rebuilding the nation on the foundations of a communitarian social ideal that evoked the traditions of village Japan. In this intrinsically romantic view, which highlighted the religious function of the emperor as high priest of the nation, Gondō held that

> the Emperor was at once more personal as an ideal and less tangible as a practical part of governance since his social role was confined to that of benevolent patriarch, rather than the source of political authority and national will as in state nationalism.
>
> (Havens 1974: 200)

Because Gondō in effect regarded Japan as 'a large tutelary shrine' (Najita and Harootunian 1988: 724), for him the absolute character of the monarchy flowed more from traditional religious origins than modern constitutional prescriptions.

Tachibana, too, ascribed to the emperor a paramount symbolic significance as high priest who mystically united the people as a religious and political community protected by the gods (Havens 1974: 266). He and Gondō believed that before this sense of community could be realized, the Emperor had to be forcibly liberated from the clutches of bureaucratic authority. Consequently they became involved in the 15 May 1932 incident, for which they were arrested. Gondō was soon released; Tachibana was sentenced to life imprisonment although in 1940 he, too, was released.

A more statist, national socialist expression of radical restorationism is found in the thought of Kita Ikki. As his *Nihon kokka kaizō hōan* (Outline Plan for the Reorganization of Japan), written in 1919, discloses, Kita likewise evinced a communitarian idealism, albeit somewhat differently. He viewed the monarch not as a divine being but a secular symbol of community, the 'people's Emperor', or *kokumin tennō*, who would serve as 'the symbol of national unity from below rather than of bureaucratic rule from above' (Kuno 1978: 76). Kita's program of revolutionary action, to prepare Japan for a confrontation with Western imperialism in Asia, called for a revolutionary coup d'état, the suspension of the constitution in the name of the emperor, military rule, and the liberation of the emperor and the people from bureaucratic control. The result, he believed, would be greater military and industrial power and social justice for the poor.[3]

Kita is significant because he influenced the young officers who led the army rebellion of 26 February 1936 (Shillony 1973: 72–80). After the uprising was suppressed, this led to his trial and execution for treason in 1937. But of interest here is that his brand of Shōwa restorationism included certain notions about the emperor which, because they superficially resembled Minobe Tatsukichi's, were all the more insidious in challenging the court's concept of constitutional government.

Specifically, Kita likewise regarded the emperor as an organ of the state. In 1906 he wrote,

> Japan's *kokutai* is not a family with the Emperor as father and the people as children but a bona fide state. The Emperor's position is not analogous to that of a main family *vis-à-vis* branch families; he is an organ of the state.

(Kuno 1978: 75)

Concerning the extensive prerogatives of the emperor, Noguchi Takehiko points out that Kita was 'perfectly aware that these imperial prerogatives were clever legal devices to ensure the supra-constitutionality of the Emperor's position and authority'. But in believing that the Shōwa Emperor would use his prerogatives to suspend the constitution for three years after a Shōwa Restoration was proclaimed, Kita held, as Noguchi Takehiko expresses it, that 'a coup d'état carried out through the exercise of the imperial prerogatives was *absolutely constitutional*' (Noguchi 1984: 445, italics Noguchi's). This 'legalistic fantasy', which collided with the Emperor's interpretation of his role as an 'organ' of constitutional government, depended on the willing cooperation of the Emperor '*as an individual* – a condition that was at once *indispensable and uncertain*' (Noguchi 1984: 445, italics Noguchi's). Neither Kita nor the rebels of 1936 anticipated the complete refusal of the Shōwa Emperor to sanction a revolutionary coup which, leading to military domination, would have destroyed the very system of constitutional government he had pledged himself to uphold.

The manner in which Kita had twisted the concept of the emperor as an organ of the state to justify a violent attack on constitutional government is illustrated in a written statement by Captain Isobe Asaichi whom Kita had influenced. As he composed his thoughts while awaiting execution for his part in the failed uprising of February 1936, Isobe wrote, 'The genrō, the senior statesmen, the people, the police, the courts, the prisons, there's nothing that isn't authorized by the Emperor–organ theory. *Shōwa Japan has finally evolved* into the era of the organ-theory'. Declaring that the rebels had thought of themselves as 'advanced thinkers who would plan and guide this evolutionary advance', Isobe explained that they had killed government leaders to '*bring Japan as the Emperor–organ state to yet a higher stage of evolution*'. But when confronted by strong opposition they found that they 'could not even defy the orders issued by the Emperor–organ state in the name of the Emperor-as-organ!' This failure, he lamented, 'is most shameful'. Isobe had nothing but contempt for the Emperor for refusing to support the rebels (Noguchi 1984: 451, italics Noguchi's).

The '26 February 1936 incident', inspired mainly by Kita's theory of revolution, was the most serious domestic political crisis in early Shōwa Japan. But it was ominously prefaced by a different kind of upheaval, the so-called 'Minobe affair' in 1935, which also bore serious implications for constitutional government. The 'emperor–organ theory incident', or *tennō kikansetsu jiken* as it is otherwise known, commenced in February that year with an attack, in the house of peers, to which Minobe had been appointed three years earlier, on his constitutional interpretation. After being accused of the crime of lèse majesté he subsequently faced months of public vilification, which was extensively reported in the media, before the incident climaxed in October when the cabinet of Prime Minister Okada Keisuke publicly repudiated his emperor–organ theory. In the interim Minobe was forced to resign in disgrace from the peers and from his post at Tokyo Imperial University. He later suffered physical abuse and retreated altogether from public life, to re-emerge after the Pacific War.

Detailed studies of the Minobe affair indicate that the crowded ranks of his critics comprised academics in the conservative Hozumi-Uesugi school of constitutional interpretation, prominent conservative bureaucrats such as Hiranuma Kiichirō, leading members of the major parties, the military establishment including the reservists, much of the media, and it would appear, a great many ordinary citizens. His detractors commonly asserted that by portraying the emperor as merely an organ of the state, Minobe had treacherously insulted the august dignity of the imperial institution, denied the divinity of the sovereign, defiled the *kokutai*, and weakened the state with foreign theories which violated the tradition of imperial rule.

Others who were known to share Minobe's constitutional interpretation, including Ichiki Kitokurō, likewise came under severe criticism. Ichiki's subsequent resignation from the privy council presidency a year later – whereupon Hiranuma succeeded him – illustrates that the attack on Minobe 'also became an attack on court leaders and the Emperor's close advisers, ultimately encouraging the outbreak of assassinations and attempted assassinations that peaked on February 26, 1936' (Titus 1974: 131). In these circumstances, the Emperor understandably endeavored to defend Minobe whenever he could at court.

He possibly wanted to defend Minobe publicly as well. But the sheer scale and momentum of the movement to censure Minobe made this anything but 'relatively easy', contrary to one account (Behr 1989: 152). Furthermore, the Emperor may well have been prevented by Saionji from speaking out publicly on Minobe's behalf. Saionji understood that the Minobe affair involved the crucial issue of constitutional government. But he continued to believe that were the Emperor to participate openly in political controversy, this would compromise his position as a constitutional monarch above the political fray (Connors 1987: 115). During a tea party hosted by the Emperor and Empress at the palace in 1934, the Prince reportedly said that if the Emperor 'wished to set an example for the people, he should say nothing at all but should simply do so as a matter of fact. With this kind of subtle attitude, he should strive to perfect his royal virtues' (Honjō 1975: 254–5). This advice epitomized Saionji's cautious view of the Emperor in relation to politics.

Of the almost entirely isolated Minobe, the Emperor privately told his attendants at court: 'I think Minobe is not at all disloyal. Is there really anyone his equal in Japan today? To bury such a scholar would be lamentable' (Harada IV 1951: 238). In expressing his personal support of Minobe, he displayed a reasoned intellectual style which confirms the general impression that 'the Emperor's mind worked in a rational, critical, and analytical fashion' (Hane 1982: 48). This reasoned style, which may be traced to the influence of his teachers at the Tōgū-gogakumonsho, is apparent in his statements concerning Minobe to General Honjō, which Honjō recorded in his diary.

From Honjō's account, the Emperor was especially aware that Minobe's critics viewed the monarch as a god not subject to constitutional constraints of any kind. He thus went to great lengths to disavow the myths which supported this concept of the *tennō* as an absolute being with absolute powers. In his diary entry of 11 March 1935 the army chief aide-de-camp reports the Emperor as telling him 'that although there might be a difference in status between the two of us, he did not believe that physically there was any difference whatsoever. In light of this he found it highly upsetting both mentally and physically' that because of attacks on Minobe's organ theory 'he was being turned into an entity without any freedom whatsoever' (Honjō 1975: 203).[4]

Later that month Honjō told the Emperor 'the military worships His

Majesty as divinity incarnate and if His Majesty were to be treated just like any other person in accordance with the organ theory, it would create difficulties in the areas of military education and the supreme command'. However, the Emperor argued that the organ theory was entirely constitutional and therefore should be respected. Honjō wrote,

> His Majesty noted that Article IV of the Constitution states 'the Emperor is the Head of the Empire'. This shows that the Constitution is based on the organ theory. If the organ theory has to be changed the Constitution also would have to be revised.
>
> (Honjō 1975: 204)

The military's reliance on the myths of imperial divinity to discredit Minobe's organ theory is evident from a directive to the army written by General Mazaki Jinzaburō, then inspector general of military education. The document, which greatly distressed the Emperor as his long conversations about it with Honjō disclose, asserted:

> The founding deity's divine decree is as clear as the sun and the moon. There is no question about the fact that the Emperor, who belongs to one eternal line, graciously rules over us as a god manifest and that he is the central entity of state governance [the source of sovereignty].
>
> (Imai and Takahashi 4 1963: 387)

But on this crucial matter of sovereignty, the Emperor said, echoing Minobe's opinion,

> To hold that sovereignty resides not in the state but in the monarch is to court charges of despotism ... I too would gladly adopt the theory of imperial sovereignty if it did not lead to the bane of despotism ... and if it did not conflict with our national polity and history.
>
> (Honjō 1975: 206)

There was no doubt in his mind that the theory of imperial sovereignty, as Minobe's critics articulated it, would lead to despotism.

These several examples from many in the Honjō diary, indicate how firmly the Emperor believed that Minobe's organ theory was soundly based on the Meiji constitution, a point he repeated constantly, sometimes with reference not only to Minobe's arguments but also to those of Jellinek, who had influenced Minobe's views. The Emperor's studious approach to the subject once prompted Honjō to tell Mazaki and the army minister, General Hayashi Senjurō, that 'if they wanted to get involved in academic theories they should speak directly to His Majesty' about the organ theory (Honjō 1975: 208).

However, the army and Minobe's other critics continued to exert enormous pressure on the Okada government to repudiate the organ theory and, throughout the controversy, the military hammered on the theme that the theory was contrary to the belief that the Emperor was 'divinity incarnate', as

Honjō had put it. This offended the Emperor's 'rational scientific' world view, as it has been characterized in studies of his earlier education, and impelled him to say, again as Honjō records his remarks,

> that if matters of faith and belief were used to suppress scientific theories then world progress will be hindered. Theories such as evolution would have to be overturned. Of course, he said, he realized that faith and belief were important. [But] belief and science must move forward side by side.
>
> (Honjō 1975: 208)

But while science, including references to the theory of evolution, informed the Emperor's defense of the organ theory against irrational attacks, so did his interest in history, another legacy of his earlier education which he applied, albeit indirectly, to the organ theory controversy. For example, at one stage in a discussion of the theory with Honjō their wide-ranging conversation turned to why Germany had been defeated in World War I. Honjō said Germany fell 'because of the anti-statist propaganda that Great Britain and America directed against it. For this reason it was necessary to strengthen all the more the concept of *kokutai*', and hence of absolute monarchy. In contrast the Emperor replied that the defeat of Germany was attributable to more specific political factors such as the Kaiser's lack of support within Germany and destructive civil-military rivalry which enabled the German military to act unilaterally, with disastrous results (Honjō 1975: 210–11).

His implication was that abstractions such as 'national polity', and their substrate of racial myths like those evoked by critics of the organ theory, had little to do with the rise and fall of nations and thus had no meaning in rational political discourse. This was also his inference in analyzing the collapse of the Russian monarchy in 1917. He held that among other reasons, as with the ancien régime in France, the Tsarist order fell because it lacked a stable middle class (Honjō 1975: 211). His general theme was that hard evidence, not recourse to irrational beliefs, was needed in debating important issues of political history and contemporary political theory, including the organ theory.

The Emperor's defense of Minobe was motivated by political as much as theoretical concerns, however. He frequently expressed anxiety that the public clamor against Minobe would jeopardize Ichiki, and Kanamori Tokujirō, chief of the cabinet legislative bureau and an authority on constitutional law, whose similar adherence to the organ theory also eventually cost him his post after Minobe's eclipse (Honjō 1975: 203, 209, 230).

The Emperor was also acutely sensitive to the reality that in opposing the organ theory while extolling the monarch as an absolute sovereign, the army still treated him in effect as an organ of state, if only to manipulate him politically for its own purposes. On one occasion he sarcastically asked Honjō, 'What would happen if I were to take this theory about the absolute sovereignty of the Emperor in earnest, instead of a mere theory on paper?' He then reminded Honjō that the army had consistently ignored his wishes even though it professedly regarded him with awe as an absolute monarch. He said that during the Manchurian incident, 'The army would not provide me with the information I wanted from the cabinet . . . why does the army prevent me from gaining information that I require?' (Honjō 1975: 207).

His sense of frustration at being unable to prevent the army from 'burying' Minobe was reinforced by his continuing feelings, dating from the Manchurian crisis, of powerlessness towards the army generally. In July 1935, during the Minobe affair, he recalled that Mazaki had joined Araki in defying his will when they had advocated the invasion of Jehol several years earlier and asked Honjō 'if Mazaki was not like Katō Kanji in character', referring to the Admiral's intractability during the London Naval Treaty controversy (Honjō 1975: 221–2).

The problem of army defiance in foreign policy had been illustrated yet again in the so-called 'Tientsin incident' of May 1935 in which officers from the Japanese garrison, which had been stationed in Tientsin ever since the Boxer uprising in 1900, used the threat of force to successfully demand of the Peking military council that Nationalist Chinese military advisers and political elements be removed from the Peking–Tientsin area (Crowley 1966: 214–17). Sharing the Emperor's anxiety over this unauthorized intervention, Saionji pressed the Okada government to restrain the Japanese army in northern China, only to be informed that the Tientsin issue involved the powers of the supreme command and hence lay beyond cabinet jurisdiction (Connors 1987: 153). Honjō reports that the Emperor was 'gravely concerned' that the Western powers would interpret the Tientsin initiative as a new provocation and thus accuse Japan 'of having a dual civilian and military foreign policy' (Honjō 1975: 217).

The 1935 'Tientsin incident' proved to be but one episode in Japan's penetration of north China which eventually would contribute to war with China in 1937. However, it also figured indirectly in the Minobe affair when Saionji decided to cease his opposition to the Tientsin incident if, in exchange, the leaders of the control faction in the army, who at the time emphasized China as Japan's strategic priority, were willing to support Minobe against his principal critics within the army, the imperial way faction Generals Mazaki and Araki Sadao, who stressed strategic preparedness against Russia as their priority (Connors 1987: 153–4).

To strengthen the control faction, Saionji backed its initiative in July 1935 to transfer Mazaki to the supreme war council and replace him as inspector general of military education with its own man, General Watanabe Jōtarō. Having no use for Mazaki, the Emperor was pleased to approve this maneuver (Honjō 1975: 222). Saionji's intrigues, however, came to no avail. The purge of Mazaki soon led to the retaliatory assassination on 12 August of the control faction's acknowledged leader, General Nagata Tetsuzan, the director of the military affairs bureau in the army ministry, by Lieutenant-Colonel Aizawa Saburō of the imperial way faction (Crowley 1966: 266–7). Given this escalating struggle for supremacy in the army, which would eventually lead to the imperial way-inspired attempted coup of February 1936, the control faction could not afford to appear tolerant of Minobe's organ theory.

Finally, although the prime minister was personally sympathetic to Minobe and his supporters at court, the Okada cabinet yielded to public pressure to 'clarify the national polity' by officially repudiating Minobe. The government's public statement, issued on 15 October 1935, read in part,

> Any theory which, merely on the basis of foreign examples, holds that the subject of sovereignty is not the Emperor but the state and that the Emperor is an organ of the state – such as the so-called organ theory – must be strictly eradicated, for they run counter to our divine national polity.[5]
>
> (Miller 1965: 246)

It would be difficult to overstate the negative consequences for prewar Japan of this climax of the Minobe affair. In terms of constitutional interpretation, the discrediting of the organ theory meant that henceforth political discourse would be predicated on the unquestioned assumption that Japan's was an absolute, not a limited, monarchy. In terms of the ideas, emotions, and symbols of Japanese nationalism, it correspondingly meant that irrationality would prevail during the years of war which lay ahead. And in the more immediate context of what had become a virtual civil war within the military, it gave great impetus to those who would violently 'restore' an 'absolute' Emperor, not so that he could actually rule, but in order to use his authority to legitimize the 'renovation' (*kakushin*) of Japan.

Altogether, then, the 'eradication' of the organ theory 'constituted a clear victory of the military-renovationist forces over the remnants of the liberal constitutional regime' (Miller 1965: 246). The Emperor sensed this was what had happened when, during a grim review of the Minobe affair in December 1935, he asked Honjō, 'is it not likely that if ever the tide of fascism rises in Japan, the military would support the movement?' (Honjō 1975: 232–3). This question would trouble him even more when faced with the army rebellion two months later.

THE FEBRUARY REBELLION AND 'CLEANSING THE ARMY', 1936–1937

In addition to the October 1931 plot and the 15 May 1932 incident discussed in Chapter 2, radical restorationist unrest among young officers and civilian activists had been apparent in the so-called 'March incident' of 1931 in which certain young officers had conspired with Kita Ikki and Ōkawa Shūmei, another theorist of national socialism, in planning a coup d'état to anticipate such military action abroad as would occur in Manchuria. The general whom the conspirators hoped to install in power was Ugaki Kazushige, who will figure again later in this account. The March plot, however, was uncovered in advance and aborted.

Then there occurred the 'Blood Pledge Corps incident' (*Ketsumeidan jiken*) of February 1932, which resulted in the assassination, by fanatics led by the Buddhist priest Inoue Nisshō, of Finance Minister Inoue Junnosuke and Dan Takuma, director of Mitsui, who were targeted as symbols of a corrupt capitalist order. No coup was envisaged but it is notable that Gondō Seikei and Tachibana Kōsaburō were suspected of having been involved in this outburst of terrorism (Havens 1974: 297–302).

Young officers were also implicated with civilian activists in two other, abortive, coup plots: the 'Heaven-Sent Soldiers' Unit incident' (*Shinpeitai jiken*) and the 'Officers' School incident' (*Shikan gakkō jiken*), in July 1933 and November 1934 respectively. In the former, the plan was to kill the prime minister and all the cabinet, attack the headquarters of the political parties, and after declaring martial law, install a new government under an imperial prince. In the latter incident, it was intended that General Mazaki Jinzaburō would take power after a coup of comparable violence.[6]

The young officers' movement which gave rise to these incidents did not have widespread popular support. Nor did most of its participants have a clear notion of what, politically, would follow a successful coup (Shillony 1973: 76–7). Rather, they were driven primarily by 'the desire to re-enact the Meiji Restoration, antagonism toward the privileged classes, professed anti-capitalism, concern for the rural population, fervent patriotism, and a mystical belief in Japan's unique destiny' (Shillony 1973: 80).

Their idealism attracted the sympathy of key military leaders, especially those of the imperial way faction, like Araki, who once said, concerning the perpetrators of the 15 May 1932 incident,

> We cannot restrain our tears when we consider the mentality expressed in the actions of these pure and naive young men. They were not actions for fame, or personal gain, nor are they traitorous. They were performed in the sincere belief that they were for the benefit of Imperial Japan. Therefore, in dealing with this incident, it will not do to dispose of it in a routine manner . . .
>
> (Maruyama 1963: 67)

And in fact, prior to the February 1936 incident, the trials which followed earlier incidents usually ended with light punishments.

The links between the young officers and Araki are notable because Araki, who had been the choice of the October 1931 incident conspirators to take charge of the government, had done more than any other army leader to popularize 'imperial way' sentiments in the military (Shillony 1973: 31). Mazaki was no less suspected of treachery, not only by the court but by the government: in 1934 Prime Minister Okada advised Army Minister Hayashi to 'get rid of Mazaki, who is the root of the evil in the army' (Harada IV 1951: 294).

The court was further concerned that the imperial way faction had developed links with members of the imperial family itself. As was true of Prince Fushimi when he became navy chief of staff, Prince Kan'in had been backed by Araki when he was made army chief of staff. Similar connections existed with Princes Higashikuni Naruhiko (related to the Emperor through marriage to Emperor Meiji's daughter Toshiko) and Asaka Yasuhiko (married to the Shōwa Emperor's aunt Nobuko), both of whom were used by the imperial way leaders to try and influence the court. After learning that Mazaki had asked Higashikuni to convey the army's views to the Emperor, in 1933 Kido wrote in his diary, 'I am sincerely troubled by the tendency to use members of the imperial family' in this way (Kido I 1966: 234). That Higashikuni had been indirectly implicated in the 15 May 1932 incident and that Asaka broke precedent by attending the court-martial of Prime Minister Inukai's assassins, illustrated that these imperial princes could not be relied upon to help the court in coping with Shōwa Restoration radicalism (Shillony 1973: 107).

Even more alarming in this regard was the position of Prince Chichibu who, until the birth of Crown Prince Akihito in December 1933, was next in line to the throne. His advice to the Emperor during the Manchurian incident to suspend the constitution was never forgotten at court. But the court was probably unaware of Chichibu's long-standing contacts with Kita Ikki's associate, Nishida Mitsugi, who once wrote, 'My great wish was to carry out the noble task (i.e. a national reform) with the cooperation of Prince Chichibu' (Shillony 1973: 96). Chichibu was likewise close to Araki, dating from 1928 when he entered the army staff college, then supervised by Araki; there, he also met many of the young officers of the Shōwa Restoration persuasion (Shillony 1973: 98).

Furthermore, it was suspected at court that Chichibu had been involved, albeit indirectly, in the October 1931 and 15 May 1932 incidents (Shillony 1973: 106–7). On 28 May 1932 the Emperor remarked to Nara, 'I cannot feel that the radicalism of the words and deeds of the young officers is entirely unexpected. Is there not a need to turn Prince Chichibu [away from them]?' (Nara 1990b: 346). In June 1932 Kido, Harada Kumao, and Prince Konoe Fumimaro similarly expressed concern over Chichibu's 'militarist views' (Kido I 1966: 176). Saionji, too, worried about Chichibu. In 1932 he rejected a suggestion that Chichibu be appointed as lord privy seal: 'I am absolutely opposed ... to making any member of the imperial family, especially Prince Chichibu, lord privy seal' (Harada II 1950: 343).

Hence, by 1936, Chichibu represented the most potentially dangerous penetration of the court by radical restorationism (Hosaka M. 1989b). The army rebels of 1936 may have had no definite plans to put him on the throne if the Shōwa Emperor did not cooperate with their attempted coup, but they did not entirely discount this possibility (Shillony 1973: 128). Nor did Saionji discount it. He conjectured, 'Japanese history has sometimes repeated itself and one can find a considerable number of examples where, urged on by hangers-on, a younger brother has killed an older brother to ascend to the throne' (Harada VI 1951: 297).

Consequently, the court moved quickly to check Chichibu politically after the 26 February 1936 rebellion had started. Upon reaching Tokyo from his military post in Hirosaki, he was intercepted by Prince Takamatsu, who, along with the Emperor's third brother, Mikasa, remained loyal to the Emperor, and was conveyed directly to the palace, where he could not contact the rebels and where he could be pressured to help end the rebellion. Because they were also under suspicion, imperial Princes Higashikuni, Fushimi and Asaka were likewise summoned to the palace. The court's concern over Higashikuni was especially justified. Earlier, Higashikuni, reportedly in a drunken state, had been waiting in his residence to receive the rebels. Referring to himself in the third person, he had told an attendant, 'The junior officers ... are paying a great deal of respect to Prince Higashikuni. They may call on the Prince in order to win him over. If so, you must receive them with utmost hospitality' (Kido I 1966: 470).

The rebellion began in the snowy early hours of 26 February when more than 1,400 soldiers from three regiments seized control of central Tokyo and with *sonnō tōkan* ('Revere the Emperor, destroy the traitors') as their clarion call, assassinated the lord privy seal, Saitō Makoto, Finance Minister Takahashi Korekiyo, and the control faction's Watanabe Jōtarō, who had expressed some sympathy with Minobe the previous year (Shillony 1973: 135–7). Grand Chamberlain Suzuki Kantarō, Makino Nobuaki and Prime Minister Okada all narrowly managed to escape similar attempts on their lives. Meanwhile, the rebels issued a revolutionary manifesto praising the tradition of benevolent imperial rule over 'our divine country' (Shillony 1973: 146). They expected that presently, the Emperor would proclaim the Shōwa Restoration and summon General Mazaki to form a new government.[7]

When first informed of the rebellion, the Emperor reportedly said, 'So, they have finally done it. . . . It's all due to a failing in me', possibly blaming himself for not having anticipated this attempted coup (Kanroji 1975: 135). Later, he would blame senior army leaders for this failure when he asked in consternation, 'Why was an incident of this magnitude not uncovered in advance?' (Honjō 1975: 282). Knowing 'that his influence for rationality, however small, would be completely lost if a really right-wing military takeover occurred' (Sheldon 1976: 32), the Emperor at once strongly opposed this extreme extralegal challenge to constitutional government.

Even before he had an opportunity to consult with Saionji, who was at his villa in Okitsu when the rebellion erupted, the Emperor declared to the army minister, General Kawashima Yoshiyuki, 'I will give you exactly one hour to suppress the rebels'. He then telephoned frequently to see if this order was being carried out (Sheldon 1976: 24). The next day he told Honjō, 'If the insurgents refuse to obey the orders of the military supreme command, I will personally lead the troops against them'. Honjō also recalls, 'His Majesty asked me on the verge of tears to make known his wish to have the rebellion quelled as quickly as possible' (Honjō 1975: 235). Enraged by the attacks on leading officials, the Emperor said,

How can we not condemn even the spirit of these criminally brutal officers who killed my aged subjects, who were my hands and feet . . . ? To kill the venerable subjects whom I have trusted the most is like gently strangling me with floss-silk.

(Honjō 1975: 275)

Before he knew that Okada was still alive, the Emperor was pressed by Princes Fushimi and Asaka to form a new government, presumably one which would please the rebels. But this he refused to do and instead appointed Home Minister Gotō Fumio interim prime minister, until Okada appeared at court (Kido I 1966: 465–6). He was loath to directly command the rebels to surrender, on the grounds that this would recognize what he regarded as an act of 'mutineers'. But having declared martial law, he pushed the martial law authorities to crush the rebellion. For a brief period, they hesitated, as did the supreme war council, before generals of the control faction, backed by the navy and prodded by the Emperor, finally persuaded the rebels to surrender on the 29th (Shillony 1973: 135–97). They capitulated after Araki and Mazaki had informed them on the 27th that the Emperor opposed the rebellion and after Prince Chichibu had urged them to surrender on the 28th (Shillony 1973: 178, 189).

In the last anaysis, it was the failure of the rebels to capture control of the palace, and hence of the Emperor, which doomed the uprising. Doubtless,

It was the tragic irony for the rebels that among the opponents of the Shōwa Restoration was the Shōwa Emperor himself. The man to whom the rebels had expressed ultimate loyalty and who was to lead their new Japan turned out to be an uncompromising adversary of the rebellion . . .

(Shillony 1973: 172)

But though the Emperor had contributed significantly to suppressing the insurrection by proclaiming martial law, it is not the case that he acted virtually alone against the rebels, as Inoue Kiyoshi claims in arguing that he had the power to prevent Japan's subsequent drift toward war (Inoue 1975: 52–8).

Even if we were to accept that the Emperor acted virtually alone in 1936, Inoue's general proposition ignores the reality that the complex political circumstances of a major rebellion and its suppression in one historical context are very different from those of national policy-making leading to war in another; because the Emperor intervened in the one context does not necessarily mean that he could do so in the other.

The problem of the Emperor in relation to war may be deferred to the next three chapters of this book but, concerning the 1936 rebellion, Inoue wrongly overlooks the fact that the control faction, centered in the army general staff office, and the navy, were more decisive in quelling it. The role of the control faction here was particularly crucial, once it saw what was at stake in this struggle with the imperial way faction for supremacy within the army. As for the Emperor's role, the efficacy of his intervention lay in its timing, when 'no decision had been worked out yet by the military and government authorities' early in the crisis; 'it was at that stage when private pressure from the Emperor could be effective' in mobilizing opponents of the rebels (Sheldon 1978: 11). However, to reiterate, he did not suppress the rebellion by himself. Throughout, his capacity to prevail depended upon anti-rebel forces within the military itself, just as his capacity to influence Japanese foreign policy was conditional on what other elites, especially the military, decided to do.[8] This latter constraint had already been made plain in the Manchurian incident.

Yet there is no question that by asserting his authority over the military in order to defend constitutional government in the crisis of February 1936, the Emperor temporarily departed from the cautiousness toward the military that he had displayed in previous crises. Even so, it is striking that, as in the aftermath of Tanaka's dismissal, he remained highly conscious of the constitutional limits on his powers. In retrospect, he said, referring to the early hours of the uprising,

> We didn't know whether the prime minister was alive or dead; I labeled the troops insurgents so as to restore order as quickly as possible. As a constitutional monarch I overstepped my authority; I should have asked the cabinet to order their suppression.[9]
>
> (Irie 1983: 39–40)

This sensitivity, to having acted beyond the proper authority of a constitutional monarch, ultimately would govern his conduct in the aftermath of the rebellion.

The Emperor refused to dignify their treason by ordering the rebels to commit honorable suicide, although some of the ringleaders proceeded to commit *seppuku* before the troops returned to their barracks, as ordered. He similarly refused to pardon them. Instead, he expressed his resolve to cleanse the army:

> Their actions have violated the Constitution, gone against Emperor Meiji's Precepts to Soldiers and Sailors, blackened the national polity, and defiled its purity. I am gravely concerned about all this. The army should now be cleansed thoroughly ... and steps should be taken to prevent such a disgraceful incident from ever happening again.
>
> (Honjō 1975: 292)

With this sentiment loyal military leaders and all the imperial princes expressed agreement as they offered their apologies for not having foreseen the revolt. Army Chief of Staff Prince Kan'in stated,

> Now the army will be completely reformed, the prerogative of the supreme command will be strengthened, and a national army truly united and powerful will be established. In this way we shall endeavor to conform to the desires of Your Majesty.
>
> (Honjō 1975: 286)

The Emperor, however, still felt it necessary to reiterate, 'The recent incident makes it clear that it is especially important to maintain control and discipline in the army. I wish you to keep this firmly in mind and do your best' (Honjō 1975: 287).

The process of 'cleansing the army' began promisingly enough, soon after the Okada cabinet resigned to take responsibility for the rebellion and after Hirota Kōki, Okada's foreign Minister, was appointed prime minister, on 9 March 1936.[10] During the brief tenure of Hirota's cabinet, which was replaced by that of General Hayashi Senjurō in early February 1937, trials of rebel leaders were conducted, resulting in the execution of seventeen and life imprisonment for five others. In addition, General Terauchi Hisaichi, the new army minister, began an extensive control faction purge of imperial way elements in the army while at the same time compelling the cabinet to support the expansion of armaments sought by the control faction (Crowley 1966: 273–4).

While the fortunes of imperial way officers such as Mazaki and Araki fell, those of Terauchi, General Sugiyama Gen (Hajime), who had been especially instrumental in ending the rebellion, Vice-Army Minister General Umezu Yoshijirō, General Tōjō Hideki, and others of the control faction, rose. As well, Prince Chichibu was sent overseas for six months, ostensibly to represent the Emperor at the coronation of King George VI and to travel in Europe, but really to get him out of the way. It may be noted, too, that owing to the complicity of his son-in-law, Captain Yamaguchi Ichitarō, in the rebellion, General Honjō resigned on 20 March as the Emperor's army chief aide-de-camp. He was succeeded in this post by General Usami Okiie.

As they developed, it seemed at court that initiatives to cleanse the army signified Hirota's responsiveness to the Emperor's instructions to safeguard the constitution and adhere to a peaceful foreign policy (Kido I 1966: 478). Other contemporary observers, too, were optimistic that now the army would be reformed. Grew, for instance, relates that Yoshida Shigeru told him in April

> that the incident of February 26 was having a favorable and healthy effect in the army, arising largely out of the splendidly strong stand taken by the Emperor. The army was getting tired of the direct actionist element and the dissension within its ranks and a general movement was now on foot to eliminate those elements.
>
> (Dower 1979: 113–14)

Events were to prove, however, that cleansing the army had more to do with the pragmatic opportunism of the control faction in consolidating its power than with the Emperor. Whether because he did not want to foster 'the bane of despotism' by acting decisively, or because he feared residual violence on the part of imperial way faction extremists if cleansing the army went too far, in the period prior to the outbreak of war with China in the summer of 1937, after which controlling the army was virtually impossible, he did not fully grasp this opportunity to try and bring the army to heel, despite his declared intention of doing so after the rebellion had been suppressed.

His cautiousness toward the imperial way faction may be illustrated as follows. When discussions were held at court in early March 1936 on whether to disband the regiments that had participated in the insurrection, the Emperor's anxiety about provoking further trouble with the army prompted him to desist, saying 'Although the abolition of the dishonored regiments would be beneficial insofar as it would serve as an object lesson to the nation's army as a whole, only a few of the units in these regiments were involved in the incident'. He continued, 'If the regiments as a whole were to suffer the misfortune of disbandment the majority of the officers and soldiers would consider this highly unjust' (Honjō 1975: 290). Therefore, it was decided not to disband the regiments.

Initially, the Emperor also considered issuing a strong statement reprimanding the army for having 'blackened the national polity' in the rebellion, but ultimately he accepted Honjō's advice that this would be provocative. In the end a statement was released, but without reference to 'blackening the national polity' and only in the form of a message which the army minister delivered to divisional commanders, not to the army as a whole. The idea of releasing it as an imperial rescript, which would have lent it more force, was ruled out (Honjō 1975: 293–4).

Regarding Mazaki, the Emperor wanted him at least purged from active service in the army, along with Araki and other imperial way leaders (Kido I 1966: 473). But he asked Honjō 'if the Generals' unhappiness about being retired might not lead to difficulties later'. Only when the control faction insisted on the purges did the Emperor give his approval to retire the officers in question to the reserves (Honjō 1975: 287–9). Mazaki was subsequently tried for his part in the rebellion but his acquittal compromised the responsibility of the imperial way faction for it. In any case, Prince Konoe Fumimaro, who became prime minister on 4 June 1937, would later restore imperial way leaders to active service in attempting to offset the control faction which had dominated the Hirota and Hayashi administrations (Dower 1979: 114).

The Emperor was as cautious in dealing with the control faction. For example, noting Terauchi's efforts to influence the selection of Hirota's ministers, on 2 March 1936 the Emperor told Honjō, 'It seems that the army's conditions concerning cabinet members continue to be rigid. It also seems to be aggressive in regard to policy matters.' But then he said,

> Unless the military's wishes are taken into consideration, another incident like the recent incident might break out again. Accordingly, I would like to take the army's desires into careful consideration. . . . We must act with extreme caution. I, too, am pulled in two directions about this.
>
> (Honjō 1975: 237–8)

The control faction would probably have had its way in any event. But this emphasis on 'extreme caution' weakened whatever imperial influence might have been used to at least qualify its growing power. Using Terauchi as its vehicle, the control faction therefore proceeded to strengthen military leverage on the cabinet by reviving the practice, begun in the Meiji period, whereby army and navy ministers could only be senior officers in active service.[11] This rendered it possible to abort cabinets unacceptable to the army by simply withdrawing, or refusing to appoint, a service minister. The Hirota cabinet itself was terminated by the control faction when Terauchi resigned after it proved incapable of enlisting Diet support for certain national defense programs sought by the control faction (Crowley 1966: 310–13).

Significantly, the control faction also sought to emphasize the public image of the Emperor as an absolute monarch in whose name, and under whose authority, it had restored order within the army. It accordingly influenced the Hirota cabinet to ban books advocating the emperor–organ theory. Relatedly, the ministry of education produced a new influential text, entitled *Kokutai no hongi* (Principles of National Polity), which chauvinistically defined the national polity in a way that would have pleased Minobe's adversaries. Finally, under pressure from the control faction, the government introduced a new designation for the Emperor on official papers. Whereas previously he had been 'Nihon Koku Kōtei', or 'Emperor of Japan', now he was referred to as 'Dai Nihon Koku Tennō', or 'Emperor of Greater Japan'. This nomenclature was deliberately adopted to heighten the titular grandeur of the sovereign and the greatness of Japan as a strong imperial state possessing dominions overseas (Connors 1987: 177).

Thus, in the aftermath of the February 1936 rebellion, the control faction's power grew to the point where, in comparison with that of the imperial way faction earlier, 'its threat to the constitutional order was more severe since its activities appeared legal and certainly contrasted with the more visible tactic of revolutionary terror' (Najita [1974] 1980: 135). Ostensibly, that is, the control faction supported constitutional government, which it had helped to preserve in crushing the rebellion, but in seeking to exploit the theory of the Emperor's absolute powers to authorize its policies, as the army would continue to do on behalf of aggression and war in the years ahead, it actually subverted the constitutional order, particularly as the Emperor understood it in adhering to the 'Minobe way' of constitutional monarchy.

This development placed the Emperor in an inescapably difficult position, the complexty of which had already begun to assert itself earlier in his reign. If, on the one hand, he defended his vision of constitutional government by asserting his prerogatives over the military in the manner of an absolute monarch, he risked the defiance of the military, the strong likelihood of failure, and the perversion of constitutional monarchy itself. His sensitivity to this last danger explains why he so regretted overstepping his authority in dealing with the army rebellion in 1936, just as he had regretted his reprimand of Tanaka in 1929.

Alternatively, however, if he ratified policies whether he personally agreed with them or not, as a constitutional monarch was obligated to do, he risked playing straight into the hands of those who manipulated the fiction of his absolute powers to legitimize their own ends. Ultimately, it was precisely this dilemma which overtook him when in the early Shōwa period he instinctively chose this alternative course. He appears to have reasoned that by doing so he was putting political principle above expediency, which may be true. But in its own way, the decision also reflected expediency in the name of principle, to suit his own cautious nature and that of his advisers.

These advisers, too, shied away from resisting the control faction in the aftermath of the February 26 incident, as we see in their ambivalence over the question, in early 1937, of whether General Ugaki Kazushige should be made prime minister. At first, despite his complicity in the March 1931 incident, Ugaki's reputation as a reform-minded army politician, who as Hamaguchi's army minister had once advocated military retrenchment, persuaded Saionji and Lord Privy Seal Yuasa that he was a potential counterweight to the control faction. Thus, after they had advised the Emperor to this effect, on 24 January 1937, Ugaki was summoned to court and instructed by the Emperor to form a cabinet (Kido I 1966: 537).

Three days later, though, when it was clear that the control faction would not provide a service minister out of opposition to Ugaki, Ugaki proposed to Yuasa that the Emperor might order the army to cooperate. Faced with this proposition, Saionji and Yuasa now had second thoughts about involving the Emperor in a confrontation with the control faction. They therefore rejected Ugaki's suggestion. As Kido relates, 'After the lord keeper of the privy seal spoke to Ugaki concerning the impossibility of ... having His Majesty ride a boat against the rapids, General Ugaki left the imperial palace without asking the Emperor for an audience' that day (Kido I 1966: 540; Ugaki II 1970: 1126–7). Instead, Saionji recommended Hayashi Senjurō, the army's choice, as the next prime minister. Hayashi took office on 2 February but resigned in early June after his frequent clashes with the Diet made his cabinet untenable (Crowley 1966: 322).

Given the army's opposition to Ugaki, it is most unlikely that a cabinet headed by him could have dealt effectively with the control faction, had the court complied with his proposal for an imperial intervention. But, significantly, the proposal was evidently never communicated to the Emperor, such was the cautiousness of his advisers.

Even had he known of it, however, the Emperor would have followed Saionji's cautious line. The February 1936 rebellion had badly 'unnerved' the elder statesman (Connors 1987: 179). By 1937 Saionji had no stomach left for challenging the control faction over Ugaki's appointment; to him, involving the Emperor directly in a risk-laden endeavor of this kind was unthinkable. Henceforth, Saionji and the constitutional monarchists around the Emperor would gradually give way at court to 'traditionalists', epitomized by Kido Kōichi, who, appointed lord privy seal in 1940, would be 'more concerned with national unity than with substantive policies, more with discovering and having the Emperor ratify a true "national consensus" than with pursuing a specific set of domestic or foreign policies' (Titus 1974: 112).

Equally, the crisis of the February 1936 rebellion had unnerved the Emperor. He was no more inclined to 'ride a boat against the rapids' of army power than were his advisers. That would have required a degree of leadership which, because of his political convictions as a constitutional monarch with circumscribed powers, and because of his notably passive nature, he was unwilling and unable to undertake.

4 The Emperor and war, 1937–1940

'Had the Emperors exercised in fact the great powers with which they were theoretically endowed, the present dynasty could not have survived the many hundreds of years of rule with which it is credited.' Yet, Robert Craigie, who made this astute judgment, also wrote, 'it is a mistake to assume that the Crown is incapable of exerting any influence at all on the course of affairs. Much depends on the character, personality, and inclinations of the occupant of the throne and of the high officers of state' (Craigie 1946: 91–2).

The Emperor's interest in influencing affairs of state was evident to Craigie when he presented his credentials at court as Britain's ambassador to Japan in September, 1937. With the Sino-Japanese War then in its third month, Craigie noted the Emperor 'was genuinely anxious to play a useful and beneficial role in world affairs', the discussion of which caused his face to assume 'an eager, almost anxious expression, indicative of his deep concern with current events' (Craigie 1946: 46).

This chapter explores how the Emperor acted upon this concern and with what results in confronting the issues of war and peace which became increasingly critical for Japan in the 1937–1940 period. However, before pursuing this question specifically in relation to the Sino-Japanese War, armed conflicts with the Soviet Union, and Japanese policy towards the Axis Alliance and Southeast Asia in the context of the European war, it is necessary to consider his evolving political environment and how the character of the man, in so far as it can be portrayed, affected his political style and behavior in the years prior to the Pacific War.

THE EMERGENT NEW ORDER AND IMPERIAL INFLUENCE

Beginning in early Shōwa, but especially after the outbreak of the Sino-Japanese War, the major emphasis of national policy was on mobilization for possible total war, to create a 'national defense state', or *kokubō kokka*, capable of defending the empire from perceived threats abroad.

Originally, the overall goal of this policy was to neutralize 'the influence of the Soviet Union, the Nationalist government of China, and the Anglo-American nations by a diplomacy rooted in the efficacy of Japan's military force' (Crowley 1966: 195). Then, added impetus to this 'renovation' of Japan was given by Prime Minister Konoe Fumimaro's declaration in 1938 that the nation's purpose in the war with China was to construct a New Asian Order rid of Western imperialism. Two years later the momentum of mobilization led to the political establishment of a New Order within Japan itself.

The main pressures for national defense mobilization, which gradually superseded previous patterns of army factionalism, emanated from the military. But the military's program was widely supported by the civil arms of government, too. In the Diet, the mainstream parties cooperated with defense priorities even as the parties resisted the erosion of their autonomy in the course of state-led mobilization. Similarly, the defense priorities of the military and 'renovationist' bureaucrats in different ministries were firmly sponsored by the cabinets of this period, beginning with the first Konoe cabinet (4 June 1937 to 5 January 1939). This administration enthusiastically supported the 1938 national mobilization law that gave the government extensive economic controls in developing defense preparedness (Berger 1988: 129). Mobilization remained the chief priority of the cabinets that followed: those of Prime Ministers Hiranuma Kiichirō (5 January 1939 to 30 August 1939), General Abe Nobuyuki (30 August 1939 to 16 January 1940), Admiral Yonai Mitsumasa (16 January to 22 July 1940) and again, Prince Konoe (22 July 1940 to 18 October 1941).

From a national perspective, the centripetal dynamics of mobilization significantly augmented the power of the state. Yet, endemic discord within the government about the specific means to achieve enhanced military power, and even more consequentially, over how to use this power in the area of foreign policy where pressures were the greatest in this period, also produced centrifugal tendencies that seriously weakened the state from within. The continuing, divisive politics of 'elite pluralism', as Gordon Berger describes it, thus posed a constant threat to the integrity of decision-making in Japan (Berger 1988: 105, 126–37).

Civil–military rivalry was but one facet of this problem. Others included, on the military side, conflict between the army and the navy in competing for priority, conflict between the service ministries and the general staffs, and conflict between the general staffs and units under their jurisdiction. Similar rivalries characterized the various ministries on the civilian side and in addition to these horizontal cleavages between elites, vertical cleavages further disrupted consensus and the coherence of policy as senior officials were often defied by their subordinates, whose actions committed Japan to policies the leadership did not authorize.

In this confused setting alternative institutional arrangements were adopted in order to achieve consensus and coordination in the making of national policy, especially where foreign affairs were concerned. Building on earlier trends in the Saitō and Okada administrations, the 'inner cabinet', comprising the prime minister, the army and navy ministers, the foreign minister, and often the finance minister, evolved as a major center of decision-making.

Soon, however, this was superseded by the mechanism of the 'liaison conference' (*renraku kaigi*). Instituted in late November 1937, to improve communication between the cabinet and the military, it generally included the inner cabinet, the army and navy chiefs of staff, the vice-chiefs, and various military bureau chiefs who served as conference secretaries along with the chief cabinet secretary. But despite its numerical domination by the uniformed participants, which gave the military the edge in its deliberations, the liaison conference by no means reached decisions easily. On the contrary, it often was stalemated by fractious debates over foreign policy.

The Emperor, it must be underlined, did not attend liaison conferences. But he did attend the 'imperial conference' (*gozen kaigi*), revived in 1938 from Meiji precedents, which constituted another institutional mechanism to foster consensus in government. Comprising the members of the liaison conference and the Emperor, the president of the privy council, and usually the president of the cabinet planning board, the purpose of the imperial conferences was not to make policy decisions but rather, to ritually endorse the policy decisions of the liaison conferences through the formal bestowing of the 'imperial will' symbolized by the mere presence of the Emperor. The ritual nature of the imperial conference is evident in the fact that the Emperor was not expected to speak during its proceedings. Instead, it was generally understood that the president of the privy council would speak for him (Butow 1961: 170–1).

The very need for these institutional arrangements to promote consensus suggests that the prewar political order was not totalitarian, although it was undeniably authoritarian in controlling political dissent and mobilizing Japanese society for war. To be sure, the Japanese New Order of 1940, which pivoted on the new Imperial Rule Assistance Association (IRAA; Taisei yokusankai), headed by Prince Konoe, was intended to be a totalitarian configuration for the achievement of national unity and on this account, the Emperor once caustically likened the IRAA to the military regimes of the shōgunates (Yamamoto 1989: 30). But despite its absorption of all existing parties, the IRAA never evolved into an effective political organization in its own right. It primarily functioned instead as a sounding-board for the government's mobilization policies.

Hence, as Berger writes in summarizing political developments in prewar and wartime Japan, 'War therefore generated extraordinary pressures for popular and elite conformity to government policy goals, but it did not permit the reconstruction of the political order along the totalitarian lines advocated by reformist proponents of the national defense state.' The reality still held that 'Beneath the veneer of national unity, political competition remained intense among and within the political elites, and the Meiji political order strained to confine conflicts within boundaries permitting stable government' (Berger 1988: 152).

Accordingly, while the military was the dominant political elite by 1941, Japan did not have a military dictatorship. The power of the military was hegemonic, not absolute, and depended upon the acquiescence of other elites. That elite pluralism undercut the possibility of totalitarianism is acknowledged by Herbert Bix, who significantly qualifies the construct of 'Emperor-system fascism' when he writes that it 'was a transient, incomplete, composite, and "recomposed" dictatorial form, characterized by the autonomy of its component elements *vis-à-vis* one another', despite their common theoretical devotion to the Emperor (Bix 1982: 19).

Regardless of whether we refer to 'fascism', 'corporatism', or another term in analyzing the prewar Japanese political order, of central relevance to this study is the fact that the multiple conflicts generated by elite pluralism potentially enhanced the court as an informal intermediary capable of helping to resolve disputes on national policy. This role, which as before was confined to the private realm of the court and not made public, was made possible by the continuing practice of 'working through the court' as contending elites sought to have their respective policies ultimately sanctioned with the formal imperial will. In this situation, 'Although he did lack power, the Emperor was in a position to influence and to inspire those around him' while relying on 'the gravitational pull of the throne' to affect policy (Butow 1961: 176).

The intended purpose of informal imperial influence reflected a continuation of the Emperor's earlier preoccupations in dealing with foreign policy crises and was broadly twofold in nature. First, hoping to play an integrative role in a seriously fragmented context of policy-formation, he still endeavored to promote coherence and consensus in the way decisions were reached. This involved encouraging the participants in decision-making to operate within their respective spheres of constitutional responsibility, as he had always insisted they should, while fostering the rationality of policy in the sense of properly aligning means and ends when considering alternative courses of action.

Committed as he was to thinking about policy issues from the national point of view,

> The Emperor's role was to keep the consensus-making process honest. By questioning leaders in audience and by exerting pressure via his palace advisers he assured himself that any policy he ratified had been thoroughly discussed and represented a genuine consensus among the policy makers.
>
> (Titus 1974: 263)

This he tried to do even though he was prevented from participating in cabinet and liaison conference meetings, where national policy decisions were made.

Second, the evidence indicates that the Emperor wished to play an instrumental role in influencing not only the way decisions were reached but also the content of policy decisions, as he had tried to do previously. That in 1937 and thereafter he was chiefly anxious to prevent war or to limit and roll back the effects of decisions which led to war is the main theme of this chapter and the next. However, it is not suggested in this account that the Emperor was less a nationalist than the men who made decisions, that he opposed war-mobilization out of some uncompromising commitment to pacifism, or that he was impervious to the view, which finally prevailed in the government in late 1941, that Japan had to save itself through force of arms from the threat of Western power in Asia. He wanted to avoid war if at all possible but not, in the end, at the cost of empire.

Another cost which he was unprepared to pay was the viability of government within Japan. To anticipate this theme briefly here, the Emperor believed that the two purposes of attempted imperial influence were complementary: ensuring the institutional coherence of policy-making within the legal framework of the Meiji constitution was the only way to check the forces of militarism and thereby avoid war. Yet, there would be times when he had to choose between promoting consensus in policy-making and influencing the content of policy, for these objectives were not always compatible. When this most difficult decision arose, his instinct was to hold the government together, even if it meant war. The breakdown of government and public order was more fearsome to him than even the extremity of war itself.

However, the Emperor's aspirations to influence events notwithstanding, his capacity to do so was very circumscribed, as it had been in the past, and here, a number of points need to be made.

First, his influence at best was indirect, for, as noted, he was removed from the actual centers of decision-making.[1] He participated in the imperial conferences, as noted. But this only highlights

> the great difference between the *actual* and the *theoretical* force of the throne. Such power as was imputed to the Emperor in the Meiji Constitution was to be exercised in accordance with the advice of his ministers, who were thus made responsible for affairs of state. . . . While theoretically possessing the right to do many things, the Emperor was actually allowed, for the good of the state and for the sake of the imperial institution, to do very little.
>
> (Butow 1961: 173–4, italics Butow's)

The fiction that the Emperor himself 'made' decisions was upheld by the imperial conference ritual but in reality he could not intervene to alter decisions already taken: the possibility of his vetoing them was ruled out by everyone, including his court advisers, and his ratification of previous liaison conference decisions was entirely automatic (Maxon [1957] 1975: 9–10).[2] His occasional attendance of the meetings of the imperial headquarters (Daihon'ei), instituted in November 1937, was similarly a ritual matter. In these proceedings, the chiefs of staff typically discussed military operations with him, not so that he could determine policy but rather to inform him, usually in the most general terms, of military policies under consideration (Maxon [1957] 1975: 61–2).

Second, his influence was restricted in terms of the timing of its application. As long as decision-makers were divided over policy alternatives, the process of 'working through the court' gave him a certain leeway privately to affect the way they conceptualized foreign policy options. But once a consensus began to emerge, he felt obliged to go along with it and finally to ratify it with the imperial will. The judgment as to when to give way in this regard was a difficult one to make and often depended upon the advice of men closest to him at court.

Third, his advisers, however, often disagreed and vacillated over the question of what his role should be and the resultant confusion also limited his influence. Until his death in 1940, Saionji persisted in keeping the Emperor politically neutral, to preserve the ideal of constitutional monarchy and to protect him from possible physical harm after the army uprising of 1936. Kido Kōichi also wished to protect the Emperor in this way, although he was less motivated by abstract principles of constitutional monarchy than by a self-image as a palace negotiatior of policy consensus. After taking office as privy seal on 1 June 1940 he concentrated on preserving the transcendental neutrality of the throne so that the Emperor could 'ratify as accurate a consensus of national opinion as possible, regardless of where that consensus led the nation' (Titus 1974: 190). In 1940 and 1941, Kido thus decisively reinforced the Emperor's integrative intentions in exerting imperial influence, at the expense of the Emperor's endeavors to influence the substance of policy.

In contrast, Prime Minister Konoe, on whom Saionji counted to stand up to the military,[3] at times wanted the Emperor to involve himself far more directly in political matters. Behind this perception of a politically active sovereign was the elitist assumption that the nobility could still manipulate the throne politically, for Prince Konoe was head of a prestigious court family, the most pre-eminent of the five branches, or Go-Sekke, of the Fujiwara family, which had done so successfully in centuries past (Storry 1960: 9).

Writing after the Pacific War, Konoe stated, 'I felt it was my mission to control the army by every possible means without provoking it' (Crowley 1966: 323). Hoping to enlist the Emperor's assistance to this end, he went so far to suggest in June 1937 that the Emperor attend cabinet meetings, which proposal Saionji successfully opposed because it would involve the Emperor in decision-making (Connors 1987: 202). There would be other occasions when Konoe would enlist the Emperor's help in coping with the military. However, Konoe was quite inconsistent in this respect: he often would change his mind about the Emperor's role and go to great lengths to neutralize him politically, as will be seen shortly.

Fourth, as in the earlier years of Shōwa, imperial influence was circumscribed by the military's tendency at crucial junctures to present the Emperor and the government with operational *faits accomplis* and by deliberate deception, particularly on the part of the chief aides-de-camp who succeeded General Honjō: Generals Usami Okiie (1936–1939), Hata Shunroku (1939), and Hasunuma Shigeru (1939–1945). In contrast to Honjō, who for the most part conscientiously bridged the court and the army, Usami, for instance, habitually distorted the Emperor's views in relaying them to the army and often failed to pass them on at all (Harada VII 1952: 311). Hata was little better but at least he was forthright. Once, after seeing the Emperor, he admitted to the privy seal and the grand chamberlain, 'what the Emperor says does not get through. Thinking His Majesty's virtues should not be infringed, I did not comply with his orders' (Harada VII 1952: 298–9).

This poor communication with army leaders in crisis situations was compounded by the continuing contrast between the Emperor's world view and that of army officials, as Kido observed in 1939, when talking with Harada Kumao. Kido said,

> The present Emperor is a scientist and very much of a liberal as well as a man of peace. Therefore, if the Emperor's ideas are not changed to some extent, the great gap between His Majesty and the rightist groups will grow. ... In order to lead the army, but still make it appear as if we were being led by them, we must also make it seem as if we understood the army a little better.
>
> (Harada VII 1952: 339–40)

Clearly, he thought it easier to change the Emperor's ideas than the army's.

Finally, imperial influence was significantly circumscribed in different ways by the Emperor's own political style which inevitably reflected certain features of his character and temperament. While the following observations pertain mainly to the period from 1937, some apply to his earlier career on the throne as well. Largely speculative in nature owing to the problems of sources mentioned in the Introduction, they nonetheless may help to explain the Emperor's overall tendency to react passively to events rather than take the initiative in trying to shape them.

As in dealing with Prime Minister Tanaka in 1929 and Prince Chichibu in 1931, during the Manchurian incident, the Emperor was capable of vigorously expressing his personal opinions during audiences at court. His forceful conduct in the special circumstances of the 1936 army rebellion similarly demonstrated a capacity on occasion to act resolutely. Nevertheless, it seems generally true that the Shōwa Emperor was timid, 'irresolute' and 'weak-willed', that he 'cannot be called a leader of men', and that he 'avoided confrontation – unless it was absolutely necessary – and went along with what seemed to be the consensus' (Hane 1982: 49). The question is, why?

His essential passivity may be attributed to many factors. One was 'overprotectiveness' on the part of those who cared for him as a child, which doubtless dulled his 'sense of self-reliance and fostered a dependent quality in him' (Kawahara 1990: 16). Another in this same vein was the influence of such strong-willed advisers as Saionji Kinmochi. Still another, which is emphasized in this study, was the Emperor's conviction, which tied his own hands politically even as others tied them, that a constitutional monarch should always abide by and not interfere with the decisions reached by his government. More than any other single 'internal constraint', this principled idealism explains his passive acceptance of policies even when he privately disagreed with them.

But in addition, his general passivity may have resulted in particular from the ethos of the Japanese court with its stultifying routine based on precedent and protocol. More research is needed on the daily life of the Shōwa court but it is germane that foreign observers were struck by its rigid formalism, notably on the ceremonial occasions which dominated the court routine. Craigie, for instance, observed the 'remarkable efficiency with which court and other official functions are organized in Japan', finding them, however, 'over-organized' to the point of 'frigidity' (Craigie 1946: 48). Grew similarly stressed that at court 'things simply don't go wrong because every step is so precisely planned in advance and everyone knows just what to do and when to do it' (Grew 1944: 181).

This very precision in court life engendered in the Emperor a conformist preoccupation with detail and weakened his capacity for independent initiative. Like his imperial predecessors, he had been trained to fit in with these established patterns of protocol and precedent and it is not surprising that performing his duties in a strictly correct manner was an uppermost concern.

Of many examples in contemporary court records an earlier case in point is Honjō's diary entry for 22 February 1935, where he recounts long discussions involving the Emperor, court attendants, and army officials on whether regimental banners should be lowered out of respect for the visiting Manchurian Emperor when the Shōwa Emperor greeted him at Tokyo station. The army argued that to dip the banners would imply equal status for Pu-yi who was, the army thought, inferior in status to the Japanese monarch. Precedents were studied, the matter was much debated, and ultimately it was decided the banners would be partly lowered. But especially pertinent is Honjō's remark that throughout the episode, 'I was truly impressed by His Majesty's concern about minor matters ...' (Honjō 1975: 201–3).

In an environment such as this, where the 'minor matters' of precedent and protocol were so all-enveloping, it would have taken a more forceful and independent man than the Shōwa Emperor to break through the elaborate conventions of tradition, and change the way things were done on ceremonial occasions. By extension into political situations, since it was mainly during private audiences with government and military leaders in precisely this environment at court that the Emperor primarily sought to exert political influence, one may say that he was conditioned by the conformist ethos of court life not to challenge and change policies he himself found objectionable, for fear of stirring up the proverbial hornet's nest. As for his occasional outbursts of anger when he did want to change a given policy, they may well have stemmed from a frustrated lack of confidence in situations for which he had few precedents to guide him in determining how far he could go in exerting imperial influence. In compensation, it was perhaps natural that he would revert to a cautious, passive stance after venting his feelings so bluntly. Consequently, for the most part, his political interventions were unsustained and erratic in character.

It also may be conjectured that the Emperor's general, scientific approach to problem-solving, which was a prominent aspect of his political style, tended to dilute the force of his political interventions. His penchant for methodical precision even in unexpected contexts is illustrated by the following vignette, again from the Honjō diary. One day, in 1933, when the Emperor and his entourage were aboard the imperial flagship returning from naval exercises at sea, they played a game of shuffleboard on deck, in a 'carefree fashion'. 'His Majesty's team won', writes Honjō, who states, referring to the Emperor, 'During the game he observed the performance of the others carefully, exhorting his side to work as a team, disperse the opponents' disks, and as in billiards, utilize the principles of geometry, etc. He is indeed intelligent and talented' (Honjō 1975: 246–7).

When applied to the field of politics, the impression here is of a man whose passion for rational order in appreciating the 'geometry' of political situations would lead him above all to rely on logical persuasion – as in his defense of Minobe – to exert influence. In itself, such a political style was not passive. But it would predispose him passively to accept decisions once suasion had failed, rather than go on challenging them.

His reliance on suasion was often apparent in audiences with military leaders when the Emperor typically would rely on asking questions to express his objection to a particular policy, either by revealing the risks it posed in mis-aligning means and ends, or by pointing up its underlying opportunism at the expense of principle. This posing of 'counter questions' has been identified as one of many ways in which Japanese may say 'no' to a given proposal (Ueda 1974: 187), and it will be shown in Chapter 5 that while some writers have misconstrued imperial questions as signifying the Emperor's support for certain military policies, that is neither what he intended nor indeed is it how his interlocutors interpreted him.

For now, however, it suffices to say that interrogation, as a principal element of the Emperor's political style, represented an indirect, reasoned approach in registering imperial influence that could only succeed if other political actors followed the same rules of rational discourse. They mostly did not do so, preferring instead arguments that either defied logic altogether or, as was quite often the case, reflected a narrower logic based on the rationality of military strategy in relative disregard of broader political alternatives. Repeated conversations in this vein often caused the Emperor to retreat, sometimes to the extent of finally persuading himself that the policy he had opposed perhaps had certain merits.

Another aspect of the Emperor's political style was reliance on subtle indirect gesture. Unless recorded, which was rare, it cannot be known from written sources how he communicated his wishes and beliefs through facial expression, tone of voice, or posture. But on occasion the unexpected gesture, such as the reading of a poem (in 1941) during a formal conference, was meant to convey his opinion symbolically, when emotion had surpassed reason in debating policy. A simple nod of the head was intended to serve the same purpose. Grew relates that during a public speech he made in 1940 emphasizing the imperative of peace, 'The Emperor, who had preserved an almost rigid expression . . . nodded at each of my points and nodded vigorously when at the end hope was expressed that Japan would contribute to the general culture and well-being of mankind'. The French ambassador later told Grew that 'he had watched the Emperor's face and was convinced that his nods of approval were given to impress the government and the highest officials of the Empire with his own desires for peace' (Grew 1944: 353).

However, gestures of this sort at best registered only a momentary impact, despite their symbolic intent, and later could be readily ignored or forgotten by Japanese leaders who pursued different objectives. This pertains as well to the Emperor's reliance on silence, which can be another way of saying 'no' in Japanese interactions (Ueda 1974: 186–7). In certain situations, as when the refusal to speak in audience signified an imperial reprimand, the unspoken message was clear enough. But by its very nature, silence could be misinterpreted, either unconsciously or willfully, as well as ignored or forgotten.

That silence might be misunderstood as signifying imperial approval, rather than censure, worried Saionji. In 1937, for instance, Saionji opposed the idea of convening imperial conferences partly on the grounds that 'they fundamentally violate the spirit of the constitution', by which he meant that they negated the principle of cabinet responsibility for national policy (Connors 1987: 145) But he also argued that the Emperor's customary silence on such occasions would be deliberately misinterpreted by the military to mean his approval of its policies. Were this to happen, as indeed it did, Saionji believed the Emperor's 'virtue would be blemished' (Maxon [1957] 1975: 158).

More generally, the ambiguity of imperial silence is emblematic of the 'oracular sovereignty' which was characteristic of the Meiji constitution (Titus 1974: 40). As well, the use of silence, like that of the counter-question and indirect gesture, may have manifested certain residual conventions that had governed communication in Japanese court circles for centuries. Common to each of these forms, whereby the Emperor communicated his wishes, was a cultivated understatement based on traditional normative assumptions at court that the sovereign's authority was too vast to require more explicit expression or emphasis. But the shared field of political discourse at the imperial court, where the aristocracy was habituated to respond to subtle imperial understatement, was one thing, and the modern, secular, world of Japanese politics quite another. If these styles of communication at the Shōwa court mirrored long-standing traditions comprising the political culture of the Japanese aristocracy, then their indirection and inexactitude made them imperfect methods of communicating the Emperor's personal will to military leaders and politicians, for whom the political language of the court was archaic and alien, however much it faintly echoed certain features of contemporary Japanese political culture generally (Yanaga [1956] 1964: 51–62).

THE SINO-JAPANESE WAR

The clash of Japanese and Chinese forces on the night of 7 July 1937 in the vicinity of the Marco Polo Bridge near Peking, despite its prompt local settlement, proved to be the first of several spontaneous incidents in north China which eventually escalated into the Sino-Japanese War. In contrast to the Manchurian incident, they were not part of some plot to precipitate war with China. As late as June, the army general staff ordered Japanese field commanders to avoid incidents in north China (Crowley 1966: 320). This instruction was consonant with the Konoe government's policy of concentrating instead on mobilization for any confrontation that might occur with the Soviet Union, which by then had been designated as the most probable opponent on land in Japanese strategic thinking because of the rapid buildup of Soviet forces along the Manchurian border after the Manchurian incident (Hata 1976: 131). In fact, the Japanese units involved in the Marco Polo Bridge affair had been on maneuvers for which Russia, not China, was the theoretical adversary (Coox 1988: 319).

On 11 July, Konoe informed the Emperor that reinforcements would be sent to the continent but stressed it was the government's policy to localize and settle through negotiation by field commanders any and all incidents in north China (Crowley 1966: 331). Army Chief of Staff Kan'in and Army Minister Sugiyama Gen reconfirmed this policy in audience with the Emperor three days later. But as further fighting erupted, and as the Chiang Kai-shek government mobilized its forces while demanding direct negotiations with Tokyo rather than local settlements, the north China crisis quickly deteriorated.

When Nationalist Chinese planes bombed Japanese naval installations at Shanghai on 14 August, leading to massive Japanese retaliation, the crisis turned into the 'China incident', or *Shina jihen* as the Japanese called this undeclared war, which eventually merged with the Pacific War after 1941 and continued until the defeat of Japan in 1945. Japan's war with China proved to be one of the most destructive in modern history. The total number of military casualties on the Chinese side has been estimated at more than 3,217,000, plus 5,788,000 Chinese civilian dead and injured. Japanese military personnel killed in China ultimately came to 447,000, with thousands more wounded or sick (Coox 1978: 304, 308).

This was not a war the Emperor had sought nor, for complex reasons, was it a war he could end. Court attendants recall that once the fighting had begun, the Emperor took to pacing the floor, 'sometimes muttering to himself.... The pacing would continue for a long time, each step resounding painfully in our minds, so that we wished to stop up our ears' (Kanroji 1975: 127). For the Emperor, the immediate problem in the early stages of the crisis was that Prime Minister Konoe seemed confused and powerless in the face of splits within the army over Japanese policy. Leaders in the army general staff, including Kan'in, Vice-Chief Tada Shun (Hayao), and General Ishiwara Kanji, the architect of the Manchurian incident who now headed the operations division, opposed the escalation of the war. But Sugiyama, Army Vice-Minister Umezu Yoshijirō, and Field Commanders Matsui Iwane and Terauchi Hisaichi, represented the view in the army that force, not negotiations with the Nationalist government, was the only way to end the hostilities in China (Hata 1983: 254–5; Crowley 1966: 353).

In time, Konoe would embrace this belligerent position but in July he complained to the Emperor that the general staff, and in cabinet meetings the army minister, were not forthcoming on what the army intended to do in China despite his initial policy of caution. Anxious for peace, the Emperor agreed to use his influence to help coordinate relations between the cabinet and the army. Soon, he reported to Konoe Sugiyama's insistence that strategic matters falling within the right of supreme command could not be discussed in cabinet. However, on the basis of information provided for him by Kan'in, the Emperor reassured Konoe, 'the assumption is that military operations will definitely stop short of the line connecting the Yungting River and Paoting'. Konoe, though, remained dismayed by the 'wide gulf separating the cabinet and the military' and by the fact 'that the army leaders, too, were completely incapable of controlling the forces within the army' (Konoe 1946: 19–21).

Throughout the autumn of 1937, in discussions with Kan'in and Sugiyama, the Emperor continued his efforts to improve liaison between the cabinet and the army, for he, too, wanted to ascertain the army's intentions in China. In early September Sugiyama told him the army had no territorial designs on China, to which the Emperor asked, 'You say this, but can you control your subordinates?' Sugiyama said he could, whereupon the Emperor demanded that Sugiyama issue a statement indicating the army had no territorial ambitions. After Sugiyama did so, Makino told Harada it was 'a wise action to delegate responsibility to the army' in this way (Harada VI 1951: 87–8).

But with the spread of war in China, in early November Konoe again complained to the Emperor, 'I have heard nothing about army operations there. I can only watch the army do as it pleases'. Konoe's apparent impotence, and continuing controversy within the cabinet and the army on whether to negotiate with Chiang Kai-shek, then prompted the Emperor to suggest holding an imperial conference at which a peace formula could be worked out to end the fighting.

Since the last imperial conference had been held during the Russo-Japanese War, this was a rather unusual proposal, although it will be recalled that he had made it twice before, in 1933, to cope with the Jehol crisis. Clearly, he did not intend the imperial conference to be the purely ceremonial occasion which it soon became. However, as in 1933, his advisers counseled against it. Saionji reasoned, 'The army says it will set its course in accordance with the Emperor's wishes but if it cannot, what then?' If, at an imperial conference the Emperor's desires for peace were ignored, 'the authority of the Emperor would be damaged and that would be inexcusable.... It is imperative that our attitude be one of extreme caution' (Harada VI 1951: 140–1).

Thus did Saionji again move to neutralize the Emperor. But so did Konoe who, when informed of the Emperor's suggestion, agreed with Saionji in opposing an imperial conference. By then, Konoe had come to favor a policy of coercing Chiang to sue for peace on terms acceptable to Japan. He would later agree to an imperial conference only to ratify this policy, not to prepare for negotiations as the Emperor wished (Harada VI 1951: 137–8). Having earlier drawn the Emperor into a more active political role to coordinate cabinet relations with the army in limiting the war, Konoe now wanted to keep the Emperor out of decision-making so as to better manage a policy of escalation.

This was also Konoe's purpose in objecting to the Emperor's suggestion that he be permitted to speak on behalf of negotiations, in the deliberations of imperial headquarters later that month. It was preferable procedure, Konoe insisted, for the Emperor to attend, but not address, the proceedings. Because of Konoe's aristocratic prestige, the Emperor had great personal respect for him and was prepared to follow his advice.[4] But he also may have feared that if he did not defer to Konoe in determining what his role should be, Konoe would resign and thereby precipitate a political crisis at a time when policy disagreements regarding the China war demanded stability. He was probably aware that Konoe had considered resigning because of the mounting wartime pressures of his office, only to be dissuaded by Kido Kōichi, then serving as minister of education (Butow 1961: 112).

There followed, in December, the government's decision to strike a decisive blow against the Nationalists by seizing the Chinese capital, Nanking. The army general staff reluctantly endorsed this policy under great pressure from field commanders but with the caveat that Japan should still keep the door open to talks with Chiang once Nanking was taken (Crowley 1966: 358).

There already had been great loss of life in the fighting at Shanghai but the Nanking campaign, which resulted in the capture of the city on 13 December, is notorious for the spontaneous and indiscriminate slaughter and torture by the Japanese of perhaps as many as 200,000 Chinese, including civilians and soldiers (Butow 1961: 101). How much the Emperor knew of these atrocities is unclear. Edward Behr speculates that Prince Asaka, who briefly served as a divisional commander in the Nanking campaign, must have later told him about them (Behr 1989: 202). However, it is more likely that Asaka kept the outrage to himself, to avoid revealing his inability to control the troops under his command. Evidently, though, the Emperor was shown a captured Chinese propaganda film of Japanese army atrocities at Nanking (Allen 1989: 309).

But any knowledge that he had about Nanking after the event hardly implicates the Emperor in what happened there and any implication that he could have prevented the atrocities overlooks the fact that he could no more control specific military operations in the field than could the army general staff office. As Joseph Grew observed in condemning Japanese brutalities at Nanking, the field army had run wild, 'perpetrating atrocities which the Emperor himself cannot possibly desire or sanction' (Grew 1944: 236).

The 'rape of Nanking' and the sinking by Japanese aircraft of the American gunboat *Panay*, which was stationed in the Yangtze River during the Nanking campaign, in particular aroused anti-Japanese opinion in the United States, as world condemnation of Japanese aggression in China increased. Chiang Kai-shek, meanwhile, moved his government to Hankow and later thence to Chungking in the interior of China, determined to resist the Japanese. In this context, the liaison conferences of 14 December and 20 December decided to go on fighing despite the protests of General Tada, the army vice-chief of staff, who argued that Japan should now negotiate with Chiang to end the war (Crowley 1966: 360–7).

It is indicative of Konoe's opposition to negotiations that he encouraged his home minister, Admiral Suetsugu Nobumasa, whom he had invited to participate in these meetings, to belittle Tada's position. Suetsugu did so again during the liaison conference of 10 January 1938, which reaffirmed the previous decision to continue the war. At this point Tada, with the support of Navy Chief of Staff Prince Fushimi, demanded an imperial conference. James Crowley rightly underscores the paradoxical nature of this demand, noting that the army general staff

> was, in effect, seeking the support of the Throne for its approach to the China situation. Since the cabinet blamed the 'pressure of field armies' for the diplomatic impasse with the Nationalist government, Tada intended to use the Imperial Conference as a way to commit the army, through the Supreme Command, to a policy which would enable and force the cabinet to intensify its efforts for a negotiated settlement with Chiang Kai-shek.
>
> (Crowley 1966: 369)

Having had his proposal for an imperial conference rejected in November the previous year, the Emperor supported Tada's request. Konoe, now confident that he could control the proceedings, agreed to convene an imperial conference the next day, on 11 January. But when the Emperor made known his wish to address the meeting, Konoe objected, realizing that he would side with the army general staff in seeking negotiations. He asked the Emperor, as Harada recalls, 'not to make any inquiries at the conference because the prime minister would present a policy which had been decided by the government' (Harada VI 1951: 204). Saionji endorsed this advice, still resolved to protect the Emperor from the dangers of direct political involvement. Konoe's concern, though, 'was less with the integrity or protection of the Imperial institution than with the desire to achieve a hardening of Japanese policy toward China which had the appearance of Imperial approval' (Connors 1987: 204–5).

Konoe's hopes were realized: the imperial conference of 11 January ratified the government's policy of 'annihilating' the Nationalist regime unless Chiang accepted within seventy-two hours an ultimatum containing Japan's severe terms for peace, which in the event Chiang rejected. These included, among other demands, China's recognition of Manchukuo, a neutral zone in north China, Japanese military occupation of parts of central China, cooperation against the Soviet Union and war reparations to Japan (Crowley 1966: 371–2). Throughout the proceedings, the Emperor remained silent, as advised. This caused General Tada to say to Konoe, 'Even though it was a conference in the imperial presence, His Majesty said nothing. This is just like the Emperor–organ theory. From now on I want things to be decided by the imperial judgment' (Harada VI 1951: 206).

Tada manifestly blamed Konoe for orchestrating the Emperor's silence in achieving ratification of a belligerent policy toward China.[5] But whether or not his remark further represented a veiled criticism of the Emperor for sustaining the view that as a constitutional organ of the state he was obliged to ratify the decisions of the government, this indeed explains why the Emperor remained silent that day, quite apart from his personal deference to the prime minister. For, as earlier, he was resolved to maintain a 'faithful adherence to the rules of constitutional monarchy according to which his powers consisted of advising and making suggestions to the cabinet, not in the wielding of sovereign power as an absolute monarch' (Kanroji 1975: 124).

That these considerations of constitutional propriety governed the Emperor's actions was made clear on 14 January when Army Chief of Staff Kan'in sought an audience at the palace during a recess in an especially stormy liaison conference that day which had decided to reconfirm the earlier decision to crush the Nationalists now that Chiang had rejected Japan's ultimatum. Kan'in plainly wanted an imperial intervention to reverse that decision, lest Japan be irretrievably committed to all-out war in China.

However, the Emperor would not see Prince Kan'in. He later explained to Konoe, 'I judged that this might surely be a plan to overturn *what had already been determined* [by the government] and I refused to see him' (Harada VI 1951: 208; italics added). After this, Kan'in and Tada ceased their resistance to the war policy when they rejoined the liaison conference. Two days later Konoe announced Japan's mission to destroy the Nationalist government and replace it with a new regime which would cooperate with Japan. This latter intention was eventually implemented with the creation of the puppet regime of Wang Ching-wei in April 1940, as part of Japan's broad commitment to building the New Order in Asia (Usui 1983: 379–406). By then, Japan was committed to realizing the so-called 'Greater East Asia Co-Prosperity Sphere'.

Even had the Emperor seen Kan'in and agreed to intervene, it is improbable that this would have persuaded the liaison conference of 14 January to negotiate an end to the 'China incident' because by then only Kan'in and Tada advocated negotiation. Yet, the Emperor's belief, that the cabinet's decision, adopted by the liaison conference, should be followed without qualification, meant the collapse of resistance to continued hostilities in China; after this, stopping the war became impossible.

His legalistic stance enabled Konoe, who had escalated the war ironically to assert his leadership over the military as well as to defeat China, to become 'the first premier since Hamaguchi to exercise the authority of the premier actively and successfully in order to implement a basic policy decision over the adamant opposition of the general staff' (Crowley 1966: 393). But the price of this authority was the unwinnable China incident, which both Konoe and the Emperor would very soon regret.

Once it was determined that Japan would fight to the finish in China, the army general staff threw its weight behind the war and Japanese armies campaigned hard in north, central, and south China. But as the months passed, initial expectations of a quick victory in China were cancelled out by the combined resistance of Chinese Nationalist and communist forces. This military stalemate, and renewed divisions within the Japanese army leadership, prompted the Emperor to use the influence of his office to try and end the war, this time with Konoe's complete cooperation.[6] But his endeavors were no more successful than they had been in late 1937. For instance, early in June 1938 the Emperor lamented that

> Konoe came the other day and said 'I would like to guide the war to an end as soon as possible'. But today the chief of staff told me 'We will attack Hankow to the end'. One group says it wants to end the war and another says it will even attack Hankow. It is very deplorable that there is no liaison between them.
>
> (Harada VII 1952: 8)

In July, the Emperor told Kan'in and General Itagaki Seishirō, who had recently replaced Sugiyama as army minister, that he wanted peace negotiations. They, however, replied that the majority view in the army favored continued hostilities until Chinese resistance was overcome (Harada VII 1952: 32). Two months later, Konoe, still hampered by the gulf between the cabinet and the army, asked the Emperor to help ascertain whether the army would consider peace negotiations with Chiang Kai-shek. The Emperor again summoned Kan'in, and referring to debates within the army on whether to fight or negotiate, asked, 'Cannot the entire body be united by those favoring peace?' Kan'in answered that it would take time for the army to forge the consensus the Emperor desired (Harada VII 1952: 97).

The continuation of the China incident confirmed Konoe's inability to persuade the army to end a conflict he had previously advocated it should wage and he finally resigned out of frustration, in January 1939. However, the new Hiranuma cabinet, like its successors, was just as unable to end the war and the Emperor found it increasingly onerous to deal with the truculent Itagaki, who, having stayed on as army minister, persisted in defending a policy of all-out war. On 5 July 1939 the Emperor asked Itagaki to explain why Japanese units had recently clashed with British units at the British concession in Tientsin where Japanese interference with Western trading interests had already occasioned British and American protests. During the ensuing two-hour audience Itagaki proved unable to assuage the Emperor's anxiety over the alarming prospect of further incidents with Britain. As Harada writes, 'The discontent of the Emperor exploded and His Majesty very bluntly said, "There is no one as stupid as you" ', to Itagaki. Later, however, he made it clear he did not intend this rebuke to mean that Itagaki should resign and thereby bring down yet another cabinet (Harada VIII 1952: 13–14).

The Emperor's nervousness about Japan's declining relationship with the Anglo-American powers as a consequence of the China incident was soon justified when on 16 July 1939 the United States gave six month's notice that it would abrogate the 1911 Treaty of Commerce and Navigation with Japan, to protest against Japanese policy in China (Usui 1983: 364). The notice foreshadowed that the Sino-Japanese War would become an increasingly negative factor, along with others, in Japanese–American relations. But at the time, problems with America and Britain seemed less urgent than a more immediate crisis, which had unfolded to the north, with the Soviet Union.

HOSTILITIES WITH THE SOVIET UNION: CHANGKUFENG AND NOMONHAN

Although there had been no 'plot' in 1937 to conquer China, as there had been prior to the Manchurian incident, increasing pressures for war on the part of army commanders in the field were prominent in Japan's escalation of the China incident. Similar pressures, exerted by the Kwantung Army, led to Japanese hostilities with Russia at Changkufeng in 1938 and Nomonhan in 1939. These encounters, following less serious border clashes in previous years, did not end in full-scale war with the Soviet Union. But to the Emperor they dramatized the dangers of army insubordination and war with Russia even as Japan was bogged down militarily in China. He again found himself responding to events over which he had no control and which were distinctly impervious to imperial influence.

The 'Changkufeng incident' began on 13 July 1938 when Soviet troops occupied the summit of Changkufeng hill, which lay along the disputed frontier between Korea, Manchukuo, and the Soviet Union. The immediate reaction of the Kwantung Army leadership was to dislodge the Russians by force, an argument which carried weight with senior army officials in Tokyo who had always believed that Russia was the primary threat to Japanese interests on the continent. The majority of the Konoe cabinet likewise favored at least a limited military response, although the navy minister, Admiral Yonai Mitsumasa, and Ugaki Kazushige, who had replaced Hirota as Konoe's foreign minister, argued against it (Hata 1976: 144).

Angered by army plans to engage Russia militarily, the Emperor also firmly opposed the use of force at Changkufeng. On 20 July, when Kan'in and Itagaki arrived at the palace to request imperial sanction for operations at Changkufeng, the Emperor had the chief army aide-de-camp, Usami, tell them 'if you are coming for that, you need not come at all' (Harada VII 1952: 50). Nonetheless, he decided to see them, whereupon they requested imperial sanction, as he had expected. When he then asked them if they had consulted Yonai and Ugaki, Kan'in and Itagaki replied that they had the support of Yonai and Ugaki.

Knowing this to be untrue the Emperor asserted, 'The methods of the army in the past have been unpardonable. In the Manchurian incident and also in the doings at Marco Polo Bridge ... there was complete disobedience to central orders.' Condemning defiance on the part of officers who had abused the imperial prerogative of supreme command as 'arbitrary', 'sneaky', and 'altogether improper as my army', he declared, 'This is disgraceful. Nothing like that must happen this time ... you may not move one soldier without my command' (Harada VII 1952: 51).

Initially, this admonition seems to have had some effect, for later that day, after much debate, and uncertain of exactly what was going on at Changkufeng, the army general staff wired the Kwantung Army not to engage the Russians, saying 'There is no prospect of obtaining an imperial order for the use of force' (Hata 1976: 145).

The Kwantung Army, however, ignored this instruction and on 31 July attacked the Russian positions at Changkufeng. Army Vice-Chief Tada at once informed the Emperor of the hostilities. Tada told him that the Japanese units involved had not crossed the international boundary and were acting purely out of self-defense. This was false, since some had been involved in fighting across the border, in Soviet territory. But the Emperor did not know this and begrudgingly acquiesced to the Kwantung Army's *fait accompli* by approving a limited operation. However, he warned Tada that under no circumstances should it be allowed to spread beyond Changkufeng and that it should be terminated as soon as Russian troops had vacated the area (Hata 1976: 149; Coox I 1985: 134).

Ultimately, the incident was contained on 10 August through an agreement with Russia by which Japan consented to withdraw its troops in exchange for a ceasefire. This, according to Inoue Kiyoshi, was due to the Emperor's intervention, which he cites as proof that the Emperor had the power to check the army (Inoue 1975: 53). However, as Sheldon writes,

> It is doubtful that the Emperor's firm position had much direct influence on this outcome, and Inoue gives no evidence to show that it did, in this further unsuccessful effort to demonstrate that unaided, the Emperor could control the military any time he wished.
>
> (Sheldon 1978: 14)

Rather, the Changkufeng incident was brought to an end only by the reality, which the Kwantung Army finally had to acknowledge, that Soviet forces had defeated it along with units of Japan's Korea Army which had joined in on the fighting (Hata 1976: 154).

The Emperor was relieved that hostilities at Changkufeng had ceased. Nevertheless, the possibility still existed that the Kwantung Army would once again defy central orders in dealing with Soviet forces on the Manchurian border and it was for this reason that in February 1939 he told the then chief army aide-de-camp, Hata Shunroku, to investigate reports that it had unilaterally mobilized twenty-five divisions along the frontier between Manchukuo and Russia. He asked Hata, 'Are they going to do something, deliberately keeping it quiet?' (Harada VII 1952: 298).

The answer came on 11 May with news of hostilities between Japanese and Russian units at Nomonhan, near the Halha River boundary between Manchukuo and Outer Mongolia. Immediately, the Emperor instructed Kan'in to localize and settle the incident with a clearer demarcation of the border to avoid similar confrontations in the future (Hosoya 1980: 18). As it happened, the incident was contained, not by orders from Tokyo but by a Japanese retreat after suffering heavy losses.

In June fighting erupted again at Nomonhan and this time the Kwantung Army undertook an extensive air assault against Russian positions in Outer Mongolia, without authorization from Tokyo. This action impelled the Emperor to reprimand General Nakajima Tetsuzō, now serving as vice-chief of the army general staff, for violating the imperial prerogative of supreme command (Hata 1976: 165). He also instructed Kan'in to punish the Kwantung Army leadership for defying orders to cease hostilities (Coox I 1985: 281). But the fighting continued through the summer and into the autumn, with increasingly heavy losses sustained by the Japanese even after the Kwantung Army threw more of its forces into the battle.

Throughout, the Emperor refused to sanction the Kwantung Army offensive at Nomonhan although reports of Japanese suicides at the collapsing front stirred his sympathy for the troops there. Orders to the Kwantung Army to pull back were finally carried out on 7 September, bringing both a conclusion to the disastrous 'Nomonhan incident' and subsequent punitive purges in the Kwantung Army (Coox II 1985: 843–78). However, as at Changkufeng, the sharp reality of defeat on the battlefield, not the authority of the Emperor or of the government, proved fundamentally decisive in achieving Kwantung Army compliance with orders to desist at Nomonhan. For the Emperor and the Tokyo authorities, peace in the north had come none too soon because other developments had completely overshadowed the Nomonhan incident and the continuing war in China. These were the German–Soviet Non-Aggression Pact of 24 August 1939, the German invasion of Poland on 1 September, and the Anglo-French declaration of war on Germany two days later.

WAR AND DIPLOMACY: THE AXIS ALLIANCE AND THE SOUTHERN ADVANCE

Successive German victories after the outbreak of war in Europe, leading by the end of June 1940 to the conquest of France, Belgium, and the Netherlands, convinced opportunistic Japanese advocates of 'renovationist diplomacy' in the army and elsewhere in the government that by joining Germany and Italy in the Axis Alliance, and by taking advantage of greatly weakened Western possessions in Asia, Japan could proceed more quickly in building the New Asian Order. The result was the signing of the Tripartite Pact with Germany and Italy in Berlin on 27 September 1940 and the almost simultaneous military penetration of northern French Indochina, which constituted Japan's first direct challenge to a Western colony in Asia. Together, the Tripartite Pact and this 'southern advance' linked Japanese aggression in Asia to the European war in a manner which virtually ensured a future collision with the Anglo-American powers.

Historically, the Tripartite Pact grew out of the Anti-Comintern Pact, signed by the Hirota administration with Germany on 25 November 1936 with a view to political cooperation in containing the spread of communism (Ōhata 1976: 9–11). Speaking for the Emperor, Saionji had vainly condemned it as useless to Japan and worse, a dangerous challenge to friendship with the United States and Britain which the constitutional monarchists at court had always regarded as an unshakable priority in Japanese foreign policy (Ōhata 1976: 35).

This view prevailed at court in subsequent years as advocates of 'renovationist diplomacy', who constituted the 'Axis faction' in the army and the foreign ministry, pressed for the conversion of the Anti-Comintern Pact into a full-scale military alliance. The question of an alliance increasingly absorbed the attention of the Hiranuma cabinet which, at Germany's request, undertook cautious negotiations that were complicated by the unilateral diplomacy of Japan's ambassadors in Berlin and Rome, General Ōshima Hiroshi and Shiratori Toshio respectively. Eager for a military alliance, both men, especially Ōshima, went beyond instructions from Tokyo in providing assurance that Japan, under an alliance, would participate on Germany's side should Germany go to war (Hosoya 1971: 100–1).

Ōshima's conduct upset the Emperor, who in addition to personally opposing a military alliance with Germany, very much disapproved of Ōshima's unilateral diplomacy. Aware that the cabinet wished to avoid any obligation to provide military assistance to Germany, other than possibly in the event of German hostilities with the Soviet Union, in March 1939 the Emperor asked Hiranuma whether Ōshima and Shiratori would be disciplined for their independent diplomacy and what was meant by 'effective military assistance'. When Hiranuma assured him on the first point that the ambassadors would be dealt with appropriately and on the second, that assistance did not mean Japan's actual participation in war, the Emperor requested, and obtained from Hiranuma, a written statement of these responses signed by the prime minister, the foreign minister, Arita Hachirō, and other leading members of cabinet (Harada VII 1952: 325–6). This unusual request made it plain that the Emperor did not want the cabinet to depart from its cautious approach towards Germany for fear that Japan might be pulled by Germany into a war not of Japan's own choosing (Ōhata 1976: 86–7).

The government stuck to this position in the continuing talks with Germany despite friction between the Axis faction, backed by Army Minister Itagaki, and those who favored good relations with Britain and America, or at least the avoidance of war with the Anglo-American powers. That was the navy's priority, for it was not yet ready for war.

However, the maverick diplomacy pursued by Ōshima and Shiratori in Europe still concerned the Emperor. In April he told Arita, 'The actions of the ambassadors ignores the supreme authority of the Emperor' in foreign affairs, the responsibility for which had been delegated to the foreign minister (Harada VII 1952: 335). He thought it intolerable that the ambassadors had usurped this responsibility. Arita readily agreed, but said that it would be better to clarify Japan's position in discussions with Germany rather than reprimand Ōshima and risk antagonizing the army.

Later that month, as negotiations proceeded, Hiranuma asked Kido to see if he could persuade the Emperor to understand the army's advocacy of a military alliance with Germany which the army regarded as a deterrent to Russian and Anglo-American interference with Japan's New Order. However, Kido replied, 'The Emperor will hear nothing of it' (Harada VII 1952: 339). And indeed on 10 May the Emperor let it be known through his chief aide-de-camp that if Kan'in, who was due at the palace to discuss the alliance with Germany, 'ever mentions anything about participation in war, I will definitely oppose it', which he did when Kan'in spoke as expected in audience (Harada VII 1952: 359–60). He also argued with Prince Chichibu when his brother advocated the alliance (STDH 1990: 107). Still, summer brought renewed army pressure for a military alliance and when, in July, Itagaki deliberately misrepresented Arita as being sympathetic to an alliance, the Emperor scolded him, 'You know my opinions well ... but have still reported falsely that the foreign minister is in favor of a military alliance. That is very insolent of you' (Harada VIII 1952: 14).

By then, though, Hitler had decided to conclude a Non-Aggression Pact with the Soviet Union, to stabilize Germany's flank in eastern Europe.[7] The shock announcement of this treaty left the question of a military alliance with Germany in disarray and precipitated the fall of the Hiranuma cabinet on 28 August. When Hiranuma came to the palace to resign, the Emperor reportedly was furious that the government had gone so far with an issue which had been misguided all along. He was overheard shouting at the prime minister. One account states, the Emperor was 'obviously angry' and after a long meeting 'Hiranuma emerged from the room looking like a man who had been in a steam bath' (Irie 1983: 40).

Later that day, the Emperor instructed the new prime minister, General Abe, who had been chosen to moderate the army's pro-German stance, to emphasize good relations with Britain and the United States. To underline his distrust of Itagaki Seishirō, whom he thought would oppose this emphasis, the Emperor further urged Abe to appoint either Umezu Yoshijirō or Hata Shunroku as army minister (Kido II 1966: 743). This was a rare instance in which the Emperor influenced the composition of a cabinet, for Abe complied by appointing Hata.

During the brief tenure of the Abe and Yonai cabinets the matter of a military alliance with Germany was left in abeyance until the combination of Yonai's unsuccessful negotiations with the United States, which was moving toward a policy of stronger economic sanctions to protest the New Asian Order (Hosoya 1976: 202–4), and Germany's defeat of France and the Low Countries, gave it renewed impetus. Hoping that a new administration under Prince Konoe would act more positively on the alliance question, the army aborted the Yonai cabinet, through the resignation of Army Minister Hata Shunroku, on 16 July 1940 (Hosoya 1976: 194–214).[8] The Emperor criticized this maneuver but consoled himself with the thought that at least it disclosed very clearly the army's hand in political intrigue (Kido II 1966: 805). He then accepted Privy Seal Kido's nomination of Konoe Fumimaro as the next prime minister, expecting that Konoe would reassert the authority of his office in checking the army's quest for a military alliance with the Axis states.

However, Konoe, his foreign minister, Matsuoka Yōsuke, General Tōjō Hideki, the new army minister, and Admiral Yoshida Zengo, the navy minister, had already agreed privately, at an informal meeting on 19 July, to make a military alliance with Germany the first priority of the second Konoe cabinet. This conference, held in Konoe's home at Ogikubo three days before Konoe took office, also agreed to conclude a non-aggression pact with the Soviet Union which, by securing the north, would enable Japan to undertake a southern advance to bring the European colonies in Asia into the New Asian Order without, however, precipitating war with the United States if it could be avoided. The twin assumptions, that Britain would soon fall to Germany in Europe and that the United States could be kept neutral by Japan's entry into the Axis Alliance, were of particular importance in this policy blueprint of deterrent diplomacy. It was largely an army blueprint but Matsuoka would figure significantly in its implementation, with the navy ultimately following suit despite reservations concerning the implications for all-out war at sea with the United States (Hosoya 1976: 216–19).[9]

Soon after the Konoe cabinet came to power Japan therefore re-opened negotiations with Germany and moved ahead with the policy of the southern advance. The latter involved, first, diplomatic pressure, which proved largely ineffective, on the Dutch colonial government in Batavia, to secure Japanese access to oil and other raw materials in the Dutch East Indies (Nagaoka 1980). Second, it involved similar pressure, backed by the threat of force, to attain the acceptance by the Vichy government and by the vulnerable French colonial regime in Hanoi of the stationing of Japanese troops in French Indochina which in the first instance could be deployed from the south in the China war. This stationing was finally accomplished on 26 September 1940 (Hata 1980; Tsunoda J. 1980).

From its inception, the southern advance created new tensions with the United States and Britain. On 25 July, three days after the installation of the

Konoe cabinet, the United States listed oil and scrap iron as items which could not be exported to Japan without governmental approval and on 31 July an embargo was placed on aviation gasoline to Japan. These attempts to dissuade Japan from carrying out the southern advance were followed by an American protest on 7 August against Japanese demands of the French that Japanese troops should be permitted in northern Indochina (Hosoya 1976: 231).

American sanctions and the ensuing preparatory mobilization of the Japanese fleet in August made the Emperor all too aware of the heightened possibility of war with the United States as a consequence of the southern advance. In a discussion with the Emperor on 10 August concerning strategic preparations for a Japanese–American war, Navy Chief Fushimi, who did not want war himself but was preoccupied with its timing should Japan decide to wage it, pragmatically observed that 'Because at least eight months will be needed to prepare after a decision to wage war is made, the later war comes, the better' (Kido II 1966: 814). Whether even with this scenario the navy could be expected to succeed militarily against the United States had become a serious issue within the navy; Navy Minister Yoshida expressed doubts on this critical question (Tsunoda J. 1980: 257).

Such discussions reinforced the Emperor's personal determination to avoid war with the United States and Britain, not only because its outcome was uncertain but because the very idea of such a conflict contradicted his long-held belief that Japanese foreign policy should be predicated on cooperation with the Anglo-American powers. Noting that Matsuoka seemed indifferent to this priority, he found it profoundly 'regrettable to learn that no definite policy has been established toward the United States' (Kido II 1966: 814). He was also concerned by the lack of consensus within the government over the more immediate problem of coordinating the southern advance with Japan's continuing war in China. He was especially distressed that the Konoe cabinet wanted to reduce the scale of fighting in China in order to concentrate on the southern advance, while the army wanted to move south without falling back in China and the navy wanted the China incident resolved before implementing the southern advance (Kido II 1966: 812).

His dismay that Japanese foreign policy could well result in war with the United States and Britain mounted further in September with the escalation of the southern advance and negotiations for a military alliance with Germany. On 13 September the inner cabinet endorsed an army plan to station troops in northern Indochina by the 22nd with, or without, French agreement. The Emperor later told Kido he greatly disliked presenting the French with this ultimatum but Kido felt it was necessary because otherwise, French Indochina would assist China against Japan, with British and American encouragement (Kido II 1966: 821–2).

Yet since the stationing of troops was the government's policy, the Emperor gave it his sanction after Army Chief Kan'in promised that force would not be used against the French in Indochina if at all possible (Hata 1980: 184). The Emperor may also have reasoned that if it could be limited to diplomacy, which would reduce the possibility of war with the Anglo-American powers, the southern advance was preferable to renewed hostilities with the Soviet Union in the north, which he still feared in the wake of the Changkufeng and Nomonhan incidents.

Meanwhile, having been persuaded by Matsuoka that a military pact with Germany would ensure continued American neutrality in the European war and American acceptance of the New Order in Asia, during a liaison conference on 14 September, the new navy minister, Admiral Oikawa Koshirō, made it clear that the navy now supported Japan's entry into the Axis Alliance (Hosoya 1976: 238–41). However, largely at the navy's insistence, it was still agreed to qualify the pact in order that Japan could retain autonomy in deciding precisely when and where to fight on the side of its Axis partners, should war prove necessary. This Matsuoka eventually succeeded in doing five days later, through a secret protocol concluded with the German envoy Heinrich Stahmer, without Hitler's knowledge (Hosoya 1976: 241–55).

The Emperor greeted the government's commitment to a German alliance with much apprehension and a deepening sense of personal isolation and fatalism. On 15 September he expressed to Kido his opposition to the pact and his fears for its impact on Japanese–American relations. Recalling Konoe's tendency to 'give up when things become difficult', he wondered whether 'Konoe would really take the bitter medicine with me' if the treaty, combined with the southern thrust into Indochina, provoked the United States into war with Japan (Kido II 1966: 822). When Kido relayed the Emperor's anxieties to Konoe, the Prince reassured the Emperor through Kido that he would remain in office come what may (Harada VIII 1952: 346).

The issue of war with the Anglo-American powers dominated the proceedings of the imperial conference on 19 September which formally endorsed Japan's entry into the Axis Alliance on the terms negotiated by Matsuoka. It is not known whether Fushimi spoke for the Emperor on this occasion. But the navy chief's reservations about the Axis Alliance, the Indochina question, and the prospects of war with the United States certainly reflected those of the Emperor.

In particular, Fushimi questioned Japan's capacity to fight a major war in Asia given the drain on national resources caused by the conflict in China and uncertain access to oil in the Dutch East Indies. To reduce the risk of war arising from the Axis Alliance, he urged that 'even though this alliance is concluded, every conceivable measure will be taken to avoid war with the United States' and expressed the hope 'that the southern advance will be attempted as far as possible by peaceful means' (Ike 1967: 13). He concluded, 'We must avoid war with the United States . . . I cannot ascertain the chances of victory' (Tsunoda J. 1980: 276).

However, despite Fushimi's warnings, the conference, at which the Emperor had listened silently, ended without changing the fixed course of Japanese foreign policy. The next day the Emperor, now greatly agitated by fears of war with the United States, summoned Konoe to the palace.

Concerning the Tripartite Pact, he told the prime minister resignedly, 'If there are no other means of dealing with the United States, it probably cannot be helped'. But considering that it might well lead to war with the United States, and anxious to ensure a realistic correlation of ends and means in Japanese policy, he wondered whether the navy could possibly prevail in such a massive conflict: 'I have often heard that in the map problems of the Naval Staff College, Japan is always the loser in a Japanese–American war. Can you reassure me about that?'

He further stated, 'I am very concerned over this situation. What would happen in the event that Japan should become a defeated nation? Are you ready to share the pains and toils with me?' Struck by the Emperor's palpable anxiety, Konoe recalled how Emperor Meiji had summoned Itō Hirobumi prior to the Russo-Japanese War, to express similar concerns, and that Itō had declared he was prepared to go to the front himself and die in battle, if necessary. Konoe said he was no less determined to serve the Emperor. As for the Emperor's question about foreboding wartime scenarios in the Naval Staff College, Konoe promised to investigate the matter (Harada VIII 1952: 346–8). Within a week the desperate future circumstances foreshadowed in this conversation were made more likely by the stationing of Japanese troops in northern French Indochina and the signing of the Tripartite Pact in Berlin.

Based on information obtained from a source 'closely in touch with the Imperial Court', Grew later speculated 'that the Emperor was most reluctant to approve the Pact and was finally led to do so only when Matsuoka gave the Emperor his studied conviction that war with the United States would be inevitable if the alliance with the Axis were not concluded' (Grew 1944: 354).

Grew was right about this, for after the Pacific War the Emperor acknowledged, 'Ultimately, I agreed with the Tripartite Pact but this does not mean I was satisfied with it. . . . I believed Matsuoka that it would deter the United States' (STDH 1990: 112). He therefore must have found it highly upsetting to be told in no uncertain terms by Kido on 21 September: 'we will have to oppose both England and the United States as a result of the conclusion of a military alliance with Germany and Italy' (Kido II 1966: 825). The ensuing imperial rescript announcing the Pact emphasized the imperative of achieving the restoration of world peace (Murakami S. 1983: 301–2). But at this stage the Emperor cannot have thought this would be possible.

Grew was also told, in this instance by an unidentified member of the imperial family, that the Emperor had opposed the Tripartite Pact until 'it was brought to the Emperor's attention that he might not survive a refusal' whereupon he reportedly told Konoe, 'Well, you and I will have to stand or fall together' (Grew 1944: 347). He may indeed have been constrained to accept the Pact partly because of violent threats against those who opposed an alliance with Germany and Italy. In July, a plot had been discovered in which activists who had been associated with the 1933 'Heaven-Sent Soldiers' Unit' incident planned to assassinate Prime Minister Yonai, Foreign Minister Arita, the former Lord Privy Seal Makino Nobuaki, Imperial Household

Minister Matsudaira, and Harada Kumao, all of whom had been against the alliance (Maxon [1957] 1975: 142).

Still, the Emperor would have sanctioned the Tripartite Pact even had there been no threats of violent intimidation. It would not have occurred to him to oppose a treaty legally decided upon by the government, regardless of its dark implications for the nation. Thus, still constrained by his own constitutional scruples and a coercive political environment that pressed him to go along with policies which he himself deplored and which, because of his isolation from decision-making, had been beyond his capacity to influence, the Emperor approached the New Year with a fatalistic dread of what lay ahead for Japan.

He also now faced the future unknown without Saionji, who died on 24 November 1940 at the age of ninety-one. This left Kido as his principal adviser in dealing with the formidable personalities who would be prominent in Japan's decision for war in 1941: General Sugiyama, who had already replaced Kan'in as army chief in October 1940, Admiral Nagano Osami, who would succeed Navy Chief Fushimi in April, 1941, and General Tōjō Hideki, appointed prime minister after the resignation of Prince Konoe Fumimaro in October 1941.

5 World war and the imperial will, 1941–1945

In early 1941 the Emperor continued to perform the public ritual role of nationalist icon which the government and the people expected of him. The foreign correspondent, Otto Tolischus, observed that during the 11 February Kigensetsu commemoration of the 2,601st anniversary of the founding of the empire, the Emperor and government dignitaries gathered 'in a severely plain hall built of white, knotless timber, decorated ... with branches of the Sakaki tree'. Then 'the Emperor, clad in ancient ceremonial dress, entered the innermost sanctuary and worshipped his legendary ancestress, the Sun Goddess, and his other Imperial Ancestors from whom he derives his supposed divinity'. Later that day large crowds waving flags thronged the shrines and after shouting 'banzai' three times, bowed towards the palace which 'remained mute – like the heavens' (Tolischus 1944: 18).

The Emperor was no less venerated as symbol of the nation on 29 April, his fortieth birthday. During an elaborate military review, he 'sat immobile on his white horse' as scores of tanks, artillery, cavalry and infantry paraded by and 'throughout the land, people made pilgrimages to the shrines to pray for the prosperity of the Imperial House' (Tolischus 1944: 82). Believing him to be an absolute monarch, the people naturally still assumed that he was in command, especially since the government presented its decisions as his personal decisions once they were ratified with the imperial will. The people did not know, nor had they ever known, that 'In order for the Emperor to function as a constitutional monarch, it was mandatory that the procedure of "working through the court" [to define national policy] operate in such a way as to avoid situations in which the Emperor himself would be forced to make decisions' (Imai 1973: 57).

DETERRENCE AND EXPANSION: JANUARY–AUGUST 1941

In January, the Konoe government opened a new phase in the southern advance when it agreed to Thailand's request to mediate long-standing border disputes between Thailand and French Indochina. The purpose was to strengthen Japan's hand politically in the region in order to facilitate the eventual conclusion of a military pact with Thailand and the stationing of

Japanese forces in southern as well as northern Indochina. The military calculated that once these objectives were realized, Japan would be better positioned to acquire needed raw materials in Southeast Asia, if that proved necessary to offset American sanctions. But at the time, most of Japan's army leaders did not believe that the southern advance would necessarily result in war with Britain and the United States. The navy was less sanguine on this point; it acknowledged that any Japanese threat to Western colonies in Asia might well provoke armed retaliation against Japan (Iriye 1971: 126–30).

The Emperor did not oppose the government's policy of mediation per se, but on 22 January he nervously requested Kido to keep him fully informed of diplomatic initiatives concerning the Thai-Indochinese border problem. Afraid that the army might impose a deadline on French cooperation, the following day he warned the chiefs of staff to coordinate with the foreign minister in carrying out mediation, hoping that the Konoe cabinet could restrain the military from using coercion to achieve a settlement (Kido II 1966: 851). Looking ahead, he asked Sugiyama whether any military agreement that might be reached with Thailand could be kept secret, so as not to alarm the Western powers. The army chief replied this would be difficult (Sugiyama I 1967: 162–3). In the event, a military pact with Thailand was not concluded until 21 December 1941.

In subsequent discussions with the chiefs of staff on 24 and 25 January the Emperor again made it plain that he was anxious to restrict Japan's southern advance exclusively to diplomacy. Fearing war with the Western powers in Southeast Asia, he pressed the chiefs to explain whether they had planned for that contingency with any greater care than had been the case in the now-inconclusive 'China incident' (Sugiyama I 1967: 163–4). Their failure to reassure him led to yet another audience, on 1 February, in which he asked them detailed questions to discover precisely what naval and air bases the military sought on mainland Southeast Asia (Sugiyama I 1967: 172–3). Commenting on these discussions to Kido, he criticized the opportunism of the military: 'Personally, as a matter of principle, I do not approve of acting like a thief at a fire ...'. However, he acknowledged, perhaps by way of rationalizing his inability to check the military, that 'to cope with the great changes in the world of today, mistaken benevolence would be unwise. So I approved these policies. But we have to be extremely tactful in implementing them' (Kido II 1966: 854).

The Emperor's questions regarding the military's operational plans in the event of war have been interpreted by Edward Behr as evidence for his 'positive guidance' of Japan's southern advance (Behr 1989: 231). However, the suggestion that he actively encouraged the military wrongly ignores his anxiety, dating from 1940, that the southern advance would plunge Japan into war with the Anglo-American powers and as Louis Allen writes, 'there is all the difference in the world between acquiescing in plans and initiating plans, even when acquiescence is accompanied by detailed interrogation. ... Mr Behr does not demonstrate that the Emperor initiated planning' (Allen 1989: 309).

Nor in fact did the Emperor invariably acquiesce. His purpose in asking questions was not to encourage war but to warn military leaders about this danger by highlighting how far they were ready to risk war, whether they truly intended to adhere strictly to diplomacy in the evolving southern advance, and whether, if their policies resulted in war, their preparations were such that Japan would prevail. General Sugiyama certainly appreciated the Emperor's desire to avoid war. In a note which he appended to the record of a similar discussion with the Emperor in July, he wrote, 'His Majesty's questions today indicated that he is filled with a desire to avoid recourse to force no matter what. I plan to use whatever opportunity that may arise to change his thinking on this question' (Sugiyama I 1967: 278). Indeed, for Sugiyama, the problem was that the Emperor did *not* provide 'positive guidance' in implementing the southern advance.

In April, however, the court seemingly had reason to hope that Japan might yet avert a wider war than that which still raged in China. First, to deter the Soviet Union, Matsuoka negotiated a Neutrality Pact with the Soviet Union in Moscow, on 13 April (Hosoya 1980). Welcoming the agreement as a means of avoiding a recurrence of border clashes with the Soviet Union, 'The Emperor was pleased', as Shigemitsu Mamoru, then Japan's ambassador to Britain and formerly ambassador to Russia from 1936 to 1938, wrote later (Shigemitsu 1958: 214). However, Matsuoka failed to inform the Emperor that he had discovered greater tension than expected between Russia and Germany, while touring Europe that spring (Shigemitsu 1958: 214).

Secondly, it momentarily appeared that tensions with the United States might be eased through the informal talks which had commenced in April between Admiral Nomura Kichisaburō, Japan's ambassador in Washington, and the American secretary of state, Cordell Hull. Expectations of progress in this connection were awakened when, on the 16th, Nomura cabled a promising 'Proposal for Understanding'.

Drafted in the first instance by private individuals on both sides who participated indirectly in the talks, and tentatively discussed by Nomura and Hull, this document contained substantial American concessions to Japan, including American mediation of the war in China. Accordingly, on the 18th, the liaison conference decided to accept it as a basis for further discussions with the United States, upon the strong recommendation of Konoe. Three days later the Emperor said that he was pleased and surprised by the new flexibility of the American government, which, Kido recalls, he attributed 'to the virtue of the Tripartite Pact' (Kido II 1966: 870).

The Emperor's optimism concerning the 'Proposal' soon ebbed. After returning from Moscow on the 22nd, Matsuoka rightly suspected what neither the Emperor nor the government had realized, namely that the 'Proposal' was not an official submission by the American government, an important point that Nomura had failed to communicate (Hosoya 1971: 102–3). Matsuoka therefore persuaded the government to dismiss the document and to take an uncompromising line towards the United States. The Washington talks continued into the summer, but without any positive results. The issues, which proved incapable of resolution, included from the American point of view, Japan's war of aggression in China, its membership in the Axis Alliance and its penetration of Indochina, and from the Japanese side, American sanctions, the accelerating buildup of the US armed forces and, more broadly, American opposition to the New Asian Order.

In June, the deliberations of the cabinet and the military on policy priorities were suddenly upset by ambassador Ōshima's cable from Berlin, on the 5th, predicting that Germany and the Soviet Union soon would be at war. This message precipitated a tense liaison conference two days later which debated whether Japan should temporarily abandon the southern advance and strike at Russia if a German–Russian war erupted. Matsuoka insisted, contrary to Ōshima, that no such war would take place and the meeting ended with a decision to wait and see (Hosoya 1980: 91–3).

The debate on Japanese priorities intensified when, at the liaison conference on 16 June, Matsuoka abruptly reversed himself and argued vehemently that Japan should lay aside the southern advance and fight alongside of Germany against Russia in a war he now felt certain would occur. He particularly opposed General Sugiyama's demand that Japan should press ahead with its policy of acquiring military bases in Indochina. Holding that Japan's obligation to Germany under the Tripartite Pact took priority, he added that in any case to occupy Indochina would be an act of 'bad faith' which he was loath to recommend to the Emperor (Ike 1967: 56). The meeting ended inconclusively.

'Operation Barbarossa', Germany's invasion of Russia on 22 June, greatly exacerbated this debate concerning Japan's priorities and it renewed the Emperor's fear that Japan would be drawn by the Tripartite Pact into a world war. On 25 June Matsuoka told the Emperor that Japan should immediately go to war against Russia and eventually against the Anglo-American powers as well. Kido writes that afterwards

> The Emperor asked me whether, if we follow Mr Matsuoka's foreign policy, it would result in the positive penetration by our army and navy into both the south and the north, whether this was agreed upon by the supreme command and the government, and whether we had enough national power to meet such a huge military operation.

(Kido II 1966: 884)

Extremely agitated, the Emperor then demanded to see Konoe, who later recalled, 'His Majesty, astounded at Matsuoka's talk, summoned me at once'. The prime minister placated the Emperor by saying that Matsuoka had articulated a purely personal view, not the cabinet's (Sheldon 1976: 19, note 65). And indeed that same day the liaison conference decided not to invade the Soviet Union for the time being, in order to emphasize the southern advance.

The chiefs of staff jointly reported this decision to the Emperor, with

Konoe present. On this occasion they did not refer to war with the Anglo-American powers as a likely consequence of acquiring new bases in Indochina. But in actuality they had not ruled out the use of force if it proved necessary to implement the bases policy (Butow 1961: 211, note 53). During a crucial imperial conference on 3 July, which sanctioned the liaison conference decision of 25 June with the imperial will, it was openly acknowledged that in expediting the southern advance Japan 'would not be deterred by the possibility of being involved in a war with Great Britain and the United States' (Ike 1967: 78). Still, hopes were expressed that the Tripartite Pact would deter the United States from challenging Japan militarily. At this, 'The Emperor seemed to be extremely satisfied', Sugiyama noted afterwards (Ike 1967: 90).

Konoe now relied upon achieving a breakthrough in the Washington talks that would relieve the pressure of American economic sanctions on Japan, which was also the Emperor's desire (Shigemitsu 1958: 234). But, to accomplish this, the truculent Matsuoka had to be replaced with a more flexible foreign minister. Thus, with the Emperor's support, Konoe reorganized the cabinet on 16 July and appointed the more moderate Vice-Admiral Toyoda Teijirō as foreign minister (Oka 1983: 134).[1] However, Japanese–American relations deteriorated critically once Japan acted upon the decision to escalate the southern advance.

In brief, on 14 July Japan demanded that the French Vichy government permit the stationing of Japanese troops in southern Indochina and the establishment of eight Japanese air and naval bases at Saigon and Camranh Bay. A reply was requested by 19 July but when that deadline passed without one, Japan demanded French compliance by the 22nd or else force would be used. Ultimately, the French yielded and Japan's goals were achieved. In response, the American government, calculating that only further sanctions could deter Japan in Southeast Asia, froze Japanese assets in the United States on 25 July, as did the British and the Dutch East Indies governments shortly thereafter (Nagaoka 1980: 236–40). Furthermore, on 1 August, the United States imposed an embargo on oil exports to Japan and proposed the neutralization of Indochina.

The Emperor followed these momentous developments with growing perturbation. On 22 July he declared to Sugiyama, 'I think it is impossible to use force in Indochina' and repeatedly questioned Japan's capacity to do so while burdened by the war in China (Sugiyama I 1967: 276–8). Three days later Kido observed that 'The Emperor is now in a state of dread concerning relations between the United States and this country' (Kido II 1966: 894).

This sense of foreboding grew all the more when the Emperor met with Navy Chief Nagano Osami on 31 July. Although like his predecessor, Prince Fushimi, Nagano said that Japan should avoid war with the United States if possible, he asserted that American sanctions meant Japan would have to decide upon war sooner than later, before its material strength ebbed and capitulation to the United States became inevitable. Upon hearing the Emperor's account of Nagano's views, Kido 'was filled with trepidation by the imperial anxiety that a war against the United States would be a hopeless one' (Kido II 1966: 896).

The American oil embargo moved the Emperor to summon Nagano again, on 1 August. He stated bluntly, 'Fushimi said war with Britain and the United States should be avoided. Are you changing this?' Nagano replied, 'Not in principle, but it would be best if we act sooner than later because supplies are dwindling by the day' (Sugiyama I 1967: 286). The urgent tone of these exchanges reveals that 'The oil embargo had a tremendous psychological impact upon the Japanese. The ambivalence and ambiguities in their perception of world events disappeared, replaced by a sense of clear-cut alternatives', war and peace (Iriye 1981: 28). It was in this desperate setting that the Emperor would henceforth display not 'a considerable capacity for ruthlessness and guile' based on approval of war (Behr 1989: 258), but rather a heightened resignation that a decision by the government for war was increasingly likely, if not yet a complete certainty.

JAPAN'S DECISION FOR WAR: AUGUST–DECEMBER 1941

Shaken by the new American sanctions, on 6 August, the Konoe administration communicated through ambassador Nomura several concessions to the United States designed to revitalize the Washington negotiations. Without mentioning withdrawal from China or the American proposal for the neutralization of Indochina, they included a promise not to deploy troops in Southeast Asia outside Indochina, a withdrawal from Indochina after settling the China incident, and a guarantee of neutrality for the American-held Philippines, all in exchange for an American willingness to resume trade relations and help ensure Japanese access to needed raw materials. Also, with the Emperor's encouragement, Konoe proposed to the United States that he and President Roosevelt should personally confer in seeking solutions to the crisis in Japanese–American relations. Japan's suggested concessions, and this proposal for a summit conference, would be the subject of fruitless discussions in Washington until early October, when the United States finally rejected both (Lu 1961: 191–207).

On 11 August, the Emperor fatalistically told Kido Kōichi that 'Regardless of whether the meeting between Prime Minister Konoe and the president is successful, if the United States does not accept Japan's proposals in a simple and straightforward manner, a most serious decision will have to be made'. Of the imperial conference which would ratify it he said, 'Previous imperial conferences have been extremely formal but now I want to ask questions until I fully understand'. He manifestly wanted to play an active role in the imperial conference to ensure that diplomacy would be given the maximum chance of success in dealing with the United States. This intention, however, would be frustrated, as will be seen shortly.

The Emperor also suggested to Kido that whereas in the past the imperial conferences had been attended by middle-ranking officers who had acted as secretaries, now attendance should be limited to the prime minister, the foreign minister, the army and navy ministers, the chiefs of staff, the president of the cabinet planning board and the president of the privy council, as well as himself (Kido II 1966: 901). He was thus aware that senior officials in the armed services had been pushed by these military 'secretaries', who were themselves under similar pressure from pro-war junior officers to take a strong stand on behalf of war preparations and indeed war itself, as other studies have since demonstrated (Maxon [1957] 1975: 151–6).

The likelihood of war was vastly increased when, during a strained seven-hour meeting on 3 September, the liaison conference adopted an army–navy agreement that the government should decide on war with the United States if by the last ten days of October there was no prospect of success in the Washington negotiations (Ike 1967: 129–33). The cabinet, in turn, endorsed this policy the following day and an imperial conference was scheduled for 6 September, to declare the decision as the imperial will.

On the 5th, after Konoe informed him of these developments, the Emperor asserted it was very wrong to impose deadlines on diplomacy and that war should not take precedence over negotiations. Konoe replied diplomacy would be given equal priority with war preparations; war would come only if diplomacy failed. He suggested that the Emperor consult the chiefs of staff about this matter, in advance of the impending imperial conference (Butow 1961: 253).

Nagano and Sugiyama were therefore summoned to see the Emperor, with Konoe present. During this meeting the Emperor asked them how long it would take for Japan to prevail over the United States in the event of war. When Sugiyama predicted three months would be needed to establish initial control of the southern Pacific, the Emperor sharply reminded him that in 1937 he had predicted three months would be sufficient to subdue China. China was vast, Sugiyama began to explain, but the Emperor interjected, 'If you call the Chinese hinterland vast, would you not describe the Pacific as even more immense? With what confidence do you say "three months"?' The chiefs answered evasively but promised that Japan would resort to war only if diplomacy failed (Butow 1961: 254–5).

The Emperor still suspected that the military was subordinating the priority of diplomacy to that of war, and without any faith in the rationality of Japanese war planning, he reiterated to Kido on the morning of 6 September that he wanted to ask questions at the imperial conference, which would take place within the hour. Kido at once objected and suggested instead that privy council president Hara Yoshimichi should ask questions for the Emperor on all aspects of Japanese policy toward the United States. However, agreeing that the conference was criticial, Kido said that at the end of the meeting 'It would be very desirable to give an imperial warning [*gyokeiku*] to the supreme command to cooperate with the government in order to attain a successful conclusion to our negotiations with the United States' (Kido II 1966: 905).

At the ensuing conference, Nagano justified the proposed deadline with the familar argument that the depletion of oil and other strategic resources would preclude the defense of the empire if the Washington negotiations trailed on indefinitely; Sugiyama agreed, but promised that diplomacy would be seriously pursued to the end; and Hara repeatedly asked for reassurances that diplomacy would take precedence over war preparations (Ike 1967: 133–51). Finally, the Emperor broke his customary silence and read aloud a poem, composed by Emperor Meiji on the eve of the Russo-Japanese War, which he said signified his desire to emulate his grandfather in working for peace.

As he later explained to Kido, he had been disappointed that the military representatives at the conference had not answered Hara's questions concerning the primacy of diplomacy satisfactorily. The poem, he inferred, had been his 'warning' to put diplomacy first (Kido II 1966: 905):

> All the seas, in every quarter,
> Are as brothers to one another.
> Why, then, do the winds and waves of strife
> rage so turbulently throughout the world?
>   (Butow 1961: 258)

That the Emperor had so unexpectedly broken with the convention of his silence at imperial conferences momentarily stunned the participants. After a brief interval when no one spoke, Nagano found his voice and declared that diplomacy would be emphasized, as the Emperor desired. Yet the Emperor's intervention and this reassurance notwithstanding, the conference ended by endorsing the government's deadline policy. The reading of a poem, which reflected the Emperor's tendency to understate his convictions through indirect gesture, had scarcely been a strong 'imperial warning'. But a more forceful intervention would have made little difference at this stage, for the policy presaging a decision for war if negotiations failed had already been fixed and the military was determined to press ahead with war preparations (Maxon [1957] 1975: 171). In effect, a time-bomb now ticked in Japanese diplomacy.

It began to tick even louder once the liaison conference decided on 25 September to bring the deadline forward, to 15 October, at the urging of the chiefs of staff (Ike 1967: 177). In early October, Konoe's hopes of avoiding war faded even more after word came on the 2nd that the United States had rejected Japan's proposals made in early August, including his proposed summit meeting with Roosevelt. At this point the Prince's thoughts turned to resigning if he could not dissuade the military from war.

On 12 October Konoe made a final attempt to do so by consulting with Army Minister Tōjō, Navy Minister Oikawa, Foreign Minister Toyoda, and Lieutenant-General Suzuki Teiichi, president of the planning board, at his residence in Ogikubo. But Tōjō only continued to argue that Japan could never capitulate to the United States while Oikawa maintained an enigmatic reluctance to say whether the navy was fully ready for war (Butow 1961: 270–6).

While this left Konoe struggling with himself over whether to resign, on 13 October, as the deadline neared, the Emperor wearily told Kido all hope for diplomacy was lost and that consideration should be given by the government to composing an imperial rescript declaring war. He regretted that the people had not understood his desire for peace, as expressed in previous rescripts, and insisted that this one indicate clearly that he had always wanted peace. He also discussed wartime relations with Germany, underlining the danger to Japan should Germany ever seek a separate peace with the United States and Russia. Meanwhile, he said, procedures for ending the war through diplomacy should be studied right away. Judging from Kido's account of this conversation, the Emperor's mood was one of complete resignation (Kido II 1966: 914).

Then, Konoe threw matters into such confusion, by signalling his intention to resign, that the 15 October deadline passed without a war decision. Before resigning on the 16th, Konoe advocated Prince Higashikuni Naruhiko as his successor, to unify the government. However, this suggestion was opposed by Kido and the Emperor, both of whom held that an imperial prince should not be appointed if there were any prospects of war. Instead, Kido recommended General Tōjō Hideki as the next prime minister. Anticipating that Konoe's resignation offered an opportunity to wipe the slate clean and revive negotiations in Washington without a deadline, Kido believed that only Tōjō had the stature to check pro-war sentiment in the army while new negotiations were attempted. The Emperor readily agreed (STDH 1990: 117–18), and on the 17th asked Tōjō to form a government. Immediately after this audience, Kido informed Tōjō it was the Emperor's desire that the government proceed with negotiations without being bound by the results of the 6th September imperial conference (Kido II 1966: 915–17).

Konoe has been widely criticized for resigning. For example, Suzuki Kantarō, who as prime minister was instrumental in encouraging the Emperor to intervene on behalf of ending the war in 1945, later claimed Konoe should have orchestrated an imperial intervention to prevent war in 1941 (Shimomura 1948: 155–6). However, Konoe judged that the military was too committed to a war decision to accept an imperial intervention for peace and that peace now depended not upon developments in Japan, but rather upon success in the Washington negotiations. He thought that by resigning he could defuse the time-bomb in Japanese diplomacy and thereby renew the negotiations. Since the Emperor came to accept Konoe's resignation in this light, one may agree with Iriye who suggests, 'That war did not come until December was primarily due to the efforts of the nonmilitary, including Prime Minister Konoe and the Emperor himself, to try to avoid an open clash with the United States' (Iriye 1971: 134).

Nonetheless, having once implored Konoe to stand with him in adversity, the Emperor must have been discouraged by Konoe's resignation. But he did not regard the appointment of Tōjō as damaging to what little hope remained for peace. On the contrary he was prompted to say to Kido, 'There's a saying, isn't there? You cannot get a tiger's cub unless you brave the tiger's den' (Kido II 1966: 918). This remark has been misinterpreted as signifying that the Emperor was ready for war and viewed Tōjō as a wartime leader (Behr 1989: 279–80). More accurately, it meant that the risk of appointing Tōjō had been justified by his assurances that he would try to avert war by complying with the instruction to resume the Washington negotiations unfettered by a deadline.

Tōjō intended to stand by these assurances, although he personally did not think that the American position could be softened. To Sugiyama, who opposed further negotiations, he declared, 'His Majesty will not permit us to cease all diplomatic negotiations and decide on war. I do not have the courage to request His Majesty to approve such a policy' (Hane 1982 : 68). That Tōjō was committed to continuing the Washington negotiations at the Emperor's request was Grew's impression. He maintained this was why Tōjō had nominated Tōgō Shigenori, a career diplomat and known moderate, as foreign minister (Grew 1944: 462). And in fact, through Nomura and later Kurusu Saburō, who was sent to Washington to assist Nomura in November, Tōgō worked hard to reach a settlement with the United States (Tōgō 1956).

Unfortunately, though, the two sides were as polarized as ever and by the end of October the military revived its pressures for a war decision subject to a new diplomatic deadline (Butow 1961: 318–20). By then the Emperor had been informed by Nagano of the heavily guarded operational plans to attack the American naval base at Pearl Harbor.

Exactly when the Emperor first heard about these plans in October is difficult to determine but one authoritative study estimates it was sometime during the period 20–25 October (Prange 1982: 309).[2] He appears not to have objected to the plans themselves, which were the responsibility of the chiefs of staff. Rather, he was far more preoccupied with trying to prevent the necessity of their implementation in the first place.

But the critical decision for war or peace lay with the government, not the Emperor. It was debated at great length during a strained 17–hour liaison conference which began in the morning of 1 November and ended at 1:30 a.m. on the 2nd. Again, judging that the passage of time would fatally deplete Japan's stocks of strategic resources, the conference finally decided that negotiations would continue until the end of November and that if they failed, a decision for war with the United States would be made on 1 December (Ike 1967: 200–7). Prime Minister Tōjō and the chiefs of staff immediately reported this resolution to the Emperor, whose grim face revealed his acute distress now that a time-bomb would again tick in Japanese diplomacy. He strongly urged them to do their utmost to assist the foreign ministry's efforts in Washington (Butow 1961: 324).

On 2 November the Emperor heard more from the chiefs of staff concerning the timing of the Pearl Harbor attack, which would occur early in the morning on Sunday 7 December, Hawaii time, and plans for the seizure of Malaya and Hong Kong (Sugiyama I 1967: 386–8). Two days later, he attended a meeting of the supreme war council and was similarly briefed in general terms concerning impending war operations. He was still worried that the military had not fully anticipated the problems of total war and later asked Kido whether plans had been made to deal with the interdiction of oil supplies by enemy forces in Asia (Kido II 1966: 921).

On 5 November he attended the imperial conference which declared the decision of 1–2 November as the imperial will. During the proceedings he remained silent and made no attempt to warn the government of the disaster that war would bring, because military leaders were manifestly committed to war, having utterly refused to compromise on any of the intractable issues that stood between Japan and the United States.

The conference devoted much discussion to two proposals, 'A' and 'B', presented by the foreign ministry as a last-ditch position in the Washington talks. In brief, 'A' included the eventual withdrawal of troops from China (excepting certain areas such as northern China, Hainan Island, and also Inner Mongolia), the withdrawal of Japanese forces from Indochina after the end of the war in China, and assurances that Japan would continue to interpret its obligations under the Tripartite Pact in a way not to provoke the United States. 'B' involved the following: Japan and the United States would agree not to advance militarily in Southeast Asia (excepting Indochina) and the South Pacific; the two countries would guarantee mutual access to resources in the Dutch East Indies; American sanctions would be lifted and trade resumed; and the United States would not interfere in the China conflict (Ike 1967: 209–11).

Neither proposal, it was recognized, stood much chance of success. Hara Yoshimichi regretted that war was being given a higher priority than diplomacy but he reflected the mood of the conference when he stated, 'it is inevitable that we must decide to start a war against the United States' once the negotiations failed, which he expected would happen shortly (Ike 1967: 236). No thorough consideration was made at this or any other prewar conference as to whether Japan actually had the means to survive the coming war. Nor did the participants seriously contemplate that Japan might prevent war by yielding on those issues to which the Americans attached such great importance. Abrogation of the Tripartite Pact, evacuation of Indochina and total withdrawal from China were now all unthinkable options for the Japanese government, the Emperor included. Inflexibility, illogicality, and no little fatalism prevailed (Maruyama 1963: 84–134).

Secretary of State Cordell Hull rejected the first proposal when it was presented on 10 November. On 22 November the liaison conference resolved that if he rejected proposal 'B', which Nomura and Kurusu had submitted on the 20th, that would mean war. Thus, war was ensured when the so-called 'Hull note' of 26th November dismissed Japan's last proposals. Everyone in the government, including Foreign Minister Tōgō, saw the American reply as an unacceptable ultimatum (Kase 1950: 62). The Emperor now told Kido, 'it is inevitable that worse should come to worse' (Kido II 1966: 925).

Still, in anticipation of a decision for war, he asked to see the *jūshin* ('elder statesmen'; former prime ministers) to hear their opinions. At the liaison conference the next day it was agreed that on the 29th the *jūshin* would confer at the palace with the prime minister and several other members of cabinet, and then meet with the Emperor during lunch (Ike 1967: 259). Kido's summary of what the former prime ministers said, with Tōjō present, indicates that while Konoe thought the breakdown of negotiations should not necessarily require a war decision, otherwise the *jūshin* were resigned to war (Kido II 1966: 926–7).

On 30 November, the day before the imperial conference to confer the imperial will upon the war decision, Kido found the Emperor profoundly dismayed by an audience he had just had with Prince Takamatsu. His brother had told him that even at this late stage, navy leaders were pessimistic about the outcome of the war and that it must be avoided. On Kido's advice, the Emperor immediately summoned Nagano and Navy Minister Shimada Shigetarō, who had replaced Oikawa in the Tōjō cabinet, and questioned them, with Tōjō present, about the navy's views. However, they replied with sufficient optimism about Japan's wartime prospects for the Emperor to inform Tōjō he was ready for the imperial conference to take place (Kido II 1966: 928).

There is no doubt that the Emperor had finally reconciled himself to the inevitability of war. In 1946, he remembered feeling that the American embargo on oil had driven Japan to the limits of endurance. Such was the extremity of the crisis that the military had clamored for war now or never, while Japan still had the physical means to defend itself. 'If at the time I had suppressed the advocacy of war, public opinion would have questioned why Japan, possessing a powerful army and navy, should submit to the United States and I felt that a coup might occur' (STDH 1990: 118–19).

This fear of a coup arose from the violent incidents of recent years. As late as August 1941, a Shintō priest, evidently angry with Hiranuma for not preventing Matsuoka's removal from the Konoe cabinet, had shot Hiranuma in the neck and jaw, and the police had uncovered plots to assassinate Prime Minister Konoe in September. From then on, Kido Kōichi and others in the Emperor's entourage had received strengthened police protection. A pro-war coup could well have been attempted at any time during these months prior to the final decision for war (Butow 1961: 251–2).

However, in addition to political necessity dictated by his fear of a coup, the Emperor's constitutional interpretation impelled him to accept the inevitability of war. He recalled in 1946, 'As a constitutional monarch in a constitutional political system, I had no choice but to sanction the decision by the Tōjō cabinet to begin the war'. He explained, 'If I were to have sanctioned it because I personally liked it, or if I had not sanctioned it because I personally disliked it, I would have been no different from a tyrant' (STDH 1990: 144–5). In retrospect, he said, 'I probably would have tried to "veto" the decision for war, if at the time I had foreseen the future'. However, 'There would have been a great rebellion within the country, the men whom I trusted around me would have been killed and my own life would not have been guaranteed.' An attempted intervention against war would have failed and 'in the end, a furious war would have developed, resulting in a tragedy several times greater than the recent war' (STDH 1990: 145).

Thus, at the imperial conference of 1 December, during which the war decision was sanctioned with the imperial will, 'Believing at the time that even if I opposed it, it would be pointless, I did not say a word' (STDH 1990: 120). Perhaps his sense of relief that the government had reached a consensus after so many protracted debates over the issue of war or peace explains why, as the minutes state, 'His Majesty nodded in agreement with the statements being made, and displayed no signs of uneasiness. He seemed to be in an excellent mood, and we were filled with awe' (Ike 1967: 283).

Yet there was no little irony in Tōjō's remark that, '*Once His Majesty reaches a decision* to commence hostilities, we will all strive to repay our obligations to him ... and set His Majesty's mind at ease' (Ike 1967: 283, italics added). The fiction that the imperial will for war represented the Emperor's personal will was upheld even though Tōjō and everyone else present that day knew perfectly well that the imperial will for war was not the Emperor's personal will and that the government, not the Emperor, had decided upon war. As Katō Shūichi has written of government decisions that ostensibly represented the Emperor's will, 'The words of the Emperor were not the words of the Emperor. The Emperor played the role of the Emperor' (Katō 1974: 210). Other than in a ceremonial sense as legitimizer, he had been peripheral to the Japanese decision for war.

Moreover, he was peripheral to three further developments on the day of the Pearl Harbor attack, 8 December Japan time. Briefly, the first relates to President Roosevelt's last-minute peace message to the Emperor. Tōgō informed Kido at the palace that the message had arrived through Ambassador Grew, whereupon Kido advised Tōgō to consult the prime minister about it before presenting it to the Emperor. He allowed, however, that 'the Emperor would not mind granting an audience even at midnight', if Tōjō approved (Kido II 1966: 932).

Tōgō showed the message, a copy of which Grew had given him, to Tōjō, who dismissed it as offering no new concessions.[3] Tōgō then saw the Emperor at 3 a.m. and after discussing the message, gave him the text of what would be the imperial reply to Roosevelt, which Tōgō had hastily prepared in consultation with Tōjō. Thus, in later handing to Grew what Tōgō represented as the Emperor's reply, Tōgō in fact gave him Tōjō's and his own reply. It was essentially a rebuff although it did say, 'Establishment of peace in the Pacific ... has been my most cherished desire ...' (Tōgō 1956: 221–2; Grew 1944: 493).

Second, it is well-known that Japan's long final note to the United States was delivered to Hull by Nomura and Kurusu one hour after the Pearl Harbor attack had commenced, owing to the note's late arrival in Washington and problems in typing it up for presentation to Hull. That it was not communicated to Hull prior to the attack greatly angered the Emperor, for he had made it clear that he wanted Japan to conform with international procedures by declaring war before hostilities began (Butow 1961: 377–86).

Third, the imperial rescript issued on 8 December declaring war, and announcing it to the Japanese people, was drafted by the cabinet, not by the Emperor. It presented the government's justification for war, citing provocations by China, the United States, and Britain toward the empire. However, the rescript did state, as the Emperor had wanted, 'It has been truly unavoidable and far from Our wishes that Our Empire has now been brought to cross swords with America and Britain' (Murakami S. 1983: 310). As he later told Kido, memories of friendly relations with the British royal family, dating from his visit to Britain as Crown Prince, made war with that country especially painful for him personally (Kido II 1966: 1,237).

WAR AND SURRENDER, 1941–1945

Japan's successful attack on Pearl Harbor sank five American battleships, damaged three others, destroyed 188 American aircraft, and left 2,403 American military and civilian personnel dead. Kido, who was very pleased, records that the Emperor reacted to this news calmly (Kido II 1966: 933; Kanroji 1975: 129). However, when Japan did well elsewhere early in the war, for example in capturing Hong Kong (25 December 1941), Manila (2 January 1942), Singapore (15 February), Batavia (6 March), and Rangoon (8 March), the Emperor often expressed satisfaction over Japanese victories. To illustrate, on 9 March, he enthusiastically recited Japan's triumphs so far, noting that 'The results of the war are coming too quickly' (Kido II 1966: 949).

At times his zeal was such that even his close confidants found it excessive. On 26 June 1942, he proposed sending congratulations to Hitler for German victories in north Africa. Kido objected that this was unnecessary since Japan had not received similar congratulations for its victories from the German leader (Kido II 1966: 970–1). Yet, to put the Emperor's satisfaction into perspective, that he was pleased with Japanese conquests once the war had begun was not inconsistent with having opposed the war in the first instance but rather was natural and what one would expect of any sovereign whose country was fighting to survive a total war. Similarly natural were his expressions of profound concern when Japan suffered defeats, beginning with that of the Battle of Midway in June 1942, or when wartime problems such as supplying Japanese troops in far-flung theaters became critical (Kido II 1966: 966–7, 1,052).

Throughout the 'Greater East Asia War', as the Japanese referred to it, the Emperor routinely received battle reports and followed the progress of the fighting from a map room in the palace. He regularly approved campaign decisions made by the high command, although his approval was mostly perfunctory, and given the enormous complexity of the war, it is difficult to believe that he knew of every Japanese operation or wartime activity.

However, at times, by his own admission in 1946, he actively associated himself with specific campaign decisions. For instance, he sanctioned Japanese operations in the battles of the Philippines and Okinawa, expressly sharing the military's desperate hope for a decisive victory that would compel the Allies to offer favorable terms for ending the war (STDH 1990: 129–30).

Furthermore, 'In his capacity as Supreme Commander (*daigensui*), the Emperor often appeared in public in uniform, riding his white horse. He reviewed troops, attended ceremonies, and bid farewell to departing soldiers and sailors'. Through these public acts, 'he bestowed on the war the legitimacy and the aura which the military desired and helped to make it a "holy war" (*saisen*)' (Shillony 1981: 42). And, when opening the wartime sessions of the Diet, he issued rescripts, prepared by the government, exhorting the nation to make greater efforts to prevail over the enemy.

Because of his public identification with the war, he has been described as a 'warrior king' (Behr 1989: 318). Yet, as a wartime symbol of national unity, the Emperor was a 'warrior king' only in the same putative sense in which King George VI played this role. Sarah Bradford's observation concerning the King could well apply to the Shōwa Emperor, too:

> The King was now, as Head of State and Commander-in-Chief of the Armed Forces of Great Britain and the Empire, a war leader, but, as he was well aware, he had no more real power actually to affect the course of war than he had as a midshipman [in his youth].
>
> (Bradford 1989: 304)

But, as Bradford adds, 'It was, however, still his duty to advise, to counsel, and to warn' the government (Bradford 1989: 304), and this, also, characterizes the Emperor's wartime role. Despite his public persona as a 'warrior king', from a very early date in the war, he endeavored to use his influence to end the fighting through a negotiated settlement, as he had anticipated in his remarks to Kido on 13 October 1941, well before the war began. As early as 12 February 1942 he emphasized to Tōjō, 'I assume you have given full consideration to not losing any opportunity of ending the conflict. It is undesirable to have it prolonged in vain, for the sake of human peace'. He added, 'I fear that the quality of our troops will decline if the war is prolonged' (Kido II 1966: 945).

Shigemitsu Mamoru recalls that after he was appointed foreign minister in April 1943, 'The Emperor's will was crystal clear: he desired peace at the earliest moment ... I constantly conferred with the Emperor on the subject of the war situation and the restoration of peace'. Shigemitsu wanted to enlist the support of the *jūshin* in seeking peace. Mostly, though, he placed his hopes on an extraordinary, unprecedented, imperial intervention, believing 'There was nothing for it but to await the moment when the Emperor gave an absolute command that the war must cease (between ourselves we called it the Voice of the Sacred Crane)'. He felt, however, that this could only happen when Japan renounced its obligations to its Axis partners (Shigemitsu 1958: 300–2).

Certain *jūshin* by then were as anxious as Shigemitsu and the Emperor to terminate the war. Konoe, for instance, had told Prince Higashikuni on 1 May 1942 that it was imperative to end the war in order to avoid the threat of an internal communist revolution against the imperial institution, a threat which would grow if the war went on too long. The immediate question in this context was what should be done about Prime Minister Tōjō, who was clearly determined to fight to the finish. In 1943, with Japan increasingly on the defensive, Kido learned from Okada Keisuke that a movement was afoot to remove Tōjō from office as the first step toward ending the war. Kido was non-committal about this but agreed to keep the Emperor informed of developments (Shillony 1981: 51–2).

In some respects, Tōjō 'had become a virtual dictator ... who had shorn the Emperor of the vast vestiges of power and had left him only in the role of a god who was in Tōjō's keeping' (Tolischus 1944: 277). But, regardless of the fact that he also served as army minister and held several other cabinet posts during the war, Tōjō himself believed that his powers were insufficient to lead the war effort. He was especially frustrated by increasingly poor coordination between the services which historians have since confirmed was a major problem throughout the conflict (Coox 1988: 379). After the war he complained that, due to army–navy rivalry, 'I did not hear of the Midway defeat till more than a month after it occurred. Even now I do not know the details. There was no proper unity in operations right up to the finish' (Shigemitsu 1958: 271).

The court, too, was aware of rivalry between the army and the navy, as when the Emperor felt obliged to admonish both services for wrangling over the allocation of new aircraft, in February 1944 (Kido II 1966: 1,087). It was to deal with this dilemma of coordination that on 21 February that year Tōjō also appointed himself army chief of staff in place of Sugiyama; Navy Minister Shimada likewise now also served concurrently as navy chief, in place of Nagano.

These initiatives to gain greater control, however, only quickened the 'movement', or more properly, the conspiracy, against Tōjō, who became increasingly vulnerable politically after the loss of Saipan on 7 July 1944 (Shillony 1981: 53–6). Already, this conspiracy included Konoe, other *jūshin* and key members of the imperial family, especially Princes Takamatsu and Higashikuni. They frequently agreed among themselves that unless Tōjō was made to take responsibility for the war, the Allies would hold the Emperor responsible for it, with fatal results for the prestige and survival of the imperial institution (Konoe 1968: 11,15, 35–6, 48).

But whether the Emperor would cooperate was a major problem. In November 1943, he declared to Takamatsu, 'I will not receive reports about overthrowing the Tōjō cabinet ...' (Hosokawa I 1953: 8). Later that month, he told Takamatsu, 'It is said that Tōjō is no good, but who would be better? If there is no one better, is there no alternative but to cooperate with the Tōjō cabinet?' (Hosokawa I 1953: 43).

The bonds between the Emperor and Tōjō were in fact unusually strong (Hasegawa 1986: 189).[4] Although the Emperor very much wanted to end the war, he depended upon Tōjō to manage the war effort until such time as peace became a realistic possibility. Similarly, Tōjō depended upon the Emperor to support him against his critics. Certain hardliners in the army had long been dissatisfied with his wartime leadership ('Daihon'ei kimitsu sensō nisshi' 1971: 371). There were even some in the army who, believing that the war was futile, were secretly plotting to kill him so that a 'peace cabinet' could be formed (Shillony 1981: 62). Rumors of similar plots in the navy, to assassinate Tōjō and Shimada to this end, alarmed Tōjō's critics in court circles. They were appalled by the prospect of such violence, notwithstanding their opposition to Tōjō (Hosokawa II 1953: 254).

Prince Takamatsu in particular found the Emperor's reluctance to see Tōjō leave office frustrating and their personal relationship consequently soured. During an argument with the Emperor, which took place on 13 June 1944, Takamatsu, alluding to widespread anti-Tōjō sentiments, stated that the Emperor was unaware of what was going on outside the government. The Emperor strongly denied this and complained irritably of the undesirable tendency of the princes to speak out about politics (Hosokawa I 1953: 222).

The brothers argued again in July. According to Prince Kaya (a cousin of the Empress and Higashikuni's nephew), the Emperor angrily rebuffed Takamatsu, exclaiming, 'I will not listen to the prattling of an irresponsible imperial prince'. This outburst persuaded Kaya that the Emperor was perhaps suffering from a nervous breakdown (Konoe 1968: 77).

The Emperor's impatience with Takamatsu manifested his belief, based on past experience, that the imperial princes should not interfere in sensitive political matters. But, as mentioned earlier, his reluctance to dislodge Tōjō primarily stemmed from his conviction that Tōjō was the only leader capable of dealing with the immediate problem of army–navy coordination. He probably also feared that Tōjō's supporters in the army might violently protest if Tōjō were removed. Certainly, the participants in the anti-Tōjō conspiracy openly worried among themselves about this possibility; they often referred to the danger of an attempted coup reminiscent of the February 1936 rebellion (Hosokawa II 1953: 269). This consideration preoccupied Kido when in June 1944 he rejected Konoe's advice that the Emperor should help to oust Tōjō. Kido believed this could only be attempted if the war went so badly for Japan that the Emperor was forced to intervene in order to end it, at which time an imperial prince could be appointed prime minister (Kido II 1966: 1,079).

However, after the fall of Saipan, Kido agreed with Konoe and Higashikuni on the urgency of replacing Tōjō, even if it required the extreme step of persuading the Emperor to abdicate. For, after the loss of Saipan, the Emperor persisted in defending Tōjō, believing that he was indispensable to the war effort and that Tōjō was too well-known, by virtue of the many contacts he had made with Japanese sympathizers throughout Asia, to force him from office (STDH 1990: 127). Hence, Higashikuni wrote in his diary that perceiving the Emperor to be immobilized concerning the vital question of Tōjō's removal, it was decided on 8 July 1944 that 'the present Emperor should abdicate, the Crown Prince should succeed him, and Prince Takamatsu should be appointed Regent', all to clear the way for Higashikuni's replacement of Tōjō as prime minister in order to negotiate an end to the war (Higashikuni 1968: 135).

Several days later, Takamatsu endorsed this scenario (Higashikuni 1968: 136). However, it was never acted upon because rumors of a military plot against the Emperor made it imperative to protect him in office. As Konoe told Kido, 'It seems to me that the army is planning to transfer the Emperor to Manchuria or even replace him with another imperial prince who opposes his peace plans' (Konoe 1968: 52–3).

Accordingly, having abandoned the idea of working for the Emperor's abdication, Kido and Konoe decided to press the Emperor, through the agency of Princes Takamatsu, Higashikuni, and Asaka, to assist in obtaining Tōjō's resignation (Konoe 1968: 50–2). At first, on 13 July, the Emperor urged Tōjō, through Kido, to appease his critics by removing the unpopular Shimada as navy minister, although it was understood that Shimada would continue to serve as navy chief.[5] Tōjō agreed to this but later that day, after further conferences with his advisers at court, the Emperor summoned Tōjō and informed him that the Princes had advised the 'strengthening of the supreme command'. In response, Tōjō, who was reportedly 'awed', submitted his resignation on the 14th as army chief and moreover had Shimada resign his post as navy minister (Konoe 1968: 73).

He also tried to reorganize the cabinet. But when none of these initiatives proved acceptable, and knowing that he no longer had the Emperor's support, Tōjō submitted his resignation as prime minister on 18 July (Shillony 1981: 63–4). That same day, the *jūshin* met with Kido to select a new prime minister and after considering whether to recommend an imperial prince, rejected the idea and decided instead on General Koiso Kuniaki, judging that he could better manage the problem of army-navy coordination and suppress any violent reaction to Tōjō's removal that might ensue within the armed forces (Kido II 1966: 891–2).

The confusion surrounding Koiso's actual appointment scarcely augured well for his administration. It had been expected, as Konoe had suggested to Kido, that he would form a national-unity cabinet with Admiral Yonai as deputy prime minister. Yonai, in fact, was expected to share power equally with Koiso and for this reason, they were summoned to see the Emperor together. Prior to this audience, Kido told them that Koiso would be prime minister but when the audience took place the Emperor did not clarify this and instead urged them to cooperate on wartime operations and to avoid war with the Soviet Union. Only afterwards did Kido make it definite that Koiso would form the new cabinet (Butow [1954] 1967: 32–3).

What is more, for reasons that remain unclear, neither the Emperor nor

Kido indicated that the cabinet should endeavor to end the war (Butow [1954] 1967: 33, note 13). Perhaps each of them assumed the other had instructed Koiso and Yonai to this effect.[6] Or, perhaps they thought a negotiated end to the war could not be attempted until Japan's failing wartime position had been improved, which in the first instance partly depended on overcoming the problem of army-navy rivalry. In any case, contrary to the hopes of the anti-Tōjō coalition, Tōjō's removal and Koiso's appointment did not bring the termination of the war any closer. Rather, the Koiso cabinet devoted itself to continuing, not ending, the war, largely due to the insistence of Sugiyama, who took office as army minister, General Umezu, the new army chief of staff, and his naval counterpart, Admiral Oikawa Koshirō.

Even as a war leader, however, Koiso was ineffective. On 8 August he established a new supreme council for the direction of the war (Saikō sensō shidō kaigi), in effect a small war cabinet including the prime minister, the service ministers, Foreign Minister Shigemitsu, and the chiefs of staff. But this more streamlined version of the liaison conference, which became an imperial conference when the Emperor attended its deliberations at the palace, failed to harmonize the army and the navy and Koiso was routinely ignored by both services in reaching operational decisions (Shigemitsu 1958: 342; Shillony 1981: 69–70). As for the anticipated cooperation between Koiso and Yonai in national affairs, it never eventuated.

Ultimately, Koiso resigned in April 1945, partly in connection with the so-called 'Miao Pin affair', which may be summarized as follows. Koiso, aware that the Emperor had long wanted peace in China, approved a secret visit to Tokyo on 16 March 1945 by Miao Pin, who, representing himself as Chiang Kai-shek's envoy, engaged in private discussions with Prince Higashikuni concerning how to end the war in China (Higashikuni 1968: 180–1). On 27 March Higashikuni informed the Emperor through Kido of Miao's mission, quoting Miao to the effect that Chiang trusted only the Emperor in negotiating peace with Japan (Kido II 1966: 1,182).

But Foreign Minister Shigemitsu, who hitherto had not been consulted about Miao's peace probe, had serious reservations about the authenticity of his credentials (Shigemitsu 1958: 331–2). The Emperor, too, doubted Miao's reliability (STDH 1990: 131). Accordingly, on 2 April he asked Koiso to clarify the circumstances of Miao's visit, and after Koiso replied unsatisfactorily, told him to 'send Miao Pin back to China' (Akashi 1978: 277). Burdened by new Japanese defeats in the war and by the court's disapproval over the Miao Pin affair, Koiso then resigned with his cabinet on 5 April, a day also notable for the shock of Soviet criticisms of the Russo-Japanese Neutrality Pact (Shillony 1981: 176).

Perhaps Shigemitsu ought to have advised the Emperor to explore the potential of Miao's visit but the fact is that Japan's deteriorating position in the war during the tenure of the Koiso cabinet was such that a comprehensive peace settlement covering all theaters of war, not just China, was an urgent necessity. Not only had Japan lost the costly Battle of the Philippines, in which special attack forces (*tokkōtai*, e.g. the *kamikaze*) had been widely used for the first time in futile suicide missions, Iwo Jima had fallen, Okinawa had been invaded by American troops (on 1 April; it would fall by the end of June) and American planes now bombed Japanese cities with impunity day and night (Coox 1988: 364–5).

The first enemy air attack on Japan proper had been the Doolittle raid of 18 April 1942, in which bombs were dropped on Tokyo, Kobe, Osaka, and Nagasaki (Coox 1988: 350). Expectations of further attacks had spurred plans in July 1944 to evacuate the Emperor from Tokyo. But he had opposed this saying, 'If I leave the capital, the nation will succumb to defeatism ...' (Kido II 1966: 1,131). Nor would he leave Tokyo after the massive fire-bombing of the city on 9–10 March 1945, which claimed the lives of perhaps as many as 90,000 people (Daniels 1975). The Emperor and Kido witnessed the devastation at first hand when they toured the capital on 18 March. The spectacle of mass destruction reminded the Emperor of the World War I battlefields he had seen in France as a youth (Kido II 1966: 1,178).

Hence, by the time Koiso resigned, it was obvious at court that his successor should be someone unequivocally committed to peace. Moreover, the Emperor's personal determination to end the war quickly had been buttressed by many former prime ministers whom he had secretly consulted in individual sessions staggered at intervals in January and February so as not to arouse army hostility toward the growing peace movement which now pivoted on the *jūshin*.

Of particular interest here is Konoe's memorial, which he submitted to the Emperor when they met on 14 February. In brief, Konoe urgently argued that to prolong the lost cause of the war would expose the monarchy to the threat of communist revolution which in his opinion was inevitable given the social dislocations and war-weariness that were now so evident within Japan. The nation had no choice but to rely on the mercy of the enemy whose postwar political interests, he predicted, would hardly be served by a communist revolution in Japan. He stated, 'Even if we surrender unconditionally, I feel that in America's case she would not go so far as to reform Japan's *kokutai* or abolish the imperial house' (Dower 1979: 265).

After listening intently, the Emperor fully agreed with this analysis, for he was no less concerned than Konoe to preserve the imperial institution, especially from the threat of communism. But he did not concur with Konoe's further suggestion that General Mazaki Jinzaburō could be relied upon to control pro-war fanatics in the military. He had never trusted Mazaki and did not wish to see anyone from the imperial way faction in power after they had caused so much havoc in the February 1936 uprising and earlier (Dower 1979: 265).

As it turned out, after consulting with the *jūshin*, Kido recommended Admiral Suzuki Kantarō to replace Koiso (Kido II 1966: 1,188–94). Suzuki was nominated, despite his advanced age (he was eighty) and partial deafness, because his prior service as grand chamberlain meant he would appreciate and act upon the Emperor's desire for peace. With his naval background, it was also hoped that Suzuki could hold the armed services in line while peace initiatives were carefully set in motion.

To ensure that he clearly understood that his mandate was to extricate Japan from the war, Suzuki was explicitly instructed by the Emperor and Kido on this point (Butow [1954] 1967: 63–4). He took office on 7 April and in an address to the Diet that day stated, 'For many years I served near the imperial throne and I am very deeply impressed by the great concern His Majesty the Emperor has for the peace of the world ...' (Kase 1950: 150). This implied that his government would work for peace although Suzuki never said so explicitly, lest he antagonize Army Chief Umezu, Admiral Toyoda Soemu, who had replaced Oikawa as navy chief, and General Anami Korechika, the new army minister, all of whom were set on continuing the war.

These men would pose formidable obstacles to peace but the presence on the cabinet of the more moderate Tōgō Shigenori, as foreign minister, and Yonai Mitsumasa, as navy minister, provided significant support for the peace initiatives Suzuki would undertake with the full backing of the court and the *jūshin*, Tōjō excepted.

The need for this 'peace party' to act decisively would soon be dramatized by the burning down of the imperial palace during an air raid on 25 May, forcing the Emperor and Empress to take refuge in the underground bomb shelter, located near the imperial library, now his residence and headquarters. He was appalled by the conflagration, although relieved that it had not spread to the imperial sanctuary where the sacred jewel and a replica of the sacred mirror were housed (Kawahara 1990: 119–23). The fiery destruction of the palace seemed to symbolize the increasing political vulnerability of the imperial institution the longer the war continued.

The peace party had already regarded Germany's surrender, and the end of the European war on 8 May, as the signal to end the 'Greater East Asian War', eventually through the Emperor's intervention. As one of them put it, 'Our source and strength was the throne, the influence of which we now tried to exploit on behalf of peace' (Kase 1950: 147). But first they pursued other options. On 8 May, Foreign Minister Tōgō issued a public statement releasing Japan from the terms of the Tripartite Pact (Kase 1950: 127). Then, supported by Suzuki and Yonai, he managed to persuade the supreme council for the direction of the war to open discussions with the Soviet Union with a view to enlisting Russian mediation to end the war. This led to informal talks between Hirota Kōki, selected for the task, and Jacob Malik, the Soviet ambassador to Japan, beginning on 3 June.

Umezu, Toyoda, and Army Minister Anami reluctantly agreed to this initiative on the council because they were extremely anxious to ascertain whether Russian denunciations of the Neutrality Pact meant that Russia would soon enter the war against Japan, and because it had been agreed that Russian mediation would only be proposed tentatively and as a last resort (Butow [1954] 1967: 82–5). However, they insisted on 6 June that the council undertake comprehensive plans for the final defense of Japan in hopes of forcing the Allies to offer Japan favorable terms of surrender, including in particular guarantees about the future of the monarchy. These conflicting policies, of negotiations with Russia and preparations for a final defense, were duly ratified as the imperial will at a council meeting on 8 June attended by the Emperor.

The determination of Japan's military leaders at this stage of the war to make a last defensive stand so dismayed Kido Kōichi that later on the same day, he recorded in his diary a plan to end the conflict forthwith. In a long entry acknowledging Japan's virtual defeat and the necessity of saving the monarchy from destruction, Kido wrote, 'I believe we have no alternative ... but to solicit a courageous imperial decision' to stop the war.

More specifically, agreeing that the way to peace was through Russian mediation with the United States, Kido proposed that the Emperor issue an imperial message (*goshinsho*) which would make it plain that the Emperor, who had always wanted peace as stated in the imperial rescript declaring war, 'has decided, in view of the impossibly heavy war damages we have sustained, to bring the war to a close on "very generous terms" '. These would include Japan's unilateral evacuation of occupied territories throughout Asia and the neutralization of the Pacific (Kido II 1966: 1,209).

Kido informed the Emperor of this plan on 9 June and the Emperor at once requested him to help put it into effect (Kido II 1966: 1,209–10; Kase 1950: 180). Several days later Kido told Suzuki and Navy Minister Yonai of the plan and they, too, endorsed it. Significantly, the plan involved a more active role for the Emperor in giving sharper priority to formal negotiations with Russia, now being explored tentatively between Hirota and Malik. Having been informed on 12 June by Admiral Hasegawa Kiyoshi, whom he had asked to study the navy's strength, that the navy could not carry on much longer, the Emperor and Tōgō agreed on 20 June that Russian mediation to end the war was absolutely essential.[7] However, it still remained to persuade Anami, Umezu, and Toyoda on the supreme council for the direction of the war to support this objective without subordinating it to a final desperate defense of Japan. Therefore, the Emperor undertook to use his influence to bring them around when the council met again on 22 June.

He opened these proceedings by gently observing that despite the decision to resist an enemy invasion, other ways had to be found to terminate the conflict, and then asked the council to study this problem (Tōgō 1956: 297). This cannot be described as a dramatic assertion of imperial influence for peace, given the typical circumspection of the Emperor's remarks. Nor did it dissuade the hardliners from wanting to continue the fighting. But it at least produced a reconfirmation of the previous decision to approach the Soviet Union.

By July, however, it was clear that due to Malik's skepticism, the Hirota–Malik talks had failed to pave the way for formal negotiations between Japan and the Soviet Union. Accordingly, on 7 July Suzuki and Kido agreed that the only way to break this impasse was to send a special envoy to Moscow with an imperial letter seeking negotiations with Stalin (Kido II 1966: 1,215). Suzuki suggested, with Tōgō's backing, that the Emperor should request Konoe to undertake this mission, which the Emperor did five days later. Recalling that the Emperor had asked him earlier to share the tribulations of high office, Konoe readily assented. The Emperor later told Kido, 'I believe Konoe is firmly resolved this time', to serve the throne in adversity (Kido II 1966: 1,217). For his part, the Prince observed that the Emperor was under immense strain that day: 'He had come out of the bomb shelter to the temporary audience chamber with his usually neatly combed hair unkempt, looking pale and terribly haggard' (Oka 1983: 176).

The Emperor wanted Konoe to go to Russia as soon as possible. But like the proposed summit conference between Konoe and Roosevelt in 1941, the Konoe mission to Moscow never materialized because the Russians, having undertaken in the Yalta Agreement of 11 February 1945 to enter the war against Japan several months after the defeat of Germany, were in no mood to help Japan end the war. The Japanese government, of course, did not know of this Russian undertaking, hence its futile pursuit of Soviet mediation.

Then came the shock of the Allied Potsdam Proclamation on 26 July, which concluded, 'We call upon the government of Japan to proclaim the unconditional surrender of all Japanese armed forces. . . . The alternative for Japan is prompt and utter destruction' (Butow [1954] 1967: 244). When informed by Tōgō Shigenori of the Potsdam Proclamation 'the Emperor said without hesitation that he deemed it acceptable in principle' (Kase 1950: 210). He later recalled, 'I thought the Japanese race would be destroyed . . . I thought we had to make peace even if I had to sacrifice my own life' (STDH 1990: 140–1).

However, the failure of the Allies to provide assurances guaranteeing the future of the monarchy triggered intense debate on the supreme council for the direction of the war, with Suzuki, Tōgō, and Yonai advocating Japan's acceptance of unconditional surrender and Anami, Umezu, and Toyoda advocating the continuation of the war, to save the imperial house. Finally, Suzuki capitulated to the hardliners and adopted a policy of *mokusatsu*, or silence. Suzuki himself intended this to signal an interim non-committal response to the Allies but they interpreted *mokusatsu* as Japan's outright rejection of the Potsdam Proclamation. Accordingly, 'Japan's failure to accept the Potsdam terms literally altered the surface of the earth' (Iriye 1981: 264): on 6 August and 8 August, respectively, Hiroshima and Nagasaki were obliterated by atomic bombs.

More than forty years later, in December 1988, as the Shōwa Emperor lay dying, the mayor of Nagasaki, Motoshima Hitoshi, criticized him for failing to end the war sooner than he did and thereby spare the people of Nagasaki and Hiroshima the horror of the atomic bombs. On this account, Motoshima said, the Emperor bore a share of responsibility for the war (*The Independent*, 13 December 1988: 11). For voicing this criticism, the mayor was later shot and wounded by a right-wing fanatic, on 18 January 1990. But he survived, and so does the controversial question he raised: could the Emperor have intervened, as he would do later, to insist upon Japan's acceptance of the Potsdam terms of surrender, before the atomic bombs were dropped?

Perhaps, had the Japanese known about the existence of these new weapons and the preparedness of the American government to use them. But in late July neither the Emperor nor the government knew this and it is most doubtful whether, at that time, the prime minister could have persuaded the military to accept anything other than *mokusatsu*, for the only alternative the military would consider was an outright rejection of the Potsdam Proclamation (Butow [1954] 1967: 145). As a turning-point in human history, the atomic bombs were morally unjustifiable and at that point in the war, militarily unnecessary. However, together with Russia's subsequent entry into the war against Japan, politically they created, albeit not immediately, the extreme national emergency that made it possible for the Emperor to intervene effectively on behalf of surrender. Even then, it took two imperial interventions to end the war.

Tōgō recalls that, staggered by the reported scale of destruction wrought by the atomic bombs, the Emperor told him on 8 August

> that since we could no longer continue the struggle, now that a weapon of this devastating power was used against us, we should not let slip the opportunity [for peace] by engaging in attempts to gain more favorable conditions. Since bargaining for terms had little prospect of success at this stage, he said, measures should be conducted to insure a prompt ending of hostilities.
>
> (Tōgō 1956: 315)

Similarly, during a morning meeting with Kido on 9 August, the Emperor told the lord keeper of the privy seal to impress upon Prime Minister Suzuki the urgency of ending the war right away (Kido II 1966: 1,223).

Yet, as before, and despite the atomic bombs, in its meeting that afternoon without the Emperor present, the supreme council for the direction of the war was completely deadlocked on whether to surrender with the issue of the monarchy's future still unresolved. Even when the news arrived that the Soviet Union had declared war (it would soon invade Manchuria and hurl the Kwantung Army into full retreat), Anami, Umezu, and Toyoda still held firm that in order for Japan to surrender, the Allies would have to guarantee the preservation of the imperial institution and make other concessions: Japan's voluntary evacuation from Asia and the Pacific, the handling by Japan alone of those who had been responsible for the war,[8] and an Allied pledge not to occupy Japan (Kido II 1966: 1,223). Suzuki, Tōgō, and Yonai forcefully objected, but to no avail, and the meeting broke up without a decision.

Shigemitsu Mamoru, who was in frequent contact with Kido at the time despite being out of office himself, recalls they now agreed the time had come to encourage the Emperor to make the 'courageous imperial decision' to bring the war to a close that Kido had envisaged in early June; that is, the

Emperor would intervene directly to this end when the council resumed its deliberations later that day, with the Emperor present. Shigemitsu writes, the Emperor 'accepted Kido's recommendation and signified his readiness to issue an imperial order as soon as the government desired him to do so. His Imperial Majesty so informed the Prime Minister in person'. Tōgō, meanwhile, drafted a surrender proposal for presentation to the council. It omitted the pre-surrender conditions advocated by the 'hawks' on the council although it did stipulate that the Emperor's prerogatives be retained (Shigemitsu 1958: 360).[9]

Suzuki knew that for the Emperor to intervene during an imperial conference would depart from the precedent of political neutrality observed so consistently by the Emperor on such occasions in the past (Handō 1985: 330–1). Yet, being deadlocked, the council obviously could no longer function in making national decisions and the imminent destruction of Japan promised by the Potsdam Proclamation seemed to justify anything that could stop the war. Thus, when the council re-opened its deliberations in the bomb shelter near the imperial library, at 11: 30 p.m. on 9 August, the Emperor was poised for his first direct intervention to conclude the war.

As expected, Anami and the chiefs of staff vigorously opposed Tōgō's surrender proposal. After a long indecisive debate, Suzuki turned to the Emperor at the head of the table and asked for his judgment on whether Japan should accept the terms of the Potsdam Proclamation. The Emperor stood up and addressing the now-silent and fraught meeting, said with considerable emotion, 'I have given serious thought to the situation prevailing at home and abroad and have concluded that continuing the war can only mean destruction for the nation and a prolongation of bloodshed and cruelty in the world'.

He then reviewed recent developments in the war and expressed his grief that the people and his armed forces had suffered so much. 'Nevertheless', he said,

> the time has come when we must bear the unbearable. When I recall the feelings of my Grandsire, the Emperor Meiji, at the time of the Triple Intervention, I swallow my own tears and give my sanction to the proposal to accept the Allied Proclamation on the basis outlined by the Foreign Minister.[10]

> (Butow [1954] 1967: 175–6)

Following these remarks, he left the chamber and Suzuki closed the meeting at 2:30 a.m. on 10 August, declaring to the stunned participants, 'His Majesty's decision ought to be made the decision of this conference as well'. It became official policy after automatic ratification by the cabinet and supreme command shortly afterwards (Butow [1954] 1967: 176–7).

But the Emperor's intervention that night did not prove decisive. The council still wanted guarantees from the Allies regarding the Emperor's prerogatives. Consequently, on 10 August, the government cabled the

American secretary of state, James F. Byrnes, accepting the Potsdam Proclamation's terms of surrender 'with the understanding that the said declaration does not comprise any demand which prejudices the prerogatives of His Majesty as a Sovereign Ruler' (Butow [1954] 1967: 244). This proviso was accompanied by statements underscoring the Emperor's desires for peace, in hopes of reinforcing any inclination on the part of the Allies to accept Japan's position on the monarchy.

However, in his reply the next day Byrnes stated, 'From the moment of surrender the authority of the Emperor and the Japanese government to rule the state shall be subject to the Supreme Commander of the Allied powers' and that 'The ultimate form of government of Japan shall, in accordance with the Potsdam Declaration, be established by the freely expressed will of the Japanese people' (Butow [1954] 1967: 245). In short, the American reply still left the future of the monarchy open to question.

This ambiguity, especially over whether the 'government of Japan' in this context included the Emperor, perplexed the Japanese leadership. The Emperor agreed with Tōgō and others that the future of the imperial institution would not be made subject to the 'will of the people' and that there was nothing in the Byrnes letter to imply a serious threat to the monarchy. Suzuki was not entirely sure of this but finally accepted Tōgō's interpretation. What counted more at this juncture, however, was the persistent belief of Anami and the chiefs of staff that Byrnes' ambiguity was completely unacceptable.

Predictably, this pro-war faction threw the deliberations of the supreme council for the direction of the war into a confused stalemate at its next meeting on 13 August, whereupon it was decided to reconvene in the bomb shelter the next day with the Emperor present, making the meeting an imperial conference. By then, at a meeting of the imperial family council on the 12th, the Emperor had obtained the personal support of the imperial Princes for a decision to surrender (Higashikuni 1968: 200–1; Butow [1954] 1967: 196–7).[11] By then, too, Kido, Suzuki, and Tōgō had anticipated with the Emperor that he would intervene again to end the war, as he had done on 9–10 August.

He was now even more anxious to do so. Referring to American propaganda leaflets that explained the government's acceptance, conditional on retaining the Emperor's prerogatives, of the Potsdam terms on 10 August and the tough Byrnes reply of 11 August, he later remembered being convinced that 'If these leaflets fell into the hands of the troops, a "coup d'état" [protesting unconditional surrender] would have been inevitable' (STDH 1990: 143). He had believed that unless he intervened to ensure the acceptance of the Potsdam terms, the nation would have been completely destroyed (STDH 1990: 145).

Thus, at the conference on 14 August, which was again stalemated, the prime minister invited the Emperor to render a judgment on whether Japan should surrender under the conditions stipulated in the Potsdam Proclamation, as clarified by Brynes. The Emperor told the very tense meeting,

> I have listened carefully to each of the arguments presented in opposition to the view that Japan should accept the Allied reply as it stands without any further clarification or modification, but my own thoughts have not undergone any change. . . . In short, I consider the reply to be acceptable.

After virtually repeating what he had said on 9–10 August about the course of the war and the suffering of the people, he ended,

> It is my desire that you, my Ministers of State, accede to my wishes and forthwith accept the Allied reply. In order that the people may know of my decision, I request you to prepare at once an Imperial Rescript so that I may broadcast to the nation.

(Butow [1954] 1967: 207–8)

This time, in contrast to the situation in December 1941, the formal imperial will reflected the Emperor's personal will for peace. Technically, 'my decision', as he had characterized it, was more advice or counsel than decision; it required cabinet endorsement to be binding. 'Yet, in the final analysis, the imperial judgment and the Supreme Command's concurrence possessed a great significance in that both overawed in *influence* what they lacked in authority' (Butow [1954] 1967: 177, italics Butow's). Japan's military leaders now calculated that 'It was better to surrender as a united nation than to continue fighting as a divided one' (Shillony 1981: 87).

Events were to prove that through the Emperor's intervention, Japan's 'timely surrender helped save the monarchy' (McNelly 1987: 76). But at the time, in contrast to the army leadership, not all military units immediately complied with surrender. Against the opposition of Army Minister Anami and Army Chief Umezu, radical elements of the imperial guards division in Tokyo invaded the imperial household ministry in the palace grounds in the early hours of 15 August, to destroy the Emperor's surrender recording that he had just made, and which would be broadcast on NHK radio later that day.

But they were soon suppressed by the loyal forces of the eastern district army without disturbing the Emperor, who slept through the incident, in the imperial library (Hasunuma 1956; Butow [1954] 1967: 210–18). Afterwards, Anami committed suicide to take responsibility for the insurgency. There followed many other suicides by leading military figures who were overwhelmed by Japan's defeat and by the prospect of being tried as war criminals. Among others, they included Sugiyama Gen and Honjō Shigeru, who died in September and November, respectively.

At noon, a shocked nation heard over the radio the strained voice of the Emperor reading the imperial rescript which announced Japan's defeat. Since he spoke in the stilted language of the court, not many of his listeners would have comprehended precisely what he said. But that he was addressing the nation directly for the first time was perhaps itself sufficient to convey the reality of capitulation.

The rescript had been written by many hands and approved by the Emperor and the cabinet.[12] It began,

> To Our good and loyal subjects: After pondering deeply the general trends of the world and the actual conditions obtaining in Our Empire today, We have decided to effect a settlement of the present situation by resorting to an extraordinary measure [the acceptance of the Potsdam Proclamation].

Avoiding the word 'surrender', he went on to explain that despite the courageous war effort, 'the war situation has developed not necessarily to Japan's advantage', a phrase which Army Minister Anami had insisted upon, to soften the reality of defeat (Kase 1950: 256). This adversity, and the fact that 'the enemy has begun to employ a new and most cruel bomb', made it necessary 'to pave the way for a grand peace for all the generations to come by enduring the unendurable and suffering what is insufferable'.

He then closed with consoling words in a section of the rescript which began, 'Having been able to safeguard and maintain the structure of the imperial state, We are always with ye, Our good and loyal subjects, relying upon your sincerity and integrity'. This vision, of the continuity of the imperial state, foreshadowed that the overriding priority of the Emperor and the government would be the preservation of the monarchy during the forth-coming Allied Occupation of Japan. Their commonly tearful acceptance of the rescript that day, and their subsequent passive acceptance of the Occupation, were early indications that, with some important exceptions, the people would support this endeavor.

Later, on 15 August, the government formally notified the Allies of Japan's surrender in full compliance with the terms of the Potsdam Proclamation. That evening, Kido recommended Prince Higashikuni as the next prime minister after Suzuki Kantarō resigned; Higashikuni took office the next day. On 2 September the Emperor promulgated an imperial rescript authorizing representatives of Japan to sign on his behalf the formal Instrument of Surrender. This was done that day by Shigemitsu, acting for the Emperor, and by Umezu, representing the Japanese armed forces, on the deck of the USS *Missouri* in Tokyo Bay, with reporters, American servicemen, other Allied representatives, and General Douglas MacArthur, the supreme commander for the allied powers, looking on.

The 'Greater East Asia War' resulted in perhaps as many as 1,675,000 Japanese army wartime casualties, 429,000 navy casaulties, and more than 300,000 civilian casualties in Japan, not to mention untold numbers of other Asian and Allied casualties (Coox 1988: note 52, 376–7). Given this immense suffering, it is often legitimately asked, if the Emperor was able to play a decisive part in terminating the war in 1945, could he not have prevented its occurrence in 1941?

He arguably should have tried to openly oppose the government's war decision in 1941, despite the high improbability of success and the great personal risk involved. However, the political realities he confronted in 1941 make it most unlikely that any such intervention would have succeeded. Whereas the acute paralysis that gripped the government, and the presence of a supportive peace party, politically enabled him to intervene, at the prime minister's request, for peace in August 1945, in late 1941 the government's unanimous consensus for war precluded an effective imperial intervention to prevent the outbreak of war.

But if these political realities constrained the Emperor in 1941, he also restrained himself, as he had on so many previous occasions. When the decision for war was made that year, he deliberately ruled out an attempted intervention for peace because that course of action would have conflicted with his concept of constitutional monarchy. Besides the postwar statements he made in this regard, which have already been cited in this chapter, he also summed up his position in more general terms during a conversation in February 1946 with Fujita Hisanori, the grand chamberlain. His explication to Fujita further reveals his determination at all costs, even that of war, to abide by the perceptions of constitutional monarchy that he had followed from the beginning of his reign.

He addressed the aforementioned '1945/1941' question head-on:

> Concerning the war, I tried to avoid it as much as possible. . . . But in spite of all my efforts, I failed and we plunged into war. I was truly grieved by this. It is often said that the war was ended by my efforts and if this is so, why did I not prevent the war before it began? But in fact, it was impossible.
>
> (Fujita 1961: 203)

He explained that because under the Meiji constitution, ministers of state bore responsibility for policy, 'The Emperor cannot on his own volition interfere or intervene in the jurisdiction for which the ministers of state are responsible'. Once a given policy is adopted by the government, 'I have no choice but to approve it whether I desire it or not'. To do otherwise 'would clearly be destroying the constitution. If Japan were a despotic state, that would be different but as the monarch of a constitutional state it is quite impossible for me to behave in that way'.

However, 'The circumstances at the end of the war were different from those at the beginning'. With the government too divided over war or peace to reach a decision, Prime Minister Suzuki had invited him to settle the issue. 'Here for the first time I was offered an opportunity to state my opinion freely, without infringing anyone's field of responsibility or power. Therefore, I stated my convictions, which I had been storing up, and asked them to end the war' (Fujita 1961: 205).[13]

By themselves, such explanations of where he had stood politically in 1941 and 1945 might be dismissed as simply biased and self-serving were it not for the fact that they reflect a consistency of self-image and conduct as a constitutional monarch throughout his earlier career on the throne. Nevertheless, although the Emperor regarded his sanctioning of the war decision in 1941 as an act of political integrity required of a constitutional monarch, the point remains that by sanctioning the decision, he participated in it, however indirectly, and thus shared in the collective responsibility for it, if in a formal legal sense. Because his role in ending the war in 1945 only partially compensated for this war responsibility in 1941, he would be shadowed for the rest of his life by critics who condemned him as a 'war criminal'.

6 The Emperor and the Occupation, 1945–1952

General MacArthur arrived in Japan on 30 August 1945, two days after the first American troops had landed. After a brief period in Yokohama, he established the allied powers general headquarters (GHQ) in the Dai-Ichi Mutual Life Insurance Building, across the moat from the imperial palace, on 8 September.

The next day, as the Occupation thus closed in around him, the Emperor reflected on the war in a letter to Crown Prince Akihito, who was still in Nikkō where he had been sent to escape the bombing of Tokyo. He wrote, 'Our people put too much faith in the Empire and held England and America in contempt. Our military put too much emphasis on spirit and forgot science'. The letter went on to explain, 'In the times of Emperor Meiji there were famous commanders ... but this time, as in World War I Germany, the military were high-handed and did not consider the wider situation, for they knew how to advance but not how to retreat'. Therefore, 'Swallowing my tears, I tried to save the Japanese race from extinction' ('Tennō kōgō ryōheika kara kōtaishi e no tegami' 1989: 365).

The letter did not reveal that, exhausted and discouraged by the war, he was beset by anxious indecision about whether he should abdicate. Despite his contempt for the military, he was anguished by the thought that many officers who had served the country in war would soon be tried for war crimes by the Allies. This prospect, Kido wrote in his diary on 29 August, 'was unbearable to him and he would rather assume all the responsibility himself, abdicating from the throne, than transfer them to the Allies'. Kido strongly opposed this, contending that abdication would probably not satisfy the Allies and that it 'might eventually destroy the foundation of the imperial family, with the result that advocates of a republican form of government would gain ascendancy' (Kido II 1966: 1,230–1).

Kido's argument proved persuasive for the time being, although for several years the Emperor continued to consider abdication. That he did not believe he was politically responsible for a war that he had personally tried to prevent is apparent from the extracts from his eight-hour Monologue, delivered during a series of five separate meetings at the palace with his closest advisers in the spring of 1946, which have been cited throughout this study (STDH:

1990).[1] Since the Americans had not yet formally communicated to the court their decision to exempt him from trial by the International Military Tribunal of the Far East (IMTFE), which was due to begin its proceedings in May, the Monologue was prompted by the need to prepare the essence of the Emperor's defense. Notwithstanding its inevitable bias in these circumstances, much of what he said about his prewar and wartime political role is corroborated by other sources, as earlier chapters have shown.

However, because Japanese monarchs traditionally had been idealized as the source and symbol of moral virtue, by which the performance of government should be judged, he very likely believed he should assume moral responsibility for the war. It is interesting that General Tōjō had remarked, on 28 December 1943, that contrary to constitutional scholars who mistakenly held that the Emperor possesses no responsibility,

> When I heard the Emperor's will as expressed in His Imperial decision [for war] prior to the opening of hostilities in the Greater East Asian War, I believed that He felt keenly His immense responsibility to His Imperial Ancestor, the Sun Goddess. We, His ministers, only thought about whether we could win the Greater East Asian War but I think He based His decision on a responsibility [to the gods] which was incomparably greater than any we felt.
>
> (Itō *et al.*, 1990: 526)

Leaving aside the fiction that the Emperor, and not the government, had made the decision for war in 1941, if Tōjō was right in implying a moral responsibility on the Emperor's part at the beginning of the war, then it is reasonable to believe the Emperor retained this sense of responsibility after the war.

Moreover, in 1946, the Emperor related that late in the war Prince Takamatsu had urged him to apologize at Ise Shrine to the gods for the complacency of government officials in dealing with the wartime sufferings of the people. Takamatsu even offered to pray in his stead if the Emperor found it inconvenient to go to Ise. But the Emperor recalled, 'Judging that the appointment of government officials was my prerogative, and that if they were bad it was my responsibility, I believed that it would be absurd to apologize to the gods and pray for divine punishment of the officials'. Yet, he did let Takamtasu pray at Ise for general guidance in bringing an end to the war, 'because the present difficulties of the country were due to my lack of virtue [*futoku*]' (STDH 1990: 130).

This reference to a 'lack of virtue' suggests that residues of the traditional Confucian view of the monarch as moral exemplar coexisted in his outlook with his self-image as a constitutional monarch who was not politically responsible for the policies of the government. The implication of this Confucian perception was that he should resign, to take responsibility for the misdeeds of subordinates, as many Japanese in high positions of authority have commonly done. The Emperor probably would have agreed, therefore, with the sentiments expressed by Nanbara Shigeru, the president of Tokyo University, who spoke out publicly on the issue of the Emperor's responsibility one month before the Tokyo war crimes trials commenced in 1946.

Nanbara asserted that the cabinet, not the Emperor, had been politically responsible for following the military into war. 'It was practically impossible for the Emperor, under such circumstances, to prevent war', he said. However, he argued that the Emperor bore moral responsibility for a war fought in his name and speculated, 'I believe that the Emperor is feeling most deeply the moral and spiritual responsibility to the Imperial Ancestors and to the people of this country for the outbreak of such a big war'. Nanbara thought that the Emperor should acknowledge this responsibility by abdicating, for only then could a new Japan emerge from the ashes of the war (Okubo 1948: 17).

Some members of the Japanese government felt the same way. According to Prince Higashikuni's diary, they suggested that although the Emperor was not politically responsible for the war, he was morally responsible for it to the people and to the gods and that therefore, perhaps 'it would be beneficial if he took responsibility and abdicated'. Higashikuni, who knew from Kido that the Emperor 'feels no deep responsibility for the war but wonders what he should best do for the sake of the people', was himself undecided on the matter. But he noted Kido's advice that if it proved necessary for the Emperor to abdicate, the appropriate time would be after a new constitution came into effect, or after a peace treaty had been signed with the Allies (Higashikuni 1968: 235–6).

These discussions in the government on the Emperor's possible abdication stemmed from uncertainty on Allied intentions toward the monarchy. Public opinion against the Emperor and the emperor system was very strong in all the Allied countries (Takeda 1988; Lattimore 1945). The Japanese communists, too, were eager to include the Emperor, and even the Empress, on their list of war criminals (Gayn 1948: 11). Tokuda Kyūichi and other communist leaders frequently attacked the Emperor for war crimes and demanded the abolition of the emperor system, at public rallies around the country. Whether the Occupation authorities might pay heed to these criticisms of the Emperor greatly concerned many in the Japanese government who felt that his abdication was a necessary pre-emptive step to safeguard the future of the imperial institution, whatever might happen to the Emperor himself.

This was the view of Prince Konoe, now the deputy prime minister and arguably the dominant figure in the Higashikuni cabinet. In October 1945 he told foreign journalists, 'It would be good if the Emperor were to abdicate and retire to Kyoto' (Hata 1978: 376). Konoe went so far as to have a temple in Kyoto, the Ninnaji, inspected as a possible residence for the Emperor after he left office (Morris 1960: 106, footnote 2).

Konoe possibly also reasoned that only by abdicating could the Emperor save himself from trial as a war criminal. This threat arose implicitly on 11 September 1945, when MacArthur ordered the arrest of Japanese leaders, including General Tōjō, for trial. That same day, after writing a suicide note in which he expressed his loyal apology to the Emperor for his part in the failed cause of the war, Tōjō tried, unsuccessfully, to kill himself with a bullet near his heart, in hopes of avoiding trial (Butow 1961: 451–62).

Perhaps it was to distance himself from Tōjō that, on 25 September, in his first interview with a foreign correspondent, the Emperor emphasized to Frank Kluckhohn of *The New York Times* that Tōjō had been responsible for the government's failure to communicate Japan's declaration of war prior to the Pearl Harbor attack (Okubo 1948: 10). But judging from what he said to MacArthur at their first meeting two days later, self-preservation was not the Emperor's primary concern.

MacArthur had let it be known at court that he wished to see the Emperor, but only at the latter's overt initiative, given that the Emperor represented a defeated nation (McNelly 1969: 370). Having by then concluded, contrary to Kido's advice, that the situation required him to sacrifice himself, the Emperor arranged through Foreign Minister Yoshida Shigeru to see MacArthur on 27 September (Yoshida 1962: 50). That day, he was driven to the American embassy where he presented himself formally, in cutaway, striped trousers and silk hat, to maintain his dignity on this difficult occasion. For his part, MacArthur did not wish to humiliate the Emperor; before the meeting, the general helped his aides arrange the chairs in the embassy's reception hall, to create a relaxed atmosphere (Egeberg 1989).

When the Emperor was ushered into the hall, MacArthur greeted him as 'sir' and offered him a cigarette which the Emperor, a non-smoker, nevertheless accepted, his hands shaking with nervousness as the general lit it for him. MacArthur expected the Emperor to plead that he not be indicted for war crimes. However, the Emperor said, 'I come to you, General MacArthur, to offer myself to the judgment of the powers you represent as the one to bear sole responsibility for every political and military decision made and action taken by my people in the conduct of the war'.

MacArthur writes, 'A tremendous impression swept me. This courageous assumption of a responsibility implicit with death, a responsibility clearly belied by facts of which I was fully aware, moved me to the very marrow of my bones' (MacArthur 1965: 288).[2] He later told Yoshida how impressed he had been by the noble spirit of the Emperor, which prompted Yoshida to state in his memoirs, 'I have no hesitation in saying that it was the attitude adopted by General MacArthur towards the Throne, more than any other single factor, that made the Occupation an historic success' (Yoshida 1962: 50–1).

Evidently MacArthur had concluded well before this meeting that it would be best for the Occupation to retain and use the Emperor. His personal physician, Roger Egeberg, recalls that in May 1945 when they were still in Manila, MacArthur,

> poking a finger into my chest, said he wanted peace to bring democracy to Japan. Further, he thought the Emperor was a captive of Tōjō and the

warlords, that they were really responsible for the war and that Hirohito would be instrumental in permanently changing the structure of the Japanese government.

(Egeberg 1989)

Still, their encounter on 27 September served to reconfirm MacArthur's anticipation of using the Emperor as a partner in the Occupation and though their subsequent conversation was not recorded, it would appear from other sources that this theme, of partnership, dominated the discussion.

For example, Kido indicates that afterwards the Emperor reported MacArthur as having said, 'I believe Your Majesty knows about the people and important men in the [Japanese] political world, so from now on, I would like to have your advice on various matters'. The Emperor replied that he would be glad to meet with MacArthur again, at the general's convenience. They fully agreed to cooperate in preserving peace (Kido II 1966: 1,237). Four days later an official of the ministry of home affairs publicly reported on the meeting in much the same vein (James III 1985: 322). The recently published diary of the chamberlain (and later grand chamberlain), Irie Sukemasa, states that Japanese officials had gained 'an extremely favorable impression' of MacArthur (Irie II 1990: 11). After this, they were more optimistic about the future.

Thus, whereas World War II led to the downfall of monarchies in Italy, Bulgaria, Romania, Yugoslavia, and Albania, just as World War I had struck a fatal blow to monarchies in Germany, Austria–Hungary, Russia, and Turkey, it was now apparent that Japan's imperial institution and the incumbent sovereign would be retained, if only because the Emperor was needed to legitimize, in the eyes of the Japanese people, SCAP's[3] many policies for occupied Japan. This utilitarian strategy, which preserved the traditional legitimizing function of the monarchy in Japanese political life, suited the decision to administer the Occupation indirectly through the agency of the Japanese government. But it was also based on MacArthur's rather enthusiastic belief, expressed to Brigadier General Courtney Whitney, head of government section, GHQ, that 'The Emperor has a more thorough understanding of the democratic concept than almost any Japanese with whom I have talked' (Whitney [1956] 1977: 286).

Similarly, for his part, the Emperor needed MacArthur, to help defend the imperial institution from its critics within Japan and overseas. He foreshadowed his intention to seek MacArthur's assistance to this end on 29 September when, upset at criticism of the monarchy in the American press, he told Kido that he would approach MacArthur about the problem. Kido, though, held that what the American newspapers were saying did not matter as long as MacArthur was favorably inclined toward the imperial institution (Kido II 1966: 1,238).

From the outset, however, it was clear that the Emperor would not be an equal partner in the Occupation, as the famous photograph, taken of the

Emperor and MacArthur at their first meeting, suggested. To many Japanese, the grim-faced Emperor looked pitifully impotent next to the towering, relaxed American. In fact, this negative impression led Home Minister Yamazaki Iwao to penalize the newspapers which carried the photograph on the grounds that it had impugned the dignity of the imperial family. For this intervention, SCAP demanded Yamazaki's dismissal, whereupon the Higashikuni cabinet tendered its resignation in protest, on 5 October. A related factor behind the resignation was MacArthur's 'Civil Liberties Directive', issued the previous day. This memorandum compelled the Japanese government to ensure freedom of speech and political action, including the freedom to criticize the Emperor, by eliminating all repressive laws, such as the peace preservation law, and by releasing all political prisoners, among whom were many communists (Morley 1970: 159; *Political Reorientation of Japan*, hereafter PRJ, II [1949] 1970: 463–5).

Altogether, the Emperor met with MacArthur eleven times before the general was dismissed on 11 April 1951, by President Harry S. Truman, for having criticized, as commander of United Nations forces in the Korean War, Washington's concept of a limited war. As in the first encounter, no records were kept of these meetings apart from summary digests prepared by the Emperor's translators for the foreign ministry, most of which remain highly classified. While the content of their conversations is therefore unknown for the most part, an exception is their meeting on 6 May 1947 when the Emperor expressed his personal concern that Japan would be defenseless were the United States to withdraw its forces from the country. MacArthur reassured him that the United States would defend Japan with no less determination than in defending California (Hata 1978: 381).

Despite these meetings, it is improbable that the Emperor ever influenced MacArthur to do what had not already occurred to him to do during the Occupation. Instead, the main effect of their conversations was to create a supportive framework for the Emperor's indirect participation in assisting the policies of the Occupation. That he personally appreciated MacArthur's willingness to consult informally is suggested by their emotional final meeting. On the day before MacArthur left Japan, he grasped the general's hand in both of his as 'tears streamed unchecked down his cheeks. The ensuing private meeting between these two men was the most poignant of all the farewells MacArthur had to say in Japan' (Whitney [1956] 1977: 475).

During the Occupation the Emperor at times acted with notable independence, but for the most part, as in prewar and wartime Shōwa, he did not act as a free agent. His political role was still 'managed *for* him' (Titus 1980: 530, italics Titus'), not only by SCAP but by the Japanese government. Both had their own agendas for the Occupation which the Emperor had always to take into account.

OCCUPATION AGENDAS

In broad terms SCAP's initial agenda for the reform of Japan encompassed the related objectives of demilitarization and democratization. Demilitarization involved dismantling the Japanese armed forces, the repatriation of military personnel overseas, and the abolition of the military bureaucracies, including the army and navy ministries and the army and navy general staffs.

In addition, twenty-eight 'Class A' Japanese leaders were tried for such war crimes as conspiracy to wage war and crimes against humanity, by the IMTFE, from 3 May 1946 to 12 November 1948. Seven of the defendants were sentenced to death by hanging. Besides Hirota Kōki, the only civilian, they included Generals Tōjō Hideki, Itagaki Seishirō, Mutō Akira, Matsui Iwane, and two others. Sixteen, among them Kido Kōichi, Shiratori Toshio, Hiranuma Kiichirō, Koiso Kuniaki, Shimada Shigetarō, Umezu Yoshijirō, Araki Sadao, and Ōshima Hiroshi, were condemned to life imprisonment. Tōgō Shigenori and Shigemitsu Mamoru received sentences of twenty and seven years imprisonment respectively. Matsuoka Yōsuke and Nagano Osami died during the trials and the ultranationalist, Ōkawa Shumei, was declared unfit for trial due to insanity. Konoe committed suicide on 16 December 1945 rather than stand trial.[4]

The Occupation also required war reparations and conducted extensive purges of 200,000 Japanese from public office or corporate positions for having been associated, however vaguely in many instances, with the war effort. But equally far-reaching and consequential were the Occupation's initiatives on behalf of democratization, the breadth of which can only be suggested here by listing some of the major reforms that were indirectly implemented by SCAP through Diet legislation: the labor union act of December 1945; the disestablishment of State Shintō in January 1946; land reform, enacted 21 October 1946; a new constitution, promulgated on 3 November 1946 and put into effect from 3 May 1947; and educational reform, enacted in March 1947.

Taken together, these and other reforms, carried out in the first several years after Japan's surrender, constitute a major legacy of the Occupation. It was primarily an American legacy to postwar Japan, for although theoretically the Occupation was an Allied undertaking influenced by the Allied Council in Tokyo and the Far Eastern Commission in Washington, it was dominated by the United States. Predictably, therefore, when the Occupation ended as the San Francisco peace treaty of 8 September 1951 came into effect on 28 April 1952, Japan emerged as an ally of the United States in a new relationship based, significantly, on the US–Japan Security Treaty, which was also concluded on 8 September 1951.

From the beginning of the Occupation, the Americans acknowledged in principle that the form of government in Japan ultimately would be determined by the 'freely expressed will' of the Japanese people. But studies of American wartime planning for the Occupation indicate fairly consistent intentions of retaining and using the Emperor to achieve the purposes of demilitarization and democratization (Ward 1987). Accordingly, Washington instructed MacArthur to exercise his authority through the agency of the Emperor and the Japanese government with the qualification that 'The policy is to use the existing form of Government in Japan, not to support it' (PRJ II [1949] 1970: 424). In practice, however, the distinction between using and supporting the Japanese government was unrealistic and in fact MacArthur supported it in order to use it in realizing the goals of the Occupation. As mentioned, this was his general approach to the Shōwa Emperor.

Not everyone in the Occupation agreed with this approach. For example, George Atcheson, MacArthur's political adviser, thought that the Emperor should be tried for war crimes and only reluctantly deferred to MacArthur on the matter (Takeda 1988: 131–3). The American joint chiefs of staff also considered the trial of the Emperor as a distinct possibility. On 29 November 1945 they instructed MacArthur to investigate whether there was sufficient evidence to indict the Emperor (Ward 1987: 15).

In a secret telegram on 25 January 1946, MacArthur replied that 'no specific and tangible evidence' had been discovered that would implicate the Emperor in war crimes. He proceeded to argue that the Emperor's political actions had been determined by his ministers of state, who bore responsibility for the war. The general described the Emperor as 'a symbol which unites all Japanese. Destroy him and the nation will disintegrate'. He estimated that if the Emperor were tried, a million troops would be required to deal with the 'vendetta for revenge' which would surely eventuate on the part of the Japanese people (Takeda 1988: 127–8).

Ultimately, MacArthur prevailed. The Emperor and all members of the imperial family were exempted from the IMTFE proceedings even though Joseph B. Keenan, the chief IMTFE prosecutor, later acknowledged that despite the fact the Emperor had opposed war, he could well have been convicted (Minear 1972: 113). But Keenan believed that, at worst, the Emperor was 'a person of weak will'. He surmised that had the Emperor stood trial he would have taken 'personal responsibility for all the actions committed by the Japanese government neglecting all evidence to the contrary' (Takeda 1988: 141). If one recalls the Emperor's willingness, expressed earlier to Kido and again to MacArthur, to do just that, this seems a plausible conjecture.

Quite apart from MacArthur's politically motivated decision to exempt the Emperor from trial, one wonders whether he would have had a fair trial had he been indicted for war crimes. The president of the court, Sir William Webb of Australia, and most other justices representing the Allies were both biased against him and generally skeptical when the defense attempted to explain the confused, collective nature of Japanese decision-making which made it difficult to determine individual responsibility. Then, too, the court's imprecise definition of 'war crimes', above all the crime of 'conspiracy' to wage war, made harsh convictions a foregone conclusion.

For these reasons and others, including questionable rules of evidence, the IMTFE proceedings have been rightly criticized as an exercise in 'victors' justice' (Minear 1972). The anticipation that this would be the case figured prominently, it seems, in Prince Konoe's decision to commit suicide. Konoe evidently felt that it would be impossible to defend either the Emperor or himself before a court that would be incapable of impartially comprehending the complexities of policy-making in prewar Japan (Oka 1983: 190).

Nevertheless, despite the Emperor's absence, the IMTFE proceedings did touch on such controversial issues as the extent to which he had been involved in decision-making, whether he could have prevented the war, and whether he was a party to Japanese brutality towards captured Allied prisoners of war.

For instance, in his testimony on 31 December 1947, Tōjō inadvertently raised the matter of the Emperor's authority, and by implication his possible capacity to prevent the war, when he stated 'I further wish to add that there is no Japanese subject who could go against the will of His Majesty, more particularly among high officials of the Japanese government' (Takeda 1988: 142).

Pressed by Kido and other defendants to clarify himself, Tōjō told the court on 6 January 1948, 'I was then speaking to you of my feelings towards the Emperor as a subject, and that is quite a different matter from the problem of the responsibility of the Emperor'. Tōjō explained, 'War was decided on by my cabinet. . . . It might have been against his will but it is a fact that because of my advice and because of the advice given by the High Command the Emperor consented, though reluctantly, to the war' (Takeda 1988: 142).

This clarification failed to satisfy Webb and other justices. Yet, Takeda Kiyoko points out that it was consistent with an earlier oral statement Tōjō had made on 19 December. Tōjō had said,

> The Emperor never ordered . . . the Cabinet and the High Command by his free will. The advice of the Cabinet and the High Command would never be refused by him. . . . Because of this customary practice the cabinet and High Command were totally responsible for the decision of political, diplomatic, and military matters.
>
> (Takeda 1988: 143)

Given the consistency of Tōjō's testimony on 19 December 1947 and 6 January 1948, it would appear that his statement on 31 December, to the effect that 'high officials' would never contravene the will of the Emperor, was less a description of political reality than an expression of Tōjō's personal devotion to the Emperor. As Tōjō had once said in 1942, 'The Emperor is the Godhead . . . and we, no matter how hard we strive as Ministers, are nothing more than human' (Itō *et al.*, 1990: 486). Such sentiments recall the tendency, noted earlier of the men who perpetrated the Manchurian incident and the February 1936 army uprising, to profess loyalty to the throne while ignoring the personal will of the sovereign. This kind of dualistic 'ambivalence was a key which enabled the political and military authorities to administer the nation as they pleased, preventing any possible popular criticism through the use of the Emperor's name' (Takeda 1988: 144).

At another point during his testimony, Tōjō defended the Emperor from implication in the sufferings of Allied prisoners of war. He credited the Emperor with having commuted the army's death sentences for five of the eight American airmen captured during the Doolittle raid and said that the decision to execute three pilots (whose bombs had killed Japanese school children) represented a political compromise struck by himself and Sugiyama, who had wanted all eight executed (Butow 1961: 517).[5] Similarly, concerning the fate of other Allied war prisoners such as those who had worked on the Burma–Siam Railway, Tōjō stated that he had not informed the Emperor of Allied protests over their extreme maltreatment, so as not to distress him; Japanese brutality in the prison camps was the fault of local camp commanders and their men (Butow 1961: 515).[6]

The IMTFE proceedings addressed these matters concerning the Emperor only indirectly and inconclusively. But this was sufficient to renew rumors that he would abdicate, perhaps at the climax of the trials. This possibility unsettled Occupation officials who relied upon the Emperor's residual authority to facilitate the process of reform. William Sebald, head of the diplomatic section, GHQ, later remembered,

> Abdication doubtless would have left the Throne intact, under Crown Prince Akihito, then fourteen years old. . . . Yet the whole system of authority and control, symbolized by Hirohito's relationship with MacArthur, might have been destroyed suddenly, creating chaos, or, at least, great opportunities for chaos [particularly at the hands of the communists].
>
> (Sebald 1965: 165)

Consequently, when it became apparent that the Emperor was again seriously considering whether to abdicate, MacArthur undertook to dissuade him. Through his advisers, he had learned that on 8 June 1948 the Emperor had remarked, 'I, too, think that if it were possible for me to abdicate, personally I would be happy. I have a strong sense that this would help the realization of democracy in Japan, which I would like to see happen' (Hata 1978: 386). Furthermore, in late October, Sebald told MacArthur that he thought the Emperor wanted to abdicate and even speculated that the Emperor might kill himself, to take responsibility for the war (Hata 1978: 388–9). MacArthur reacted strongly to these warnings and at his request, Prime Minister Yoshida Shigeru soon prevailed upon the Emperor not to abdicate. Yoshida then drafted a letter to MacArthur, dated 12 November 1948, and signed by the director of the imperial household agency, Tajima Michiji, which conveyed the Emperor's message to the effect that he had decided against abdication (Hata 1978: 390–2).

Now, inasmuch as his retention was crucial to SCAP's agenda for the Occupation, the Emperor's political position in relation to a stronger military authority after the war resembled his subservience to the Japanese military before the war, with the major difference that SCAP called upon him to symbolize a new democratic order. But SCAP appreciated that to convert him into a symbol of democracy first required the demystification of the Emperor.

Building on the momentum of the Civil Liberties Directive, on 15 December 1945 SCAP thus issued the 'Shintō Directive', a memorandum to the Japanese government regarding the 'Abolition of Governmental Sponsorship, Support, Perpetuation, Control, and Dissemination of State Shintō' (PRJ II [1949] 1970: 467–9). Once this policy was implemented through Diet legislation, it established that, henceforth, all institutions such as Yasukuni Shrine were deprived of state patronage and obliged to reorganize as private religious corporations, that government personnel were no longer to visit them in an official capacity, and that state schools were no longer allowed to propagate Shintō ideology (Nakano 1987: 134). The dismantling of State Shintō, which had promoted the cult of imperial divinity, was intended 'to bring about as complete a separation of church and state as is consistent with our recent policy of permitting the Emperor to retain his throne', as one Occupation official put it (Nakano 1987: 129).

Other attempts to demystify the Emperor would soon follow. But here it is well to emphasize that SCAP's policy of retaining and democratizing the Emperor was also based on the pragmatic recognition that Japanese public opinion overwhelmingly supported both the Emperor and the imperial institution. To be sure, there were significant exceptions to this support, as the communists illustrated. In war-torn social conditions that made the search for food and shelter a daily preoccupation for most Japanese, it was natural that spontaneous protests would arise over issues of public welfare and that the re-emergent communist movement would try to exploit them in criticizing the Emperor.

A case in point was the demonstration of 60,000 Japanese in the imperial plaza outside the Nijūbashi bridge on 'Food May Day', 19 May 1946, when Tokuda Kyūichi, addressing the rally, pointed to the palace and exclaimed, 'We're starving. Is he?' (Gayn 1948: 227). Other demonstrators waved satirical placards, one of which read: 'The national polity is preserved. I am eating more than plenty. Go starve to death, ye my subjects; [Signed] Hirohito' (Sodei 1984: 99).

Five days later, the Emperor tried to dampen these protests by urging the people, over the radio, 'to share the burden together, to help each other in order to overcome this hard time'. But criticism of him continued. Left-wing periodicals commonly published satirical cartoons, such as one by Kondō Hidezō, who depicted an armless Emperor standing next to a farmer-like microphone with a caption, 'No time to play, only a mouth to talk and mouths to eat' (Sodei 1984: 98).

The Occupation authorities generally permitted this criticism because, as Robert Spaulding, who served in the civil censorship division, GHQ, later recalled during a panel discussion, 'our feeling was that the Emperor was fair game' at a time when SCAP wanted to 'redefine his position' in a democratic fashion (Burkman 1984: 131). However, MacArthur did issue a public warning against organized protest on 20 May, following the Food May Day demonstrations: 'I find it necessary to caution the Japanese people that the growing tendency towards mass violence and ... intimidation, under organized leadership, present a grave menace to the future development of Japan' (PRJ II [1949] 1970: 750). Over the years he grew increasingly concerned about the communists in particular. Their involvement, along with the socialists in the proletarian party and labor movements, led him to prohibit a massive general strike scheduled to occur on 1 February 1947.

Yet, as strident as they were, criticisms of the Emperor were insignificant next to the widespread public respect which SCAP sought to exploit in converting him into a democratic symbol. Even the communists came to see that they were out of tune with public opinion and gradually moderated their opposition to the Emperor, if not the emperor system. As Nozaka Sanzō, another communist leader, stated in February 1946, 'We claim to abolish the Emperor system and think of the Emperor and the Imperial family separately. The respect of the people for the Emperor is a definite fact' (Hayes 1978: 158).

The strength of this respect is apparent in national Japanese public opinion polls conducted during the Occupation. For example, in a national poll carried out on 12 November 1945 and published on 9 December, 95 per cent of the respondents favored retaining the monarchy, with the remainder seeking its abolition; there were no significant variations according to age (*Shōwa nihonshi* Supplement I 1987: 117). Popular support for the Emperor and the imperial institution remained high in subsequent years, although it declined temporarily during the war crimes trials.

Other surveys conducted early in the Occupation revealed more impressionistically that most Japanese viewed the Emperor favorably. Typical statements were: 'If there were no Emperor, we should be plunged into confusion'; 'he is like a national flag, a form of our existence'; 'I do not think that the Emperor began or is responsible for the past war ... I feel very sympathetic toward him, for his task is very difficult these days and sometimes I think he wishes that he did not occupy his position' (Smythe and Watanabe 1953: 340–2).

Many leading Japanese politicians likewise expressed support for the Emperor. To illustrate, Katayama Tetsu, leader of the Socialist Party who later formed the only socialist cabinet Japan has had, commented in December 1945, 'the Socialist Party wishes to keep the Emperor on a basis similar to the English monarchical system', as 'a figurehead' (Hayes 1978: 157). Hatoyama Ichirō, then leader of the Liberal Party asserted, 'the central pillar in the Japanese political and economic structure is His Majesty, the Emperor. We must never lose this pillar because it supports the very political life of the Japanese people' (Hayes 1978: 153). In that it echoed liberal sentiments generally Hatoyama's statement is especially relevant, for it was the liberal party movement which would soon inherit political power in postwar Japan. On the necessity of retaining the Emperor in office there would be a complete convergence of opinion between the liberals and SCAP.

Their commitment to the Emperor's retention was prefigured by the policy of the Higashikuni cabinet early in the Occupation. The unprecedented appointment of an imperial prince as prime minister signified the govern- ment's determination to use the prestige of the imperial family in ensuring Japanese compliance with the surrender rescript and thereby demonstrate that the Emperor would be essential to the Occupation. This consideration also prompted the sending of several imperial princes, on 16 August 1945, to different theaters, in order to persuade Japanese forces to yield to the Allies (Shillony 1981: 89).

Moreover, the Higashikuni cabinet mounted an extensive campaign to dissociate the Emperor from the war. On 5 September, in his first address to the Diet, the prime minister emphasized the Emperor's earlier opposition to the war and the 'extraordinary step' he had taken to end it. Asked by journalists later that month whether the Emperor had been responsible for the war and whether he had ordered the attack on Pearl Harbor, Higashikuni explained that under the constitution the Emperor was not a party to government decisions, that he scarcely knew about the Pearl Harbor attack, and that 'the Emperor bears no responsibility for the war' (Higashikuni 1968: 239–40).

Another aspect of this campaign was a meeting between Konoe and MacArthur on 4 October, when Konoe insisted that the military, not the Emperor, had plunged Japan into war. He stressed that the Emperor was indispensable to the reconstruction of Japan and warned that if the Occupation did not support politically responsible elements, Japan would fall prey to communist subversion. MacArthur, however, dwelt upon the urgency of constitutional revision to promote liberal democracy. Konoe eagerly offered his services to that end (Oka 1983: 180–2).

Thus it is clear that

> The greatest concern of Japanese leaders at the end of the war had been to preserve as much ideological and practical continuity as possible. From this point of view the decision of the Allies to respect the continuity of the imperial institution was of the greatest symbolic importance.
>
> (Morris 1960: 386)

But if the Japanese and American agendas for the Occupation agreed on the necessity of retaining the monarchy and the incumbent monarch, they diverged concerning the scope and substance of democratization. SCAP's notion of democracy bore the stamp of American liberal idealism, especially its populist variant which stressed the importance of direct popular participation in politics and the political accountability of government. By contrast, the Japanese approach to democracy arose from quite different origins and was decidedly more conservative and patrician in character. This was true of the Higashikuni cabinet, and of the liberals, when they took office.

Admittedly, like SCAP, Japanese liberals repudiated the authoritarian system that had prevailed under the political hegemony of the military in prewar Shōwa, just as they repudiated militarism and imperialist aggression. They also shared SCAP's opposition to all forms of political extremism and SCAP's evolving emphasis on the economic recovery of Japanese capitalism. However, the postwar Japanese governments 'in thought and interest harked back to the late Meiji period, when Japan was governed by the bureaucratic elite, supported by big business, and centered on the Throne' (Morley 1970: 154).

This orientation to Meiji precedents typified the Higashikuni cabinet and that of his successor, Shidehara Kijūrō, prime minister from 9 October 1945 to 22 May 1946, whose administration marked the advent of liberal rule in postwar Japan. After Shidehara fell from office as a result of the May 1946 elections (the first since the war and the first in which women exercised the right to vote), fidelity to Meiji precedents proved as strong in the case of Yoshida Shigeru, Shidehara's successor and previously foreign minister in the Higashikuni and Shidehara cabinets. Having assumed the leadership of the Liberal Party after Hatoyama was purged by SCAP, Yoshida first served as prime minister for only a year. But he returned to power on 15 October 1948, following the short-lived cabinets of Katayama Tetsu (May 1947–March 1948) and Ashida Hitoshi (March–October 1948), and remained in office until 10 December 1954. He unquestionably was the dominant figure in Japanese politics during this period.

As John Dower writes, Yoshida aspired to a 'new conservative hegemony' (Dower 1979: 309). His vision was conservative, that is, in comparison with the alternatives of proletarian democracy on the one hand and the liberal democratic vision of SCAP on the other. Above all, his was a bureaucratic, elitist notion of democracy which emphasized the controlling hand of the state and guidance of Japan by men, like himself and the business leaders who supported him, who knew best what was good for the nation. Accordingly, he would endeavor to minimize the effects of many democratic reforms introduced by SCAP. Only when SCAP embarked on a 'reverse course', subordinating democratic reform to other priorities later in the Occupation, did the tension in his relationship with SCAP over democratization lessen.

The grand chamberlains and imperial household ministers who dominated the Emperor's affairs after Kido's departure, and after SCAP abolished the office of the lord keeper of the privy seal, were as politically conservative as Yoshida, if not more so.[7] SCAP officials regarded them as 'a selfish group intent on preserving their special privileges. . . . They are fearful of any outside influence reaching the Emperor' (Takeda 1988: 134).

Their instinctive protectiveness of the Emperor was hardened by SCAP's initiatives to democratize the court. A major step in this respect was the abolition of the peerage and the reduction of imperial family members by fourteen, leaving only the Emperor's family and its branch houses comprising the members of the imperial house, as stipulated in the new imperial house law, enacted on 3 January 1947 (PRJ II [1949] 1970: 846–8). Another significant step in democratizing the court was to make the Emperor completely reliant on Diet appropriations for the operating budget of the imperial house (PRJ II [1949] 1970: 849–50). As well, there occurred a drastic reduction of the vast imperial estate, including properties, stocks, and other assets.[8] Finally, in 1947, the imperial household ministry, which still managed the Emperor's affairs, was renamed the imperial household agency (Kunaichō) and attached to the prime minister's office (Titus 1980: 565–8).

Together, these changes reduced the functions of the palace bureaucracy whose personnel were cut from 6,200 to 1,500 officials in a sweeping reorganization that eliminated various offices such as the board of rituals (although Shintō ritualists would remain on the court scene). Faced with reforms of this magnitude, it is no wonder that leading palace officials tried to preserve as much continuity as possible in protecting the Emperor's political interests as they saw them.

To summarize, the Emperor had to conduct himself bearing in mind the agendas of SCAP from one side and of the Japanese government and his palace entourage from the other. The specific ways in which he accommodated himself to SCAP's democratic reforms will be elaborated shortly. But first, how far did his views on the monarchy correspond with those of Yoshida Shigeru?

He doubtless shared Yoshida's general respect for Meiji precedents, especially as they evolved during the 1920s, in anticipating the future of the imperial institution. This orientation generally typified the postwar leadership: 'When facing the necessity to reform the state structure into a more liberal one soon after Japan's defeat, political leaders invariably took as their model the Emperor system advocated in the 1920s', as for instance by Hara Kei (Watanabe O. 1987: 40). Specifically, both men took it for granted that the constitutional ideals reflected in the 'Minobe way' were broadly congruent with the British model of constitutional monarchy which they regarded as a model for postwar Japan.

Yet they regarded the 'Minobe way' somewhat differently. Yoshida qualified it markedly by honoring the 'national polity' far more than did Minobe. For Yoshida, the *kokutai* was the theoretical keystone of Japanese political tradition and constitutional government. By contrast, like Minobe, the Emperor had never regarded this mystical concept as a central element in Japan's constitutional system and in this sense, he was more flexible than Yoshida, particularly in relation to constitutional revision. For a sovereign whose adult political consciousness had formed in the period of the Taishō regency, when the Minobe constitutional interpretation held sway at court, SCAP's elimination of the authoritarian constraints of the past represented a unique opportunity to establish his role as an 'organ' of a modern constitutional monarchy. As he told the foreign correspondent, Hugh Baille, on 25 September 1945, he very much wanted to develop a British-style constitutional monarchy in Japan (Okubo 1948: 70).

This is precisely what the British expected of him, which is why they urged his retention after the war. Craigie anticipated that he would indeed now function as 'an organ of the state', as Minobe had wanted, not as 'the autocratic embodiment of the state itself' (Craigie 1946: 167). British officials in Japan also took positive note of a statement by Konoe in October 1945 that 'the Emperor knows the application of the British constitution to the British Royal house' (Buckley 1982: 65).

The British government moreover interpreted a letter, dated 29 January 1946, from the Emperor to the distinguished English historian of Japan and member of the Far Eastern Commission, Sir George Sansom, as indicating that the Emperor would contribute to a British-style constitutional monarchy. Writing, 'I did my utmost to avoid war', he pledged, 'I earnestly desire to ... make every effort to rebuild a better nation dedicated to peace and democracy' (Takeda 1988: 158). After Sansom passed the letter on to the foreign office he received a reply stating,

> It is a fact that the Imperial House of Japan has a long tradition of respect for our own Royal House ... and I think it is generally agreed that if the Imperial House can transform itself into a genuine constitutional monarchy on the British model, its continuance will suit our interests. The present Emperor seems anxious to bring about this change ...
>
> (Takeda 1988: 160)

DEMOCRATIZATION

The Emperor justified these expectations. Without exaggerating his role in the overall history of the Occupation reforms, it is clear that he contributed significantly to the process of adapting the monarchy to liberal democracy in four key areas. To begin with, he assisted the process of demystifying the imperial institution by renouncing his so-called divinity in a rescript promulgated on 1 January 1946, using for the first time the less formal imperial style that henceforth would characterize his public proclamations.

The relevant passage occurs well into the document, the first part of which commends the five-article Charter Oath, given in full, as the basis of national reconstruction. Noting in passing the existence of 'radical tendencies' reflecting a lack of direction that the Oath might rectify, the Emperor stated simply,

> We stand by the people. ... The ties between us with our people ... do not depend upon mere legends or myths. They are not predicated on the false conception that the Emperor is divine and that the Japanese people are superior to other races and fated to rule the world.
>
> (PRJ II [1949] 1970: 470)

That same day, MacArthur publicly commented, 'The Emperor's New Year's statement pleases me very much. By it he undertakes a leading part in the democratization of his people. He squarely takes his stand for the future along liberal lines' (PRJ II [1949] 1970: 471).

It is uncertain whether the initiative for the rescript originated from SCAP or from the court. One study suggests that in the first instance Admiral Yamanashi Katsunoshin, president of the Peers' School, suggested the rescript to deflect criticism of the Emperor as a war criminal and that R.H. Blyth, an Englishman who taught on Yamanashi's staff, played a major part in its drafting, in close consultation with SCAP officials (Hirakawa 1985). Be that as it may, the specific idea of including the Charter Oath came from the Emperor, who had been taught to respect it long ago by Sugiura Shigetake. Years later, in 1977, he remarked in an interview that, in 1946, he had regarded the reference to the Oath as more important than renouncing his divinity, which he had never believed in anyway (Hirakawa 1985: 40). During the Occupation, some observers dismissed the notion that the Oath, which they felt was archaic, could possibly encourage democracy in Japan (Gayn 1948: 93). But he clearly 'intended his rescript to serve as a bridge between the new post-war era and the Meiji roots of democracy as postulated in the Charter Oath' (Takeda 1988: 115–16). Yoshida Shigeru, it may be noted, regarded the Oath in similar terms (Dower 1979: 322).

The main significance of the rescript, however, lay in the Emperor's renunciation of divinity. At last he was able publicly to disown this myth in a way that had been impossible in the prewar period, particularly during the 'Minobe affair' of 1935. But whether the Japanese were much impressed by this renunciation is doubtful. Few of them had seen the Emperor as a god in any Western, Christian sense; worship of the Emperor had always been little more than 'a formal act of profound respect' for a higher religious authority (Vining [1952] 1989: 79). Some doubtless continued to revere him in that way but the main effect of the rescript, which 'was tantamount to the revival of the organ theory', was 'not the "devaluation" but rather the enhancement of the position and person of the Emperor' as a secular sovereign (Yanaga [1956] 1964: 131, 136).[9] In short, the rescript was seminal in promoting the new image of a 'human emperor' (*ningen tennō*), or a 'people's emperor' (*shiminteki tennō*) (Nishijima 1981: 104).

The Emperor's repudiation of divinity was also important in the context of SCAP pressures on the government to revise the Meiji constitution along liberal democratic lines. Michael Schaller states, the rescript 'deflated conservative efforts to rouse public opposition to the constitutional reforms' which soon unfolded (Schaller 1985: 42). Viewed accordingly, it fore-shadowed the Emperor's general support for constitutional revision. This is a second area where he assisted in adapting the monarchy to democracy.

Why he would concern himself with at least the basic issue if not the details of constitutional revision is understandable. He had long been harassed by the ambiguous provisions for absolute and limited monarchy in the Meiji constitution. His political instincts, combined with an abiding legal-mindedness, favored a far more precise definition of his role as a constitutional 'organ of the state', again in line with Minobe Tatsukichi's interpretation. Therefore it was quite in character for him to instruct Konoe, on 11 October 1945, to study the problem of constitutional revision after the Prince had agreed to help in this regard when he saw MacArthur earlier that month (Oka 1983: 183–4).

A month later Konoe submitted a fairly progressive proposal for constitutional revision but, by then, his efforts had been discredited in a statement from MacArthur dissociating SCAP from Konoe, after it had been decided to arrest him soon for war crimes (PRJ II [1949] 1970: 91). Moreover the new prime minister, Shidehara, had already elected to by-pass Konoe by establishing, on 25 October, a new Constitutional Problems Investigation Committee, chaired by Dr Matsumoto Jōji, a specialist in constitutional law, who was assisted by some of Japan's leading constitutional theorists, including Minobe and Professor Miyazawa Toshiyoshi.

The Matsumoto committee, however, adopted only a very minimalist approach to constitutional revision and proposed few alterations to the Meiji constitution. In Yoshida's words, 'It was the desire of the government to satisfy the clauses of the Potsdam Declaration dealing with the democratization of Japan without altering the fundamental principles of national government laid down in the Meiji Constitution' (Yoshida 1962: 131–2). Consequently, after a Japanese newspaper published the Matsumoto committee's initial draft of a new constitution on 1 February 1946, MacArthur ordered the government section, GHQ, to provide the Japanese with a model draft constitution (PRJ II [1949] 1970: 102).

The result was a hastily prepared document which shocked the Matsumoto committee when its contents were revealed on 13 February: 'Dr Matsumoto sucked in his breath. Mr Yoshida's face was a black cloud' (Whitney [1956] 1977: 251). Dismayed, Yoshida called it a 'revolutionary document' because of its great contrast to the Meiji constitution (Yoshida 1962: 133). No less shocking was the veiled threat, in fact a bluff, by the Americans, that it would be necessary to adopt the GHQ draft in order to ensure that the Emperor would not be tried as a war criminal (McNelly 1987: 82).[10]

Further American threats of this kind followed and it was therefore with much anxiety that on 22 February the Japanese leadership reported the situation to the Emperor and asked for his opinion. His reaction was unequivocal. As Yoshida writes, 'It was only because ... the Emperor had himself expressed the view that there was nothing in it to which exception should be taken that we brought ourselves to accept' the SCAP draft (Yoshida 1962: 137). Consequently, the Matsumoto committee used the American draft constitution as a model to produce a Japanese draft which was published on 6 March, along with an imperial rescript which endorsed it. That same day MacArthur welcomed the 'decision of the Emperor and the government of Japan' to initiate constitutional revision on such progressive lines, implying, misleadingly, that SCAP had had nothing to do with the formulation of what was known as the 'government draft' (PRJ II [1949] 1970: 657).

Of all SCAP's democratic reforms, the new Japanese constitution, based on this 'government draft', was arguably the most important. Ever since its adoption it has provided a liberal democratic legal framework for Japanese politics and has survived numerous attempts to amend it. It is also distinctive because of the well-known article nine, which renounces 'war as a sovereign right of the nation' and forbids the maintenance of 'land, sea, and air forces, as well as other war potential'. Whether the idea for article nine came from MacArthur, Shidehara, or someone else is still debated, but it is undeniable that article nine was meant to prevent the monarchy from ever being used again to promote Japanese militarism and aggression and that it was a quid pro quo for retaining the imperial institution (McNelly 1987: 81).

In addition, besides making the Diet the highest organ of the state, prescribing responsible elected government on the Westminster model, guaranteeing basic human rights, and so forth, the constitution states in article one, 'The Emperor shall be the symbol of the state and of the unity of the people, deriving his position from the will of the people with whom resides sovereign power' (PRJ II [1949] 1970: 671). Accordingly, the new constitution created what the Japanese have called the 'symbol emperor' (*shōchō tennō*), or 'symbol emperor system' (Hasegawa 1976: 8–9), meaning an emperor deprived of all political authority and removed from government. The functions performed by him were now completely subject to approbation by either the Diet or the cabinet. As enumerated in article seven, these included the appointment of prime ministers and chief justices of the supreme court, the attestation of ministers of state, the promulgation of constitutional amendments, laws and treaties, the convening of Diet sessions and the dissolution of the house of representatives, and various other duties, all ceremonial in character (Yanaga [1956] 1964: 140). Needless to say, his former prerogative of supreme command was also eliminated.

The Emperor accepted these changes to his political role but not, it appears, without certain misgivings. Although he had no fundamental objection to being cast as a 'symbol' in this way, he hoped that he would still be given the opportunity to be consulted, to encourage, and to warn, as was true of the British monarch, in discussing affairs of state with government ministers.

This desire, to be able to register at least some informal political influence, however indirect, made him especially keen to have ministers of state continue the practice of reporting to the throne as a matter of courtesy and so that he could give his opinion even if it was not taken into account. As it happened, ministers of state generally reported informally to him and when they did not, he sometimes expressed his disappointment (Ashida II 1986: 13). It may be assumed, however, that these informal reports, some of which lapsed after the mid-1960s in any case (Watanabe O. 1990: 122), were as perfunctory as have been the routine reports by British ministers of state to Queen Elizabeth. It is unlikely that what he said to ministers of state on these occasions had much effect on them.

The Emperor also had misgivings on specific points of constitutional revision. For instance, concerning parallel changes to the imperial house law, he wanted to retain his powers to amend this law rather than see its amendment become the province of the Diet, which ultimately it did.[11] As well, he wanted descendants of court nobles to be exempt from the abolition of the peerage, but here, too, he was unsuccessful (Ashida I 1986: 90).

Apart from these reservations, however, he was quite ready to accept the new constitutional dispensation. Most Japanese, too, understood that the constitutional revisions, including those pertaining to his political position, were a natural requirement of democratization. Yet, it struck many Japanese critics of the constitution that it was anomalous to have a monarch who performed no meaningful political functions and who was no longer the head of the state (Nakamura M. 1986: 135–7). Confusion on this last point would grow over the years whenever the Emperor operated as if he were the head of state, as for instance in greeting and conferring with visiting heads of state.

However, during the Occupation uncertainties regarding his political functions mattered less than the fact that the Shōwa Emperor was strongly identified with the constitution when it came into effect on 3 May 1947, as he proclaimed with manifest sincerity, 'I rejoice that the foundation for the construction of a new Japan has been laid according to the will of the Japanese people' (PRJ II [1949] 1970: 670). That day, large crowds mobbed the imperial car in enthusiastic celebration of the occasion, while a Japanese brass band nearby incongruously played the American tune, 'Stars and Stripes Forever' (Gayn 1948: 488).

The Emperor had indeed been identified as the main sponsor of the constitution from the day he presented it, accompanied by an imperial message, to the Diet for deliberation on 20 June 1946, after it had been approved by the privy council. His endorsement of the constitution was indispensable because, technically, it would be enacted as an amendment of the Meiji constitution. Otherwise, though, he took no part in the debates leading to its final passage in the Diet on 7 October 1946.

Representatives of the government tried to interpret the constitution very conservatively in these debates. They believed, with Minobe Tatsukichi, that Japan could evolve a British-style political system without radically revising the Meiji constitution and that Japan's previous progress in this direction had faltered, not because of any defects in the Meiji constitution itself, but because of the aberration of militarism (Dower 1979: 323). They therefore argued that at least in spirit the new constitution would not fundamentally depart from the Meiji constitution. Yoshida Shigeru, for instance, held that

> As for the Imperial House, the idea and reality of the Throne had come into being among the Japanese people as naturally as the idea of the country itself; no question of antagonism between the Throne and the people could possibly arise; and nothing contained in the new Constitution could change that fact.
>
> (Yoshida 1962: 139)

Similarly, on the issue of sovereignty, Kanamori Tokujirō, the government's chief spokesman on constitutional revision and a disciple of Minobe's, claimed that while the constitution would make the people sovereign, it was valid to regard the Emperor as part of the people, in which case he retained partial sovereignty, and by extension, political authority (Dower 1979: 324).

To these conservative interpretations SCAP retorted that 'the imperial institution is no longer the source of any authority whatsoever, can exercise no powers, and is certainly not indestructible'. The Emperor had no powers of government. 'His acts of appointment, attestation, promulgation, et cetera, are nothing more than the confirmation of the acts of the representatives of the people, a confirmation he cannot withold, he must give' (PRJ I [1949] 1970: 114). Regarding his symbolic role MacArthur stated: 'In his new role the Emperor will symbolize the repository of state authority – the citizen' (Whitney [1956] 1977: 285). When Yoshida subsequently tried to persuade MacArthur to restore lèse majesté as a crime, MacArthur refused, insisting that all the people, including the Emperor and other members of the imperial family, were now equal before the law (PRJ II [1949] 1970: 679–80).

Even so, the government's minimalist interpretation took hold as a new constitutional orthodoxy (Titus 1980: 535–44). Members of the government typically held that the Emperor's authority had been preserved. One stated, 'Through the adoption of this Constitution, the Emperor will become a symbol *above* the people and the people will also realize this is their government' (Gayn 1948: 125, italics added). This is most probably what Yoshida, too, had in mind when he proclaimed that with the new constitution the Emperor's symbolic and spiritual role 'will be that much more enlarged and his position will increase in importance' (Dower 1979: 329). Thus, the 1947 constitution radically altered the Emperor's political functions, but not the way many of Japan's leaders perceived them. In the future they would often claim the Shōwa Emperor as a symbol of state authority while their critics would claim him as a symbol of democracy.

The Emperor's efforts to popularize the monarchy by going out among the people represents a third endeavor in adapting the monarchy to democracy, albeit one which, in this instance, unquestionably originated in pressures from SCAP (Ward 1987: 13–14). Reminiscent of extensive national tours undertaken by the Meiji Emperor, those of the Shōwa Emperor were a logical sequel to his renunciation of divinity, and partially overlapping as they did the evolution of the 1947 constitution, they reinforced the creation of a new, popular, 'symbol emperor'.

The Emperor's well-known travels by car or by train during the Occupation, on which he was accompanied by senior court officials, began with a public appearance in Chiba Prefecture in June 1946 and continued into 1951, taking him to almost every part of Japan on different occasions. In 1947 alone, he visited twenty-one prefectures.[12] On the itinerary were factories, villages, schools, hospitals, local government offices, department stores, even sporting events. Everywhere, he was hosted by local dignitaries. Media coverage was very extensive.

Initially, his manner was formal and stiff. He could not bring himself to shake hands with people who made the effort, preferring instead to bow, in the traditional Japanese way. One of the countless local books published about his tours, in this instance to the Fukusuke Tabi Company (makers of Japanese footwear) in Sakai in 1947, indicates that he often responded to information given him by plant managers by repeating woodenly, 'is that so?' While there, he rather mechanically exhorted the workers to increase production for the sake of economic recovery and told local union leaders he wished the union a prosperous future in contributing to Japanese democracy (Tsujimoto 1947: 30). Still, an American military official who was present, as often happened on the tours, later praised his democratic demeanor at this factory (Tsujimoto 1947: 38).

But gradually the Emperor relaxed and more often than not succeeded in communicating a genuine personal concern for the well-being of people. At an Osaka railways works in June 1947 he asked a worker how long he had been employed there and then inquired, 'Was your house burned down?', referring to the bombing of the area. 'Yes, it was', the worker replied. 'How about your family?', the Emperor asked. The worker said, 'They are all safe', to which the Emperor said, 'I know things are hard but please take heart' (*Hyōgoken gyōkōshi* 1948: 48). At a hospital in Himeji the Emperor similarly asked a wounded veteran about his experience in the war and then stated warmly, 'I am very sorry for you. I hope you will recover soon' (*Hyōgoken gyōkōshi* 1948: 128). Such exchanges were typical.

It is true that the Japanese people saw from these tours that

[the Emperor] was short, slight, and round-shouldered, that his co-ordination was so poor he seemed constantly on the verge of toppling over. He was weak-chinned. . . . Apart from a stubby mustache his beard was straggly and he often needed a shave. Thick, horned-rimmed glasses shielded his weak eyes. His clothes were unkempt and his shoes scuffed.

(Brines 1948: 83)

Yet, his very ordinary and even vulnerable image drew the people to him: 'Instead of turning on him with fiery disillusionment, they now seemed anxious to mother him and protect him from the world' (Brines 1948: 84).

Their affection is apparent in many contemporary Japanese accounts. For instance, one school headmaster in Himeji said, 'This was not the Emperor who had been turned into a god but rather a very warm-hearted human Emperor'. A teacher agreed: 'The Emperor is no god, just an ordinary man. By being at one with the people, he has their deep affection' (*Hyōgoken gyōkōshi* 1948: 122). Moreover, the tours aroused sympathy from perhaps unexpected quarters. Nagai Takashi, the author of a popular book about the bombing of Nagasaki, noted after meeting him:

Although he is dressed in a suit, not the dress of a pilgrim, and although he is escorted by many attendants, I believe the Emperor feels as if he were a solitary pilgrim following the circuit of holy shrines ... to pay his respects to the souls of those who died in the war.

(Kanroji 1975: 134)

Very often, massive crowds waving Japanese flags were attracted by the tours. For instance, the American correspondent, Mark Gayn, relates that in Saitama a huge throng virtually engulfed the Emperor, trampling women and children to draw close to him and weeping hysterically (Gayn 1948: 139–40). While some people flocked to him out of simple curiosity, to many he represented endurance and continuity amid rapid change and it appears that most identified him with their hopes for a better day in the 'new Japan'. To this extent, the Emperor had proven effective – surprisingly so in view of his cloistered background – in bringing the monarchy closer to the people.

Sometimes his aides intruded, as when they wanted to keep the people from observing him through the window of his train while he took his meals. But he was reluctant to be screened away in this fashion. On one occasion, the people saw that 'with chopsticks in one hand and a napkin in the other he had come to the window to wave at them' (Irie 1983: 42). In 1974 the Emperor said, recalling his motivations while on tour, 'The people had been wounded by the war. I wanted to comfort them and get them to work for the development of Japan in a new era, so I intended to go around the country encouraging them'. He added, however, that he doubted he could go about as naturally now (Takahashi 1978: 177). And indeed, the easy mixing with the people that had typified his tours proved all too rare in later years.

The Emperor also met for the first time with the press during the Occupation, as he would in later years. Court officials prohibited controversial questions from reporters about the war. Still, his sessions with the press gave him an opportunity to display the same concern for the people as on his tours. This, too, contributed to the gradual popularization of the monarchy (Takahashi 1978: 6–10).

The Emperor's renunciation of divinity, his identification with the new constitution and his tours, were all public acts in adapting the monarchy to democracy during the Occupation. A fourth and more private endeavor in this regard was his interest in seeing that the Crown Prince received a comprehensive education which included a respect for democratic values. When the English-language *Nippon Times* announced the appointment of the American Quaker, Elizabeth Gray Vining, as tutor to the Crown Prince in October 1946 it stated, 'the present Emperor and Empress themselves possess most enlightened and democratic inclinations, indeed far more so than most of those who surround them' at court (Vining [1952] 1989: 35).

Vining, who credits the Emperor for the idea of appointing an American to this position, was not expressly meant to do more than teach English. But her memoirs disclose that she did in fact introduce her pupil to democratic ideas in the broad sense, by having him read the new Japanese constitution, books about the new United Nations, Nicolson's study of King George V, and

Abraham Lincoln's speeches. She came to admire his intellectual curiosity and growing confidence as the Crown Prince, like the Emperor, increasingly emerged as a public figure. 'Wherever he went', she observed, 'the crowds gathered. . . . He was learning fast that an imperial prince belongs not to himself but to the public' (Vining [1952] 1989: 121). As for the Emperor, Vining believed he had tried to prevent the war and was a man of peace genuinely committed to the democratic reform of Japan.[13]

In retrospect, partly by virtue of political necessity but more so by force of political conviction, the Emperor had assisted democratic reform where the imperial institution was concerned during the first several years of the Occupation. However, the overall reform process and the democratic image of the new 'symbol emperor' which he had helped to create, were increasingly subject to compromise once the Occupation entered its 'reverse course' phase, as critics of the Occupation characterize its later years.

REVERSE COURSE

'Reverse course' denotes a relative shift of emphasis, beginning in late 1947 or 1948, from democratization to the priority of rebuilding Japan as an ally of the United States in its escalating Cold War confrontation with communism in Europe and Asia. In Asia, the 'loss of China' to the communists in the 1949 revolution, and the Korean War, which commenced with the invasion of South Korea by North Korea on 25 June 1950 and ended on 27 July 1953, made it essential from the American perspective to forge a military, political, and economic alliance with Japan.

The Yoshida administration welcomed this reorientation of American policy and took the opportunity afforded by it to qualify those aspects of SCAP's earlier reforms which Yoshida believed were inappropriate for Japan. Thus, for example, his government moved to recentralize the police, reassert Tokyo's control of local government, and revive the efficiency of the zaibatsu, which the Occupation now encouraged after abandoning earlier efforts to break them up.

Yoshida also applauded SCAP's de-purge of all but a minority of people who had been purged from office earlier and he cooperated with SCAP's so-called 'red purge' of known and suspected communists in government during this period. Further measures were taken to contain the communists, and all other left-wing elements, in the proletarian party and labor movements, for this was a major priority for the government. As well, in 1951, Yoshida established a committee to review Occupation legislation across the board. This initiative previewed the government's resolve to continue on the path of reverse course after Japan recovered its sovereignty.[14]

Initially at least, Yoshida's reverse course policies did not include rearmament because he believed this would violate article nine of the constitution.[15] However, after the American envoy, John Foster Dulles, pressed him to rearm on a visit to Japan in June 1950, during which the

Korean War coincidentally erupted, the crisis in Korea pushed Yoshida into creating the new 75,000–man National Police Reserve. He insisted it was not an army. But this was not Vining's impression. She wrote disapprovingly, 'They lived in camps like soldiers, they were trained like soldiers ... and they looked like soldiers, in American army surplus khaki and marine boots' (Vining [1952] 1989: 304). In July 1954, Japan's re-emergent military, supplemented with naval and air units, became the Self-Defence Forces, or Jieitai. The Jietai were administered by the new defense agency attached to the prime minister's office (Dower 1979: 436).

The Shōwa Emperor himself was not directly involved in other reverse course developments but on the vital question of national security in the context of the Cold War, he was prepared to apply whatever informal influence he had with the Occupation authorities to ensure that Japan would be protected from the threat of communism. One example of this endeavor, his conversation with MacArthur in May 1947, has already been mentioned. Four others late in the Occupation may also be given.

First, against the background of increasing tension between the United States and the Soviet Union in Europe, and Japanese anxieties regarding American defense plans in Asia, Terasaki Hidenari, claiming to speak for the Emperor, told Sebald on 27 February 1948 that the American line of defense against communism in Asia should be drawn to include Japan, Okinawa, South Korea, and Taiwan. Terasaki said that the United States should disengage from China where the escalating struggle between the Nationalists and communists for political control lay beyond American influence. In Hata Ikuhiko's view, this advice reflected the Emperor's thoughts on the perils of over-extension which had befallen Japan earlier in the Sino-Japanese War (Hata 1978: 383–4).[16]

The second example of attempted imperial influence on security matters is more problematic with regard to the Emperor's participation. The day after the Korean War began in June 1950, Matsudaira Yasumasa, Kido Kōichi's former secretary and also formerly a chamberlain who now served as grand master of ceremonies at court, presented what he said was a 'message' from the Emperor, to Compton Pakenham, a Briton who headed the Tokyo bureau of *Newsweek*. Matsudaira had established a personal relationship with Pakenham, and with Pakenham's colleague Harry F. Kern, the foreign editor of *Newsweek* who had accompanied Dulles to Japan that year. Kern, a confidant of Dulles, headed the so-called 'Japan lobby' in the United States, a group which pressed the American government to make Japan an ally in the Cold War. The imperial message was thus intended for Kern and through him, for Dulles.

In brief, this message, which refers to the Emperor in the third person, regretted that so many Japanese officials had been purged by the Occupation and that relations between the United States and Japan had been badly served by certain 'ill-intentioned Japanese' who had misrepresented Japan to the Americans. It proposed, therefore, the establishment of an informal group of

Japanese who, trusted by the Americans, could advise the Occupation on sensitive issues without 'being penalized for their opinions' (Roberts 1979: 403). It noted pointedly that had such a group been consulted, 'the recent mistaken controversy over the matter of bases could have been avoided through a voluntary offer on the part of Japan' to the United States in the Dulles–Yoshida discussions concerning Japanese rearmament and the long-term stationing of American forces in Japan (Schonberger 1977: 356).

Kern thought that the proposal for an advisory group including people on the Japan side whose views were similar to those of the 'Japan lobby' in the United States would interest Dulles. Apparently it did, for after passing it on to Dulles, Kern noted, 'I am told Mr Dulles regards this message as the most important development of his trip'. In a later letter to Dulles, he stated that by employing the 'unofficial channel' of the Emperor's message, the Japanese 'can, if they so choose, deny everything at any time' (Schonberger 1977: 355).

It is quite possible that the message reflected the Emperor's views and that he had a hand in, or approved, its drafting. But the extent of his involvement, if any, in this episode cannot be established; it is equally possible to hold that, as John Roberts suggests, 'If the message itself was of dubious authenticity, the involvement of the Emperor ... in such a partisan maneuver is even harder to accept' (Roberts 1979: 403). What is apparent, however, is that conservatives on both sides sought to exploit the prestige of the imperial institution to establish an 'American Lobby in Japan' analogous to the 'Japan Lobby in the United States'. Whether anything came of this message is unknown, as is the identity of its author (Roberts 1979: 404–5).

The third instance of attempted imperial influence regarding defense issues, and one in which the Emperor's role is somewhat clearer, involves his meeting with Dulles when Dulles visited Japan again, in early 1951. Sebald, who was present, 'suggested the Emperor might be interested in learning what the mission had accomplished during its visit. Hirohito replied he would like this very much'. Sebald relates that Dulles then briefed the Emperor on a wide range of issues, including 'problems of security', and that the Emperor 'listened with interest, asking a number of pertinent and searching questions' (Sebald 1965: 263). Although Sebald does not disclose their specific contents, it is evident that the Emperor wished to ensure adequate American protection for Japan.

The fourth example is rather more revealing as to the Emperor's thinking on defense. According to MacArthur's successor, General Matthew Ridgway, when he first met the Emperor in May 1952, 'The Emperor asked questions freely' when Ridgway gave him a detailed briefing, using a map, of the fighting in Korea. 'He was deeply pleased, he said, at my assurance that the war in Korea could, and would, be brought to a satisfactory close ...' Ridgway further notes, 'He said he was delighted that the US had seen fit to send troops to protect northern Hokkaidō. I told him that we considered the security of Japan intimately related to our own'. The Emperor also said he had been pleased by Ridgway's 'actions in supporting the Japanese government in opposing the May Day meeting at the Imperial Plaza', a reference to anti-war demonstrations staged by the Japanese left-wing (Ridgway 1956: 227).

These expressions of the Emperor's defense concerns suggest that while the Occupation reforms had subtracted him from the formal equation of government, he still thought it appropriate for a constitutional monarch informally to be consulted, to encourage, and to warn, on the crucial issue of national security. At times in future years, as for instance in the 1973 'Masuhara affair' (discussed in Chapter 8), when made public, this stance would be criticized as compromising his political neutrality under Japan's new constitutional dispensation.

However, he had been too marginalized politically by the Occupation reforms to influence policy to any significant extent. Rather, the Emperor increasingly withdrew into the nonpolitical world of his domestic life, devoting himself to family affairs and to his scientific research which he had resumed with renewed enthusiasm after the war. Yet, any expectations he may have had of living out his reign free of public controversy were illusory. During the Occupation he, and the imperial institution he personified, inevitably were caught up in a storm of political conflict, between proponents of neo-nationalism and their critics, which greatly polarized postwar Japanese politics.

In a trenchant essay, written in 1951, Maruyama Masao stressed that defeat and foreign occupation had severely weakened, but not destroyed, Japanese nationalism. Because old values, such as patriotism, a disciplined respect for political authority, and obedient service to the state, were harder to change than institutions, in its fragmented postwar configuration nationalism retained a latent potential that had survived the Occupation's democratic reforms (Maruyama 1963: 150–1). To galvanize these values as a defense against the Cold War threat of communism was the ambition of Japanese neo-nationalists who in effect wanted to repossess the imperial institution.

Within Japan, the perceived threat of communism was magnified out of proportion in part by the Cold War and in part because the communists remained conspicuous on the political scene despite growing Occupation attempts to suppress them. To illustrate, in 1951, communists and their sympathizers were prominent in 'the most tumultuous May Day demon-strations since the surrender', as they protested at the Yoshida government's pro-American line in the Korean War and American military bases in Japan (Morris 1960: 282). Communists were likewise conspicuous among the many students who loudly protested the war and the imperial institution when the Emperor visited Kyoto University in November. Irie Sukemasa recounts how they 'kept singing the "International" in a wild voice' that day, when the police were needed to clear them from the Emperor's path (Irie III 1990: 27).

At the popular level of neo-nationalism in this volatile context, many anti-communist groups, typically attracting demobilized war veterans and what Maruyama describes as various 'anti-social elements' (Maruyama 1963: 150), arose and became increasingly active. To cite but one, the Japan Revolutionary Chrysanthemum Flag Association (Nihon Kakumei Kikuhata

Dōshikai) made the protection of the Emperor from communism its primary mission when its members acted as an unofficial, self-styled bodyguard, frequently marching in advance of the imperial motorcade during the Emperor's tours (Morris 1960: 87–8).

Extremism of both the left and the right repelled most Japanese but to the Yoshida government, that of the left was especially alarming. Hence, it undertook to mobilize the monarchy as a neo-nationalist symbol of state control, to foster public respect for state authority while isolating and containing left-wing dissent. How far the Shōwa Emperor himself agreed with this policy cannot be established from the available sources. He had always regarded communism as a menace to the state. On the other hand, the government's manipulation of the monarchy in this way evoked memories of prewar Japanese authoritarianism and undermined his own efforts to contribute to postwar democracy. In all likelihood, therefore, he greeted the government's neo-nationalist campaign during the Occupation and thereafter ambivalently.

This campaign focused less on the Emperor per se than on restoring the sub-symbols of monarchy which had buttressed popular respect for state authority in prewar Japan (Nishijima 1981: 118–19). For instance, in 1950 Amano Teiyū, the minister of education, urged an all-Japan conference of educators to enhance the students' patriotic spirit by having them honor the flag, Hi no maru, and sing 'Kimi ga yo' on national festival days (Nishijima 1981: 138).[17] Amano also advocated that the schools should inculcate respect for the traditional moral authority of the Emperor as the symbol of the *kokutai* (Dower 1979: 355).

In the setting of postwar democratization, these were highly controversial initiatives, for Amano manifestly ignored the Occupation reforms that had been designed to break the prewar connection between national festival days, educational courses, and the Emperor. In future years, the government would vigorously promote the patriotic revival of Kigensetsu, formerly prohibited by SCAP, and national ethics classes in the schools. And, as it would later persist in doing, during the Occupation the government defended the use of imperial era-names against those who opposed the continuation of this traditional practice as contrary to the spirit of democracy in postwar Japan (Nishijima 1981: 146).

Most emblematic of this manipulation of imperial sub-symbols were fledgling efforts to rehabilitate Yasukuni Shrine. In October 1948 the Emperor paid his first postwar visit to the Shrine, to honor the souls of Japan's war-dead (Morris 1960: 135). Since he now had no political authority, this was interpreted as a strictly private act of worship, as were the Shintō rituals he still performed at court where it was maintained that these were purely the religious concern of the imperial family and bore no relationship to politics or the state. Nonetheless, the readiness of Yoshida to permit, indeed encourage, this visit, signified Yoshida's determination to rehabilitate Yasukuni. Yoshida himself visited Yasukuni three years later, albeit in a private unofficial capacity, when he joined 70,000 Japanese paying homage to the war-dead at the Shrine (Nishijima 1981: 161). With the issue of the separation of church and state at stake, inevitably Yasukuni would remain the focus of acute public controversy in post-Occupation Shōwa.

There were also strong indications that the new 'people's emperor' was gradually being 'remystified' behind a restored 'chrysanthemum curtain', to the extent that 'if somebody dares to take off the mystic veil of the Emperor-system, he has to expect pressure or revenge of all kinds', on the part of the extreme right-wing (Smythe and Watanabe 1953: 343). In addition, the imperial household agency drew criticism for trying to 'make the Emperor into a demi-god again'. To cite a somewhat later example, when Prince Chichibu died on 4 January 1953, after a long illness, the agency prevented the Emperor from attending his funeral on the grounds that for him to attend would violate court precedent. This aroused complaints that such traditional precedents undermined the democratization of the monarchy. A typical criticism ran,

> The Emperor seems to be almost a prisoner. We wish the people surrounding him would try to relax the yoke harnessed to the Emperor. . . . To the bigoted bureaucracy, this [chrysanthemum] curtain is very useful – for consolidating their status and privileges. This constitutes an unhappiness not only for the Emperor himself but for all the Japanese people.
> (Smythe and Watanabe 1953: 344)

It would be misleading to exaggerate the public impact of these different initiatives to dress the Emperor in old clothes. Tsurumi Shunsuke recalls that children scarcely recognized the Japanese flag and many mistook 'Kimi ga yo' only for a song that one sang at sumō tournaments (Tsurumi S. 1984: 64). Similarly '*kokutai*' was often mistaken for an abbreviation of '*kokumin taiiku taikai*', a reference to the annual National Athletic Competition (Gluck 1985: 284).

More fundamentally, most Japanese were simply too caught up in postwar democratization to be attracted to neo-nationalism based on restored imperial sub-symbols which recalled early Shōwa authoritarianism, militarism, and war. Still, as the Occupation ended, it was abundantly evident that however long the Shōwa era was destined to last, the prospects for the development of democracy in Japan would at times be held hostage to a darker past, as would be the Shōwa Emperor, who emerged from the Occupation a much contested symbol.

7 The politics of imperial symbolism, 1952–1970

The first two decades of post-independence Shōwa witnessed the extraordinary speed of Japan's economic recovery from the war. By the mid–1950s, prewar levels of production had been restored, and between 1955 and 1965 the economy grew at an annual rate of 9.5 per cent, which rose impressively to an annual average of 12.3 per cent in the late 1960s (Hata 1984: 21). In the early 1970s, 'only the United States and the Soviet Union had economies that in terms of gross national product were bigger than Japan's' (Stockwin 1975: 1).

The basic policy guideline for this dramatic turnabout in the nation's fortunes was the 'Yoshida doctrine', named after Yoshida Shigeru, who retired from office in December 1954. Its priorities were economic growth as the foremost national objective, a program of light rearmament coupled with a low diplomatic profile to avoid entanglement in sensitive international problems, and reliance upon the United States for national defense (Pyle 1987: 246–7). From its inception in 1955, following the merger of the liberal parties, the Liberal Democratic Party (LDP), which then began its uninterrupted domination of government down to the present day, adhered to the 'Yoshida doctrine' as its blueprint for Japan.

Economic success came at a high political price, however. During the 1950s, the Japanese Communist Party (JCP) and the Japanese Socialist Party (JSP) relentlessly attacked Yoshida's successors, Prime Ministers Hatoyama Ichirō (1954–1956), Ishibashi Tanzan (1956–1957) and Kishi Nobusuke (1957–1960), for reviving Japanese capitalism and militarism while subordinating Japan to American interests in the Cold War.

The resultant unprecedented polarization in Japanese politics finally climaxed in the massive protests of May–June 1960 against the renewal of the security treaty. This upheaval forced Kishi, who had undermined parliamentary procedure during Diet deliberations on the treaty, to resign shortly after he had managed to obtain its ratification on 19 June. In the immediate aftermath of the treaty crisis, political tensions remained high. Kishi was stabbed, but not seriously wounded, in July by a mentally disturbed right-wing fanatic and in October, the viewing public witnessed on television the

shocking assassination of the JSP chairman, Asanuma Inejirō, a strong
opponent of the treaty, by a right-wing youth (Packard 1966: 304–5, 321).[1]

However, as Kishi's successors, Ikeda Hayato (1960–1964) and Satō Eisaku
(1964–1972), successfully applied the 'Yoshida doctrine' to economic
development, political conflict gradually yielded to a relative calm as Japan
passed into the new era of 'economism' (Hidaka 1985: 71). Against this
background, the completed construction, begun in 1959, of the spacious
new Fukiage palace in 1961 symbolized the national priority of economic
growth. Built at public expense, and consisting of two floors and an
underground level, it contained residential apartments and a large library for
the Emperor's personal use. In addition to the cream-colored palace, a new
palace hall, with a total of 250,000 square feet for official functions, was
completed in 1968, and sections of the palace grounds were turned into public
parks, as if to reduce the distance between the monarch and the people
(Kawahara 1990: 188–9).

Just as the new palace betokened Japan's economic achievements, so too
did the Emperor, in his capacity as constitutional 'symbol of the state and of
the unity of the people', represent Japan's new democracy by conscientiously
performing the strictly ceremonial functions required of him by the 1947
constitution. In 1964 alone, for example, he signed 1,390 documents relating
to matters of state, including the promulgation of 594 laws, ordinances, and
treaties, the attestation of diplomatic appointments, the recognition of
foreign diplomatic credentials, and so forth. He also signed another 1,733
documents concerned with the affairs of the imperial household agency, sent
many personal telegrams and letters to foreign heads of state, and held 189
audiences in addition to numerous receptions at the palace (Titus 1980: 574).

However, what the 'symbol emperor' stood for in Japanese political life was
conditioned by the reality that 'It is the needs, the hopes, and the anxieties of
men that determine the meanings' of symbols (Edelman 1967: 2); 'The
meanings . . . are not in the symbols. They are in society and therefore in men.
. . . There is nothing about the symbol that requires it to stand for only one
thing' (Edelman 1967: 11).

Inevitably, therefore, the Emperor found himself still subject to the same
combination of concurrent and overlapping pressures, to determine what he
represented politically, which were apparent during the Occupation: the
impulse to portray him as a popular and democratic constitutional monarch
close to the people, and the impulse to project him as a venerable neo-
nationalist icon of state authority and control. His position calls to mind the
deity of doors and gates, Janus, to whom the Romans prayed when passing
through, as it were, to a new beginning. Like Janus, depicted with two faces,
one looking forward and one looking backward, the Emperor, though not a
god, represented different things to different people as he stood figuratively
at the gate of Japan's future.

His Janiform image was the work of many hands, including principally the
government, the imperial household agency, and the mass media. Each

participated in both the popularization of the Emperor and his rendering as a neo-nationalist symbol.

The government sought to popularize him so that he would symbolize to the Japanese people and to the world Japan's postwar democratic evolution and the country's re-emergence as a responsible member of the international community closely associated with the Western democracies. Equally, it had a major interest in 'selling' the Emperor as a neo-nationalist symbol of its superintendency of Japan, to help ensure the control of radical dissent, particularly from the far left, and public acceptance of its policies. The coherence and consistency of the government's intentions in this respect ought not be overstated. Yet, there is strong evidence to suggest that in pursuing the politics of cultural nationalism centered on the Emperor and related imperial sub-symbols, the government deliberately manipulated the monarchy to its own political ends.

Adapting to the democratic trends of the times, the imperial household agency cooperated in popularizing the Emperor and the imperial institution for the same reasons that motivated the government. The agency especially encouraged the mass media to link the Emperor with the goals of democracy, peace, and international goodwill (Titus 1980: 575). This was the manifest emphasis of Usami Takeshi, agency director since 1950, and of the grand chamberlain, Irie Sukemasa who, as a virtuoso of public relations, composed the 'human emperor song' (Takahashi 1978: 74).

But the agency still maintained the 'chrysanthemum curtain' taboo against criticism of the Emperor and the imperial institution and by so doing, contributed to his neo-nationalist image over the years. As before, whenever he met with the press, agency officials routinely screened questions to him in advance and abruptly intervened if reporters persisted in touching upon politically sensitive topics. This happened, for instance, on 20 August 1954, following the Emperor's tour of Hokkaidō, where he had been greeted at various venues by representatives of the Self-Defence Forces. Usami sharply terminated the interview when the Emperor was asked whether to associate with the Jieitai did not compromise his new constitutional position as a people's monarch who no longer had any links with the military (Kyūtei kishadan 1955: 44).

The agency's vigilance in preserving the sanctity of the Emperor even extended to what it regarded as objectionable fiction, as its criticism of *Chūō kōron* (The Central Review) for publishing Fukazawa Shichirō's short story, 'Fūryū mutan', or 'Elegant Beauty', in its December 1960 issue, indicates. Fukazawa caused offense by having his dreamer-narrator enthusiastically witness the palace slayings by an angry mob of the Crown Prince and Princess, followed by the decapitation of the Emperor and Empress. Predictably, this story also incensed the ultranationalist far right, inspiring an attack on the publisher's household which resulted in the stabbing to death of his maid and his subsequent public apology for printing the story (Nathan 1974: 184–5).

The mass media, in turn, actively popularized the Emperor partly out of enthusiasm for democratic reform but also for reasons of commercial gain, since the bigger the public's appetite for news and information about the Emperor, the greater the market profits. Along with television, which dates from 1953 in Japan, and newspapers, the new popular weeklies stimulated a growing fascination with the imperial family. It was typical that after one weekly magazine carried a story about the Emperor's eating habits in 1957, workers on a holiday excursion were overheard discussing this topic with passionate interest (Kōsaka 1982: 146).

However, the media's habitual use of honorifics when referring to him communicated the impression that he stood apart from ordinary people (Mori 1979: 557). Hence, whether unwittingly or by design, the media often reinforced his neo-nationalist image. Even without this ingrained deference, their reliance on the imperial household agency for information about the Emperor, and threats from ultranationalist monarchists who acted as if lèse majesté were still a crime, constrained critical reporting about him. The intimidation of the media in the 'Fūryū mutan' incident was by no means unusual (Matsu'ura 1974).

Thus, different agencies, governed by a mixture of motives, participated in the 'selling' of the Emperor, one way or another. Although the popular and neo-nationalist dynamics of this process were entwined, in this account they are discussed separately, to better elucidate their impact. Put succinctly, although the Emperor's democratic and popular 'face' proved to be more sharply sculpted than his neo-nationalist 'face', still, by 1970, there existed no little ambiguity over precisely what the 'symbol emperor' symbolized politically in the 'new Japan' of the postwar Shōwa period.

THE POPULAR EMPEROR

The popularization of the Shōwa Emperor, which resembled on a smaller scale the popularization of Queen Elizabeth after her coronation in June 1953, unfolded through myriad descriptions and visual images emphasizing such themes, among others, as his earnest devotion to peace, to democracy in performing his constitutional duties, to scientific research and to family.

Typically, his public image as a man of peace was highlighted in stories of his role in ending the war and of his sympathy for the wartime sufferings of the people. His dedication to democracy was similarly underscored in stories of his cooperation with MacArthur in helping to build new foundations for political democracy during the Occupation and of how seriously he now took his constitutional responsibilities, going every weekday morning to his office in the imperial household agency building to attend to the routine affairs of the court.

Accounts of how he spent Saturday mornings doing research in his laboratory also reinforced his reputation as a '*kagakusha tennō*', or 'scientific Emperor', who by the time he died, was well-known in the international scientific community for his published works, notably on hydrozoa. His image as a serious scholar served to accentuate the compatibility of the imperial institution with modern scientific and technological progress in postwar Japan (Kyūtei kishadan 1955: 99).[2]

Given that historically the court had comprised a world closed to the public eye, possibly of greatest interest to the Japanese people were the oft-repeated stories of the Emperor's personal daily life in the palace which created and consolidated his image as a family man. Typical were vignettes of how he enjoyed watching the news, sumō wrestling (his favorite sport) and dramas on television with his family in the evenings, and of how he enjoyed playing family parlor games. That he had the same range of emotions as any family man was also conveyed by accounts, for example, of how he and the Empress sat by the bed of their eldest daughter, Shigeko (Teru-no-miya) on the night she died at the imperial household agency hospital on 23 July 1961. This was a 'human emperor' with whom the people could identify.

Elizabeth Gray Vining recalls, after visiting the imperial family again in 1957, that they 'were warm, natural and lovable people, a united family who took delight in being together'. She noted their easy laughter and their generosity, as when the Empress, herself an artist, took pleasure in giving Vining a gift of scarves on which she had painted wild flowers (Vining 1960: 26–8). Vining, and others, have also noted the close personal relationship between the Crown Prince and the Emperor, who dined together at the palace on Friday evenings and enjoyed discussing history and their mutual interest in science, for the Crown Prince was a student of ichthyology (Iizuka 1984: 141–3). Altogether, such homely images of daily life at court encouraged the people to idealize the Emperor as a model family man. The overriding impression was that 'the nation's first family are bound together by the bonds of affection, mutual respect, and awareness of their collective responsibility to the Japanese people as a symbol of a democratized, peaceful, and modern Japan' (Titus 1980: 557).

How far the Emperor himself approved his popularization as a middle-class family man is unknown. But as a monarch who had spent his earlier career on the throne obliged to play the role of a 'living god' which he had personally repudiated, the chances are that he preferred this new postwar image as a people's monarch even if that image was taken to extremes. Certainly, his popularization was a highly commercial and contrived process, as it had to be, to reconcile the old aristocratic ethos of the court with new images of his middle-class life. Thus, it was noted, 'The members of the imperial family take on the aspects of stars with a pre-packaged public image as models of the ideal life. They are like store-window mannequins portraying a happy family surrounded by attractive furniture' (Miura and Yamamoto 1989: 13). In the commercial realm of public relations, the Emperor increasingly resembled Queen Elizabeth, whom critics have likened to 'a colour photograph covering a large box of chocolates' (Rose and Kavanagh 1976: 573).

Nevertheless, there was a sufficient correspondence between many of these popular images and the reality of his daily life to implant the general idea that, in him, people could see a reflection of their increasingly middle-class lifestyles and aspirations. There were, however, limits on how far the Emperor could be popularized.

Besides his remembered association with authoritarianism in prewar Japan, in certain personal respects he was rather hard to 'sell' as the 'people's emperor'. Unlike the Empress, who sparkled in conversation, his public manner was generally rigid and formal, far more so than that of his brothers, who were more outgoing. In this sense, too, he resembled Queen Elizabeth, of whom John Grigg writes,

> In general, she is not good at responding with animation and warmth to a popular feeling. . . . She seems to wave, smile, and accept favours in a predetermined manner and with a deliberately self-imposed restraint, as if it were undignified to show surprise or enthusiasm.
>
> (Grigg 1969: 54)

Not that popular affection (*shin'ai*) for him was insignificant. It motivated many of the people, numbering nearly 400,000, who greeted him at the imperial palace plaza on New Year's Day in 1954, or the more than 300,000 who did likewise two years later when one foreign witness observed 'the enthusiastic shouts of banzai when the Emperor and Empress made their appearance and the feeling of affection that was manifested' (Yanaga [1956] 1964: 131, foonote 7). 'Affection' was evenly reflected in national public opinion polls during the 1960s as well. For instance, 40 per cent said *shin'ai* described their feelings toward the Emperor in a 1961 poll, 38 per cent in a 1963 poll, 52 per cent in a 1965 poll, and 33 per cent in a 1969 poll (*Shōwa nihonshi* Supplement I 1987: 118).

Yet the same polls also reflected a combination of other feelings for the Emperor. On the one hand, 24 per cent of the respondents in both the 1961 and 1963 polls, 8 per cent in the 1965 poll, and 33 per cent in the 1969 poll chose traditional 'reverence' (*sūhai*) or 'respect' (*sonkei*) to describe their feelings toward him. On the other, feelings of 'hostility', or *hanjō*, were insignificant: 1 per cent in 1961 and 1963, 4 per cent in 1965, and 3 per cent in 1969. In the middle, however, was a sizeable category of people who expressed their 'indifference' (*mukanshin*) towards the Emperor. They constituted 30 per cent in the 1961 poll, 33 per cent in the 1963 and 1965 polls, and 29 per cent in the 1969 poll (*Shōwa nihonshi* Supplement I 1987: 118). The steady growth of this indifference would pose a major problem for the Shōwa Emperor later in his reign.

One constant, however, in the national polls of the 1950s and 1960s, was a prevailing popular desire to maintain the imperial institution as it had been redefined in the 1947 constitution. To illustrate, in a 1952 poll, 82 per cent expressed this view. Similar results in polls taken in 1957 and 1965 recorded 87 per cent and 83 per cent respectively (Tsurumi S. 1984: 143, footnote 29).[3]

Some Japanese persisted, though, in wrongly identifying the Emperor as the nation's 'head of state'; 13 per cent clung to this view in another 1965 poll, for instance (*Shōwa nihonshi* Supplement I 1987: 119).

The fact that popular opinion generally revealed a mixture of sentiments concerning the Emperor suggests a certain 'fragmentation of national symbolism' that to some extent qualified his public persona as a popular, democratic symbol (Morris 1960: 147–8). In this context, it was important for the future of the monarchy that the Crown Prince proved to be much easier to popularize than the Emperor. Because he was young and untainted by association with political authoritarianism in prewar and wartime Japan, the Crown Prince offered a fresh face to symbolize the 'new' Japan. His growing public prominence is comparable to that of Prince Charles, later, in Britain.

Beginning with his 'coming of age ceremony' (*seinenshiki*) at the age of eighteen and his investiture in 1952, which caused 'great rejoicing throughout the nation' (Yanaga [1956] 1964: 132), there was much public interest in the Crown Prince. Admittedly, although extensive, media coverage and court public relations concerning the Crown Prince did not match the hype surrounding Prince Charles' investiture at Caernavon Castle in July 1968, for which British television repeatedly screened the film, 'The Royal Family', showing 'the women's magazine side of royalty in a reasonably chatty but over-long way' in blending 'nostalgia, patriotism, and humour to give the appearance of reality' (Duncan 1970: 212–13).

Still, there is no doubt that the Japanese mass media made the Crown Prince a 'star'. When he represented the Emperor at the Queen's coronation in 1953, 'the Japanese public listened to radio broadcasts and scanned the papers for every bit of news that could be found regarding his doings' (Yanaga [1956] 1964: 132). This interest continued, albeit with diminishing enthusiasm owing to their frequent occurrence, when the Crown Prince represented the Emperor on many trips overseas in future years. By the time he succeeded his father in 1989, he had visited thirty-seven different countries. Some of these trips strengthened relations between the Japanese and other monarchies, for example in Britain, Denmark, Sweden, Norway, Jordan, Saudi Arabia, Thailand, and Iran (until the Iranian revolution in 1979), but all of his excursions abroad helped to make him much more of an 'international person' with a 'well-defined international sense' than his father had ever been (Iizuka 1984: 144).

Above all, however, it was the Crown Prince's marriage to Miss Shōda Michiko in 1959 which ensured his place in the limelight. The story of how the young couple met on a tennis court at Karuizawa in August 1957 and of their unfolding romance reads like a fairy tale, for he was the handsome Crown Prince and she was the daughter, not of aristocracy, but of Shōda Hidesaburō, the president of the Nisshin Flour Milling Company. Their's was not the usual marriage arranged by the court, but a 'love marriage' which entranced a people who had become keen to experiment with new, more liberal, practices by the time the imperial household agency announced her 'selection' on 27

November 1958. The people were similarly interested many years later in Miss Kawashima Eiko, the daughter of a professor of economics and the bride of the present Emperor's second son, Prince Fumihito (Aya-no-Miya, or Prince Aya, born on 30 November 1965), when they were married on 29 June 1990.

As in this more recent ceremony, the wedding of the Crown Prince and Shōda Michiko on 10 April 1959 featured the private performance of Shintō rites in the palace sanctuary and a public ceremony which was seen on television by millions of Japanese, including the Emperor and Empress, for it was not the custom for them to attend personally. The wedding, 'one of the most popular events in postwar times' (Kōsaka 1982: 146), was marred only by an incident which took place afterwards as the young couple made their way to the Tōgū palace where they would reside. A nineteen-year old right-wing youth, apparently objecting to the bride's commoner background and her family's Catholic faith, threw a stone at their car, missing his target. He then tried to clamber aboard, whereupon he was seized by security police (*Shōwa nihonshi* Supplement I 1987: 133).

But to the overwhelming majority of Japanese, the Crown Prince and Princess were a 'dream couple' and Michiko, whose commoner status was approved by 87 per cent of the people polled soon after the wedding (Nishihira 1980: 84), quickly became the focus of a virtual 'Michiko boom' resembling the 'Diana Boom' which would accompany Prince Charles' marriage to Diana Spencer. In keeping with the mood of the times, the theme selected for the court's New Year's poetry submissions in 1960 was, appropriately enough, 'romantic love'. One teenage girl entered this typical poem:

In the stream
Flowing toward us
As a beam of light,
You and I stood
Together,
Dipping our hands in
Water.
            (Kishida 1983: 46)

Stressing that Japan's political evolution under the 1947 constitution saw the creation of new social values, Titus writes 'When Princess Michiko married the Crown Prince she wedded new Japanese middle class values to the imperial institution for the first time in Japanese history. The outpouring of public approval was virtually an approval of those values'; the marriage 'reinforced the new meaning of the Japanese monarchy in Japan's postwar democratic order' (Titus 1980: 576–7).

John Hall similarly emphasizes the democratic imagery of the monarchy in evaluating the general thrust of popularization during the first two decades since independence, when he states that the increasing

stability of postwar politics, the growing economic prosperity, and the new public image of the imperial family all contributed to the acceptance of the new constitutional formula and a return of the monarch to a position of popularity of a vastly different sort from the prewar style.

(Hall 1968a: 61)

Hall further writes that by the time the Emperor officially opened the Tokyo Olympic Games in 1964, 'a basic change in the relationship between monarch and people was being ritualized'. For, 'as he stood before his countrymen in the great Olympic Stadium it seemed no longer that it was simply through him that the fiercest feelings of pride were drawn from the hearts of the Japanese', as in earlier Shōwa (Hall 1968a: 62). They could also take pride in Japan's progress since the war simply by looking at the physical signs around them of Tokyo's rebirth, including new modern thoroughfares and the new stadium itself. That is, the Tokyo Olympics were 'a festival in celebration of Japan's postwar recovery' (Kōsaka 1982: 236), of which the Emperor himself was a positive symbolic reflection.[4] This is also how he was widely regarded when he opened the Osaka Exposition in 1970 (Irokawa 1983: 31).

Irokawa Daikichi, though critical of the monarchy, acknowledges that its popularization enabled it 'to align itself with a mass society, a modern civil society' which now accepted 'the image of a warm imperial family and the Emperor as a democratic monarch'. However, Irokawa notes perceptively that for many Japanese this acceptance arose from a nostalgic 'search for communality' in a more and more impersonal and competitive society where 'the loneliness of alienation' was not uncommon (Irokawa 1983: 31–2). It was precisely this yearning for a sense of community which had the potential to make them receptive to neo-nationalist emotions and ideas in postwar Japan.

NEO-NATIONALISM AND THE EMPEROR

Japan's postwar prime ministers subscribed to Yoshida Shigeru's liberal nationalism in seeking to continue the nation's historic quest for 'wealth and power' within the framework of the American alliance. But this very strategy posed the risk of appearing too subservient to the United States and not suprisingly, therefore, his successors, beginning with Hatoyama and Kishi, 'were faced with the need to work out policies that would appeal to the people's nationalism' – expressed in demonstrations against American military bases in Japan – 'in order to break away from the image of subordination to America'. Accordingly, during their tenure in office, 'Japan shifted further to the right then it has at any other time since the war' (Hata 1984: 20).

This shift was especially noticeable under Kishi, the first postwar prime minister to receive the backing of right-wing ultranationalist extremists. To his left-wing critics, Kishi's endeavors to rearm Japan, revise and renew the defense treaty with the United States, strengthen the police, revise the constitution, and restore the sub-symbols of the prewar *tennōsei*, all made him an especially dangerous threat to postwar democracy (Packard 1966: 52).

Ikeda was more moderate politically and embraced a less controversial form of neo-nationalism as he concentrated on the priority of rapid economic development. Yet he, too, equated the Emperor with the traditional *kokutai* and encouraged the revival of imperial sub-symbols (Crump [1989] 1991: 191–2). The neo-nationalism of Satō, Ikeda's successor, was stronger and more obvious. The slogans of his administration were 'based on the ideology of nationalism. Being extremely vague and nebulous, they include problems of national power, national interests, national defense, national prestige, national traditions and culture, thus representing nationalism in its daubed, theatricalized form' (Latyshev 1973: 10).

Their resolve to persist with Yoshida's 'reverse course' policies in qualifying the reforms of the Occupation predisposed these LDP prime ministers to use the monarchy virtually to achieve 'a planned reaction' against left-wing radicalism as they sought to promote a national consensus for the priorities set forth in the 'Yoshida doctrine' (Ōtsuki 1976: 119). In this, they had the support of right-wing organizations which operated as an 'auxiliary force' in seeking the revival of Japanese ultranationalism (Morris 1960: 419).

It must be emphasized that, in significant contrast to the far right, the government did not seek to restore the prewar fiction of 'absolute monarchy' which was, for instance, the goal of the well-known novelist, Mishima Yukio, who often denounced 'the pseudo-political system called Western con-stitutional monarchy' (Nathan 1974: 234). The government quickly dissociated itself from Mishima's anachronistic ultranationalism when on 26 November 1970 he startled the nation by committing ritual suicide at the Ichigaya headquarters of the army Self-Defence Force in Tokyo, after exhorting an indifferent assembly of soldiers to rise up and protect the Emperor from civilian authorities whom he accused of leading Japan into decadence (Nathan 1974: 274–81).

The government preferred a 'quasi-emperor system' attuned to the new political context of postwar Japan and the interests of the LDP and its main supporters, big business and the majority of relatively conservative rural voters (Hasegawa 1976: 8). What is more, it wanted a 'respectable' neo-nationalism with a political pragmatism which the far right did not evince. Adopting a middle course intended to appeal to the middle class, the government popularized the Emperor at the expense of offending the far right, while also projecting him as a neo-nationalist symbol in ways that alienated the far left.

To the government, these were complementary, not contradictory, objectives. In the liberal ideology of the LDP, a popular constitutional monarchy was as compatible with 'respectable' nationalism in Japan as it was in Britain. Moreover, it seemed quite within the boundaries of the new constitution to apply a neo-nationalist interpretation to the Emperor as the 'symbol of the state and of the unity of the people', to emphasize his residual authority and their patriotic membership in a political and social community held together by traditional values and institutions. Japan's leaders reasoned that by encouraging the people's identification with a popular monarchy, it would be easier to mould their affection for the Emperor into a general respect for the state.

And here, a certain 'politics of nostalgia' came into play. To illustrate its potential, a survey of people who had seen the 1957 movie, 'Emperor Meiji and the Great Russo-Japanese War', revealed that this film, which celebrated Meiji's paternal qualities more than those of a warrior sovereign, appealed to most viewers because it recalled for them 'the good old days', when the virtues of unselfishness and moral reciprocity had allegedly prevailed in society (Morris 1960: 138–9). Writing in 1960, Ivan Morris observed that this kind of nostalgia was the basis of 'home consumption nationalism', geared to 'a conformist respect for established authority' (Morris 1960: 395). The government wished to harness this sentiment in striving to restore vestiges of the traditional family system, which to many Japanese the Emperor represented, along with a general 'full-scale return to traditional customs, institutions, principles, and relationships that made Japan powerful in the past' (Morris 1960: 400–1).

Certain features of the imperial house made it readily susceptible to nostalgic manipulation. One was the perception, by itself politically benign, that the imperial house was a patron of learning and the arts. As the present Emperor once said, 'The traditions of our imperial house are not military. They are cultural and scholarly' (Iizuka 1984: 146). But there were conservative Japanese who would have agreed with Mishima, if not with his extreme ultranationalist vision, who had held that because the emperor was the 'preserver of court culture', which for Mishima signified the essence of Japanese cultural tradition, 'without the Emperor the Japanese people have no *identification*' (Nathan 1974: 233, italics Mishima's).

The ritual traditions of the imperial house, as on the occasion of court Shintō ceremonies, or *saishi*, likewise served the government's neo-nationalist purposes. Under the constitutional separation of church and state the Emperor carried out acts of worship at court, at Ise, or at other shrines, as 'private functions of the court', assisted by Shintō ritualists who were court employees but not public servants (Bock 1990: 38). Even so, his priestly function continued 'to exert a latent but powerful force within Japan's indigenous culture' (Irokawa 1983: 29). As ceremonies uniting, in effect, nature and culture, these rituals had the potential to foster a 'psychological collectivism' among some Japanese who followed their observance through media coverage (Nishijima 1981: 106). Very likely, this was their impact on many older people when contemplating the funeral ceremony of the Emperor's mother, Empress Dowager Teimei, who died on 17 May 1951, or the rites for the investiture and wedding of the Crown Prince. These ceremonial occasions catered to a sense of popular nostalgia for the idealized cultural traditions of the court (Ishida 1974: 228).

It was natural, therefore, for the government to encourage the study of, and respect for, the traditional imperial myths which were still embedded in court rituals (Nishijima 1981: 200–1). Indeed, this emphasis on the study of myths was prominent not just in the schools but also in the educational manuals used by the Jieitai from the 1950s onwards (Yamauchi 1976: 105–6). The same desire to develop popular respect for imperial myths, while fostering a new spirit of emperor-centered nationalism, informed the government's campaign to revive the tradition of Kigensetsu (Empire Day) as a national holiday.

In undertaking this project, the government took its cue from Yoshida's declaration in 1951, 'I would like to revive Kigensetsu to strengthen the people's spirit of patriotism after independence' (Nishijima 1981: 175). Backed by such right-wing groups as the Kigensetsu Hōshukukai (National Foundation Day Celebration Association), formed in 1953, the government repeatedly submitted bills in the Diet to restore Kigensetsu, only to see them thwarted by the opposition, which resisted this 'reverse course' campaign to set aside the Occupation's prohibition of Kigensetsu. Finally, however, the government prevailed, with the passage of a law in 1966 which revived Kigensetsu under a new name, Kenkoku Kinenbi, or National Founding Day. By 1967, when the legislation took effect, the Satō administration had determined that the festival would fall on 11 February, the old Kigensetsu date (Nishijima 1981: 173–80).

Kigensetsu was the only imperial sub-symbol to be fully restored in the period under discussion, although the government labored assiduously to rehabilitate others. To wit, the ministry of education constantly urged schools to fly the flag and sing the national song on important days in the school calendar (Nishijima 1981: 138). That some progress was made here is indicated by national polls taken in 1964 which showed that 69 per cent of those surveyed supported the public display of the Hi no maru, with 71 per cent favoring 'Kimi ga yo' (Watanabe A. 1977: 120). These high figures of approbation probably reflected more a diffuse sense of cultural, rather than political, pride, occasioned by Japan's hosting of the Olympic Games that year. But from the government's point of view, the distinction did not much matter, for cultural pride heralded the awakening of political nationalism in Japan.

The government's sustained initiatives to rehabilitate Yasukuni Shrine were even more indicative of its determination to promote the spirit of nationalism in post-independence Japan. If it were just a question of paying tribute to Japan's war dead, the government could have focused on the Tomb for Unidentified War Victims at Chidorigafuchi, or the Peace Park at Hiroshima (Hardacre 1989: 159). The government's focus instead on Yasukuni was thus deliberate, for Yasukuni was a rallying point for Japanese nationalists, as it is today.

Its campaign began in March 1956 with the first of many bills to restore state patronage of Yasukuni. Over the years these bills were successfully resisted by the opposition parties. They continued to resist when, in order to avoid contravening the constitutional separation of church and state, the government argued from 1960 that Yasukuni was a non-religious juridical person, and hence qualified for public funds.

Significantly, the government involved the Emperor indirectly in its Yasukuni campaign by encouraging him to attend various functions sponsored by pro-Yasukuni groups, as when he appeared at the fifteenth anniversary meeting of the Japanese Association for the Bereaved Families of War Dead, at Kudan Hall in Tokyo on 18 September 1962, or when he attended the first government-sponsored commemoration of the war dead on 15 August, the anniversary of Japan's surrender, in 1963. The opposition parties protested at this association of the Emperor with respect for the war dead. They also objected when veterans' groups, the conservative Association of Shintō Shrines, and such ultranationalist organizations as Seichō no Ie (House of Growth), all of which were monarchist proponents of a 'Shōwa Restoration', backed the government's Yasukuni initiatives (Nishijima 1981: 163–5; Murakami S. 1980: 130–2).

The opposition also criticized the government's political manipulation of the Emperor and imperial family in foreign affairs. In 1959, with the renewal of the security treaty looming, it was widely anticipated that 'the LDP might use the political calm surrounding the Crown Prince's wedding to whisk the Treaty through the Diet' (Packard 1966: 106). Thus, they were prepared for Kishi's efforts to mobilize the prestige of the imperial house on behalf of treaty ratification in the Diet, after he signed the revised treaty in Washington on 19 January 1960.

The next day Kishi announced a plan, endorsed by President Eisenhower, whereby the Crown Prince and Princess would exchange visits with Eisenhower, ostensibly to commemorate the centennial of diplomatic relations between Japan and the United States, but really to create an atmosphere conducive to treaty renewal. Specifically, the imperial couple were to visit the United States in mid-May, with the president due to visit Japan around 19–20 June, soon after the anticipated ratification of the treaty. At once, the opposition attacked the plan, perceiving that Kishi's purpose was to use the advance publicity for this exchange to influence Diet deliberations on ratification (Hara Y. 1988: 325, 403).

However, Usami Takeshi, the director of the imperial household agency, blocked Kishi's proposal by arguing passionately that to send the Crown Prince and Princess to America that spring would unwisely embroil the monarchy in the political crisis over ratification. Usami's resistance persuaded Kishi to postpone their trip until September, on the pretext that the Crown Princess needed more time to recover after giving birth, on 23 February, to the present Crown Prince, Naruhito, or Hiro-no-miya, known at court as Prince Hiro (Takahashi 1987: 112–13).[5]

As for Eisenhower's trip, it was cancelled on 16 June because of tumultuous anti-treaty demonstrations in Tokyo, including one six days earlier in which Eisenhower's press secretary, who had arrived in Japan ahead of the president, was mobbed by anti-treaty protestors (Hara Y. 1988: 408–9). The court was relieved that Eisenhower would not be visiting Japan. Had he come, and had the Emperor greeted him at Haneda Airport and accompanied him on the journey into Tokyo as planned, it would have been difficult to ensure the Emperor's safety, not to mention Eisenhower's (Packard 1966: 293). The grand chamberlain, Irie Sukemasa, wrote in his diary that the cancellation of the president's trip 'is not the very best [outcome], but it is better than the very worst' (Irie III 1990: 270).

Notwithstanding this denouement, the government would continue to exploit the monarchy in diplomacy, as will be seen in the next chapter. Its general readiness politically to manipulate the Emperor and other members of the imperial family is also apparent in the area of constitutional revision, although here, the government moved more cautiously.

It had emphasized constitutional revision ever since the LDP first advocated, in 1955, 'the voluntary revision of the Constitution to insure Japan's full-fledged independence' (Ward 1965: 405). It especially wanted to revise article nine, to put the Jieitai on a more secure legal footing which would make it easier to develop Japanese military strength. To facilitate revision, it successfully sponsored a bill in June 1956 to establish the commission on the constitution, or Kenpō Chōsakai, to be headed by Professor Takanayagi Kenzō, a leading expert on constitutional law. The commission began its work in 1957 and after a prolonged investigation into the issues of constitutional revision, submitted its final report on 3 July 1964.

By then, however, the government had decided to quieten down its intensive political offensive on behalf of constitutional revision. The upheavals over the security treaty in 1960, the determination of the opposition parties to defend the constitution as it stood and opinion polls showing strong public opposition to constitutional revision, had alarmed the Ikeda cabinet, which wanted a calmer political environment for implementing its priority of heightened economic growth. Furthermore, LDP proponents of military development now discerned that this policy could be pursued incrementally, without revising article nine. Finally, and perhaps most important, the commission's investigation had made it very reluctant to recommend major revisions of the 1947 constitution (Fukui 1968 : 51–65).

Specifically, its final report rejected the view, expressed by one conservatives cholar and commission member, that article one, dealing with the Emperor, should be revised because 'the adoption of the principles of popular sovereignty in the present constitution was completely against the will of the Japanese people.' Speaking for the commission's majority, Takanayagi asserted that the concept of popular sovereignty was now virtually universal in all monarchical and republican forms of government alike. He held that Japan should emulate Britain, where 'through the political good sense of the English people the monarchy has been solemnly preserved against a background of substantial popular sovereignty' (Maki 1980: 245–9).

However, while it did not recommend the revision of article one, the commission did accept the view, articulated repeatedly during its public hearings, that the term 'symbol' left the emperor's role unclear in key respects and thus required clarification through a revised statement of his functions.

The commission agreed that his public 'acts in matters of state' as stipulated in article seven – e.g. convocation of the Diet, dissolution of the house of representatives, attestation of ministers and so forth – were all subject to cabinet control. It judged that 'the general interpretation is that the cabinet, through the imperial household agency as an upper-level administrative organ, bears responsibility for them'.

However, the commission noted that in foreign affairs, 'it is unclear as to whether the emperor does represent the nation internationally' (Maki 1980: 254). In attesting the appointment of ministers and ambassadors, or in receiving foreign heads of state, for example, the Emperor virtually performed as a head of state and was perceived in this light by most countries, as when he greeted the Ethiopian Emperor, Haile Selassie in November 1956, the Shah of Iran in May 1958 and the King of Nepal in April 1960, to cite several of many instances. The final report stated, 'Therefore, the provisions relating to the Emperor's role in affairs of state should be completed by a reference to his role in foreign relations where as "head of state" he would represent the state in general matters' (Maki 1980: 382).

On another issue relating to the emperor's symbolic role, the commission asserted, concerning his ceremonial functions, that the constitutional separation of church and state still left it unclear as to 'what actions can be taken in regard to these ceremonies, as acts of state, which are inseparably related to former traditional religious rites'. Here, the difficulty was that 'the imperial house possesses a private character in addition to the public one recognized by the Constitution. Private affairs arising from this private character are deeply influenced by the Emperor's role as a symbol', whether they involved court rituals, imperial visits, imperial audiences or whatever (Maki 1980: 89–90).

On this problem, ultimately the commission upheld the position that the rites which the Emperor performed at court or at the great shrines were private acts unrelated to state affairs. However, it recommended, contrary to article eighty-nine, that public money should be spent on the maintenance of such shrines as Yasukuni and Ise because they 'are not simply for individual worship but possess an intrinsically national character'. As Takayanagi said, 'if it is made clear that the intent is not to grant special privileges to Shintō', the state could maintain the important shrines as 'cultural assets' (Maki 1980: 333–4). In recommending revisions to make this clear, the commission in effect compromised the separation of church and state.

But as a whole, the final report was notable for its circumspection regarding the emperor. The commission seems to have taken seriously the warning, given at one of its public hearings, that if his powers were increased through a revised statement of his functions, 'persons in certain positions would evade their responsibilities and there might be a danger that advisory organs close to the Emperor and outside the cabinet might be revived' (Maki 1980: 195). As commissioner Mano Tsuyoshi, a supreme court justice from 1947 to 1958, asserted, placing the emperor in a nonpolitical position makes possible the continuation of the emperor-system. To place him again in a position of political power or even to inch in that direction are matters which we, who have experienced . . . the manipulation of the emperor-system in the past, must oppose as a matter of course.

(Maki 1980: 252)

Similarly, commissioner Rōyama Masamichi held that any revision of the powers of the monarch would jeopardize the supremacy of the Diet, 'the highest organ of state power' (Maki 1980: 294–5). Nakasone Yasuhiro, then an LDP member of the lower house, and later, prime minister from 1982 to 1987, concurred, saying that apart from appointing the prime minister on the advice of the cabinet, the emperor 'should be freed of functions involving power or from involvement in difficult procedural issues related to the interaction of the organs of state'. He saw the emperor's role as restricted to the 'support of peace, the promotion and protection of the arts and learning, and the development of international goodwill' (Maki 1980: 255).

The circumspection of the commission prompted the government to note, but not act upon, the final report, although it remained ostensibly committed to constitutional revision as a future objective. What the Shōwa Emperor himself thought about the report can only be guessed. He may well have personally favored his redefinition as 'head of state', to clarify in legal terms the role he already played in practice. But on other questions, such as a return to imperial sovereignty, he was probably skeptical, due to their connotation of prewar authoritarianism.

Whether he sought the restoration of state patronage of the shrines is very doubtful. To be sure, concerning Yasukuni, for instance, Thomas Crump speculates that 'Given his devotion to the memory of his grandfather, the Meiji Emperor, he could hardly have been expected to repudiate so important a monument of the Meiji era'. Furthermore, on the occasion of the spring and autumn festivals that were always celebrated there, an imperial message (*gosaimon*) was read out at Yasukuni by an imperial messenger, in keeping with tradition. However, Crump adds that this 'is about the extent of the imperial patronage in the period after 1952; there is no suggestion that the government's policy of reinstating Yasukuni was in any way a response to the will of the Shōwa Emperor' (Crump [1989] 1991: 196).

Nor is there any evidence that he personally favored the restoration of other imperial sub-symbols, such as Kigensetsu. On the contrary, if we recall his skepticism, deriving from the influence of Shiratori Kurakichi in his youth, concerning the validity of national myths, it is likely that he agreed with Prince Mikasa's open letter, written in January 1958, opposing the restoration of Kigensetsu on the grounds that this would impede an objective understanding of ancient myths in Japan's cultural tradition. For taking this position, Mikasa was heavily criticized by ultranationalist extremists and special bodyguards had to be assigned to protect him (Morris 1960: 122, note 2).

These points are worth making because some commentators too easily assume, without producing convincing evidence, that the Emperor had a vested interest in restoring the ceremonial practices of the old emperor system (Watanabe O. 1989: 285–6). But not all critics of the imperial institution see the Emperor as a willing participant in the government's campaign to rehabilitate the monarchy in a neo-nationalist direction. Kobayashi Naoki, for instance, acknowledges that it cannot be demonstrated that the Emperor himself approved of this manipulation. But he rightly points out that the Emperor's personal feelings in this matter were irrelevant, for the government exploited the Emperor and the imperial institution pretty much as it pleased (Kobayashi N. 1976: 24). It simply did not need his personal approval to restore the sub-symbols of imperial authority.

Yet, despite all of its efforts, the government found in the 1960s that the people were mostly indifferent to its restoration policies. Ironically, this indifference owed much to the government's success in sponsoring impressive economic growth, for material prosperity in turn produced a new social ethos, that of 'indulgence of the self, neglect of the public', which conflicted with the government's emphasis on 'sacrifice of the self in the service of the state' (Hidaka 1985: 68). What has been described as Japan's ascendant 'new middle mass' increasingly cared more about matters of economic interest than about 'conventional ideological politics' (Murakami Y. 1982: 45). And as the 'corporate ideology of economic growth', epitomized by Japan's large companies, thus took hold, it gradually led to 'the decline of nationalism' in this decade (Watanabe O. 1989: 282–3).

This reorientation impeded the process of reconverting the emperor into a neo-nationalist icon. Still, that process had proceeded far enough to partially blunt his simultaneous popularization as a democratic symbol, with the result that by the late 1960s, the complex politics of imperial symbolism had engendered much the same kind of ambivalence toward him as one finds among the British people, who 'would like the Queen to be at one and the same time grand and common, extraordinary and ordinary, grave and informal, mysterious and accessible, royal and democratic' (Blumler *et al.* 1971: 158).

This confusion of expectations amid rapid social change challenged both those who upheld the emperor as a popular, democratic symbol and those who upheld him as a traditional, neo-nationalist symbol. Some Japanese who saw him in the former terms were troubled by the perceived shortcomings of a democratic political system that permitted the LDP's overwhelming domination of government. They wondered, 'If we don't have a stable society which largely satisfies the people, what can be symbolized by the Emperor?' For many, the answer to this question was found in contemporary Britain, where they believed the monarchy 'is a symbol of a social system in which liberal democracy actually reigns' (Fukuda 1963: 27).

On the other hand, those for whom the emperor was primarily a symbol of neo-nationalism still hoped that the country might yet rediscover a political sense of national pride even in the age of 'economism'. This commitment is markedly apparent in the Satō administration's elaborate preparations for the Meiji centennial in 1968. The organizing committee for the centennial anticipated that the observances that year would celebrate Japan's transformation from an obscure feudal country into a great nation during the Meiji era. The minutes of one of the committee's many meetings added, in part,

> The goal which has inspired our people up to now, 'to catch up to Europe and America, even to overtake them', has lost some of its earlier urgency now that our material culture has attained the level of Europe and America. . . . Is not now the opportune time to reassess those Eastern virtues which we have neglected for so long?
>
> (Hall 1968b: 713)

Similarly, a ministry of education document on the importance of the Meiji centennial stated:

> The feelings of respect and love for the Emperor are indissolubly related to the feelings of respect and love for Japan. In other words, to respect and love the Emperor, the symbol of the Japanese state, is to respect and love the state of Japan.
>
> (Latyshev 1973: 11)

Thus, when he opened the centennial observances during a grand ceremony held at the Nihon Budōkan in Tokyo on 23 October 1968, the Emperor had been given a major symbolic role in this national celebration of Japan's progress since 1868. Standing in front of a raised national flag, he addressed the audience of assembled Japanese and foreign dignitaries. After alluding to Japan's 'remarkable development as a modern state during the past one hundred years', and praising the 'wisdom and courage' of Japan's leaders since the Restoration, he said,

> Our history of those one hundred years, and the present situation at home and abroad, lead me to believe that we must exert ourselves to build a better future with original ideas, keeping in mind the lessons and experiences of the past.
>
> (Naikaku sōridaijin kanbō 1969: 142)

Then, 'Kimi ga yo' was sung and Prime Minister Satō delivered a longer speech, emphasizing that Japan's rapid emergence since the Restoration was singular in modern world history; whereas the advanced Western nations had taken three centuries to achieve progress in the industrial revolution, Japan had taken much less time. Great sacrifices had been made along the way. But the country could look back with even greater pride on its modern history. Significantly, neither Satō nor the Emperor referred to the cycle of war and social inequalities that had scarred the historical saga of modern Japan.

Other speeches followed and after the hall resounded with three 'banzai' cheers for the nation, the opening ceremony ended. Over the ensuing months, there were countless public exhibitions, musical and theatrical performances, television and radio documentaries and dramas, regional and local festivals, sporting events, and shrine services, all devoted to the centennial. Those few citizens aged over 100 years received special commendations. Centennial stamps and coins were produced. A ship was fitted out for a 'Japanese Youth Goodwill Cruise' to mark the occasion. Cigarette packs and a host of other objects carried special commemorative messages, and so forth (Naikaku sōridaijin kanbō 1969).

However, for all of this activity, the centennial did not arouse the patriotic spirit and national pride the government had hoped for in sponsoring these events. Because the centennial came and went without addressing the lessons of war, to which reference was seldom made, and without reaffirming the democratic ideals proclaimed in the 1947 constitution, it was greeted by the intense criticism of historians, the cynicism of the left, and the general indifference of the public (Hall 1968b).[6]

But while the people, in this age of 'economism', were mostly apathetic toward domestic political issues, on the issue of Okinawa's political reversion from American to Japanese control, they were very much aroused. Public opinion, inflamed by the American use of bases on Okinawa in waging the Vietnam War, 'put the Satō Government under increasing pressure to secure the return of Okinawa, preferably with the bases and their nuclear weapons removed' (Stockwin 1975: 228). Satō himself had contributed to these popular expectations by remarking, on a visit to Okinawa in 1965, 'the postwar era will not be over until Okinawa comes back to Japan' (Etō J. 1973: 64).[7]

Ultimately, after prolonged negotiations with the United States, it was announced in the Nixon–Satō communique of 21 November 1969 that Okinawa would revert to Japan by 1972, which it did, on 15 May 1972. But by 1972, other problems had developed in Japanese–American relations that were to intensify greatly over the years. Part of the government's response in coping with them would involve the 'symbol emperor' in ways which perpetuated controversy, at home and abroad, about what he symbolized politically.

8 The Emperor and the imperial institution in late Shōwa Japan, 1970–1989

The 'Nixon shocks' in the summer of 1971 made that year 'a landmark in Japanese–US relations, delimiting the honeymoon years of the cold war consensus from the recurring crises and uncertainties' which lay ahead (Hellmann 1988: 364). First, in July, without consulting Prime Minister Satō in advance, the president announced that he would visit Peking in February 1972. Satō was stunned by this abrupt signal of a fundamental reorientation in America's China policy, which Japan had hitherto followed by maintaining diplomatic relations with the Republic of China (Taiwan). After a speedy reassessment of Japanese foreign policy, it fell to his successor, Tanaka Kakuei, who held office from July 1972 to December 1974, to recognize instead the People's Republic of China, in September 1972 (Welfield 1988: 318–20). As it turned out, Japan took this important step seven years ahead of the United States.

Second, in reaction to escalating trade competition with Japan, Nixon announced in August 1971 a new economic policy which greatly upset Japan's political and business elites: the dollar would be floated in terms of gold and a 10 per cent surcharge would be applied to imports. The purpose of these measures was to force an upward revaluation of the yen in exchange for lifting the surcharge, in order to reduce the competitiveness of Japanese imports into the American market. This objective was realized, albeit temporarily, through an agreement reached that December (Stockwin 1975: 218).

The 'Nixon shocks' ultimately did not shake the government's resolve to continue close economic, political, and strategic ties with the United States. However, at the time, they were sufficient to trigger a sober and comprehensive reconsideration of relations with America. Japan's political leaders now believed that the United States had taken Japan's cooperation for granted in developing a new China policy and that it was openly treating Japan as an economic adversary. Within the LDP, doubts even extended to the military reliability of the alliance. Whereas prior to the 1969 general election a survey of LDP candidates indicated that 99 per cent favored the military alliance as it stood, a similar survey in December 1972 revealed that only 44.5 per cent held this opinion, with 47.8 per cent advocating either changes to the security treaty or its abrogation (Welfield 1988: 299).

Concerns that Japan was newly vulnerable to outside pressures were further heightened by the 1973 oil crisis, which exposed the dangers to Japan when overseas supplies of needed strategic materials, of which petroleum was the most crucial, were disrupted. Faced with a four-fold jump in oil prices, the government emphasized exports to finance the purchase of oil, with the consequence that the Japanese–American trade imbalance favoring Japan soon 'grew out of all proportions. By the end of 1974, at the time of the collapse of the Tanaka cabinet, it stood at $US 1.69 billion. By 1977 it had reached $US 7.99 billion. By the end of the decade it had increased sixfold to $US10.41 billion' (Welfield 1988: 330). It would rise even more dramatically later, to $US 80 billion, by 1987 (Welfield 1988: 445).

Beginning in the 1970s, there were increasingly strident calls in America for protection against Japanese automobiles, color television sets, computers, and other imports. In response, the Japanese succumbed to a 'siege psychology' and a 'rightward shift' based on the perception that the United States and other advanced industrial countries were using Japan as a 'punching bag' (Komiya 1979: 75–6). As Etō Jun wrote in late 1973, the American government 'operates consistently on a policy that has no faith in Japan, and tries to make Japan its scapegoat ...' In pondering the future of the American alliance, he challenged the Japanese 'to adjust our psychological bearings, get rid of the "postwar complex", and squarely face the reality of Japan as a big power' (Etō J. 1973: 74).

Many Japanese, however, were distinctly reluctant to abandon their 'postwar complex'. When Satō proclaimed in 1972 that 'the postwar period ended with the return of Okinawa', as he had predicted in 1965, a national opinion poll showed that only one-third of the Japanese people agreed with him (Watanabe A. 1977: 113). Nor were many Japanese ready to think of their country as a 'big power'. In a 1971 poll, which asked respondents to say what Japan should be known for in the future, just 9 per cent answered as an economic superpower and 3 per cent as a military power. Most, 53 per cent, wanted the country to be known as an advanced welfare state, while 20 per cent answered, as a significant donor of foreign aid (Watanabe A. 1977: 122).

This imperviousness of the growing 'new middle mass' to visions of national power constituted a major problem for the government as it grappled with serious trade frictions with the United States. How to develop strong nationalist support for the state as it addressed these frictions likewise preoccupied Japanese business leaders. During the 1960s, they had not primarily relied upon the government to safeguard Japan's economic interests abroad. But this attitude changed in the late 1970s as Japanese investments overseas soared:

Firms began to look to the state to ensure the protection of capital resources overseas. ... For Japan to become a global power, it was necessary for the people to agree to measures for protecting Japanese interests by military and political means should these be endangered. To do this the business community saw the need from the end of the 1970s to encourage nationalism.

(Watanabe O. 1989: 283)

Earlier in the decade and thereafter, the imperative of a new nationalism was fervently advocated by veterans' associations which had strong connections with the Self-Defence Forces, and by a growing number of ultranationalist organizations, estimated at 500 with a membership of around 120,000 in 1973. Furthermore, in 1973 an extreme right-wing group, the Seirankai, or 'Young Storm Association', was formed within the LDP. Notably, it drew its members chiefly from the party factions of Fukuda Takeo and Nakasone Yasuhiro (Welfield 1988: 431). Fukuda was to serve as prime minister from December 1976, when he followed Miki Takeo, Tanaka Kakuei's successor, to December 1978. Nakasone, as mentioned, became prime minister in 1982, following the cabinets of Ōhira Masayoshi (1978–1980) and Suzuki Zenkō (1980–1982).

These neo-nationalist pressures significantly affected the political position of the Emperor during the 1970s and 1980s. To preview the themes of this chapter, the government surpassed its earlier endeavors to promote him at home as a neo-nationalist symbol, around which the country could unite in protecting its interests overseas. At the same time, it took new steps to promote him abroad as a popular symbol of Japanese democracy and goodwill, in order to soften international criticism of Japan. As a consequence of this latter policy, he unexpectedly re-emerged from political obscurity in the 1970s, to become once again a focus of international attention.

THE EMPEROR IN THE 1970s

'The imperial household agency does not use the words "imperial house diplomacy" [*kōshitsu gaikō*]', its director, Usami Takeshi, often reiterated (Takahashi 1987: 110). In his opinion, diplomacy as such was the exclusive province of the foreign ministry; the tours of the Emperor and other members of the imperial family were strictly ceremonial, and non-political, contributions to international goodwill.

It was somewhat disingenuous of Usami to make this distinction, but as he had disclosed during the 1960 treaty crisis, he consistently regarded anything that might be construed as 'imperial house diplomacy' as too controversial to justify involving members of the imperial family. Still, despite his reservations, the imperial household agency cooperated with the government in choreographing the two important international tours undertaken by the Emperor in the 1970s, to Europe in the autumn of 1971, and to the United States, in the autumn of 1975.

The broad purpose of the European tour, during which the Emperor was accompanied by the Empress, a large retinue of palace officials, and seventy-one representatives of the Japanese media, was to express Japan's goodwill when he met with European heads of state or circulated among the European people (Date 1975: 71). More pragmatically, the Satō cabinet reasoned that this exercise in public relations would help reduce the isolating effects on Japan of the recent 'Nixon shocks' and create an atmosphere conducive to the expansion of Japanese trade with Europe. A related objective was to assist in mending the damage to Japanese–American relations caused by the 'Nixon shocks', by having the Emperor stop along the way in Anchorage, Alaska, where it was arranged that he would briefly meet with Nixon.

The Emperor's plane departed Japan on 27 September and upon arrival in Anchorage, it was greeted by President and Mrs Nixon. While it was being refueled, the Emperor and Nixon exchanged pleasantries in a private room. According to one account (Ebitsubo and Kamiya 1971: 118–24), Nixon suggested that his guest could slip into a kimono while he put on a terrycloth bathrobe, before they had tea, sitting on the floor, Japanese-style. 'The emperor said that if it was all right with the President, he would prefer to sit in a rocking chair and have some hamburgers sent up ...' While eating, they continued to speak about mundane matters, including their personal tastes for movies. Nixon said he admired 'Rashomon' nearly as much as 'Patton'. For his part, the Emperor said he admired King Kong films. Soon, the plane was ready and the meeting ended. Although nothing of political substance had been discussed, which was appropriate given that the Emperor was not permitted by the 1947 constitution to engage in policy matters, this exchange in Anchorage was reported in the American press as a successful display of goodwill on both sides.

In Europe, the tour included stops in Copenhagen (28 September), Brussels and other points in Belgium (29 September–1 October), Paris (2–4 October), London (5–8 October), The Hague (8–10 October), Geneva (10 October), and Bonn for several days before returning to Japan on 14 October. Among other dignitaries, the Emperor met with King Frederick IX in Denmark, King Baudouin in Belgium, and Queen Elizabeth. In France he also made a point of visiting the Duke and Duchess of Windsor, having always retained fond memories of Edward's visit to Japan in 1922. Throughout, imperial household agency spokesmen stressed the ceremonial nature of these meetings. But the impression that the Emperor acted as Japan's head of state when meeting with European heads of state invariably aroused criticism in Japan among those who regarded this as an insidious subversion of the constitution.

The Emperor's time in England recalled scenes from his 1921 visit. He rode to Buckingham Palace in a horse-drawn carriage, this time accompanied by the Queen and Prince Philip. He was also reinstated as an honorary Field Marshal in the British army and as a Knight of the Garter. And, he was received into the Fellowship of the Royal Society, to which he had been elected a member in May that year, in recognition of his scientific research (Corner 1990: 258). In all of these ceremonial respects, the tour was probably most gratifying for him personally, for it renewed nostalgic memories of his first visit and enabled him to go some way in transcending memories of Japan's war with Britain.

Yet, in Britain and on the Continent, he found that transcending the war was far more difficult than he had perhaps imagined. In Denmark, demonstrators protesting at Japan's role in World War II threw faeces at him and distributed handbills condemning him as a war criminal (Kawahara 1990: 194). In the Netherlands, where anti-Japanese sentiments were even stronger, he was greeted by placards which read, 'Hirohito Go Home!', 'Murderer!', and the like. Elsewhere in Holland, student protestors called him a 'fascist' and at one demonstration, threw a bottle which smashed the windshield of his car. They also burned the Japanese flag and broke windows at the Japanese embassy residence where he stayed (Kawahara 1990: 194).

Similarly, in England, a symbolic tree of Anglo-Japanese friendship he had planted in Kew Gardens was soon chopped down and hydrochloric acid poured on its roots, to protest Japanese brutality towards British prisoners of war. In Germany, he was pelted with tomatoes and greeted by placards declaring of him, 'Hitler killed six million Jews while he killed fifty million Asians' (Sheldon 1978: 5).

As if to offset these demonstrations, the Emperor's public statements repeatedly emphasized his goodwill towards Europe. In Belgium, for instance, he told a dinner party hosted by King Baudouin,

> This past half century has been a time of many difficulties and harsh testing, both for Japan and myself. As an Emperor who symbolizes the unity of the Japanese state and of the Japanese people, and who hopes for world peace, it gives me great pleasure to meet again with your country.
>
> (Yuri and Higashi 1974: 345)

Nevertheless, wherever he went, it was widely noted that he did not apologize for the war. A typical criticism, in the *Daily Telegraph*, ran, 'The emperor's words were filled with an empty geniality, as if relations between our two nations have always been fine. Why did we hear no expression of regret [for the war]?' Another critic wrote in the *Guardian*,

> The emperor who stood and spoke at Her Majesty's banquet last night is the same one who ruled when British soldiers were taken prisoner and used to build the Burma Railroad. The past cannot be swept aside in the name of protocol surrounding an official visit.
>
> (Kawahara 1990: 195)

His failure to apologize for the war while he was in Europe was highlighted by the fact that during an interview with foreign journalists in Tokyo prior to the tour, he had expressed an apology for Japan's part in the war (Sheldon 1978: 29, note 42). His silence in Europe on this major issue was not of his own doing, however. What the Emperor said, or did not say, during the tour was determined by the imperial household agency and foreign ministry (Kawahara

1990: 195). As Sheldon writes, 'The Emperor's visit to Europe offered an opportunity for a gesture of reconciliation but it was let slip, no doubt by government request'. He continues,

> Perhaps to avoid damage to the image of the imperial institution which it is committed to protect, the government must have asked the Emperor to remain silent about the war. Thus, he did not speak about the past, but about the present and future, in hopeful generalizations. Perhaps government leaders expected that time had eroded unpleasant memories. In this they seem to have miscalculated, although we do not know how far they shared the general shock felt in Japan at the demonstrations of anti-Emperor (and anti-Japanese) feelings remaining in Europe.
>
> (Sheldon 1979: 159)

Demonstrations against him in Europe had observedly unsettled the Emperor. In a later interview with foreign correspondents in Tokyo, described in the 17 November 1971 issue of the *Guardian*, he nervously twisted his fingers when asked about his role in the war, which his European tour had raised again. He replied,

> In this country my grandfather Meiji established constitutional government and I have acted with the wishes of Meiji . . . as a constitutional monarch. I acted in that way during the war and at other times. I have heard comments about my role, but there are many things I really did not know personally.
>
> (*Guardian* 17 November 1971)

Regarding the events leading to the decision to surrender in 1945, he said that prime minister Suzuki Kantarō had 'left everything to my discretion to make a decision . . . but that decision was taken on the responsibility of the prime minister'. A reporter then asked if he planned to abdicate. The Emperor replied simply that the Japanese constitution made no provision for abdication.

Because his European tour stirred up bitter memories of the war, it was scarcely the public relations success the cabinet and the imperial household agency had hoped for. Perhaps it was to compensate for this disappointment that the court went out of its way to welcome Queen Elizabeth and Prince Philip when they visited Japan in May 1975. Reporters noted that when he received the Queen at the palace, the Emperor wore his insignia as a Knight of the Garter, a reminder, in effect, of his symbolic rehabilitation and good standing at the English court (Takahashi 1978: 202).

The Queen, however, who was more adept at public relations, overshadowed the Emperor. The Japanese were impressed by the fact that, on her own initiative, she rode from the Imperial Hotel to the National Theater in an open car, close to the enthusiastic crowds lining the road (Kawahara 1990: 195). Once, when asked in Britain why she had so few bodyguards, the Queen answered that the people were her bodyguard (Takahashi 1978: 168). Her more confident relationship with the people, even in Japan, contrasted sharply with the Emperor's. While the great majority of Japanese were either pro-monarchy, or indifferent, an active minority of left-wing radicals constituted an ever-present physical threat to members of the imperial family.

This threat was vividly illustrated when the Crown Prince and Princess visited Okinawa, to open the Okinawa Oceanic Exposition in July 1975. A security force of 3,800 police was mobilized to protect them, although mainly, they were greeted by cheering crowds holding Japanese flags. However, protestors, blaming the Emperor, whom the Crown Prince represented, for the wartime sufferings of many Okinawans, threw milk bottles from the third floor of a hospital, narrowly missing his car. A Molotov cocktail was also thrown in their direction as he and the Crown Princess prayed at the Himeyuri monument to the war dead. Meanwhile, in Tokyo, demonstrators threw Molotov cocktails at the defense agency building and the police apprehended four left-wing extremists who broke into the imperial palace grounds to protest about the tour (Takahashi 1978: 270–3).

Incidents of this kind dramatized the imperative of strong security for the Emperor and others in the imperial family whenever they traveled about in Japan. To illustrate the typical scale of security precautions, during a four-day trip to Ibaraki Prefecture in May 1976, 5,600 police were posted on the streets to protect the Emperor along the route. It had already been checked in advance, with agents interviewing staff and examining rooms at hotels where he would spend the night. (Takahashi 1978: 149–59). On the occasion of this tour and others, they routinely went so far as to measure out how many steps he would take and exactly where he would stand, when disembarking, for example, from the imperial train, so that his position could be screened from would-be protestors (Takahashi 1978: 160).

But concerns for the Emperor's security, and disappointments caused by his 1971 European tour, did not prevent the government from attempting another exercise in 'imperial house diplomacy' when it decided to send the Emperor and the Empress to the United States in 1975. This was in response to a long-standing American invitation, first extended by President Nixon and later renewed by his successor, President Gerald Ford, to help improve Japanese–American relations in the context of worsening trade tensions.

Originally, Prime Minister Tanaka had wanted this tour to take place in October 1973, to dampen the smouldering effects of the 'Nixon shocks'. But Tanaka deferred to Usami Takeshi, who, 'beside himself with anger', strenuously objected (Kawahara 1990: 197). Usami feared that if the Emperor went to the United States, he would be plunged into the same turbulent controversies that had marred his recent European tour. Alluding as well to other political controversies that had engulfed the Tanaka administration, he protested, 'A trip to the United States would be bad at a time when we are so divided' (Takahashi 1987: 114).

Tanaka, however, persevered, and after arrangements were negotiated with the Nixon administration, it was announced in February 1974 that the Emperor would visit the United States in the autumn of 1975. Once Nixon resigned in August 1974 over the Watergate scandal, arrangements for the tour were later reconfirmed by Tanaka and President Ford when he visited Japan in November that year. Details on the Japanese side were subsequently handled by Prime Minister Miki Takeo after Tanaka resigned under a cloud of scandal in December. By then, left-wing 'struggle' rallies opposing the tour had erupted in various parts of Japan and when the Emperor visited Ise to 'report' the impending tour, as remained the custom for key events in his schedule, Molotov cocktails were thrown in protest, scorching a shrine gate there (Takahashi 1978: 169).

Both the Japanese and American governments stressed that the tour would be a purely ceremonial and non-political gesture of friendship between the two countries. For instance, Secretary of State Henry Kissinger wrote, in a long memo on 1 October to President Ford, that the Japanese were anxious to make the tour a success and to avoid any incidents that recalled the war. He observed that 'The Emperor himself considers the visit a symbolic pilgrimage to express his and the Japanese people's deep sense of gratitude for the assistance we rendered Japan following its defeat'. From all reports, 'The Emperor and Empress appear almost childishly excited and delighted with the prospect of visiting the US'. Kissinger further pointed out that some Japanese still considered the Emperor and the monarchy to be controversial, while others, especially young people, regarded both with considerable indifference. He anticipated that the visit would improve the Emperor's standing in Japan and that it would have the result of 'reminding the Japanese people of the presence of the Imperial Family in their midst'.[1]

The Emperor was similarly briefed in advance by palace advisers and various interviews with American correspondents before he left Japan enabled him to practice what he would say to the American media when in the United States. One interview was with Bernard Krisher, the Tokyo bureau chief for *Newsweek*.

He told Krisher that the purpose of his trip was to 'deepen the friendly relations between our two countries'. In response to questions about the historical continuation of the imperial institution, he attributed its survival to the fact that 'the imperial family has always given first thought to the welfare of the people' and said, concerning the problem of indifference towards the imperial house, 'generally speaking, the Japanese people have a respect for the imperial family'.

Krisher then asked him to compare his prewar and postwar roles. The Emperor answered, 'I don't think there has been any change, spiritually, in my prewar and postwar roles'. He explained, 'I feel I have always acted in strict observance of the Constitution'. When asked the perennial '1945/1941' question about his war responsibility, he answered it in the same familar terms as on many other occasions. He had intervened to end the war only at the invitation of the prime minister when it had become evident the government was incapable of deciding whether to surrender or carry on fighting. 'Now, at the time of the outbreak of the war and also before the war, when the Cabinet made decisions, I could not override their decisions. I believe this was in accordance with the provisions of the Constitution.' In reviewing his long career in office, he went on to say, 'The saddest time, without doubt, was the last war'.

Finally, on whether the imperial family would ever be more open and closer to the people of Japan, he remarked, 'This is my constant hope but it may not always be so easy to achieve, owing to the circumstances of the times'. Had he ever wished to leave the palace and do as he pleased, as a common man, if only for one day? 'That has been my desire, deep in my heart. Perhaps something like Mark Twain's "Prince and the Pauper". If I were to realize such a wish, however, perhaps the conclusion might turn out the same as in the story' ('A Talk With the Emperor of Japan' 1975: 56).

The aircraft bearing the Emperor and Empress and their entourage landed in Hawaii on 30 September, with Mr and Mrs Ford on hand to greet them. From Hawaii, the imperial couple flew to Williamsburg, Virginia for a rest before proceeding to Washington. As it happened, the only difficulty he encountered on the tour occurred in Virginia, when the Emperor sent the Japanese consul general of Atlanta, Chiba Kazuo (a future ambassador to Britain) to lay a wreath at the MacArthur Memorial, located nearby in Norfolk, rather than do so himself. This occasioned indignant letters of protest to President Ford from Memorial officials and a letter from MacArthur's wife, Jean, who also refused to attend a formal banquet in the Emperor's honor, held later in Washington.[2] The Emperor, however, did visit her in her New York apartment, where he expressed his great personal admiration for the general.

Otherwise, until he left Hawaii on 13 October, the tour went smoothly. Politically and symbolically, the high point was a statement he made when returning the president's toast at a banquet, hosted by the Japanese embassy in Washington, at Smithsonian Castle.

> It has been my wish for many years to visit the United States. There is one thing in particular which I have hoped to convey to the American people . . . that is, to extend in my own words my gratitude to the people of the United States for the friendly hand of goodwill and assistance their great country afforded us for our postwar reconstruction immediately following that most unfortunate war, which I deeply deplore.
>
> *(Public Papers of the President: Gerald R. Ford 1975* II 1977: 607)

The wording of this last phrase ('*fukaku kanashimi to suru* . . .', in Japanese), which he was to repeat in many speeches during his American tour, had been carefully worked out by Japanese embassy officials in Washington, in close consultation with the foreign ministry. They were concerned that in expressing his strong dismay over the war, the Emperor should say nothing which could be interpreted as indicating responsibility on his part for it (Takahashi 1978: 219). They must have felt relieved, therefore, when the Americans widely took the Emperor's statement as an acceptable apology for the war, which he had not made during his European tour. As Henry Catto, Ford's chief of protocol (and more recently, the American ambassador to Britain, now retired) later recalled, the Emperor had made 'to our surprise, a moving and dramatic apology for the attack on Pearl Harbor' (Catto 1989).

The Shōwa Emperor would not make a similar public apology to any other country and for this, he would be held in contempt by many people around the world.[3] But it seemed that in the United States at least, he had at last generally managed to put the war behind him. The American media reported his 1975 tour sympathetically, as did the Japanese correspondents who had accompanied him. The reporter, Takahashi Hiroshi, for instance, believed it had been effective in smoothing relations with the United States (Takahashi 1978: 22).

The success of the Emperor's 'imperial house diplomacy' was due not only to his apology but also to his capacity to appear at ease and 'human' in a variety of situations which recall to mind the personal touch he often displayed when touring Japan during the Occupation years. He seemed genuinely to enjoy watching a professional football game at Shea Stadium in New York. He beamed with delight when chatting with the Volz family during a tour of their farm in Illinois, where he enjoyed riding a tractor and cuddling farm animals. Similarly, he was pleased to pose at Disneyland with Mickey Mouse standing in the background. He always treasured the Mickey Mouse watch that was given to him on this occasion. After he died, it was placed in his casket, along with a current list of sumō champions, copies of some of his scientific publications, and an old German microscope (Sayle 1989: 29).

Probably the Emperor most enjoyed his visit in Massachusetts to the Wood's Hole Oceanographic Institute and the Marine Biological Laboratory where, 'glued to a microscope, he spent two hours at his favorite pastime' and left only reluctantly (Catto 1989). By the time he flew home from Hawaii on 13 October (his plane avoiding a route over Pearl Harbor), he had made a positive impression on many American observers. As Catto wrote, referring to the war, 'It almost seemed Fate had miscast his role and that of his artist wife, thrusting them into a maelstrom far from their liking' (Catto 1989).

Most Japanese reactions to the tour were likewise favorable but critics of 'imperial house diplomacy', such as Hasegawa Masayasu, charged that 'The Liberal Democratic Party has made use of the visit to America of the Emperor and Empress to divert the people's gaze from Japan's political and economic crisis under its subservience to the United States' (Sheldon 1979: 340, note 10). Similarly, once back in Japan, during a televised interview with reporters on 31 October, the Emperor still found himself having to answer probing questions about the war. Asked what he would say to Japanese who had lost loved ones in the war, he expressed his sorrow for their tribulations, which he felt keenly every 15 August, and added, 'Now I rejoice that these same people, who suffered so much, have contributed to Japan's development'.

Then, a reporter asked him whether his apology for the war when in the United States could be taken to signify 'an expression of your responsibility for the war?' He replied awkwardly, 'As for the subtle nuances of my remark [in Washington], not being a specialist in things literary, I am afraid they are beyond me. I am not really able to respond to your question'. Another question concerned the bombing of Hiroshima. He replied, 'I feel that it was truly regrettable that the atomic bomb was dropped. But in the midst of a war, and however tragic it may have been for the citizens of Hiroshima, I believe it was unavoidable' (Kawahara 1990: 201). After the interview ended, he was overheard to say uneasily to an assistant, 'I wonder whether I said enough?' (Takahashi 1978: 14). Usami Takeshi, for one, felt that he had said too much, and anxious that the Emperor had unwittingly conveyed a somewhat nonchalant attitude towards the victims of Hiroshima, later tried to qualify the Emperor's remarks accordingly (Kawahara 1990: 201–2).

Judging from a later poll, though, the majority of Japanese were satisfied with the Emperor's performance that day. Seventy-five per cent of respondents had witnessed the interview on television or had read about it in the press and of these, 42 per cent, the largest single category, said the interview had made them feel 'affection' for the Emperor. But others voiced less positive reactions: 21 per cent said he had appeared 'pathetic' and 12 per cent said they were 'indifferent' toward him; 7 per cent said the interview was of no significance, and 6 per cent said it had made them 'hostile' toward him (Nishihira 1980: 86).

After his American trip, the Emperor dropped out of the international spotlight and back into relative obscurity, where he remained until he died in January 1989. Yet, a minority of Japanese, for whom he still symbolized the war, continued to demonstrate against him. In November 1976, left-wing extremists threw Molotov cocktails into the palace grounds to protest against the government-sponsored commemoration of his fiftieth year on the throne (Sheldon 1979: 340). For them, it did not matter that he deeply regretted the war, as when he told the 7,500 politicians, bureaucrats, and foreign guests, who had gathered at the Nihon Budōkan to pay him tribute,

> When I think of the many people, and their families, who sacrificed their lives during the war, and when I further see that the wounds of that war remain with us today, the grief it causes me is almost more than I can bear.

> (Kawahara 1990: 205)

At times, during the 1970s, the Emperor inadvertently contributed to the controversy which continued to flare around him, as the 'Masuhara affair' in the late spring of 1973, indicates. Ever since 1961, when the commanders of the Self-Defense Forces were granted the right to be received in audience with the Emperor, his relationship with the growing Japanese military establishment had been a sensitive public issue (Watanabe O. 1990: 124). Thus, when in May 1973 the press reported a statement by Masuhara Keikichi, director general of the defense agency, which disclosed certain remarks the Emperor had made to him during a private meeting, critics of the Emperor protested vociferously that he had violated his constitutional position as a monarch who had no say on defense issues. According to Masuhara,

> His Majesty ... said that it cannot be thought that the strength of the Self-Defense Forces, when compared to that of neighboring countries, is very great, but what do you say about the fact that newspapers and the like are writing as if we are constructing huge forces? Furthermore, His Majesty said that the problems of defense are very difficult but it is very important to protect the country. Do not copy the bad aspects of the old military. Adopt its good points and do your best.
>
> (Sheldon 1978: 32, note 49)

At once, the imperial household agency condemned Masuhara for violating the convention of not publicly revealing what the Emperor said privately and the government accused him of misrepresenting the Emperor. Under this intense pressure, Masuhara resigned on 29 May. However, this scarcely satisfied the Emperor's critics who believed that he had improperly sought to influence national defense policy (Kobayashi N. 1976: 16–17).

It is impossible to know whether, or how far, Masuhara had misrepresented the Emperor, who had unwisely expressed certain concerns regarding national security, as he had done from time to time during the Occupation. But even if 'Masuhara exaggerated a noncommittal remark of the Emperor's into one of support for the Self Defence Forces ...' (Sheldon 1978: 31), that the incident aroused much protest indicates the extent to which controversy still attached to the Emperor, because of lingering memories of the war and the government's postwar efforts to manipulate him politically.

On occasion, off-hand remarks by cabinet members revealed the importance of the imperial institution to the government's overall policies. Such was the case in 1973 when Nakasone Yasuhiro, then minister of transport in the Tanaka cabinet, stated to the Shah of Iran, 'Japan is a monarchy in East Asia; you are a monarchy in West Asia' (Sheldon 1979: 349, note 6). For carelessly implying that the Emperor's powers were comparable with the Shah's, Nakasone was roundly condemned by the left-wing parties in the Diet.

But criticism, however strident in the 1970s, did not prevent the government from continuing its expedient promotion of imperial sub-symbols which invariably revived memories of prewar authoritarianism. Again, Yasukuni Shrine dominated its agenda as the government persisted in introducing bills to restore state patronage of Yasukuni. Although these bills were still repeatedly blocked by the opposition in the Diet, the prime minister and other cabinet officials regularly supported this legislative campaign by visiting Yasukuni on 15 August, beginning in 1975 with Prime Minister Miki Takeo (Murakami S. 1980: 159). It increasingly appeared that these visits were undertaken in an official, rather than a private, capacity but this would not be openly acknowledged until Nakasone Yasuhiro became prime minister.

Nor did it go unnoticed in the media that the Emperor's occasional, private visits to Yasukuni were being used by the government to support its proposed shrine legislation. Anticipating his visit in 1975, the *Asahi* commented, 'It would give the impression that Yasukuni Shrine was a national institution and could be used as evidence that the bill presently under consideration by the government, was an established fact . . .' The newspaper continued, 'Added to the visit of Prime Minister Miki on August 15, it would exploit the Emperor's status to provide further precedents for the government's proposed bill' (Powles 1976: 492).

In 1978 the Yasukuni authorities decided to enshrine the spirit of Tōjō Hideki and other Class A war criminals, although this did not become widely known until later (Hiro and Yamamoto 1986: 73). As well, the neo-nationalist rehabilitation of Yasukuni was subtly extended to include Ise Grand Shrine. In 1973 the traditional ritual rebuilding of Ise every three years was resumed after a long hiatus and Princess Kazuko, the Emperor's third daughter, was made the temporary chief priestess at Ise, thereby reviving the ancient customary links between the imperial house and Ise (Murakami S. 1980: 158). Furthermore, it was at Ise, on the occasion of the Emperor's private visit in 1974, that the prewar custom of *kenji dōza*, wherein the Emperor was accompanied on tour by the sacred sword and jewel, was revived. It had been expressly prohibited by the Occupation authorities (Takahashi 1978: 180–2).

The government was active on other familiar fronts, too, in the 1970s. For example, it continued to advocate the patriotic use of the flag and 'Kimi ga yo' and it pursued legal sanction for the hitherto customary use of imperial era names on official documents. After introducing legislation to that end for many years, it finally succeeded when, in June 1979, a bill authorizing era names was passed by the Diet (Nishijima 1981: 148–56).

Yet another, albeit rather different, facet of government policy, to reawaken a spirit of nationalism, involved the control of historical information relating to the wars of the early Shōwa period. This control was accomplished through the controversial vetting, by the ministry of education, of history textbooks for use in the schools, to delete or qualify references to Japanese aggression. The government manifestly wanted the postwar generation of Japanese to take pride in the nation's achievements since the war without feeling guilty for the havoc Japan had wrought throughout Asia and the Pacific earlier.

The desire to erase memories of the war also explains why, in 1970, a number of conservative LDP members, including Genda Minoru, who had led the attack on Pearl Harbor, joined Hayashi Fusao, who was well-known for his pro-Japanese reinterpretation of the war, and other prominent nationalists, in advocating, at a meeting held in Hiroshima, the removal of the inscription on the Atomic Bomb Cenotaph. They objected to the inscription, which in translation reads, 'Rest in peace, the mistake shall not be repeated', because it implicitly blamed Japan for bringing about the war, and thus the destruction of Hiroshima. Predictably, the Japanese peace movement demonstrated vigorously against any alteration of the words and when the Emperor visited Hiroshima in April 1971, it staged massive rallies there, to oppose the *tennōsei*, its prewar connections with militarism, and its perceived connections with rearmament in postwar Japan (Kurihara 1974).[4]

Sustained protests of this kind, on a variety of issues raised by the attempted 'neo-nationalization' of the Emperor and the imperial institution during the 1970s, reflected strong and active resistance to the government's promotion of a nationalist consciousness. But mainly, the government's neo-nationalist initiatives foundered on the seas of public indifference.

To illustrate, two polls taken by NHK in 1973 and 1978 included the question, 'Do you feel respect for, favorable feeling to, indifference to, or antipathy toward the Emperor?' In 1973, 42.7 per cent of respondents indicated they were indifferent, while 33.3 per cent said they respected him and another 20.3 per cent indicated they felt favorably toward him. Only 2.2 per cent said that antipathy characterized their feelings. In the 1978 poll, 44.1 per cent expressed indifference; the responses for the other categories were roughly comparable with those in the 1973 poll (Murakami Y. 1987: 78).[5] A perspective on this high level of indifference is suggested by Tsurumi Shunsuke, who believes that the materialistic 'postwar egotism' which remained characteristic of Japanese society served 'as a negative guideline for the Japanese people in making decisions on national and diplomatic policies', including the government's neo-nationalist initiatives (Tsurumi S. 1984: 124).

Faced with this public apathy, the question of how Japan could maintain its position in an increasingly competitive world without developing a strong sense of nationalism remained a pressing concern to the country's conservative leadership at the dawn of the 1980s.

THE LAST YEARS OF SHŌWA

On 24 June 1972 the Emperor had become the longest-reigning Japanese monarch, exceeding by one day his grandfather's record of 16,618 days. Other Shōwa landmarks followed in the 1980s. In 1985, he became the longest-living monarch at the age of eighty-four. In 1986, he celebrated his sixtieth year in office and on 29 April, his birthday, during special ceremonies sponsored by the government in his honor, he stated,

> While I have been praying for world peace and the good fortune of the people, before I knew what was happening, these have come to pass. In these sixty years, when all is said and done, the most abominable thing was World War II. What pleased me the most was the splendid recovery after the war, through the efforts of the people, which built the prosperity we know today. . . . As I contemplate here the sixty years of Shōwa and think of the sacrifices of the people in the last war I am grieved and again feel a reverence for peace.
>
> (Handō 1989: 459)

The central theme of these reflections, his identification with the people, was later said by the present Emperor to be the traditional concern of the

Japanese sovereign: 'The emperor is not in a position to move politics. Traditionally, he stands on the spiritual position of sharing the joys and the suffering of the people' (*The New York Times*, 8 January 1989: 6). Whether or not the Shōwa Emperor had always shared the people's joys and sufferings is perhaps debatable. At times, he had, as at the end of the war and during the Occupation; at other times, especially earlier in his career, his patrician outlook had made him less than caring about the lives of ordinary people.

However, where his political position is concerned, it is true that he had not been able to 'move politics'. Rather, he had been moved by politics, which continued to be the case in the 1980s as the government stepped up its efforts to mould him as a neo-nationalist symbol.

Of all Japan's postwar prime ministers, Nakasone Yasuhiro went to the greatest lengths in using the imperial institution to build what one of his critics somewhat extravagantly described as a 'symbol emperor system-empire', or '*shōchō tennōsei teikoku*' (Amano 1987: 307). Far more than his predecessors, Nakasone was a skilled practioner of symbolic politics who advocated the recovery of national identity to meet the economic and political challenges confronting Japan in the 1980s.

When he took office in 1982, Nakasone discerned a pervasive crisis of confidence in the minds and hearts of the Japanese people. As he stated a year later,

> A large number of Japanese today have a feeling that the nation is plunging more deeply into a period of crisis and confusion such as has never been experienced before.... There is worry as to what is going to happen to Japan, an uneasy sense that perhaps the nation has already reached an impasse, that growth may be over, and decline imminent.
>
> (Nakasone 1983: 12)

Nakasone's solution to this crisis was a 'grand design' which, intended to replace the 'Yoshida doctrine', coupled inspiring new visions of Japan as a global leader and 'international state' with those of a 'new liberal nationalism in Japan' contingent on the 'transformation of national consciousness' (Pyle 1987: 254–62). Notwithstanding the latent tension in this 'grand design' between Nakasone's emphasis on the 'internationalization' (*kokusaika*) of Japan and nationalism, to him, both goals were crucial to the imperative of 'settling the accounts of postwar politics', or '*sengo seiji no sōkessan*', as he often put it (Amano 1987: 291).

Here, Nakasone echoed Etō Jun's call in 1973 for the Japanese to set aside their 'postwar complex' and to see their country as a 'big power'. In 1982, he held 'that true independence is impossible as long as a nation chooses to depend in large measure on the military power of another country for its territorial security' (McCormack 1986: 47). Therefore, Nakasone called for revision of article nine of the constitution to facilitate a more rapid expansion of Japan's armed forces. He also advocated military appropriations exceeding the 1 per cent of gross national product that had been allocated in the past.

This 1 per cent barrier was soon surpassed, in 1988, under his successor, Takeshita Noboru; that year, Japan's expenditures on defense came to the equivalent of $41 billion which, according to some calculations, was the world's third highest.[6]

Furthermore, as a self-proclaimed internationalist devoted to maintaining the security treaty, Nakasone promised the Americans, when he visited Washington in 1983, that Japan would be 'a big aircraft carrier' capable of clearing the Sea of Japan in the event of hostilities with the Soviet Union (Pyle 1987: 266). He clearly felt that Japan should undertake military and political responsibilities commensurate with its status as an economic superpower.

Significantly, Nakasone sought to stimulate popular support for his 'grand design' by stressing the importance of the monarchy to the people. This was true in 1986, for instance, when the government opportunistically encouraged the commercial production of countless commemorative objects, such as special rings, pendants, watches, model toy cars and trains and ten million commemorative gold coins issued by the Bank of Japan, to arouse public interest in the official celebrations of the Emperor's sixtieth year in office. But Nakasone's political expediency was even more illustrated by the timing of these celebrations.

Ten years earlier, the fiftieth anniversary observances had occurred in November, to mark the month of the Emperor's formal enthronement in Kyoto. But in 1986 they were deliberately scheduled to take place in April so that the LDP could profit from the patriotic atmosphere they were expected to create as the party headed for the upper house election in July. The government then decided on this account to dissolve the Diet and hold general elections that summer. The outcome was an increase by thirty seats of the LDP's majority in the lower house. Ishida Takeshi writes, 'How much of the LDP's success was due to the government's manipulation of the ceremony commemorating the sixtieth anniversary of the Emperor's reign is impossible to measure, but many analysts agree that it must have had some effect' (Ishida 1989: 55).

Nakasone was no less expedient in anticipating how the Emperor's death could be used to foster public respect for the imperial institution, and by extension, for the government as chief mourner. Planning for 'X-day', the Emperor's death, had begun in 1981 and much care had already gone into the way the event would be announced, and how he would be eulogized in many television programs reviewing his long reign. By 1986, the grey-haired sovereign appeared increasingly hunched and frail, his face sagging with age, his progress when walking, slow and labored. Thus, calculating that his death could not be far off, the Nakasone cabinet intensified its coordination with the media in preparing the news coverage for 'X-day', in hopes of using the occasion both to honor the Emperor and publicize the virtues of the imperial institution (Hosaka, H. 1987).

Knowing that the Crown Prince would soon be emperor, Nakasone also sought to exploit his increasingly high profile by announcing, in April 1986, an agreement with the president of the Republic of Korea, Chun Du Hwan, for the Crown Prince and Princess to visit South Korea in mid-October, to help improve Japanese–Korean relations. However, their trip had to be cancelled, supposedly because the Crown Princess would need more time to recovery from impending surgery. In actuality, it was cancelled because of protests in Korea and Japan against the proposed tour, which, its critics claimed, would obscure memories of Japan's colonial exploitation of Korea in the past (Takahashi 1987: 116).

Besides these initiatives, Nakasone and his cabinet continued the long-running LDP campaign to encourage public respect for the sub-symbols of monarchy. 'Kimi ga yo' and the Hi no maru flag were of course promoted but Yasukuni Shrine remained the most important single cause. Together with cabinet colleagues, Nakasone regularly visited Yasukuni on 15 August, to complement the government's continuing, but still unsuccessful, attempts to enact a Yasukuni Shrine bill in the Diet. Indeed, in 1985, Nakasone became the first Japanese prime minister since the war to make it quite clear that his visits to Yasukuni were official, not private, in character (Sugiyama K. 1986: 71).

In the event, however, the government was forced to tone down its pro-Yasukuni initiatives once the Yasukuni issue became a serious problem in Japan's relations with its neighbors. In 1985 Nakasone's August visit to Yasukuni caused even more of a political uproar than usual because it implied government support for the earlier inclusion of Tōjō's name on the Shrine list of spirits, which was now widely reported in the context of intense criticism from the governments of the People's Republic of China and North and South Korea.

Nakasone responded to their denunciations of a revived Japanese militarism by publicly expressing his understanding of their views. But his almost apologetic effort to be conciliatory upset the right-wing groups which had cultivated ties with him. They consequently staged a large rally, with many LDP politicians present, at Kudan Hall in Tokyo, demanding state support of Yasukuni. Subsequently, the cabinet decided to proceed more carefully on this issue and on 15 August 1986, Nakasone was conspicuous for his absence from the Shrine (Hijikata 1987: 186–96).

The Nakasone government also ran into trouble with other Asian states when the ministry of education approved a controversial history textbook for classroom use. This text, which had been sponsored by the right-wing National Congress to Safeguard Japan, was entitled, *Shinpen nihonshi* (A New History of Japan), and reflected a revisionist attack by conservative historians in the 1980s on the 'Tokyo Trials' interpretation of Shōwa history, which had blamed Japan for the war. The book was particularly controversial because it qualified important wartime incidents, such as the invasion of China, as strategic advances, while omitting others altogether.[7] So great was the protest in the People's Republic of China that Nakasone felt compelled to personally fly to Peking to apologize for its publication.

Within Japan the *Shinpen nihonshi* ignited similar protests over its historical distortions of the war and its positive portrayal of prewar State Shintō, which furnished additional support for the rehabilitation of Yasukuni Shrine. Inevitably, the controversy over the book's suitability for use in the schools indirectly involved the imperial institution because of its historical links with State Shintō in general and Yasukuni in particular. Hata Ikuhiko speculates that the book's praise of Yasukuni, and by extension, its defense of old notions of imperial divinity, had surely offended the Emperor: 'The National Congress's tacit affirmation of the Emperor's divinity must be a great annoyance to the Emperor, who is a biologist and an admirer of Darwin' (Hata 1986: 77).

As prime minister, Nakasone is remembered for his attempted administrative reforms and his outspoken 'presidential style' at home and abroad, as when meeting with the American president, Ronald Reagan, with whom he was on a first-name basis (Muramatsu 1987: 333). During the Nakasone–Reagan era, relations with the United States generally improved, especially due to greater cooperation in defense matters. Still, 'The increasinglyi ntimate strategic cooperation of the 1980s did not necessarily demonstrate the "inevitable harmony" of Japanese and American interests', given the serious problems which remained over trade (Welfield 1988: 447).

However, of particular relevance to this study is that Nakasone, for all of his rhetoric, did not achieve the 'transformation of national consciousness', focusing on the Emperor and the imperial institution, that he had envisaged. As the preceding discussion indicates, because of protests within Japan and overseas, Nakasone was forced to retreat on many of his neo-nationalist initiatives.

He knew, of course, that an active minority opposed the monarchy; amid the celebrations marking the sixtieth year of Shōwa, left-wing extremists again threw Molotov cocktails into the imperial palace grounds and fired shots near the Akasaka imperial estate (Takahashi 1987: 124–5). Nevertheless, he liked to claim, with typical passion, that 'The great majority of the people love Japan and wish to defend the centrality of the emperor system' (Takahashi 1987: 117). Or, as he said in 1986, '99 per cent' of the Japanese people strongly supported the monarchy (Araki 1986: 155).

But did the 'majority' of Japanese enthusiastically support the imperial institution, as he alleged? It would seem that they did not, if public opinion polls are any indication. Most Japanese still wished to maintain the imperial institution in the symbolic sense defined in the constitution. But separate polls sponsored by the *Yomiuri* and *Asahi* newspapers in 1986 showed that over one-third were 'indifferent' to it (Araki 1986: 166). Even Prince Mikasa had seemed indifferent to the imperial institution when, in April 1982, he requested permission from the imperial household agency to withdraw his status as a member of the imperial house in order to undertake various 'social activities' more freely. Mikasa was obliged to reconsider, after the agency brusquely reminded him that there was no provision in the imperial household law for taking such a step (*Asahi*, 24 April 1982: 1).

In short, Nakasone found that many Japanese were too apathetic towards the imperial institution to be stirred by his monarchist rhetoric. Indeed, this apathy persisted after he left office in 1987. A June 1988 NHK poll revealed, for instance, that although 28 per cent of respondents recorded feelings of 'affection' towards the Emperor, with another 22 per cent feeling at least 'favorably' towards him, a high 47 per cent indicated that they were 'indifferent' to the Emperor and the imperial institution (Ishida 1989: 47).

It is possible, of course, to interpret this widespread indifference as a positive indication that the Emperor and the imperial institution had won acceptance as legitimate fixtures on the Japanese political scene, to the point where they were simply taken for granted. To that extent, his position resembled that of Queen Elizabeth.

On the other hand, and probably far more so than in Britain, public indifference also suggested a fundamental lack of commitment to the imperial institution on the part of people who had yet to be convinced that it was either necessary or important in Japanese political life. To Mori Kōichi, it was apparent that despite the government's promotion of the 'common fantasy' of emperorism, most Japanese would 'not fight or risk their lives to protest the abolition of the emperor-system. The emperor-system simply does not mean that much to people today' (Mori 1979: 558). One suspects that many Japanese, especially young people, would have agreed with Mori.

It is striking that a great many Japanese remained generally indifferent towards the Emperor even after it became known in 1987 that he was very ill. The earliest signs of his illness had dated from 23 August when he vomited blood after eating, as he continued to do in early September. On 22 September, he underwent intestinal bypass surgery (misleadingly announced as surgery for chronic pancreatitis). He was subsequently forced to delegate all official functions to the Crown Prince but recuperated sufficiently to greet the people as usual at the New Year in 1988. However, only 87,000 people gathered at the palace that day. As Watanabe Osamu points out, although this was by no means a negligible number, many more might have been expected to express their concern for his health on that occasion (Watanabe O. 1989: 278).

The Emperor gained strength until September 1988 when, on the 20th, he again vomited large measures of blood. After that, he was kept alive only by massive blood transfusions. At this point, a general mood of voluntary 'self-restraint' (*jishuku*) began to spread among the people, to express their sympathy. In keeping with this mood, department stores withdrew ceremonial foods used on festive occasions, shoppers increasingly stayed home, and trade generally declined. A worried government had the Crown Prince publicly declare, on 8 October, 'An excess of *jishuku* does not accord with the common sense of His Majesty' (Watanabe O. 1989: 279).

Meanwhile, Japanese went to the palace and other designated points around the country to sign one of the many get-well books (*kichō*) that had been made available. By November, six million had signed their names

(Watanabe O. 1989: 277). Yet, indifference to the Emperor's physical decline persisted beneath the surface of *jishuku*: only 29,000 people assembled at the imperial palace plaza to offer New Year wishes in 1989, as he lay gravely ill in the imperial household agency hospital (Watanabe O. 1989: 278).

This indifference cannot have been for lack of information, especially during the final stage of the Emperor's illness. Day and night, the media carried detailed reports of his deteriorating condition, including his blood pressure, heart beat, blood transfusions, vomiting, and even the nature of his stool. This intensive reporting offended the conservative, Nishibe Susumu, who believed that it constituted an 'invasion of privacy'. Nishibe wrote, 'When we call the Emperor a symbol we are saying that he manifests a concept of some element of the sacred, however we choose to define that. What is the purpose of bandying about a sacred symbol's vital signs?' (Nishibe 1989: 23).

As the Emperor's condition deteriorated dramatically in the first week of 1989, the public mood of concern deepened. When he finally died, aged eighty-seven years and nine months, of duodenal cancer, at 6:37 a.m. on 7 January 1989, massive crowds began gathering solemnly at the imperial palace plaza and during the next several days, four million people signed condolence books in his honor. Now the nation was swept by a solemn spirit of mourning and even greater displays of *jishuku*: weddings, holiday trips, and public events were cancelled one after another; employees, public officials, and athletes displayed black arm-bands; shoppers bought only necessities; and the media were given over to programs eulogizing the Emperor as a symbol of Japan's postwar regeneration, while recounting the principal events of his reign, as had been planned.

This outbreak of '*tennō* fever' following the death of the world's longest-reigning monarch astonished many observers, one of whom exclaimed, concerning 'all these young people' who assembled at the palace in 'jeans and short skirts', 'The schools haven't taught anything about the Emperor in all the years since the war, yet we have this response' (Miura and Yamamoto 1989: 13). Even ardent monarchists were taken aback. One states, 'The majestic scale of this scene came as a great surprise, not only to the left-wing intellectuals who are anxious about any "return to the *Tennō* system" but even to such self-proclaimed conservatives as myself' (Watanabe O. 1989: 276–7).

But the scale of this '*tennō* fever' should not be exaggerated. There were many Japanese, especially young people, who preferred to rent videos rather than watch television programs about the Emperor. Then, too, it has been plausibly suggested that the outward observation of *jishuku* on the part of many Japanese was mostly perfunctory and contrived. Contrived, that is, by the media in reporting it so extensively, by the imperial household agency in extolling the Emperor, by the LDP in using *jishuku* to enhance party discipline, and by big business, to encourage disciplined conformity among employees (Watanbabe O. 1989: 279–87). In an *Asahi* poll on 8 February, 57 per cent of respondents accused the media of overselling the Emperor, and only 28 per cent said that the outpouring of public affection for him had been genuine and spontaneous; 5 per cent feared that the attention given him in death prefigured a return to prewar emperorism (Sakamoto 1989: 17).

Some foreign observers were likewise persuaded that Japanese elites had contrived to exploit the Emperor's death for their own political purposes. The English anthropologist, Brian Moeran, who was in Tokyo shortly before the Emperor died, later wrote, 'The LDP was anxious to divert media attention from its members' involvement in illegal share purchases in what is now known as the "Recruit Affair" ' (Moeran 1989: 62). The LDP had good reason to be worried about this 'affair', which later contributed directly to the downfall of Prime Minister Takeshita, in June 1989, leaving other LDP leaders, including Nakasone, tainted with scandal.

Yet, many people genuinely mourned the Emperor's passing. Older Japanese nostalgically remembered how, after the war, he had encouraged them to rebuild their lives and their country. For them, he had personified their resilience and that of Japan through the vicissitudes of Shōwa history. And, he had personified traditions from an earlier agricultural age which were all the more valued because Japan was now an overwhelmingly urban, industrial society. It was not lost on many country people, or on city folk who retained strong links with their former villages, that as he was dying he reportedly asked attendants whether the rice harvest had been good (Ōtsuka 1989: 68).

Nostalgia also seems to have typified some of the young people who expressed regret at his death. As one teenage girl said, 'I like the Emperor because he doesn't seem to be soiled by the world' (Ōtsuka 1989: 68). Other Japanese similarly praised his 'royal innocence' and 'extraordinary self-abnegation' (Yamazaki and Kōsaka 1989: 17). Whether or not it is true that such nostalgia for the Emperor 'comes from the soft side of the Japanese psyche – the same place where they feel homesickness and sadness' (Miura and Yamamoto 1989: 14), the fact that some Japanese saw it in these terms indicates the depth of their personal identification with the Shōwa Emperor.

In this setting of contrasting emotions, the transition from Shōwa to the new era of 'Heisei' ('Achieving Peace') unfolded quickly. At his first televised public appearance on 10 January, the new Emperor said of his father, 'His heart was always with his people as they surmounted difficulties'. Using the more familiar term, '*minasan*' – which the Shōwa Emperor had avoided in preference for '*mina*', (that is, without the honorific suffix denoting respect for 'all of you', the people) – he then said, 'I wish to work with all of you to abide by the constitution' (*The Independent* 10 January 1989: 12). This promised continuity, from father to son, of commitment to constitutional monarchy, and early signs that the new Emperor would continue to popularize the imperial institution by bringing it closer to the people, inspired expectations within Japan of a more democratic and publicly accessible monarchy in the years ahead (Hosaka M. 1989a: 629–32).

But before the Japanese could focus fully on the future they had to lay the past to rest by burying the Shōwa Emperor, whose televised funeral, with the world watching, was held on a cold rainy day, on 24 February.[8]

It was a reflection of Japan's acknowledged status as an economic super-power that, altogether, 164 foreign countries and twenty-eight international organizations were represented at the ceremony, which took place in the Shinjuku Imperial Gardens in Tokyo, before the Emperor's remains were later interred in the Musashino Imperial Mausoleum, next to those of the Taishō Emperor. Fifty-one foreign heads of state, including the American president, George Bush, the French president, François Mitterand, other presidents, prime ministers, kings and princes from around the world attended, as did representatives of the People's Republic of China, the Soviet Union, and many other countries, large and small, of diverse political persuasions. On the Japanese side, all the political parties were represented among the many dignitaries from all walks of life, including the outspoken critic of the Emperor, Mayor Motoshima Hitoshi of Nagasaki.

After a hearse carrying the Emperor's coffin had made its way to the site through the streets of Tokyo, as a crowd of 200,000 people witnessed its journey, the funeral ceremony began with a procession of Shintō priests bearing his coffin in a large palanquin, which was escorted by unarmed members of the Self-Defense Forces. Accompanied by members of his family, the former Crown Prince, now Japan's 125th Emperor, followed, as gongs, bamboo flutes, and drums evoked the ancient traditions of the imperial house.

It was then announced that there would be two services, in accordance with the constitutional separation of church and state. The first was a Shintō ritual, a private ceremony of the court, which the socialists and communists who were present chose to boycott, in conspicuously protesting against the remembered links between the imperial house and State Shintō, which they associated with authoritarianism and war in early Shōwa history.

The second was a secular state service at which Takeshita Noboru, the last of the thirty-two prime ministers whom the Emperor had seen in office during his reign, delivered the first of two eulogies, stating that after 'that deplorable war', the Emperor had 'worked for world peace and human welfare'. In the other eulogy, presented by the chief justice, the Emperor was described as 'a much-beloved and familiar figure' whose desire to uphold the rule of law was now served by the judiciary. After he spoke, the foreign heads of state, led by King Baudouin II of Belgium, each bowed in succession before the imperial coffin. It was noticed by some that when it was his turn, Prince Philip, representing the Queen, bowed only slightly, as if not to bow at all.

For the most part that day, greater Tokyo was quiet, as the majority of its residents remained at home to watch the funeral on television. However, an estimated 100,000 people participated in rallies where they denounced the deceased Emperor as a fascist war criminal (Sayle 1989: 25, 28). Peripheral though they might have been, these demonstrations represented a persistent, intense criticism, on the part of a small but vocal minority in Japan, of the Shōwa Emperor and his reign.

A more reasoned criticism had been expressed earlier, prior to his death, at various campuses in Tokyo, of which Meiji Gakuin University is the foremost example. In November and December 1988, the staff and students at Meiji Gakuin had conducted seminars on the Emperor's career, the past and present role of the emperor system, and on the current practice of *jishuku*, which they perceived as a subtle form of manipulated nationalism that might one day lead Japan again down the path to militarism and war. Their theme, that the Shōwa era should be remembered objectively for the wars Japan had fought in the Emperor's name, led to threatening letters and telephone calls to the university president and his colleagues in January from ultra-nationalists who resented even the slightest criticism of the Emperor (*Prime* 5: 1989). This was the kind of angry reaction that lay behind the shooting of Mayor Motoshima a year later.

The dead Emperor was lavishly praised by the Shintō religious press, but like the staff and students at Meiji Gakuin, other religious organs, whose readers remembered the repressive past of early Shōwa, used the occasion of his death to comment critically on the monarchy and the way it had been exploited politically. In its 11 January 1989 issue, the Buddhist newspaper, *Chūgai nippō*, pondered the future with this statement:

> For the greater part of the long history of Japan, have not the Emperors belonged to a symbolic emperor system? The continuance from now on into the future of more than forty postwar years of uncontested rule by the Liberal Democratic Party, in which the symbolic emperor is made to shine ever brighter over popular sovereignty, is hardly a welcome prospect.
> (*Bulletin of the Nanzan Institute for Religion and Culture* 13 1989: 20)

Likewise, the 22 January issue of the *Catholic Weekly* warned, referring to the government's neo-nationalist policies, 'When made subservient to total-itarian tendencies and the power of the state, the presence of the Emperor as a "symbol of the unity of the people" harbors the danger of menacing and violating the "inalienable rights" of the individual' (*Bulletin of the Nanzan Institute for Religion and Culture* 13 1989: 22).

The Japanese Communist Party reacted to the Emperor's death more aggressively with this statement on his historical significance:

> We are called upon to speak out in deep emotion of the tens of millions of victims of the war of aggression and harsh domestic rule who cannot speak any more. The Emperor Hirohito bears the heaviest and supreme responsibility for the war of aggression.
> (*The New York Times* 8 January 1989: 6)

Evidently, many of his countrymen agreed that war responsibility could be attributed to the Emperor, although few of them would have said so in terms as strident as the JCP's. A Jiji Press poll in February revealed that more than 52 per cent of the respondents took this position, with 29 per cent saying he bore no responsibility for the war. However, the same poll also found that the issue of his war responsibility had come to matter less over the years: 66 per cent of the respondents, including at least some who held him responsible in some measure for the war, still professed respect or affection for him (Dower 1989: 8). If this poll is any indication, to many of his countrymen, perhaps the Emperor, in death, had finally transcended the war.

Overseas, governments and the mass media commonly voiced polite expressions of regret at his passing and here and there, we find eloquent foreign testimonies to his 'war innocence'. For instance, Laurens van der Post, who had personally suffered at the hands of the Japanese during the war, asserted,

> I say, with all the knowledge and passion of conviction I possess, that it is false to regard the dead Japanese emperor as a war criminal. He did all that a person in his position in the overlooked context of his day could do to steer his inflamed and powerful army away from war.
>
> (*The Times*, 25 January 1989)

But in Europe, Australia, and elsewhere, although less so in the United States, the Emperor was bitterly condemned for the Asian–Pacific War. To illustrate, in Britain, when it reported the news of the Emperor's illness on 21 September 1988, the *Sun* proclaimed in its frontpage headline, 'Hell's Waiting For This Truly Evil Emperor' and the *Star* that day described him as 'The Sinking Sun of Evil'. In the wake of his death, this climate of opinion made it unthinkable for the Queen to attend the Emperor's funeral, as various commentators had advocated. Such was the outcry from British ex-servicemen, whose ranks included former prisoners in Japanese wartime camps, that only after intense public debate was it decided to have Prince Philip represent her. Even his attendance was widely opposed.

How far these condemnations of the Emperor expressed the views of most people around the world is impossible to determine, but similar outcries were heard in many other countries where opinion against him ran strong. As a result, some foreign governments did not dispatch their highest statesmen to his funeral. In the Netherlands, it was decided to send the minister for foreign affairs, Hans van den Broek, instead of a member of the Dutch royal family. Australia was represented by the governor-general, William Hayden, not by Prime Minister Bob Hawke. New Zealand sent the governor-general, Sir Paul Reeves, not Prime Minister David Lange. The New Zealand minister of defense, Bob Tizzard, was quoted as even saying that the Emperor 'should have been shot or publicly chopped up at the end of the war' (*The Washington Post*, 11 January 1989: 1).

Thus, it was quite plain that despite the passage of more than four decades since Japan's surrender, for many people across the globe in 1989, the Shōwa Emperor had by no means outlived the war.

Conclusion

The study of the Shōwa Emperor and his career highlights the importance of paradox in history. He was a modern scientist on a throne shrouded in pre-modern mythology. He began his reign wanting an 'illustrious peace', only to find his country soon at war. His career, lasting sixty-two years, was nearly as long as Queen Victoria's and spanned nearly two-thirds of the twentieth century, yet is mostly remembered for its first two stormy decades, from December 1926 to August 1945.

Finally, he was called 'emperor', but was no Tsar or Kaiser capable of exerting personal rule. Throughout, he was less important for what he did than for what other elites did in his name, which broadly characterizes his political role and place in Shōwa history. It remains for this Conclusion briefly to summarize and extend the book's more specific interpretations, starting with the issue of his 'war responsibility'. For 'Placing the Shōwa emperor in national history means dealing with the war' (Gluck 1990: 16).

THE EMPEROR'S WAR RESPONSIBILITY

Had the Emperor been tried, it would have been logical for the IMTFE to convict and sentence him for formally sanctioning nearly every act of Japanese aggression and war in the 1931–1945 period, including, for example, the participation of Japanese army units from Korea in the Manchurian incident; the Japanese invasion of Jehol in 1933; the escalation of war with China in 1938; Japanese operations at Changkufeng in 1938; and the fateful decision for war which led to Japan's attack on Pearl Harbor in 1941. In addition, he sanctioned other Japanese initiatives which contributed in different ways to war: Japan's withdrawal from the League of Nations in 1933; Japan's entry into the Axis Alliance in 1940; and Japan's southern advance into French Indochina in 1940 and 1941.

For such critics of the Emperor as David Bergamini and Inoue Kiyoshi, his formal sanctions were emblematic of his deeper participation in a Japanese conspiracy to wage war. The strong implication is that he was as bloodthirsty as Kaiser Wilhelm II who, following the battle of Tannenberg in September 1914, 'proposed to kill 90,000 Russian prisoners of war by driving them onto the barren spit of land in the Baltic Sea known as the Kurische Nehrung, and letting them starve to death' (Röhl 1982: 31).

The intense passions pervading this interpretation are readily understandable when we recall the carnage wrought by Japan in the Emperor's name. Yet, this interpretation is untenable. It ignores, as this study has shown, that he personally opposed, and tried to use his influence privately at court to prevent, the acts of aggression that he ultimately sanctioned as representing the formal imperial will. He 'was absolutely consistent in using his personal influence to induce caution and to moderate, and even to obstruct, the accumulating, snowballing impetus towards war' (Sheldon 1976: 2). In retrospect, his only major success was the part he played at court in assisting the Hamaguchi cabinet on behalf of the London Naval Treaty in 1930.

Still, concerning the Emperor's war responsibility, Ishida Takeshi writes,

> since under the Meiji Constitution only the Emperor, as the supreme commander of the Imperial Army, was empowered to control the army, the Emperor cannot be absolved of responsibility for Japan's invasion of China in the 1930s and other Asian countries in World War II, though it is true that these actions were planned by the militarists.
>
> (Ishida 1989: 50)

Similarly, Ōnuma Yasuaki concedes that the Emperor opposed war but agrees that he was accountable for war because the war crimes tribunal 'regarded as criminal not only positive acts but also "disregard" of the "legal duty" to prevent breaches of the laws of war ...' (Ōnuma 1984: 66). That the Emperor was accountable, not for acts of commission in conspiring to wage war, but for acts of omission in failing to prevent it, is therefore the central issue in considering his war responsibility. Could he have done more, should he have tried to do more, to oppose war?

For the historian, because of the methodological problems it poses, this question is as difficult to answer as it is necessary to ask. Not to ask it would imply a determinist view in which history is invariably governed by impersonal forces and structures over which individuals have little or no control; pushed to an extreme, the responsibility which individuals share for historical outcomes would be ignored.

On the other hand, to ask it implies a voluntarist view that individuals invariably matter more than impersonal forces and structures in the making of history. This assumption runs the twofold risk of over-simplifying the complexities of historical causation and making too much of individual responsibility for historical outcomes. Furthermore, it often leads to over-reliance on indirect and inconclusive evidence in making dubious counterfactual claims about what might have happened had individuals acted differently (Lukes 1977: 24).

Clearly, an approach is needed which addresses the intricate interaction of impersonal forces, structures and individuals in shaping historical events and processes (Röhl 1982: 11). Here, 'the problem that then confronts us has at its center the network of dependence within which scope for individual decisions opens to the individual, and which at the same time sets limits to his possible decisions' (Elias 1983: 30). The preceding chapters have considered this problem in probing how the Emperor perceived his political role, how he acted upon his perceptions, and with what consequences, while also exploring why his personal intentions for peace were so much at variance with the effects of his war-sanctioning.

More particularly, as foreshadowed in the Introduction, this book has emphasized the combination of 'external' and 'internal constraints', in the sense suggested by Lukes, that defined the political 'opportunities' available to the Emperor and his 'abilities' to respond to them when confronted by the issue of war in early Shōwa history. These constraints were both positive and negative: positive, in that some plainly obstructed action, and negative, in that some comprised 'an absence, such as lack of resources, strength, skill, or knowledge, that, equally, prevents a potential option from being realized' (Lukes 1977: 11). To reiterate Lukes' overall perspective, it is necessary to see a career such as the Emperor's in terms of 'a dialectic of power and structure, a web of possibilities for agents, whose nature is both active and structured, to make choices and pursue strategies within given limits, which in consequence expand and contract over time'. To ask whether the Emperor could have acted otherwise is to ask what an individual could reasonably be expected to have done in a given set of situations (Lukes 1977: 28).

The formidable 'external constraints' on the Emperor make it unreasonable to hold that he could have done more to oppose war or that had he done more, war could have been averted. By way of a brief recapitulation, first, it was always clear that 'The emperor was to be neither a political partisan nor a policy maker. He was to ratify decisions produced by governmental leaders with the Imperial Seal' (Titus 1974: 56). He did not attend meetings of the cabinet or the liaison conferences, where decisions were made. Only when Japan's leaders competed in the process of 'working through the court' to declare the imperial will was he given opportunities to influence policy-making. Although he certainly was manipulated, especially by the military, he was no robot, for he exerted influence as he advised, encouraged, and warned. But his influence for peace was ignored, leaving him to confer automatically ritual sanction in the imperial conference on decisions reached elsewhere by others beforehand, as he was expected to do. Throughout prewar and wartime Shōwa, 'Far from being his personal decision-making powers, therefore, the Emperor's prerogatives were the source of authority for rule by others' (Titus 1974: 15).

Second, the military, which set the pace in developing a 'national defense state' and in determining Japanese foreign policy, not only ignored his opposition to war, it often presented him and the government with the *fait accompli* of war, only perfunctorily reported to him its strategic plans and operations, and frequently withheld information from him.

This last point bears directly on a question that is often asked: how much did the Emperor know about the military's policies and projects? What he could have done about what he knew is a more important issue, but that aside, we are left to speculate concerning the information at his disposal. Whether, and how far, he was fully informed of the 'Rape of Nanking', for instance, was discussed in Chapter 4. But did he know about such other infamous operations as the biological warfare experiments on prisoners of war that were carried out by the army's Unit 731 in Manchuria (Williams and Wallace 1989)?

Probably not. It is true that Unit 731 was established, as an 'epidemic and water supply unit', under the authority of the imperial seal. However, the imperial seal was used to authorize a great many wartime activities of which the Emperor was unaware and it has not been established that he knew of the Unit's true purpose, which is unlikely, given the army's consistent deceitfulness in dealing with him. As Gavan McCormack writes, in an otherwise critical assessment of his career, 'The peculiar tragedy of Hirohito's life was to have been born and raised at the center of a web of deceit', which he continued to experience, and complain about, throughout the early Shōwa period (McCormack 1989: 20).

Third, the Emperor's advisers constrained him in significant ways and on occasion, they, too, deliberately deceived him, as when, in 1931, Prince Saionji told the foreign minister, 'It is not necessary to lie but tell the Emperor things that will please him in order to ease his mind'. Moreover, on other occasions when he wanted to convene an imperial conference with the intention of speaking out against war, his advisers opposed the idea and thereby negated whatever imperial influence for peace he might have applied.

In 1939, Harada Kumao told the new prime minister, Hiranuma,

> It is regrettable to know that no knowledge of His Majesty's intelligence and virtues is being transmitted to the people.... For instance, in politics, it is the wish of the Emperor to respect and guard strictly the spirit of the Constitution, but this cannot be told to the people.... The Emperor's ideas are not at all evident either in politics or diplomacy ...

Harada continued,

> If one should explain that it is the Emperor's desire to conduct a completely constitutional government, it is said that Saionji, Makino, or other immediate officials do what they please behind the scenes by using the name of the Emperor. As a result, the spirit of the Constitution is ignored and matters are conducted in such a way that the Emperor's wishes cannot be conveyed to the people.
>
> (Harada VII 1952: 278–9)

For all Harada's regret, he and other members of the court circle were mostly to blame for failing to communicate the Emperor's political wishes to the public and insofar as their fear of violence caused them to keep him out of controversial situations, the violent incidents of the early 1930s on the part of Shōwa Restoration extremists constituted a fourth, and very significant, 'external constraint' on the court, including the Emperor.

Fear of violent reprisals from the imperial way faction partly explains why he failed to follow through on his pledge to 'cleanse the army' following the suppression of the February 1936 rebellion. Similar fears of a possible coup also figured in his sanction of the decision for war in 1941. Throughout the prewar years of Shōwa, fear of 'riding a boat against the rapids', not only of army power but also of war-inspired popular nationalism, traumatized, and effectively neutralized, the Emperor and his advisers.

Finally, the most important 'external constraint' on the Emperor was the contradictory nature of the Meiji constitution. At best, 'Every constitutional monarchy has an element of ambiguity. In most cases the authority of the monarchy has been eroded in stages over time, so the limits of its power are not entirely clear' (Yamazaki and Kōsaka 1989: 17). This was true of Britain, too. For instance, Harold Nicolson writes of King George V that though he was determined to 'act strictly in accordance with his duties and responsibilities as a Constitutional Monarch', he 'was often driven by the winds and tides of events into these zones of uncertainty, and was obliged to determine, with little more than the stars to guide him, which was the true constitutional course to pursue' (Nicolson 1952: 155).

What made the Meiji constitution especially ambiguous was its provisions for both absolute and limited monarchy, to the point where, in 1932, the American political scientist, Kenneth Colegrove, justifiably preferred to call the Japanese system not a constitutional monarchy but a 'constitutional autocracy' (Colegrove 1932: 642). The Emperor's contradictory powers gave rise to an acute symbolic dissonance whereby the people saw him as an absolute monarch while Japan's political elites paid lipservice to the idea that he was a constitutional monarch. Until, that is, this latter perception was buried once and for all in prewar Shōwa by the 'Minobe incident' of 1935. Thereafter, imperial absolutism became national orthodoxy, not so that the Emperor would actually rule but so that the power of others who ruled in his name would be unassailable.

The confused and uncertain powers which the constitution ascribed to him forced the Shōwa Emperor to improvise in opposing the military and war. To be sure, article LV, which established the principle of ministerial responsibility, entitled him to expect that ministers of state would pay heed to his advice, warning, and encouragement in many areas of national policy. But whether they would do so was never guaranteed and in any case, where his relations with the military were concerned, article XI mattered more because it gave him the right of supreme command. It is this article which prompts the view that he should have been held accountable for failing to control the military, and in particular, the army and navy chief of staff offices.

Yet whether article XI ensured his control of the military was questionable. It, and article XII, which enabled the Emperor to determine the organization and peace standing of the armed forces, were originally meant 'to prevent cabinet intervention in affairs related to military strategy and operations; also to prohibit Diet interference in determining the military strength needed for national defense. They were not framed to provide an institutional base for the Emperor's direction of military affairs' (Banno 1990b: vi).

Regardless of its original purpose, article XI conceivably could still have been used by the Emperor to try and control the military. However, this would have been extremely difficult because 'there was absolutely no provision holding the supreme command responsible to the Tennō for its decisions or vice versa' (Yamamoto 1976: 67). To recall Masuda Tomoko's similar point about article XI, 'there was no clear definition regarding either the scope of the right of supreme command or the person responsible for exercising it'. Thus, the Shōwa Emperor did not know how far he could go in using his supreme command prerogative to control the military. He evidently thought that the chiefs of staff should be responsible to him in the same way as ministers of state were responsible to him for their policies (Yamamoto 1976: 68). But his concept of ministerial responsibility clashed with their political irresponsibility as the chiefs of staff repeatedly usurped his authority.

What does such usurpation signify when it comes to assessing the 'emperor system' in prewar Shōwa Japan? Many Japanese, and a minority of Western, historians have typically 'subsumed all aspects of the modern Japanese state and society under the category of "emperor system", or *tennōsei*, seeing it as the capstone' of power (Jansen 1977: 612). But 'The construct of the emperor-system state ... is of little utility in terms of detailed historical inquiry, for it exaggerates the unity, strength, and rigidity of the Japanese state from 1890 to the nation's defeat' (Garon 1986: 301).

Given the prevalence of 'elite pluralism' and all of the political divisions discussed in Chapter 4, which made prewar Japan anything but totalitarian, if the 'emperor system' means anything, its distinguishing feature was its amorphousness. Takeyama Michio captures this reality when he writes, 'The history of the early Shōwa era demonstrates the absence of control. The government and the military were divided ...' (Takeyama 1984: 61); 'the emperor-system had become nominal and the insubordination of the military had usurped the Emperor's authority' (Takeyama 1984: 62).

To compensate, the Emperor, especially under Kido's guidance, tried to unify the complicated process of national policy-formation, ultimately by sanctioning the government's decisions with the formal imperial will. But to unify in this ritual sense was not to exercise control, and although the imperial institution may have served 'to hinder effective fascist control' (Bix 1982: 5), it could not prevent war. One may say of the Emperor in relation to war as Oka Yoshitake says of Saionji in relation to fascism,

Saionji saw only one sure basis for resistance: the palace. That was the final irony. Only the palace remained firm against the tidal wave of military fascism that seemed to innundate everything else. But it could never become a force in politics. Powerless to save anything but itself, Saionji's last bastion still left him miserably broken.

(Oka 1986: 223)

In sum, the combination of 'exernal constraints' mentioned above make it doubtful that the Emperor could have done more to prevent war. But again, should he have tried to do more, and if so, why did he not do more, to prevent it? It is in pondering this problem that the 'internal constraints' discussed in this book, which arose from his personality, temperament, political style and political beliefs, are important.

The rigid upringing of the emperors in the Heian period was 'hardly designed to encourage the development of a vigorous personality, let alone any determination to challenge the political status quo' (Morris [1964] 1969: 46). Nor had much changed by the Tokugawa period when 'The training of imperial children bred in them habits of docility and rigidly patterned behavior' (Webb 1968: 122). Since rigid courtly precedents of protocol and ritual still obtained during his childhood, it is not surprising that his upbringing left the Shōwa Emperor a passive person who always was inclined to 'play by the rules', as when he performed Shintō rites whose underlying myths he personally rejected, or sanctioned war, despite his private hopes for peace.

This early conditioning to be passive was a long-term 'internal constraint' on his 'ability' to oppose war. Another was his scientific, rational world view as a marine biologist who was most at ease in his laboratory and when collecting specimens in Sagami Bay or elsewhere in Japan. Believing in the 'geometry' and orderly evolution of politics and government, which to him seemed comparable to the ordered and evolutionary patterns of the natural world, he was not the sort of man who could face, and deal effectively with, the reality of violence in domestic political life and foreign policy. His reliance on logical argument, and what Honjō Shigeru observed as his scholarly, almost pedantic, manner, made little impact on military men who subscribed to the different rationality of strategic ends and means and who were set on war.

It should be remembered, however, that although he was a naturalist who respected the sanctity of life, as when he once despaired that an officer had given him a pair of cranes which had been shot for his pleasure (Honjō 1975: 252), he was not a pacifist. Despite his instinctive preference for international cooperation, the Shōwa Emperor was himself a nationalist whose abiding concern with national security ultimately made him susceptible to the argument in late 1941 that, encircled, Japan had to go to war to save itself and its overseas possessions.

This book has also speculated that there were aspects of the Emperor's political style, including in particular his indirection and understatement, which rendered him more passive than assertive in expressing his opposition to war. It was suggested that these tendencies may have reflected certain general features of the political culture of the Japanese aristocracy. This political culture deserves more research than it has so far received but in some respects, as for instance its emphasis on self-control rather than open expression of feelings, it resembles the political culture described by Elias in his study of the court of Louis XIV.

Historically, for example, the oracular reputation of Japanese monarchs, based on their sacerdotal function and religious authority, may have made it possible for them to communicate their wishes largely through inference and understatement, to courtiers whose aristocratic training made them receptive to the import of subtle gesture. Elias, who sees similar patterns of aristocratic communication in France as aspects of a certain 'court rationality', describes communication at the French court in terms of Gratian's maxim, as follows:

> The substance is not enough, circumstance also is needed. A poor manner spoils everything, disfigures even justice and reason. A fine manner, by contrast, adds to everything; it gilds a refusal, softens the bitterness that lies in truth, smooths the wrinkles of age. The 'how' does much in all matters ...
>
> (Elias 1983: 109, note 42)

There existed at the Shōwa court a similar emphasis on 'a fine manner' which led the Emperor to rely upon questions to 'gild a refusal' and 'soften the bitterness that lies in truth' when indirectly registering his dismay over war plans put forward by Japan's military leaders. But, as mentioned, the 'court rationality' arising from this political style conflicted with the military rationality of his interlocutors, who dismissed it as archaic and irrelevant when analyzing what was required to protect Japan's national interests.

Another feature of aristocratic political culture in Japan which possibly impinged on the Emperor's 'ability' to oppose war is the ancient Chinese emphasis, translated into Japan, on the normative 'non-assertion' of monarchy. Herschel Webb quotes Han Fei Tzu as having written in the third century BC: 'The sceptre should not be shown. For its inner nature is non-assertion'. The sage-king merely 'remains empty' and relies on his ministers to govern: 'If the ruler has to exert any special skill of his own, it means that affairs are not going right'. Webb comments that in Japan, 'The *ideal* of non-assertion remained influential' (Webb 1968: 157, italics Webb's).

To the extent that it influenced the Shōwa court, then this ideal helps to explain the Emperor's passive political style. And insofar as the Shōwa court was influenced by the ancient Japanese tradition in which emperors primarily used their religious authority to legitimize the secular power and policies of others, this tradition, too, informed his scrupulous sanctioning of policies, including those that led to aggression and war.

A final characteristic of the modern Japanese aristocracy which throws light on the Emperor's political passivity was a fundamental ambivalence towards political power. This was true of Saionji and even more of Prince Konoe Fumimaro, who, unlike Kido Kōichi and others comprising the new 'merit' aristocracy, traced their lineages back across the centuries, yet were nervous about having and using power.

Saionji once said, 'I don't go against the trend of the times and I don't follow it' (Oka 1986: 82). Consequently, when he 'came to imposing his will on others, he was very disinclined to do so and this made him appear rather passive' (Oka 1986: 182). As for Konoe, who often considered resigning whenever serious problems arose, when once asked by Harada Kumao to make himself available as prime minister, Konoe said bluntly, 'I do not want the job' (Oka 1983: 43). When pressed to become head of the Imperial Rule Assistance Association, he at first hesitated, remarking in 1938, 'I don't have the courage to lead a new party and I know that it would be chaos if I accepted the job' (Oka 1983: 93). After Japan's defeat in 1945, he reflected on his insecurity and weakness of will, stating, 'I am a child of fate . . . I have been surrounded by rightists and leftists and those in between . . . no, I have allowed them to surround me and that is what has brought this fate upon me. It is my own fault' (Oka 1983: 190).

The Shōwa Emperor would have understood and sympathized with Saionji and Konoe. That he relied heavily upon Saionji for advice was due to his own lack of confidence. That he repeatedly worried whether Konoe would stand by his side in adversity likewise attests to his own fear of standing alone. Whether he thought of himself as lacking inner strength is unknown but others certainly did. His father-in-law once told the Empress: 'The Emperor is weak-willed, so it is necessary for the Empress to help him from behind the scenes. You must be strong . . .' (Kojima II 1981: 58).

Perhaps the Emperor unconsciously used his constitutional scruples to disguise his inability to stand up to the military. Be that as it may, a major theme in this study has been the importance he consistently attached to upholding the example of Emperor Meiji as a constitutional monarch. The late Edwin Reischauer wrote in 1975, 'Since the present Emperor has always been a conscientious Constitutional monarch, it really is not proper to inquire what his own particular views may have been, even under the old system' (Reischauer 1975: 10). However, precisely because the Emperor so diligently operated as a constitutional monarch, it is absolutely essential 'to inquire what his own particular views may have been', if we wish to understand how, more than any other, this 'internal constraint' led him to tie his own hands politically even while others tied them.

'World history gives us many examples of rulers who sought to expand their own power, but very few have approved of limiting their own authority' (Kawahara 1990: 67). Kaiser Wilhelm II epitomizes the former. He once told a group of German admirals, 'All of you know nothing; I alone know something, I alone decide'. In 1891, he also told the Prince of Wales, 'I am the sole master of German policy and my country must follow me wherever I go' (Röhl 1982: 29). The Kaiser, of course, was famous for exaggerating his role. But he was undeniably significant in plunging Germany and the whole of Europe into World War I (Kennedy 1982).

By contrast, the Shōwa Emperor was one of the 'very few' sovereigns who, for reasons of political conviction, made it a point to operate strictly as a limited monarch. The sources of this determination were discussed in Chapter 1. Sugiura Shigetake encouraged him to respect the principles of constitutional monarchy in emulation of Meiji. Later, after observing for himself the theory and practice of constitutional monarchy in Britain during his tour of Europe in 1921, the then Crown Prince 'conceived his own role as that of a constitutional monarch in the British mould, automatically sanctioning any bill approved by the cabinet', with King George V as his model (Ueyama *et al.* 1989: 47).

This stance was in turn greatly reinforced by Saionji and his circle of constitutional monarchists who advised him during the Taishō regency and thereafter, well into the 1930s. Under their influence, he especially 'refrained from exercising the prerogative of supreme command ... Deferring to parliamentary democracy based on constitutional government, he did not take the initiative' (Takeyama 1984: 62). Finally, through these advisers, and directly when Minobe Tatsukichi lectured at the palace, Minobe further strengthened the Emperor's resolve to function as a constitutional monarch with limited powers. The Emperor may not have followed Minobe's constitutional interpretation in every detail. But he firmly embraced Minobe's concept of the emperor as an 'organ' of the state.

He thus insisted on the rule of law, the principle of ministerial responsibility, and the need at all costs to avoid what he often referred to as 'the bane of despotism'. There is no question that 'In his own interpretation of the Constitution, the Emperor at all times acted constitutionally and it would have been out of character and contrary to his convictions about the rule of law to do otherwise' (Sheldon 1976: 38).

At times, in crisis situations, he acted and spoke as if he saw the possibility of using the absolute powers ascribed to him in the Meiji constitution to defend constitutional government, as when he reacted strongly to the exceptional political crisis of the February 1936 army insurrection. Furthermore, it will be recalled that during the Changkufeng crisis, he declared to the war minister and the army chief of staff, 'you may not move one soldier *without my command*'. And, when reflecting on the decision for war in 1941, he said in 1946, 'If at the time *I had suppressed* the advocacy of war' the public would have been incensed and a coup might have taken place. These statements suggest a more assertive model of imperial action.

Nevertheless, he deliberately rejected this model and instead virtually 'absolutized' the model of constitutional monarchy as he understood it (Yamamoto 1989: 19). Thus, after dismissing Tanaka Giichi in 1929, and after helping to suppress the 1936 army rebellion, he worried that he had gone too far as a constitutional monarch. If anything, his determination to uphold his limited powers grew all the more as other elites sought to exploit his absolute powers in declaring the imperial will. He believed that

> As the symbol of the unity of the nation, he must not divide the nation by opposing policies which represented the combined wisdom of his constitutionally responsible ministers of state. He might not personally feel that those policies were correct or necessary; yet, if he were so advised by the cabinet and the Supreme Command, his duty would be clear and incontrovertible. The will of the state must be the will of the Emperor.
>
> (Butow [1954] 1967: 230)

After Japan's defeat, Prince Konoe regretted that the Emperor had not boldly challenged the military:

> Out of reserve, the Emperor seldom expresses his own views. Prince Saionji and Count Makino taught His Majesty not to take the initiative, in adherence to the British-style constitution, but the Japanese Constitution exists on the premise of the Emperor's personal administration.

The Emperor, Konoe complained, should have asserted his prerogative of supreme command to control the military. He concluded, 'If the Emperor merely gives encouragement or advice as in England, military affairs and political diplomacy cannot advance in unison' (Sheldon 1976: 37–8).

Konoe had exposed the contradictory nature of Japan's 'constitutional autocracy' but his criticism of the Emperor was self-serving. Konoe himself blocked the Emperor when he wanted to take the initiative: for example, when he told the Emperor not to speak at the crucial imperial conference of 11 January 1938, which ratified the decision to 'annihilate' the enemy in China. In fact, knowing of the Emperor's constitutional scruples, Konoe deliberately used the principle, that a constitutional monarch should not interfere with government policy, to prevent him from openly opposing all-out war in China. Kido, too, neutralized the Emperor politically in this way. When testifying on trial after the war, he said, 'I used to counsel the Emperor to approve [policy], trusting the government in accordance with constitutional government' (Maxon [1957] 1975: 159).

In his study of King George V, Harold Nicolson asks, 'Can any public issue arise therefore in which the King has to exercise personal initiative or reach an independent decision?' (Nicolson 1952: 165). This very question concerned the King. Replying to the view of Prime Minister Asquith that the monarch must always accept the advice of his ministers, the King stated in a letter, dated 22 September 1913:

> Fully accepting this proposition, I nevertheless cannot shut my eyes to the fact that ... the people will, rightly or wrongly, associate me with whatever policy is adopted by my advisers, dispensing praise or blame accordingly as that policy is in agreement or antagonistic to their own opinions.
>
> (Nicolson 1952: 302)

Regarding his prerogative to change his advisers, he asked, pointedly, 'Should the Sovereign *never* assert that right?' (Nicolson 1952: 302; italics the King's).

The Shōwa Emperor was too much of a strict constructionist in interpreting his constitutional role to be deflected by this kind of question. He 'was actually downright stubborn in his observance of the Constitution' (Miura and Yamamoto 1989: 12). Accordingly, he refused on 14 January 1938 to see the army chief of staff, Prince Kan'in, even though he knew that Kan'in shared his own opposition to the Konoe cabinet's pro-war stance on China. Of Kan'in's intentions, he said, 'I judged that this might surely be a plan to overturn what had already been determined [by the government] and I refused to see him'.

The same consideration convinced him that he had no choice as a constitutional monarch but to sanction the decision for war in 1941. There is thus a certain validity in Kamishima Jirō's remark, 'It is probably correct to say that he conducted himself generally in accordance with the "organ theory" ' and that 'on that account, the war broke out' in December 1941 (*Shōwa nihonshi* Supplement I 1987: 33). Ironically, however, his sanction served perfectly the interests of the militarists and it mattered little that he sanctioned war thinking that this was required of him as a constitutional monarch while to them he sanctioned it as an absolute monarch who, a god himself, spoke for the gods in commanding the destiny of imperial Japan.

After Japan attacked Pearl Harbor the Emperor, as 'manifest deity', was used by the government to sponsor Japan's 'holy war' and encourage the people in hard times. Yet his own constitutionalism still led him to support General Tōjō Hideki's leadership even after the war went badly for Japan and a 'peace party' had emerged, for he believed that it would be improper for a constitutional monarch to depose a prime minister, as he had once deposed Tanaka. And when he intervened to end the war in August 1945, he did so only at the request of the prime minister, after the government had reached a complete impasse in debating whether to carry on with a lost cause. His intervention was critical in ending the war but even at that point, 'the Emperor was only the instrument and not the prime mover, of Japan's momentous decision' to surrender (Butow [1954] 1967: 232).

Looking back on the prewar years of Shōwa,

> Should the Emperor have betrayed his own principles of Constitutional monarchy, which also served to preserve the Imperial institution by putting it, at least publicly, above politics? Should he have taken an inflexible stand, and suffered the consequences, including the probable assassination of his most trusted advisers, and his own captivity, or at least the loss of what freedom he had to influence politics?
>
> (Sheldon 1978: 35)

The Emperor's consistent and principled adherence to constitutional monarchy was his strongest point and in modern times it would be strange indeed to criticize any sovereign for not acting in effect despotically. Also, if it takes a despotic intervention to avert the crisis of war, the crisis has probably already passed the point of no return in any case. All the same, however, in view of the terrible consequences of war fought in the Emperor's name, there is a strong case that, whatever the risks, he ought to have subordinated his constitutional principles to expediency, on the chance that a dramatic refusal to sanction war might have caused those who favored war to think twice.

The last chance to intervene with any hope of success was in the early stages of the Sino-Japanese War when there existed the potential, however slim, for mobilizing the caution of the army general staff to challenge the belligerent policy of Prime Minister Konoe and the generals who supported it. That the chance was missed made this arguably the darkest episode in the Emperor's career.

By late 1941, it was simply too late to intervene for peace with the United States and its allies, given that there was too much of a broad consensus on the part of military and civilian leaders that Western sanctions made war absolutely necessary. A failed imperial intervention for peace in 1941 might have ennobled him in the tradition of fallen heroes, which Ivan Morris has characterized as 'the nobility of failure' in Japanese history (Morris [1975] 1980). But few men and women in history are cut out to be heroes and the Shōwa Emperor was not one of them.

The Emperor sanctioned war, but to conclude, this study confirms that 'Hirohito was neither the bloodthirsty tyrant that David Bergamini has described, nor the reckless reactionary depicted by Inoue Kiyoshi' (Shillony 1981: 41). Nor was he Edward Behr's devious sovereign who turned a blind eye to aggression while cleverly contriving to let others take responsibility for war. Rather, he exemplified what is more commonly found in history, major figures who, politically, were 'mediocre rather than great' (Elias 1983: 126). In the last analysis, the Shōwa Emperor was the unwilling symbol, not the maker, of chaos and catastrophe.

BEYOND WAR: THE LEGACY OF SHŌWA

Over the years, many Japanese have insisted that although it is hard to prove the Emperor's political responsibility for war, except in the formal sense that he sanctioned war, his moral responsibility for war is beyond question. But whether they think the Emperor's war responsibility was moral or political, or both, for some Japanese, this question has been subsumed into the more basic and complex issue of whether the Japanese people as a whole were also historically responsible for war.[1]

For example, rejecting the idea that the Emperor should be made a scapegoat, Nishibe Susumu wrote in 1989, 'We must ask how the Japanese people could possibly demand that the Emperor take responsibility for a war that they themselves supported, or at best did nothing to prevent'. Whereas the Emperor had been preoccupied with the tragedy of the war, the Japanese people had mostly forgotten it. They 'should be the last ones to point a finger at the Emperor' (Nishibe 1989: 24).

Sakamoto Yoshikazu similarly argues,

> the responsibility for the atrocities committed by the Japanese Imperial Army against the people of the Allied Powers during the last war cannot be borne, even in part, by the Emperor: it should be borne by the Japanese people as a whole.
>
> (Sakamoto 1989: 12)

Yet, Sakamoto insists, 'But to say that everybody is responsible amounts, for all practical purposes, to saying that nobody is responsible. By absolving the Emperor of war responsibility one absolves oneself, and vice versa' (Sakamoto 1989: 12).

In this perception, the Emperor's exemption from trial as a war criminal, which allowed him to escape his war responsibility, also permitted the Japanese people to escape their own historical accountability for war. His escape recalls how Kaiser Wilhelm II evaded judgment by abdicating and fleeing to the Netherlands after World War I, where he lived until 1941. However, as important a parallel with the Kaiser is the Japanese people's abdication of their war responsibility, which they have never fully confronted, and may never confront, now that the Shōwa era is over.

The contrast with Germany since World War II is revealing. The German people appear less self-conscious today when singing their national anthem and displaying their flag, perhaps because they have dealt more openly and honestly with their prewar and wartime history. But in Japan, where, in April 1990 the ministry of education at last made it mandatory for schools to display the flag and sing 'Kimi ga yo' on important occasions in the school calendar, many Japanese refuse to do so, because these imperial sub-symbols represent the unresolved issue of collective responsibility for war.[2] In Germany, the ghost of the past has been at least partly exorcized. In Japan, it has generally been ignored.

Where historians are concerned, however, their preoccupation with the particular question of the Emperor's war responsibility, though justifiable in view of its undeniable interpretative importance, has prevented them, first, from thoroughly researching the Emperor and Shōwa Japan since 1945 and, second, from reflecting more broadly on significant patterns of continuity and change in the long sweep of prewar and postwar Shōwa history. The following brief summary of themes in this book's discussion of the 1945–1989 period therefore goes beyond the issue of war responsibility in speculating about the historical evolution of the imperial institution throughout the Shōwa era.

During the Occupation, the Emperor's public association with early Shōwa authoritarianism and war made it hard to believe that his retention on the throne augured well for democracy in postwar Japan. And in truth, it might have been to Japan's advantage had he been permitted to abdicate, as he wished, for had a new reign begun, Japan's immediate postwar transition to democracy would have been less encumbered by a violent and authoritarian past.

Nevertheless, he survived the war, if only because it suited the Occupation authorities, and in a century that has witnessed the collapse of many monarchies around the world, his political survival illustrates that 'the less politically significant a monarch, the better his chances of survival; the more politically active a monarch, the less chance that his throne will survive' (Rose and Kavanagh 1976: 567). For, under the 1947 constitution, which made the Diet 'the highest organ of state power' (article forty-one), he was reduced as a 'symbol emperor' to the purely ceremonial role that Prime Minister Hara had wished for the monarchy in the Taishō period.

However, the Emperor's divorce from government notwithstanding, he contributed to three long-term developments since 1945, as shown in

Chapters 6–8. First, now eager to reign unequivocally as a constitutional monarch, he actively assisted the adaptation of the imperial institution to democracy. In particular, he endorsed the process of constitutional revision that led to the 1947 constitution and he helped to demystify the monarchy, by publicly renouncing his so-called 'divinity' in 1946 and by bringing the monarchy into a closer relationship with the people during his postwar domestic tours. Democratic political practice in Japan since 1945 has been seriously flawed by elitism, corruption and the negative effects of sustained one-party rule. But Japan's postwar political system is incomparably more pluralistic than in the past and to the extent that the Shōwa Emperor participated in its evolution, this was a significant contribution.

Second, by exhorting the nation to strive for economic growth, and by publicly representing the achievement of prosperity, as when he opened the 1964 Tokyo Olympics, the Emperor broadly participated in the rise of Japan as the economic superpower it is today. The 'price of affluence' in the continuing 'age of economism' has been high: the pollution of the environment in Japan and offshore where Japanese industries were established in Asia, insensitivity on the part of the materialistic 'new middle mass' to social problems, and trade conflict with the West, especially the United States. Yet, Japan's rapid postwar recovery and subsequent economic development is manifestly the most significant aspect of postwar Shōwa history in which the Emperor was involved, albeit indirectly, as a proponent of Japanese capitalism.

Third, and relatedly, he played an important part in generally encouraging Japan's political and military, as well as econonic, cooperation with the United States, not only by fostering Japanese–American goodwill during his 1975 American tour but by accentuating the importance to Japan of the American alliance. This was a natural priority for him, given his life-long plea for international cooperation with the Anglo-American powers, his personal opposition to war with them, and his sympathy with their Cold War aversion to communism. Whether, as it evolved, the American alliance was a positive force in Asian affairs has been questioned by those who believe that it led to the exploitation of many countries in the region. Whether, too, Japan's steady rearmament over the years is good for Japan, for the United States, or indeed for anyone else, may also be questioned. But it is certain that the alliance assisted Japan's reintegration into the world community after World War II, which is exactly what the Emperor wished to see happen even if he himself had little directly to do with the political history of its development.

By associating the imperial institution with these political, economic, and military developments after the war, the Shōwa Emperor 'served as a metaphor of change for the Japanese nation' (Coaldrake 1989: 29). In this, he reflected the fact that, historically, a major function of monarchy is 'to legitimize change; it conceals or at least makes easier for the nation as a whole to accept measures of a fundamental nature' in the direction of change (Thompson and Mejia 1971: 17).

However, it is no less true that a monarchy may function to block, or delay the pace, and limit the scope, of change by serving as the rallying point for conservatives who fundamentally resent democratization (Rose and Kavanagh 1976: 79). Accordingly, it is suggested here that the dual capacity of monarchy symbolically to promote and yet resist change characterized the political role of the Emperor and of the imperial institution in Shōwa history since 1945 and constitutes the principal long-term legacy of Shōwa to Japan in the Heisei era and beyond. To further clarify this legacy requires a brief discussion of the dynamics of secularization in the evolution of Japanese 'civil religion',[3] beginning with earlier developments for the sake of a broad historical perspective.

In an insightful essay on interwar Japan, Bernard Silberman states that 'the role of the Imperial will as the condition of secular society in Japan suggests the validity of the concept of ... civil religion', as applied to the 1920s and 1930s (Silberman 1974: 453). He traces the growing 'secular conception of economic relationships', the 'primacy of secular values' in Japanese thought, and the corresponding ascendancy of bureaucratic 'legal-rationality' in the interwar years to the historical 'breakdown of consensus about the natural character of authority and social behavior' (Silberman 1974: 451).

Ironically, Silberman explains, the Meiji leaders had contributed to this breakdown. After overthrowing the Tokugawa regime, which had justified its power on Confucian perceptions of the natural order

[they] could not claim that the new government represented the true natural order of politics. In their appeal to the Imperial will they had implicitly argued that there was no natural order, only a natural commitment to Imperial will that superseded all existing political and social relationships.

(Silberman 1974: 451)

The result in interwar Japan was a basic tension between 'a secular conception and a view of society in which no behavior was exempted from the claims of Imperial will by virtue of its natural morality' (Silberman 1974: 445). This latter view, which the Meiji leaders and their successors in effect substituted for the defunct Tokugawa view of natural order, in order to legitimate state power, comprised the basis of the 'civil religion of nationalism', to recall Coleman's phrase. What is more, if 'secularization is the decline of community' in that the concept of 'society', which 'ceases to depend on supernatural concepts', supersedes the concept of community based on religious 'taboos and prescriptions, legitimated by reference to supernatural order' (Wilson B. 1976: 265–6, 267), then the invented civil religion of interwar Japan was fundamentally a reaction to secularism. Hence, well before World War II, the 'Japanese state had been not merely a secular entity. It had been a sacred church as well ...' (Holtom 1947: 176).

In the 1930s this civil religion, pivoting on the *tennō* as the ultimate symbol of community, became increasingly coercive, to eradicate sectarian interest and political dissent of whatever kind. Its insistence on communitarian values reflecting the orthodoxy of emperorism also compensated for the growing disjunction between the agrarian myths of State Shintō and the reality of social change that had attended economic development. In Gluck's account, 'Between 1910 and 1935 the proportion of gainfully employed workers in the industrial and service sectors of the economy increased steadily, and the urban population doubled, until 30.8 per cent were living in cities of over 50,000' (Gluck 1985: 282). The crisis of total war, from 1941 to 1945, only papered over this and other disjunctions as the civil religion of Japanese nationalism reached its frenzied extremes.

During the Occupation, however, the postwar disestablishment of State Shintō and the constitutional separation of church and state dismantled the 'sacred church' of civil religion and removed the imperial will as the 'condition of secular society'. One writer sees this as a crucial transition from 'latent' secularization in prewar to 'manifest' secularization in postwar Japan, defining political secularization as a process of 'desacralization' in which 'Political authority has ceased being an agency representing the supernatural, and the legitimate authority of state power has become based upon law, such as a Constitution, instead of depending on religious sanction' (Nakano 1987: 124). Because it produced 'a radical change in the religious meaning the state used to have', 'the new Constitution of Japan became the source of law and authority, so that Japan for the first time became a constitutional country in the modern sense of the word' (Nakano 1987: 133).

The postwar separation of church and state left the Japanese monarch more of a secular sovereign than his counterpart in British civil religion who, during the official coronation ceremony, receives the crown from the Archbishop of Canterbury while also taking possession of St Edward's staff, and the sceptre with the cross, along with the other royal regalia which mark him or her as 'Defender of the Faith' (Nicolson 1952: 201–2). But since in prewar and wartime Shōwa the formal imperial will had been declared by others without regard to his personal will, and since he himself had never believed in the myths propagated by State Shintō, the Shōwa Emperor had little difficulty in accepting these secular changes. Nor did most Japanese, as they adjusted to a new postwar political settlement which placed sovereignty in their hands. Indeed, 'The enthusiasm with which many Japanese abandoned *kokutai* for democracy in the short space of several months suggests, among other things, that prewar ideology [e.g. emperorism] had overreached itself' (Gluck 1985: 284).

Significantly, the political secularization of the imperial institution foreshadowed the deepening social secularization of postwar Japan, typified, for instance, by the primacy of the rule of law, the economic rationality of the marketplace, the pursuit of science which the Emperor personified in his published research, a meritocratic emphasis on education as the ladder of success, and the growing sophistication of a large reading and travelling public who, through the acquisition of knowledge about the wider world, grew increasingly skeptical of official orthodoxies. This picture should not be overdrawn of course.[4] Nonetheless, in comparison with prewar Shōwa, the far greater levels of industrialization, urbanization, and overall prosperity helped to make postwar Japanese society far more secular.

However, politically, 'authority exercised in the name of the people' is subject to the 'ever-recurring paradox between elitism and populism' (Bendix [1978] 1980: 599), and postwar Japan was no exception. The political secularization of the monarchy and other postwar democratic reforms were anathema to conservative Japanese for whom the myths of State Shintō and the mystical concept of *kokutai* had been the essence of the state and of Japanese national identity. Thus, successive Liberal Democratic Party governments undertook to restore the imperial sub-symbols of the past in hopes of gradually reconstituting significant elements of the former 'civil religion of nationalism'.

As in prewar Japan, the wide ranging neo-nationalist initiatives discussed in Chapters 6–8 represented a reaction to the 'loss of community' engendered by social secularization. Amid the impersonality, materialism, and egotism of 'economism', the proponents of neo-nationalism therefore played to latent popular nostalgia for the idealized values of communal solidarity which were believed to have existed in the past. Since this nostalgia found a ready focus in the imperial house, the orchestrated neo-nationalist campaign to revive such symbols as Yasukuni Shrine invariably threatened to accentuate the conservative, at the expense of the progressive, functions of the imperial institution. Richard Rose and Dennis Kavanagh observe, concerning monarchy in general, 'If anything, it appears that a reigning monarch is expected to be a symbol of a morality that is being abandoned, setting a standard for admiration because such behavior is rarely found in the workaday world' (Rose and Kavanagh 1976: 565). This is pretty much what neo-nationalists expected of the 'symbol emperor'.

As a means of arousing a national consciousness both befitting an economic superpower and necessary to protect Japanese national interests at a time of mounting strain in foreign relations, their monarchical revivalism peaked during the tenure of the Nakasone cabinet in the early 1980s. Yet, as they had been all along in postwar Shōwa, the 'new middle mass' were indifferent to the imperial institution and to the Shōwa Emperor, whom they probably regarded by then as a 'superannuated symbol', as Thomas Carlyle once characterized King George IV (Firth 1973: 90). Consequently, the government's emperor-centered neo-nationalism never elicited the anticipated popular response in postwar Shōwa.

Even so, despite this public apathy, the government had managed over the postwar Shōwa decades partially and incrementally to reconstitute aspects of 'civil religion' in Japan, as with the restoration of Kigensetsu, the legalization of era names, the promotion of Yasukuni Shrine, the thin distinction between private court Shintō rituals and secular state services such as occurred at the Shōwa Emperor's funeral, and, more recently, the use of the flag and 'Kimi ga yo' in schools. Consequently, 'religious legitimation of political power still does have some effects' in Japan today, however indirect they may be (Nakano 1987: 137). This is why, in some quarters, the imperial house 'continues to excite controversy ... on a far deeper and more divisive level than would be the case for such ostensible equivalents as the British royal family' (Napier 1989: 71).

Echoing this controversy overseas, Bob Tadashi Wakabayashi has recently asked, 'can anyone categorically state that an imperial comeback – in some form or other – is totally impossible?' (Wakabayashi 1991: 57). This question, which is part of the Shōwa legacy to the future, could conceivably turn out to be more important than it is now, especially if the further development of Japanese wealth, power and influence in world affairs meets with greater resistance than at present, provoking a sense of isolation and crisis in Japan. Robert Bocock states, 'no doubt if there were a national crisis, the symbolism of the monarchy would re-emerge as one of the major symbols of English nationalism' (Bocock 1974: 106). Given its adaptability in the past, and depending upon how it is used politically, the imperial institution has the similar potential to symbolize a resurgent Japanese nationalism in the future far more than it did in postwar Shōwa.

Yet, it is as generally true in modern Japanese history as in modern British history that, as David Cannadine writes, the invention of monarchical tradition connotes 'not so much the re-opening of the theatre of power as the premiere of the cavalcade of impotence' (Cannadine 1985: 121). Seen in this light, rather than achieving an imperial 'comeback' redolent of prewar Shōwa, it is more probable that as it continues its postwar evolution along British lines, the imperial institution will have as its primary function in the Heisei era simply that of 'a tradition-maintenance service' (Miura and Yamamoto 1989: 14), preserving ornamental traditions in Japanese political life that are increasingly obsolescent.[5] Its relevance to democracy is more contested than in Britain. But, 'Ultimately, the question of whether democracy is to be practiced in Japan does not depend on whether the Emperor system continues to exist; it depends entirely on the will of the people' (Takeyama 1964: 26).

Notes

INTRODUCTION

1 The sacred sword itself was housed in the Atsuta Grand Shrine and the jewel, in the imperial palace sanctuary. The third part of the regalia, the sacred mirror, was housed in Ise Grand Shrine; a replica never left the imperial palace sanctuary.

2 'Shōwa' is often translated as 'enlightened peace.' But 'illustrious peace' is used here, to better distinguish it from the translation for 'Meiji', the reign name of Hirohito's grandfather, which is usually rendered in English as 'enlightened rule'. The term, 'Shōwa', selected by the privy council in an emergency meeting soon after the Taishō Emperor died, was an adaptation of a passage from the Chinese *Shu Ching*, or Book of History, which reads, 'The hundred clans are *illustrious*, the ten thousand nations are in *harmony*' (Kawahara 1990: 45, italics Kawahara's). Note that 'Taishō' signified 'great justice'.

3 The *daijōsai* was preceded by the *sokui-rei*, a ceremony in which the emperor appeared in his first official audience. There is a throne in Japan, the *takamikura*, used in the *sokui-rei* ceremony. But because the Japanese sovereigns do not otherwise use a throne, the terms 'throne' and 'enthronement' are best used metaphorically.

4 The books by Inoue, Bergamini, and Behr have been widely criticized for seriously distorting evidence in portraying the Shōwa Emperor. Sheldon's critique is the most revealing on Inoue (Sheldon 1978). Of the many equally negative reactions to Bergamini's work, James Crowley's is especially recommended (Crowley 1971). The main problem with Behr's study, apart from the fact that because he does not read Japanese, he had to rely on a team of Japanese researchers whose use of sources was highly selective, is its over-reliance on inference (Large 1991b).

5 Even Japanese historians who are critical of the Shōwa Emperor have attested to the reliability of this evidence (Sheldon 1976: 2, footnote 3).

6 As found in the *Kojiki* (Record of Ancient Matters, compiled in 712) and the *Nihongi* (History of Japan, compiled in 720).

7 W.G. Beasley's study of this movement and its outcome is especially recommended (Beasley 1972).

8 The phrase is suggested by Eric Hobsbawm. Broadly, it refers to the 'formalization' and 'ritualization' of values and institutions to achieve the legitimation of power and authority (Hobsbawm 1985). David Cannadine has written an intriguing essay on 'invented tradition' in the evolution of the British monarchy from 1820 to 1977 (Cannadine 1985).

9 The following quotations from the constitution and the edict of promulgation are from *Meiji Japan Through Contemporary Sources*, Vol. 1 (Center for East Asian Cultural Studies 1969).

10   The reign of my Lord,
      A thousand ages, eight
      thousand ages;
      So long that a tiny pebble
      Will grow into a rock
      All covered with moss

                    (first verse; Malm 1971: 264)

11 Taishō also ranked first, with 289 votes, in a 1924 poll of 1,439 women workers at the Tokyo Muslin enterprise who were asked a similar question (Nakamura M. 1986: 130).

12 Note that the term, '*tennō*', literally, 'heavenly sovereign', dates from the sixth or seventh century. '*Heika*' (His Majesty) or '*tennō heika*' (His Majesty the Emperor) are commonly used to refer to the emperor (Ueyama *et al.* 1989: 48). His sole name, his given name, is seldom used, nor is it the practice in Japan to use nicknames for him. Another term, '*kōtei*', is commonly used in Japanese to refer to the monarchs of other countries.

1 THE MAKING OF THE SHŌWA EMPEROR

1   Sadako appears to have favored Chichibu, perhaps because he was more outgoing and expressive (Hane 1982: 51).
2   Fushimi was the heir to a distinguished cadet branch of the imperial family; his daughter was the wife of the Shōwa Empress's brother. Shillony provides concise information on the composition of the imperial family (Shillony 1981: 38–9 and footnote 88, p. 187).
3   In the late nineteenth and early twentieth centuries, busts of Lincoln, Napoleon, and Darwin were commonly kept in many private libraries in England and in America, too.
4   The foreign ministry kept a detailed official record of the tour (Gaimushō 1969: 757–81). Popular magazines also devoted special issues, complete with maps and photographs, to the tour. A good example is *Fujin gahō* [Ladies Graphic], published in September 1921.
5   Note that Shikama Kōsuke, whose diary is the basis of this narrative, was the naval aide-de-camp.
6   The others were the Princesses Hisa-no-miya Sachiko (10 September 1927), Taka-no-miya Kakuzo (30 September 1929), and Yori-no-miya Atsuko (7 March 1931). After Akihito, the Empress gave birth to Prince Yoshi-no-miya Masuhito (or Hitachi, 28 November 1935) and Princess Suga-no-miya Takako (2 March 1939). Princess Shigeko died in 1961, Princess Sachiko in 1928.
7   Saionji departed from this pattern for several years in the early 1920s when he recommended the formation of 'transcendental' or non-party cabinets in order to stabilize the volatile political situation which prevailed after Hara's assassination.

2 JAPANESE AGGRESSION AND THE LIMITS OF IMPERIAL INFLUENCE, 1926–1933

1   Tanaka died shortly thereafter of heart failure, a disappointed man.
2   Note that the Mayer-Oakes book is a reliable English translation of volume I of the Harada papers dealing with the London Naval Treaty controversy.
3   The point that, by promoting these men the court sought to appease the army politically, calls into question Behr's unfounded implication that the court promoted them because it approved their actions in the Manchurian incident (Behr 1989: 126–7).

4 'Arbitrary decision and execution' in reacting flexibly to the exigencies of combat (Shimada 1984: 243).

5 The Emperor later composed a poem of tribute to Shirakawa for limiting the fighting at Shanghai but it was kept secret because the chief aide-de-camp, Honjō Shigeru, believed it would offend the army (Kido I 1966: 542). Kawahara observes that in the poem the Emperor 'had praised Shirakawa's bravery in *avoiding* war, not *waging* it' (Kawahara 1990: 58, italics Kawahara's).

6 Two rather vague exceptions, both addressed to Japanese troops, were an 'imperial instruction' (*chokuyu*) and an imperial rescript, dated 4 January and 8 January 1932 respectively, which, while praising the soldiers' martial spirit, emphasized the theme of their loyalty to the Emperor in a general manner intended to encourage their obedience to his authority (Murakami S. 1983: 272–3).

7 The Emperor had discussed the problems of the League and Jehol with Army Chief Kan'in on 26 January and had stated his view that if Japan were to fight in Jehol, this would jeopardize 'all of the success we have accomplished so far', by which he meant the avoidance of further trouble with the League. In another exchange that day, with Uchida, who foreshadowed that Japan might have to withdraw from the League, the Emperor asked where this would leave the mandated islands under Japan's control. Uchida's vague reply caused him to lose confidence in the foreign minister (Kido I 1966: 215–16).

8 At one stage when Araki watered down a palace draft the Emperor told him, 'That is not what I mean. I mean there must be no further changes in the imperial rescript in cabinet meetings' (Kido I 1966: 229). However, this directive was ignored (Sheldon 1976: 8–9).

3 THE CHALLENGE OF SHŌWA RESTORATION RADICALISM, 1931–1937

1 The 1932 Theses contained the first systematic analysis of the 'emperor system' as such. Germaine Hoston has provided the best discussion in English of different prewar Japanese interpretations of the '*tennōsei*' (Hoston 1986: 179–222).

2 Income from the imperial estate, which included 3,226,388 acres in 1940, is estimated at nine million yen. The Emperor's capital investments, managed along with his estate by the imperial household ministry, stood at about fifteen million yen. In addition, he received 4,500,000 yen annually from the national treasury (Titus 1974 : 66–8).

3 The standard biography of Kita in English is by George Wilson (1969).

4 In 1946 the Emperor recalled this conversation, albeit with some confusion, as follows: 'Was it Honjō . . . ? He called me a god, so I told him I am not a god, because the structure of my body is no different than that of a normal human being. I continued to tell him that it is a nuisance to be called such' (STDH 1990: 104).

5 Inoue Kiyoshi misleadingly suggests that the Emperor agreed with the government's final condemnation of the organ theory (Inoue 1975: 46–7). Charles Sheldon has shown how Inoue's determination to argue that the Emperor assisted fascism led him to misrepresent, or omit, key passages in the Honjō diary and the Harada papers (Sheldon 1978: 16–17).

6 This summary of incidents is based on Ivan Morris' account (Morris 1960: 431–4).

7 The recently-published diary of the chamberlain, Irie Sukemasa, contains a dramatic account of the rebellion (Irie I 1990: 54–7).

8 Another unfounded claim concerning the Emperor and the 1936 army rebellion is that he deliberately allowed the uprising to take place so that in suppressing it he could purge Araki and Mazaki while eliminating the imperial way faction (Bergamini 1971: 621). He indeed wanted to purge Araki and Mazaki, especially after the incident. But to suggest that he somehow let the rebellion occur flies in the face of all

evidence. On the contrary, it is clear that he was too surprised, shocked, and threatened by this massive assault on the constitutional order to risk anything so cynical as tolerating the rebellion for ulterior reasons. He was as opposed to the rebellion as was King Juan Carlos of Spain when he resolutely opposed the coup attempted by Lieutenant Colonel José Antonio Tejero on 23 February 1981.

9   The Emperor spoke in similar terms in 1946 when he recalled the rebellion (STDH 1990: 104).

10 Hirota's name was suggested in the first instance by Ichiki Kitokurō and conveyed to the Emperor through Saionji (Connors 1987: 175).

11 This provision had been set aside in 1913, without, however, altering previous practice (Shillony 1973: 210, footnote 3).

4 THE EMPEROR AND WAR, 1937–1940

1   As a typical earlier illustration of his distance from policy-making, Prime Minister Okada was surprised to discover in 1934 that the Emperor did not know of key decisions on defense spending made the previous year by the Saitō cabinet (Maxon [1957] 1975: 97).

2   Technically, imperial sanction was finalized after the ceremonial imperial conference and after the cabinet and military high command had met again to certify the 'decision' which had been 'reported' to the Emperor during the *gozen kaigi*. At this point the Emperor would sign the relevant state document, making the policy decision official (Butow 1961: 172–3).

3   Saionji had accordingly recommended Konoe as prime minister after the 1936 army uprising but Konoe had declined, ostensibly on the grounds of ill-health. He had not wanted to take office for fear that with the imperial way faction weakened, it would be impossible to cope with the control faction (Oka 1983: 40–1).

4   The Emperor's tendency to defer to Konoe may also have been due to the fact that Konoe was ten years older. The Prince, in turn, was inclined to treat the Emperor in a familiar, casual manner which contrasted with the stiff formality observed by most others at court (Oka 1983: 49–50).

5   Tada's complaint belies Inoue Kiyoshi's judgment that the Emperor could have spoken out against the war policy (Inoue 1975: 93–5); Tada correctly perceived that the Emperor was not a free agent, due to Konoe's manipulation and Saionji's conviction that the Emperor should not speak at the imperial conference.

6   This discussion of the Emperor in relation to the Sino-Japanese War is based on evidence which refutes Behr's unfounded statement that the Emperor's only criticism of the generals was '*that they were not winning the war fast enough*' (Behr 1989: 192, italics Behr's). His assertion that 'Far from deploring the escalation of the war, after Nanking, the Harada memoirs show that the Emperor used his influence to keep it going' (Behr 1989: 228) is equally unfounded. The Harada memoirs show just the opposite.

7   On 22 August Hitler blamed the Emperor for Japan's failure to conclude an alliance with Germany. He told his military leaders, 'The Emperor is the companion piece of the later Czars. Weak, cowardly, irresolute, he may fall before a revolution' (Coox II 1985: 896).

8   Hata, who had personally opposed an alliance with Germany, was pressed to resign by Kan'in (Komiyama 1977).

9   Regarding Matsuoka, it should be noted that the Emperor had tried to dissuade Konoe from appointing him as foreign minister, believing Matsuoka to be too headstrong and remembering that he had led the Japanese delegation in walking out of the League of Nations in 1933. The Prince, however, refused (Oka 1983: 98).

5 WORLD WAR AND THE IMPERIAL WILL, 1941–1945

1 When Japan attacked Pearl Harbor, Matsuoka acknowledged that his diplomacy of deterrence, grounded in the Tripartite Pact, had been a complete failure (Lu 1961: 119).

2 Due to an erroneous translation of a passage found in the Sugiyama papers (Sugiyama I 1967: 370), Bergamini wrongly claimed that the Emperor first heard of the navy's plan to attack Pearl Harbor and ordered it to be researched, in January 1941 (Bergamini 1971: 737, note 1). The passage in question does not mention the Emperor (Large 1990: 73–4; Crowley 1971: 66).

3 Essentially, this was true, for in expressing his personal hopes for peace the president mainly reiterated American objections to Japanese expansionism, especially in Indochina, which he said the United States would not invade if Japanese forces were withdrawn from the region (Grew 1944: 488–9).

4 Even in 1946 the Emperor defended Tōjō as a conscientious administrator whose reputation as a tyrant had been unjustified (STDH 1990: 123–4). A good general study of their relationship is Kamei (1988).

5 (Itō, *et al.*eds., 1990: 462). This source comprises diaries kept by Tōjō's private secretaries (Large 1991a).

6 The Emperor might have left it to Kido to clarify this imperative after he himself met with Koiso and Yonai, just as, it will be recalled, he had Kido instruct Tōjō to ignore the mid-October 1941 war deadline.

7 Interestingly, Tōgō discovered on this occasion that Suzuki had failed to inform the Emperor of the Hirota-Malik conversations, which Tōgō proceeded to recapitulate at some length (Butow [1954] 1967: 118)

8 This was in response to the Potsdam Proclamation's statement that 'stern justice shall be meted out to all war criminals' (Butow [1954] 1967: 243).

9 Kase relates that it was Hiranuma Kiichirō who, after being invited to participate in the council's deliberations, insisted upon this proviso concerning the retention of the Emperor's prerogatives (Kase 1950: 243).

10 This quotation (Butow [1954] 1967: 175–6) is based on recollections by some of the participants of what the Emperor said. He later summarized his statement to Kido (Kido II 1966: 1,223–4). The Triple Intervention, by Russia, France and Germany, denied Japan the Liaotung Peninsula after the Sino-Japanese War of 1894–1895 and occasioned a sense of national humiliation in Japan.

11 Only Prince Asaka hinted that the war should be continued, to preserve the 'national polity'. But the Emperor believed that the only way to save the *kokutai* was to surrender (STDH 1990: 141).

12 Butow presents a full English text of the rescript (Butow [1954] 1967: 248; see footnote 44, page 208 for a brief discussion of those who participated in the various stages of its drafting).

13 Fujita's rendering here is a slight revision of the original version, which appeared in *Taihei*, October 1955.

6 THE EMPEROR AND THE OCCUPATION, 1945–1952

1 The Monologue was recorded and preserved by one of those present, Terasaki Hidenari, who had served in the Japanese embassy in Washington prior to the Pearl Harbor attack. It was delivered on 18, 20, and 22 March and twice on 8 April 1946 (Large 1991a).

2 The notes made by his interpreter make no reference to the Emperor's statement but there is little reason to doubt MacArthur's account of it, given the Emperor's desire, as Kido noted on 29 August 1945, to assume responsibility (Kawahara 1990: 147–8).

3 While the term stands for MacArthur, the supreme commander of the allied powers,

it is often also used to denote the Occupation regime comprising MacArthur and his staff.

4   None of these men served out their sentences. For instance, Shigemitsu was released in 1950 and returned to public life as foreign minister in 1954; Kido was released in 1953 due to illness and died in 1977. Note that trials of Class B and C war criminals were also conducted by the Allies throughout Asia.

5   Tōjō's account seem plausible. First, that he had struck a compromise with Sugiyama after arguing that clemency be shown to all the pilots is confirmed by the Emperor's own recollections in 1946 (STDH 1990: 124). Second, and more importantly by way of corroboration, that the Emperor had wanted the pilots to be treated with 'courtesy' is confirmed by wartime general staff papers which noted that he hoped that if Japan treated them mercifully, Japanese prisoners of war in Allied camps would be treated mercifully ('Daihon'ei kimitsu sensō nisshi' 1971: 364). Apparently his innate timidity, and reluctance to challenge Sugiyama for fear of upsetting relations between the army chief and Prime Minister Tōjō during the war, kept him from insisting upon clemency for all the Doolittle pilots, which he had the right to do in such cases.

6   Shigemitsu, however, states in his memoirs that he had informed the Emperor of the situation in the camps. Repelled by reports of inhumane treatment of prisoners, the Emperor had demanded that it be ended at once, but to no avail (Shigemitsu 1958: 347).

7   Three men served as grand chamberlain during the Occupation: Fujita Hisanori, in office from 1944 to May 1946, Ogane Mosujirō, to April 1948, and Mitani Takanobu, who remained in office for many years after the Occupation. The imperial household ministers were Ishiwata Sōtarō (who had replaced Matsudaira Tsuneo in June 1945), to January 1946; Matsudaira, who returned, to serve until June 1948; Tajima Michiji, to October 1950; and Usami Takeshi, who like Mitani, held office well into the post-Occupation period. For the backgrounds and personalities of these men, see accounts by Takahashi and Vining (Takahashi 1978: 61–77, Vining [1952] 1989).

8   To illustrate the extent of this reduction, the more than three million acres of imperial lands as of 1945 were cut to under 7,000 acres (Titus 1980: 567). However, the Emperor retained a personal fortune of ten million yen which, according to one source, was 'twice as much as the wealthiest zaibatsu saved out of defeat' (Brines 1948: 86).

9   It was rather ironic that while the Emperor rejected his former image as a god, there were some Japanese who regarded MacArthur as an almost supernatural figure. When other Japanese criticized these sentiments toward the general as excessive, GHQ officials censored them.

10 Yoshida attributed SCAP's haste on constitutional revision to the belief that unless the matter were handled quickly, the Far Eastern Commission, under Soviet influence especially, might interfere and thereby jeopardize the future of the monarchy (Yoshida 1962: 134–6).

11 Prince Mikasa voiced the Emperor's objections in this regard during the final session of the privy council on 8 June 1946 (McNelly 1987: 86).

12 Takahashi gives a full list of tours with dates (Takahashi 1978: 171).

13 Vining's appointment ended in 1950. Her memoirs, originally published in 1952, are valuable for their recollections of life at court and of the Occupation generally. Although they disclose a strong identification with the imperial family, they are for the most part objective.

14 This discussion of Yoshida's policies is based on Dower's book (Dower 1979: 305–68).

15 MacArthur shared Yoshida's reluctance to see Japan undertake rearmament. Note, however, that others in GHQ cooperated with activists in the defunct imperial army to try and promote the development of a new Japanese military establishment (Dower 1979: 387).

16 It transpired that after the Chinese revolution the United States defined its defense

commitments in Asia along the lines suggested. But specifically how the American government reacted to the Terasaki–Sebald exchange when Sebald reported it is unknown.

17 In May 1947 SCAP granted permission to fly the flag after previously prohibiting its display (PRJ II [1949] 1970: 138). The author is unaware of any SCAP move to prohibit the Japanese national song.

7 THE POLITICS OF IMPERIAL SYMBOLISM, 1952–1970

1 Earlier, on 17 June, the socialist politician, Kawakami Jōtarō, had been injured by stabbing, for his opposition to treaty renewal (Packard 1966: 301).

2 The Emperor published his first book, on hydrozoa, in 1967. Over the years, he published seven more on this topic, the last in September 1988, along with a number of books on other subjects relating to his interest in marine biology. For a detailed discussion of his scientific career, see Corner's article (Corner 1990).

3 Judging from a 1968 Glasgow poll, in which 69 per cent responded affirmatively to the question of whether Britain needed the Queen, with 27 per cent opposed and the rest unsure, it appears that pro-monarchist feelings were rather stronger in Japan than in Britain (Rose and Kavanagh 1976: 552).

4 The Emperor's association with the material prosperity of postwar Japan is ironically suggested by the fact that in the one direct, and unsuccessful, attack on him in this period, the weapon used was a *pachinko* ball – itself a symbol of Japan's booming entertainment industry – thrown by a middle-school youth from the crowd greeting the Emperor on New Year's 1969. Evidently the boy had been motivated by reading about how Japanese soldiers had starved to death in New Guinea during the war and blamed the Emperor for their tribulations (*Shōwa nihonshi* Supplement I 1987: 133).

5 Note that the present Emperor and Empress have a third child, besides Princes Naruhito and Fumihito: Princess Sayako, or Nori-no-miya, born on 18 April 1969.

6 For instance, virtually every issue of the historical journal, *Rekishigaku kenkyū*, in 1968 includes strong criticism of the government for using the centennial to obscure the harsh realities of modern Japanese history and for exploiting the event to foster public respect for Yasukuni Shrine and other sub-symbols of the old imperial order.

7 The situation of Okinawa resembled that of the 'northern territories', the four islands north of Hokkaidō, occupied by the Soviet Union since 1945.

8 THE EMPEROR AND THE IMPERIAL INSTITUTION IN LATE SHŌWA JAPAN, 1970–1989

1 The Kissinger memo, located at the Ford presidential library in Ann Arbor, Michigan, is filed under 'Co 75 Japan Executive PR7–1, 10.1. 75'.

2 The letters are filed under 'Co 75 Japan Executive, 10.2. 75–10.9. 75' and Ford's reply to Mrs MacArthur, under 'Co 75 Japan Executive PA2/MX 503, 10.2. 75–10.9. 75', at the Ford presidential library.

3 The Emperor did express regret for the war in many private conversations with world leaders, according to his translator, Mazaki Hideki. For instance, during a conversation with President Corazon Aquino in 1986 he repeatedly apologized for 'the trouble the Japanese army had caused the people of the Philippines' (Mazaki 1991: 56). But it fell to the present Emperor to make the first public apology to an Asian country. At a banquet in honor of the South Korean president on 24 May 1990, he said, 'I think of the sufferings your people underwent . . . which were brought about by my country, and cannot but feel the deepest regret' (*The Independent*, 25 May 1990: 12).

4 By the mid-1970s Japan had become a formidable military power despite its lack of

nuclear weapons. Welfield's study contains a detailed analysis of Japanese military development in this period and since the war generally (Welfield 1988).
5 Similar results were obtained in many other polls (Nishihira 1980: 89–96).
6 Most of this money was spent on sophisticated weapons; the number of Japanese combat personnel is relatively small in comparison with other major military powers (Drifte 1990: 35).
7 There have been more recent Japanese claims that the 'Rape of Nanking' never took place (Watanabe S. 1991: 78–9).
8 The following account of the funeral is based on the first-hand impressions of Murray Sayle (Sayle 1989).

CONCLUSION

1 There is a large and still growing literature in Japanese on this problem. A thoughtful sample is Ienaga Saburō's book, *Sensō sekinin* (1988).
2 For a recent sketch of a Japanese music teacher, whose objections to 'Kimi ga yo' caused her to be transferred to another post, see *The Independent*, 20 June 1991: 17.
3 'Civil religion' is used here as Robert Bellah defines it: 'a set of beliefs, symbols, and rituals' which, despite the theoretical separation of church and state, still to some extent confer 'the religious legitimation of the highest political authority' (Bellah 1970: 171). In the United States, for instance, the marks of civil religion include the inscription, 'In God We Trust' on coins, prayers to God during official 4th of July commemorations of independence, and descriptions of the Republic's cause in wartime as a reflection of God's will. In Britain, where church and state are indivisible, the anthem, 'God Save the Queen', is one aspect, among many, of civil religion.
4 For example, the process of secularization has been qualified by the expansion of such 'new religions' as Sōka Gakkai ('Value-Creation Society'), which has supported the Komeitō, or 'Clean Government Party', since the latter was founded in 1964.
5 This applies to the *daijōsai* rituals, recently performed in Tokyo, on 22–23 November 1990, to mark the accession of the present Emperor. The government's decision that these rites should be conducted without modification mostly reflected the LDP's 'search for legitimacy' (Crump [1989] 1991: 224). They were generally received in Japan as private rites of the court which had no public or state ramifications. Accordingly, as Thomas Crump writes concerning their political significance, 'A chapter of Japanese history has been closed, and it is beyond anyone's power to open it again' (Crump [1989] 1991: 225).

Bibliography

'A Talk with the Emperor of Japan.' (1975) *Time*, 29 September 1975: 56.

Akashi, Yōji. (1978) 'A Botched Peace Effort: The Miao Pin *Kōsaku*, 1944–1945', in A.D. Coox and H. Conroy (eds) *China and Japan: Search for Balance Since World War I*, Oxford: ABC–Clio.

Allen, Louis. (1989) Review of Edward Behr, *Hirohito: Behind the Myth*, *Japan Forum* 1, 2: 306–10.

Amano Keiichi. (1987) '"Sengo seiji no sōkessan" to "X-dē" kōgeki', in Suga Takayuki (ed.) *Ronsō: nihon tennōsei*, I, Tokyo: Shashoku shobō.

Araki Moriaki. (1986) 'Tennō to "tennōsei" ', in Rekishigaku kenkyūkai (eds) *Tennō to tennōsei o kangaeru*, Tokyo: Aoki shoten.

Ashida Hitoshi. (1986) *Ashida nikki*, 1–2, Tokyo: Iwanami shoten.

Bagehot, Walter. (1969) *The English Constitution* [1st edn 1867], London: New Thinkers Library.

Banno, Junji. (1990a) 'Emperor, Cabinet and Diet in Meiji Politics (1880–1913)', *Acta Asiatica* 59: 59–76.

—— (1990b) 'Foreword', *Acta Asiatica* 59: iii–x.

Beasley, W.G. (1972) *The Meiji Restoration*, Stanford, Calif.: Stanford University Press.

Beckmann, George M. and Okubo, Genji. (1969) *The Japanese Communist Party 1922–1945*, Stanford, Calif.: Stanford University Press.

Behr, Edward. (1989) *Hirohito: Behind the Myth*, London: Hamish Hamilton.

Bell, David V.J. (1975) *Power, Influence, and Authority: An Essay on Political Linguistics*, Oxford: Oxford University Press.

Bellah, Robert N. (1970) *Beyond Belief: Essays on Religion in a Post-Traditional World*, New York: Harper and Row.

Bendix, Reinhard. (1978) *Kings or People: Power and the Mandate to Rule*, 2nd edn 1980, Berkeley, Calif.: University of California Press.

Bergamini, David. (1971) *Japan's Imperial Conspiracy*, New York: William Morrow.

Berger, Gordon M. (1988) 'Politics and Mobilization in Japan, 1931–1945', in Peter Duus (ed.) *The Cambridge History of Japan*, Vol. 6 (The Twentieth Century), Cambridge: Cambridge University Press.

Bix, Herbert P. (1982) 'Rethinking "Emperor-System Fascism": Ruptures and Continuities in Modern Japanese History', *Bulletin of Concerned Asian Scholars* 14, 2: 2–19.

Blacker, Carmen. (1990) 'The *Shinza* or God-seat in the *Daijōsai*: Throne, Bed, or Incubation Couch?', *Japanese Journal of Religious Studies* 17, 2–3: 179–97.

Blake, Robert. (1969) 'The Crown and Politics in the Twentieth Century', in Jeremy Murray-Brown (ed.) *The Monarchy and Its Future*, London: Allen and Unwin.

Blumler, J.G., Brown, J.B., Ewbank, A.J. and Nossiter, T.J. (1971) 'Attitudes to the Monarchy: Their Structure and Development During a Ceremonial Occasion', *Political Studies* XIX, 2: 149–71.

Bock, Felicia G. (1990) 'The Great Feast of Enthronement', *Monumenta Nipponica* 45, 1: 27–38.
Bocock, Robert. (1974) *Ritual in Industrial Society: A Sociological Analysis*, London: Allen and Unwin.
Bradford, Sarah. (1989) *George VI*, London: Weidenfeld and Nicolson.
Brines, Russell. (1948) *MacArthur's Japan*, New York and Philadelphia: Lippincott.
Buckley, Roger. (1982) *Occupation Diplomacy: Britain, the United States and Japan 1945–1952*, Cambridge: Cambridge University Press.
Bulletin of the Nanzan Institute for Religion and Culture 13 (1989).
Burkman, Thomas W. (ed.) (1984) *The Occupation of Japan: Arts and Culture*, Norfolk, Va: General Douglas MacArthur Foundation.
Butow, Robert J.C. (1954) *Japan's Decision to Surrender*, 5th edn 1967, Stanford, Calif.: Stanford University Press.
—— (1961) *Tōjō and the Coming of the War*, Princeton, NJ: Princeton University Press.
Cannadine, David. (1985) 'The Context, Performance and Meaning of Ritual: The British Monarchy and the "Invention of Tradition" ', in E. Hobsbawm and T. Ranger (eds) *The Invention of Tradition*, Cambridge: Cambridge University Press.
Catto, Henry. (1989) 'And His Gracious Apology', *The Washington Post*, 8 January: C7.
Center for East Asian Cultural Studies (compilers) (1969) *Meiji Japan Through Contemporary Sources* I (Basic Documents, 1854–1889), Tokyo: Tōyō Bunko.
Coaldrake, William H. (1989) 'Japan at the End of an Era: How Should We React?', *Current Affairs Bulletin* [Sydney] (February): 29–30.
Colegrove, Kenneth. (1932) 'The Japanese Emperor', *American Political Science Review* XXVI, 4: 642–59.
Coleman, John A. (1970) 'Civil Religion', *Sociological Analysis* 31, 2: 67–77.
Connors, Lesley. (1987) *The Emperor's Adviser: Saionji Kinmochi and Pre-war Japanese Politics*, London: Croom Helm.
Coox, Alvin D. (1978) 'Recourse to Arms: The Sino-Japanese Conflict, 1937–1945', in A.D. Coox and H. Conroy (eds) *China and Japan: Search for Balance Since World War I*, Oxford: ABC–Clio.
—— (1985) *Nomonhan: Japan Against Russia, 1939* Vols 1–2, Stanford, Calif.: Stanford University Press.
—— (1988) 'The Pacific War', in Peter Duus (ed.) *The Cambridge History of Japan* Vol. 6 (The Twentieth Century), Cambridge: Cambridge University Press.
Corner, E.J.H. (1990) 'His Majesty Emperor Hirohito of Japan, K.G.', in *Biographical Memoirs of Fellows of the Royal Society* 36: 243–72.
Craigie, Robert. (1946) *Behind the Japanese Mask*, London: Hutchinson.
Crowley, James B. (1966) *Japan's Quest for Autonomy: National Security and Foreign Policy 1930–1938*, Princeton, NJ: Princeton University Press.
—— (1971) Review of David Bergamini, *Japan's Imperial Conspiracy*, *The New York Times Book Review*, 24 October: 2, 66.
Crump, Thomas. (1989) *The Death of an Emperor: Japan at the Crossroads*, London: Constable (2nd edn 1991, Oxford: Oxford University Press).
'Daihon'ei kimitsu sensō nisshi'. (1971) *Rekishi to jinbutsu*, September: 333–73.
Daniels, Gordon. (1975) 'The Great Tokyo Air Raid, 9–10 March 1945', in W.G. Beasley (ed.) *Modern Japan: Aspects of History, Literature, and Society*, London: Allen and Unwin.
Date, Munekatsu. (1975) *Tennō no gaikō*, Tokyo: Gendai kikakushitsu.
Dower, John W. (1979) *Empire and Aftermath: Yoshida Shigeru and the Japanese Experience, 1878–1954*, Cambridge, Mass: Harvard University Press.
—— (1989) Review of Edward Behr, *Hirohito: Behind the Myth*, *The New York Times Book Review*, 8 October: 8–9.
Drifte, Reinhard. (1990) *Japan's Foreign Policy*, London: Routledge.
Duncan, Andrew. (1970) *The Reality of Monarchy*, London: Heinemann.

Duus, Peter. (1968) *Party Rivalry and Political Change in Taishō Japan*, Cambridge, Mass: Harvard University Press.

Ebitsubo Isamu and Kamiya Naoyoshi (eds) (1971) *Gaikokujin no mita tennō*, Tokyo: Hara shobō.

Edelman, Murray. (1967) *The Symbolic Uses of Politics*, Urbana, Ill.: University of Illinois Press.

Egeberg, Robert O. (1989) 'How Hirohito Kept His Throne', *The Washington Post*, 19 February: D5.

Elias, Norbert. (1983) *The Court Society*, Oxford: Blackwell.

Etō, Jun. (1973) 'Japan's Shifting Image', *Japan Interpreter* VIII, 1: 63–75.

Etō, Shinkichi. (1974) 'Japan's Policies Toward China', in J.W. Morley (ed.) *Japan's Foreign Policy 1868–1941: A Research Guide*, New York: Columbia University Press.

Firth, Raymond. (1973) *Symbols: Public and Private*, Ithaca, NY: Cornell University Press.

Fujita Hisanori. (1961) *Jijūchō no kaisō*, Tokyo: Kōdansha.

Fukuda, Kan'ichi. (1963) 'The Fate of Monarchy in the Twentieth Century', *Journal of Social and Political Ideas in Japan* 1, 2: 25–8.

Fukui, Haruhiro. (1968) 'Twenty Years of Revisionism', in D.F. Henderson (ed.) *The Constitution of Japan: Its First Twenty Years, 1947–1967*, Seattle: University of Washington Press.

Gaimushō (eds) (1969) *Gaimushō no 100–nen* I, Tokyo: Hara shobō.

Garon, Sheldon M. (1986) 'State and Religion in Imperial Japan, 1912–1945', *Journal of Japanese Studies* 12, 2: 273–302.

Gayn, Mark. (1948) *Japan Diary*, New York: William Sloane.

Gluck, Carol. (1985) *Japan's Modern Myths: Ideology in the Late Meiji Period*, Princeton, NJ: Princeton University Press.

—— (1990) 'The Idea of Shōwa', *Daedalus* 119, 3: 1–26.

Grew, Joseph. (1944) *Ten Years in Japan*, New York: Simon and Schuster.

Grigg, John. (1969) 'A Summer Storm', in Jeremy Murray-Brown (ed.) *The Monarchy and Its Future*, London: Allen and Unwin.

Hall, John W. (1965) 'The Historical Dimension', in J.W. Hall and Richard Beardsley (eds) *Twelve Doors to Japan*, New York: McGraw-Hill.

—— (1968a) 'A Monarch for Modern Japan', in R.E. Ward (ed.) *Political Development in Modern Japan*, Princeton, NJ: Princeton University Press.

—— (1968b) 'Reflections on a Centennial', *Journal of Asian Studies* XXVII, 4: 711–20.

Handō Kazutoshi. (1985) *Seidan: Tennō to Suzuki Kantarō*, Tokyo: Bungei shunjū.

—— (1989) 'Shōwa tennō hachijū shichinen no kiseki', *Bungei shunjū*, March Special Issue [Oinaru shōwa]: 442–59.

Hane, Mikiso. (1982) 'Introduction', in Hane, Mikiso (ed. and trans.) *Emperor Hirohito and His Chief Aide-de-Camp: The Honjō Diary, 1933–1936*, Tokyo: University of Tokyo Press.

Hara Kei. (1965–1967) *Hara Kei nikki*, 1–6, Tokyo: Fukumura shuppan kabushiki kaisha.

Hara Yoshihisa. (1988) *Sengo nihon to kokusai seiji: anpo kaitei no seiji rikigaku*, Tokyo: Chūō kōronsha.

Harada, Kumao. (1950–56) *Saionji-kō to seikyoku*, 1–9, Tokyo: Iwanami shoten.

Hardacre, Helen. (1989) *Shintō and the State, 1868–1988*, Princeton, NJ: Princeton University Press.

Hasegawa Masayasu. (1976) 'Tennōsei no hōteki shomondai', *Hōritsu jihō* 48, 4: 8–15.

—— (1986) 'Shōwa shi to tennō no sensō sekinin', in Bunka hyōron henshūbu (eds) *Tennōsei o tou*, Tokyo: Bunka hyōron.

Hasunuma Shigeru. (1956) 'Senritsu no hachi jūshi jiken', *Bungei shunjū*, October Special Issue [Tennō hakusho]: 192–9.

Hata, Ikuhiko. (1976) 'The Japanese–Soviet Confrontation, 1935–1939', in J.W. Morley (ed.) *Deterrent Diplomacy: Japan, Germany, and the U.S.S.R. 1935–1940*, New York: Columbia University Press.

—— (1978) 'Tennō no shinsho', *Bungei shunjū* October: 374–92.

—— (1980) 'The Army's Move into Northern Indochina', in J.W. Morley (ed.) *The Fateful Choice: Japan's Advance into Southeast Asia, 1939–1941*, New York: Columbia University Press.

—— (1983) 'The Marco Polo Bridge Incident, 1937', in J.W. Morley (ed.) *The China Quagmire: Japan's Expansion on the Asian Continent 1933–1941*, New York: Columbia University Press.

—— (1984) 'The Postwar Period in Retrospect', *Japan Echo* XI, Special Issue [The War and Japan: Revisionist Views]: 12–21.

—— (1986) 'When Ideologues Rewrite History', *Japan Echo* XIII, 4: 73–8.

Havens, Thomas R.H. (1974) *Farm and Nation in Modern Japan: Agrarian Nationalism, 1870–1940*, Princeton, NJ: Princeton University Press.

Hayes, Michael P. (1978) 'The Japanese Press and the Emperor, 1945–46', in Gordon Daniels (ed.) *Proceedings of the British Association for Japanese Studies* 3, 1: Sheffield: Centre for Japanese Studies.

Hellmann, Donald C. (1988) 'Japanese Politics and Foreign Policy: Elitist Democracy Within an American Greenhouse', in Takashi Inoguchi and Daniel Okimoto (eds) *The Political Economy of Japan*, 2 (The Changing International Context), Stanford, Calif.: Stanford University Press.

Hidaka, Rokurō. (1985) *The Price of Affluence: Dilemmas of Contemporary Japan*, Ringwood, Victoria: Penguin Books Australia.

Higashikuni Naruhiko. (1968) *Higashikuni nikki*, Tokyo: Tokuma shoten.

Hijikata Tomio. (1987) 'Yasukuni kōgeki no gendankai', in Suga Takayuki (ed.) *Ronsō: nihon tennōsei* I, Tokyo: Shashoku shobō.

Hirakawa, Sukehiro. (1985) 'R.H. Blyth and Hirohito's Denial of the Divine Character of *Tennō*', in J.W.M. Chapman and David Steeds (eds) *Proceedings of the British Association for Japanese Studies*, Sheffield: Centre for Japanese Studies.

Hiro, Sachiya and Yamamoto, Shichihei. (1986) 'Yasukuni Shrine and the Japanese Spirit World', *Japan Echo* XIII, 2: 73–80.

'Hirohito: "A Happy Experience"' (1975) *Time*, 6 October: 42, 44.

Hobsbawm, Eric. (1985) 'Introduction', in E. Hobsbawm and T. Ranger (eds) *The Invention of Tradition*, Cambridge: Cambridge University Press.

Holtom, D.C. (1947) *Modern Japan and Shintō Nationalism: A Study of Present-Day Trends in Japanese Religion*, Chicago: University of Chicago Press.

Honjō Shigeru. (1975) *Honjō nikki*, Tokyo: Hara shobō.

Hosaka Hisato. (1987) 'X-dē wa ika ni enshutsu sareruka', in Suga Takayuki (ed.) *Ronsō: nihon tennōsei*, I, Tokyo: Shashoku shobō.

Hosaka Masayasu. (1989a) 'Chichi shōwa tennō no sensō sekininron ni yanda koro', *Bungei shunjū*, March Special Issue [Ōinaru shōwa]: 628–33.

—— (1989b) *Chichibu no miya to shōwa tennō*, Tokyo: Bungei shunjū.

Hosokawa Morisada. (1953) *Jōhō tennō ni tassezu*, 1–2, Tokyo: Isobe shobō.

Hosoya, Chihiro. (1971) 'Retrogression in Japan's Foreign Policy Decision-Making Process', in J.W. Morley (ed.) *Dilemmas of Growth in Prewar Japan*, Princeton, NJ: Princeton University Press.

—— (1976) 'The Tripartite Pact, 1939–1940', in J.W. Morley (ed.) *Deterrent Diplomacy: Japan, Germany, and the U.S.S.R., 1935–1940*, New York: Columbia University Press.

—— (1980) 'The Japanese-Soviet Neutrality Pact', in J.W. Morley (ed.) *The Fateful Choice: Japan's Advance into Southeast Asia, 1939–1941*, New York: Columbia University Press.

Hoston, Germaine A. (1986) *Marxism and the Crisis of Development in Prewar Japan*, Princeton, NJ: Princeton University Press.

Hyōgoken gyōkōshi. (1948) [Held in the Gordon W. Prange Collection, University of Maryland, College Park, Maryland].

Ienaga Saburō (1988) *Senso sekinin*, Tokyo: Iwanami shoten.
Iizuka Akio. (1984) 'Kōtaishi: sono shirarezaru nichijō', *Bungei shunjū* May: 134–47.
Ike, Nobutaka (ed. and trans.) (1967) *Japan's Decision for War: Records of the 1941 Policy Conferences*, Stanford, Calif.: Stanford University Press.
Imai, Seiichi. (1973) 'Cabinet, Emperor, and Senior Statesmen', in D. Borg and S. Okamoto (eds) *Pearl Harbor as History: Japanese–American Relations 1931–1941*, New York: Columbia University Press.
Imai Seiichi and Takahashi Masae (eds) (1963) *Gendaishi shiryō*, 4, Tokyo: Misuzu shobō.

Inoue Kiyoshi. (1975) *Tennō no senso sekinin*, Tokyo: Gendai hyōronsha.
Irie, Sukemasa. (1983) 'My 50 Years with the Emperor', *Japan Quarterly* XXX, 1: 39–43.

—— (1990) *Irie Sukemasa nikki* (Irie Tametoshi, gen. ed.), 1–3, Tokyo: Asahi shinbunsha.

Iriye, Akira. (1965) *After Imperialism: The Search for a New Order in the Far East 1921–1931*, Cambridge, Mass: Harvard University Press.
—— (1971) 'The Failure of Military Expansionism', in J.W. Morley (ed.) *Dilemmas of Growth in Prewar Japan*, Princeton, NJ: Princeton University Press.
—— (1981) *Power and Culture: The Japanese–American War, 1941–1945* Cambridge, Mass: Harvard University Press.
Irokawa, Daikichi. (1983) 'The Subject Mentality', *Japan Quarterly* XXX, 1: 28–38.
Ishida, Takeshi. (1974) 'Sengo no tennōsei', in Kuno Osamu and Kamishima Jirō (eds) *'Tennōsei' ronshū*, Tokyo: San'ichi shobō.
—— (1989) 'The Emperor Problem in a Historical Perspective', in Yoshikazu Sakamoto (ed.) *Prime* [International Peace Research Institute Occasional Papers, Meiji Gakuin University], 5: 47–56.
Itō Takashi, Hirohashi Tadamitsu, and Katashima Norio (eds) (1990). *Tōjō naikaku sōridaijin kimitsu kiroku*, Tokyo: Tokyo daigaku shuppankai.
James, D.C. (1985) *The Years of MacArthur*, 3, Boston: Houghton Mifflin.
Jansen, Marius B. (1977) 'The Presidential Address: Monarchy and Modernization', *Journal of Asian Studies* XXXVI, 4: 611–22.
Kamei Hiroshi. (1988) *Shōwa tennō to Tōjō Hideki*, Tokyo: Kojinsha.
Kanroji, Osanaga. (1975) *Hirohito: An Intimate Portrait of the Japanese Emperor*, Los Angeles: Gateway.
Kase, Toshikazu. (1950) *Journey to the Missouri*, New Haven, Conn.: Yale University Press.
Katō Shūichi. (1974) 'Tennōsei ni tsuite', in Kuno Osamu and Kamishima Jirō (eds) *'Tennōsei' ronshū*, Tokyo: San'ichi shobō.
Kawahara, Toshiaki. (1990) *Hirohito and His Times: A Japanese Perspective*, Tokyo: Kōdansha International.
Kawai, Kazuo. (1960) *Japan's American Interlude*, Chicago: University of Chicago Press.
Kennedy, Paul. (1982) 'The Kaiser and German *Weltpolitik*: Reflections on Wilhelm II's Place in the Making of German Foreign Policy', in J.C.G. Röhl and N. Sombart (eds) *Kaiser Wilhelm II: New Interpretations*, Cambridge: Cambridge University Press.
Kido Kōichi. (1966) *Kido Kōichi nikki*, 1–2, Tokyo: Tokyo daigaku shuppankai.
Kishida, Hideo. (1983) 'Utakai-Hajime: The New Year's Poetry Party', *Japan Quarterly* XXX, 1: 44–9.
Kitagawa, Joseph M. (1974) 'The Japanese *Kokutai* (National Community): History and Myth', *History of Religions* 13, 3: 209–26.
Kobayashi Naoki. (1976) 'Gendai tennōsei josetsu', *Hōritsu jihō* 48, 4: 16–29.
Kobayashi, Tatsuo. (1984) 'The London Naval Treaty, 1930', in J.W. Morley (ed.) *Japan Erupts: The London Naval Conference and the Manchurian Incident, 1929–1932*, New York: Columbia University Press.
Kojima Noboru. (1981) *Tennō* 1–4, Tokyo: Bungei shunjū.

Komiya, Ryūtarō. (1979) 'The Rightward Shift' *Japan Echo* VI, 3: 71–9.
Komiyama Noboru. (1977) 'Yonai naikaku hōkai no shin-in', in Komiyama Noboru (ed.) *Sugamo nikki* [by Hata Shunroku], Tokyo: Nihon bunka rengōkai.
Konoe Fumimaro. (1946) *Ushinawareshi seiji: Konoe Fumimaro-kō no shuki*, Tokyo: Saikensha.
—— (1968) *Konoe nikki*, Tokyo: Kyōdō tsūshinsha.
Kōsaka, Masataka. (1982) *A History of Postwar Japan*, Tokyo: Kōdansha International.
Kuno, Osamu. (1978) 'The Meiji State, Minponshugi, and Ultranationalism', in J.V. Koschmann (ed.) *Authority and the Individual in Japan*, Tokyo: University of Tokyo Press.
Kurihara Sadako. (1974) 'Hibakusha ni totte no tennō', in Kuno Osamu and Kamishima Jirō (eds) *'Tennōsei' ronshū*, Tokyo: San'ichi shobō.
Kyūtei kishadan (eds) (1955) *Tennō*, Tokyo: Tōyō keizai shinpōsha.
Large, Stephen S. (1990) 'The Shōwa Emperor and the Asian-Pacific War', *The Japan Society: Proceedings* [London] 115: 65–78.
—— (1991a) 'Emperor Hirohito and Early Shōwa Japan', *Monumenta Nipponica* 46, 3: 349–68.
—— (1991b) Review of Kawahara Toshiaki, *Hirohito and His Times* and Edward Behr, *Hirohito: Behind the Myth, Journal of Japanese Studies* 17, 2: 508–12.
Lattimore, Owen. (1945) *Solution in Asia*, Boston: Little, Brown.
Latyshev, I.A. (1973) 'Reactionary Nationalist Tendencies in the Policy of the Ruling Circle of Japan', *Asia Quarterly* 1: 3–16.
Lu, David J. (1961) *From the Marco Polo Bridge to Pearl Harbor: Japan's Entry into World War II*, Washington: Public Affairs Press.
Lukes, Steven. (1977) *Essays in Social Theory*, New York: Columbia University Press.
MacArthur, Douglas. (1965) *Reminiscences*, London: Heinemann.
McCormack, Gavan. (1977) *Chang Tso-lin in Northeast Asia, 1911–1928: China, Japan, and the Manchurian Idea*, Stanford, Calif.: Stanford University Press.
—— (1986) 'Beyond Economism: Japan in a State of Transition', in Gavan McCormack and Yoshio Sugimoto (eds) *Democracy in Contemporary Japan*, Sydney: Hale and Iremonger.
—— (1989) 'Mountains Collapse: The Death of Hirohito', *Japanese Studies Association of Australia* [Newsletter] March: 16–21.
McNelly, Theodore H. (1969) 'The Role of Monarchy in the Political Modernization of Japan', *Comparative Politics* 1, 3: 366–81.
—— (1987) ' "Induced Revolution": The Policy and Process of Constitutional Reform in Occupied Japan', in R.E. Ward and Sakamoto Yoshikazu (eds) *Democratizing Japan: The Allied Occupation*, Honolulu: University of Hawaii Press.
Maki, John (ed. and trans.) (1980) *Japan's Commission on the Constitution: The Final Report*, Seattle: University of Washington Press.
Makino Nobuaki. (1990) *Makino Nobuaki nikki*, Itō Takashi and Hirose Yoshihiro (eds), Tokyo: Chūō kōronsha.
Malm, William P. (1971) 'The Music of Meiji Japan', in D. Shively (ed.) *Tradition and Modernization in Japanese Culture*, Princeton, NJ: Princeton University Press.
Maruyama, Masao. (1963) *Thought and Behaviour in Modern Japanese Politics*, London: Oxford University Press.
Masuda, Tomoko. (1990) 'The Emperor's Right of Supreme Command as Exercised up to 1930: A Study Based Especially on the Takarabe and Kuratomi Diaries', *Acta Asiatica* 59: 77–100.
Matsumoto Seichō. (1968) *Shōwa hakkutsu*, 6, Tokyo: Bungei shunjū.
Matsu'ura Sōzaburō. (1974) 'Taikenteki tennō tabūron', in Kuno Osamu and Kamishima Jirō (eds) *'Tennōsei' ronshū*, Tokyo: San'ichi shobō.
Maxon, Yale Candee. (1957) *Control of Japanese Foreign Policy: A Study of Civil-Military Rivalry 1930–1945*, 2nd reprinting 1975, Westport, Conn.: Greenwood.

Mayer-Oakes, Thomas Francis. (ed. and trans.) (1968) *Fragile Victory: Saionji-Harada Memoirs*, Detroit: Wayne State University Press.

Mazaki Hideki. (1991) 'Shōwa tennō: Mazaki-shi akasu', *This is Yomiuri* 8: 38–134.

Miller, Frank O. (1965) *Minobe Tatsukichi: Interpreter of Constitutionalism in Japan*, Berkeley, Calif.: University of California Press.

Minear, Richard H. (1972) *Victors' Justice: The Tokyo War Crimes Trial*, Princeton, NJ: Princeton University Press.

Mitchell, Richard H. (1976) *Thought Control in Prewar Japan*, Ithaca, NY: Cornell University Press.

Miura, Shumon and Yamamoto, Shichihei. (1989) 'The Imperial Institution: Japan's Unbroken Thread', *Japan Echo* XVI, 2: 8–14.

Moeran, Brian. (1989) 'Last Days of the Emperor', *Encounter* February: 58–62.

Mori, Kōichi. (1979) 'The Emperor of Japan: A Historical Study in Religious Symbolism', *Japanese Journal of Religious Studies* 6, 4: 522–65.

Morley, James W. (1970) 'The First Seven Weeks', *Japan Interpreter*, VI, 2: 151–64.

Morris, Ivan. (1960) *Nationalism and the Right Wing in Japan: A Study of Postwar Trends*, London: Oxford University Press.

—— (1964) *The World of the Shining Prince: Court Life in Ancient Japan*, 3rd edn 1969, New York: Alfred A. Knopf.

—— (1975) *The Nobility of Failure: Tragic Heroes in the History of Japan*, London: Martin Secker and Warburg (1980 edn, Harmondsworth: Penguin).

Morton, William F. (1980) *Tanaka Giichi and Japan's China Policy*, Folkestone, Kent: Dawson.

Mosley, Leonard. (1966) *Hirohito: Emperor of Japan*, Englewood Cliffs, NJ: Prentice-Hall.

Murakami, Shigeyoshi. (1980) *Japanese Religion in the Modern Century* (H.B. Earhart, trans.), Tokyo: University of Tokyo Press.

—— (ed.) (1983) *Kindai shōchokushū*, Tokyo: Shinjinbutsu ōraisha.

Murakami, Yasusuke. (1982) 'The Age of New Middle Mass Politics: The Case of Japan', *Journal of Japanese Studies* 8, 1: 29–72.

—— (1987) 'The Japanese Model of Political Economy', in Kōzō Yamamura and Yasukichi Yasuda (eds) *The Political Economy of Japan*, Vol. 1 (The Domestic Transformation), Stanford, Calif.: Stanford University Press.

Muramatsu, Michio. (1987) 'In Search of National Identity: The Politics and Policies of the Nakasone Administration', *Journal of Japanese Studies* 13, 2: 307–42.

Nagaoka, Shinjirō. (1980) 'Economic Demands on the Dutch East Indies', in J.W. Morley (ed.) *The Fateful Choice: Japan's Advance into Southeast Asia, 1939–1941*, New York: Columbia University Press.

Naikaku sōridaijin kanbō (eds) (1969) *Meiji hyakunen kinen gyōji nado kiroku*, Tokyo.

Najita, Tetsuo. (1974) *Japan: The Intellectual Foundations of Modern Japanese Politics*, 2nd edn 1980, Chicago: University of Chicago Press.

Najita, Tetsuo and Harootunian, H.D. (1988) 'Japanese Revolt Against the West: Political and Cultural Criticism in the Twentieth Century', in Peter Duus (ed.) *The Cambridge History of Japan*, Vol. 6 (The Twentieth Century), Cambridge: Cambridge University Press.

Nakamura Masanori. (1986) 'Senzen tennōsei to sengo tennōsei', in Rekishigaku kenkyūkai (eds) *Tennō to tennōsei o kangaeru*. Tokyo: Aoki shoten.

Nakamura, Takafusa. (1987) ' The Japanese Economy in the Interwar Period: A Brief Summary', in R. Dore and R. Sinha (eds) *Japan and World Depression: Then and Now*, London: Macmillan.

Nakano, Tsuyoshi. (1987) 'The American Occupation and Reform of Japan's Religious System: A Few Notes on the Secularization Process in Postwar Japan', *Journal of Oriental Studies* 26, 1: 124–38.

Nakasone, Yasuhiro. (1983) 'Toward a Nation of Dynamic Culture and Welfare', *Japan Echo* X, 1: 12–18.

Napier, Susan J. (1989) 'Death and the Emperor: Mishima, Ōe, and the Politics of Betrayal', *Journal of Asian Studies* 48, 1: 71–89.
Nara Takeji. (1990a) 'Nara Takeji jijū bukanchō nikki', Hatano Sumio and Kurosawa Fumitaka (eds) *Chūō kōron* September: 324–46.
—— (1990b) 'Nara Takeji jijū bukanchō nikki', Hatano Sumio and Kurosawa Fumitaka (eds) *Chūō kōron* October: 338–52.
Nathan, John. (1974) *Mishima: A Biography*, Boston: Little, Brown.
Nicolson, Harold. (1952) *King George V: His Life and Reign*, London: Pan.
Nish, Ian. (1988) 'The Prince and the Principal', *International Studies* 177: 19–31.
Nishibe, Susumu. (1989) 'Defending the Dignity of the Symbolic Emperor', *Japan Echo* XVI, 2: 22–7.
Nishihira Shigeki. (1980) 'Tennō, gengō, kokka, kokki', *Jiyū* 22, 10: 82–96.
Nishijima Takeo. (1981) *Sengo no shōchō: heiwa, minshushugi, tennōsei*, Tokyo: Shinsensha.
Noguchi, Takehiko. (1984) 'Mishima Yukio and Kita Ikki: The Aesthetics and Politics of Ultranationalism in Japan', *Journal of Japanese Studies* 10, 2: 437–54.
Nomura Minoru. (1988) *Tennō to Fushimi no miya to nihon kaigun*, Tokyo: Bungei shunjū.

Ogata, Sadako. (1964) *Defiance in Manchuria: The Making of Japanese Foreign Policy, 1931–1932*, Berkeley, Calif.: University of California Press.
Ōhata, Tokushirō. (1976) 'The Anti-Comintern Pact, 1935–1939', in J.W. Morley (ed.) *Deterrent Diplomacy: Japan, Germany, and the U.S.S.R., 1935–1940*, New York: Columbia University Press.
Oka, Yoshitake. (1983) *Konoe Fumimaro: A Political Biography*, Tokyo: University of Tokyo Press.
—— (1986) *Five Political Leaders of Modern Japan*, Tokyo: University of Tokyo Press.
Okubo, Genji. (1948) *The Problem of the Emperor System in Postwar Japan*, Tokyo: Japan Institute of Pacific Studies.
Ōnuma, Yasuaki. (1984) 'Beyond Victors' Justice', *Japan Echo* XI, Special Issue [The War and Japan: Revisionist Views]: 63–72.
Ōtake Shūichi. (1986) *Tennō no gakkō*, Tokyo: Bungei shunjū..
Ōtsuka, Eiji. (1989) 'Teen-age Fans of the "Sweet" Emperor', *Japan Echo* XVI, 1: 65–8.
Otsuki Takeshi. (1976) 'Tennōsei kyōiku to kokumin', *Hōritsu jihō* 48, 4: 115–20.
Packard, George. (1966) *Protest in Tokyo: The Security Treaty Crisis of 1960*, Princeton, NJ: Princeton University Press.
Peattie, Mark R. (1975) *Ishiwara Kanji and Japan's Confrontation with the West*, Princeton, NJ: Princeton University Press.
Pelz, Stephen E. (1974) *Race to Pearl Harbor: The Failure of the Second London Naval Conference and the Onset of World War II*, Cambridge, Mass: Harvard University Press.

Pittau, Joseph. (1967) *Political Thought in Early Meiji Japan*, Cambridge, Mass: Harvard University Press.
Political Reorientation of Japan: September 1945 to September 1948, by the Supreme Commander Allied Powers, Government Section, 1–2. (1949), 1970 reprint, Westport, Conn.: Greenwood.
Powles, Cyril. (1976) '*Yasukuni Jinja Hōan*: Religion and Politics in Contemporary Japan', *Pacific Affairs* 49, 3: 491–505.
—— (1976–7). 'The Emperor System in Modern Japan: A Case Study of Japanese Religiosity', *Studies in Religion* 6, 1: 33–42.
Prange, Gordon W. (1982) *At Dawn We Slept: The Untold Story of Pearl Harbor*, London: Michael Joseph.
Prime [International Peace Research Institute Occasional Papers, 5, Meiji Gakuin University]. (1989).
PRJ: see *Political Reorientation of Japan*.

Public Papers of the President: Gerald R. Ford 1975 II (1977), Washington: United States Government Printing Office.

Pyle, Kenneth B. (1987) 'In Pursuit of a Grand Design: Nakasone Betwixt the Past and the Future', *Journal of Japanese Studies*, 13, 2: 243–70.

Reischauer, Edwin O. (1975) *The Emperor of Japan*, New York: Japan Society.

Ridgway, Matthew B. (1956) *Soldier: The Memoirs of Matthew B. Ridgway*, New York: Harper.

Roberts, John G. (1979) 'The "Japan Crowd": and the Zaibatsu Restoration', *The Japan Interpreter* XII, 3–4: 384–415.

Röhl, John C.G. (1982) 'Introduction', in J.C.G. Röhl and N. Sombart (eds) *Kaiser Wilhelm II: New Interpretations*, Cambridge: Cambridge University Press.

—— (1982) 'The Emperor's New Clothes: A Character Sketch of Kaiser Wilhelm II', in J.C.G. Röhl and N. Sombart (eds) *Kaiser Wilhelm II: New Interpretations*, Cambridge: Cambridge University Press.

Rose, Richard and Kavanagh, Dennis. (1976) 'The Monarchy in Contemporary Political Culture', *Comparative Politics* 8, 4: 548–76.

Saeki Shinkō. (1989) 'Seibutsugaku to arahitogami no hazama', *Bungei shunjū*, March Special Issue [Ōinaru shōwa]: 490–5.

Sakamoto, Yoshikazu. (1989) 'Introduction: The Essence of the Problem', in Yoshikazu Sakamoto (ed.) *Prime* [International Peace Research Institute Occasional Papers, Meiji Gakuin University] 5: 3–21.

Sayle, Murray. (1989) 'The Day They Stopped Work in Tokyo', *The Independent*, 4 March: 22–31.

Schaller, Michael. (1985) *The American Occupation of Japan: The Origins of the Cold War in Asia*, New York: Oxford University Press.

Schonberger, Howard. (1977) 'The Japan Lobby in American Diplomacy, 1947–1952', *Pacific Historical Review* XLVI, 3: 327–59.

Sebald, William J. (1965) *With MacArthur in Japan: A Personal History of the Occupation*, London: Cressett.

Sheldon, Charles D. (1976) 'Japanese Aggression and the Emperor, 1931–1941, From Contemporary Diaries', *Modern Asian Studies* 10, 1: 1–40.

—— (1978) 'Scapegoat or Instigator of Japanese Aggression? Inoue Kiyoshi's Case Against the Emperor', *Modern Asian Studies* 12, 1: 1–35.

—— (1979) 'The Left Wing and the Present Emperor's Alleged Responsibility for Japanese Aggression', in Ian Nish and Charles Dunn (eds) *European Studies of Japan*, Tenterden, Kent: Paul Norbury.

Shigemitsu, Mamoru. (1958) *Japan and Her Destiny*, London: Hutchinson.

Shikama Kōsuke. (1980) *Jijū bukan nikki*, Tokyo: Fuyō shobō.

Shillony, Ben-Ami. (1973) *Revolt in Japan: The Young Officers and the February 26, 1936 Incident*, Princeton, NJ: Princeton University Press.

—— (1981) *Politics and Culture in Wartime Japan*, Oxford: Clarendon Press.

Shimada, Toshihiko. (1984) 'The Extension of Hostilities, 1931–1932', in J.W. Morley (ed.) *Japan Erupts: The London Naval Conference and the Manchurian Incident, 1928–1932*, New York: Columbia University Press.

Shimomura Kainan. (1948) *Shūsenki*, Tokyo: Kamakura bunko.

—— (1949) 'Uchigawa kara mita tennō', in Abe Yoshishige (ed.) *Tennō no inshō*, Tokyo: Sōgensha.

Shinobu, Seizaburō. (1967) 'From Party Politics to Military Dictatorship', *Developing Economies* 5, 4: 666–84.

Shōwa nihonshi (1987) Supplement I (Kōshitsu no hanseiki), Tokyo: Akatsuki kyōiku tosho.

'Shōwa tennō no dokuhaku hachijikan'. (1990) *Bungei shunjū*, December: 94–145.

Silberman, Bernard S. (1974) 'Conclusion: Taishō Japan and the Crisis of Secularism', in Bernard S. Silberman and H.D. Harootunian (eds) *Japan in Crisis: Essays on Taishō Democracy*, Princeton, NJ: Princeton University Press.

Smythe, Hugh H. and Watanabe, Masaharu. (1953) 'Japanese Popular Attitudes Toward the Emperor', *Pacific Affairs* XXVI, 4: 335–44.
Sodei, Rinjirō. (1984) 'Satire Under the Occupation: The Case of Political Cartoons', in Thomas W. Burkman (ed.) *The Occupation of Japan: Arts and Culture*, Norfolk, Va: General Douglas MacArthur Foundation.
STDH: see 'Shōwa tennō no dokuhaku hachijikan' (1990).
Stockwin, J.A.A. (1975) *Japan: Divided Politics in a Growth Economy*, London: Weidenfeld and Nicolson.
Storry, Richard. (1960) 'Konoe Fumimaro. "The Last of the Fujiwara" ', *Far Eastern Affairs* 7, 2: 9–23.
Sugiyama, Gen. (1967) *Sugiyama memo: daihon'ei-seifu renraku kaigi hikki*, Sanbō honbu (eds), 1–2, Tokyo: Hara shobō.
Sugiyama, Kyūshirō. (1986) 'Facts and Fallacies About Yasukuni Shrine', *Japan Echo* XIII, 2: 69–72.
Takahashi Hiroshi. (1978) *Gendai tennōke no kenkyū*, Tokyo: Kōdansha.
—— (1987) *Shōchō tennō*, Tokyo: Iwanami shoten.
Takeda, Kiyoko. (1988) *The Dual-Image of the Japanese Emperor*, London: Macmillan.
—— (1990) 'The Emperor System in Modern Japan', *Richard Storry Memorial Lecture* No.3 (1989), Oxford: St Antony's College.
Takeyama, Michio. (1964) 'The Emperor System', *Journal of Social and Political Ideas in Japan* 11, 2: 21–6.
—— (1984) 'Questions on the Tokyo Trial', *Japan Echo* Special Issue [The War and Japan: Revisionist Views]: 55–62.
'Tennō kōgō ryōheika kara kōtaishi e no tegami'. (1989) *Bungei shunjū* Special Issue [Oinaru shōwa]: 362–5.
Thompson, J.A. and Mejia, A. (1971) *The Modern British Monarchy*, New York: St Martin's.
Tipton, Elise K. (1990) *Japanese Police State: Tokkō in Interwar Japan*, Sydney: Allen and Unwin.
Titus, David A. (1974) *Palace and Politics in Prewar Japan*, New York: Columbia University Press.
—— (1980) 'The Making of the "Symbol Emperor System" in Postwar Japan', *Modern Asian Studies* 14, 4: 529–78.
Tōgō, Shigenori. (1956) *The Cause of Japan*, New York: Simon and Schuster.
Tolischus, Otto D. (1944) *Tokyo Record*, London: Hamish Hamilton.
Toriumi, Yasushi. (1980) 'Was the Emperor Meiji Really a Puppet?', *Japan Echo* VII, 2: 107–17.
Tsujimoto Noboru (ed.) (1947) *Kōei* [Held in the Gordon W. Prange Collection, University of Maryland, College Park, Maryland].
Tsunoda, Jun. (1980) 'The Navy's Role in the Southern Strategy', in J.W. Morley (ed.) *The Fateful Choice: Japan's Advance into Southeast Asia, 1939–1941*, New York: Columbia University Press.
Tsunoda, Ryūsaku, Wm. Theodore de Bary, and Donald Keene (compilers) (1960) *Sources of Japanese Tradition*, New York: Columbia University Press.
Tsurumi, Kazuko. (1970) *Social Change and the Individual: Japan Before and After Defeat in World War II*, Princeton, NJ: Princeton University Press.
Tsurumi, Shunsuke. (1984) *A Cultural History of Postwar Japan*. London: KPI.
Ueda, Keiko. (1974) 'Sixteen Ways to Avoid Saying "No" in Japan', in J.C. Condon and Mitsuko Saitō (eds) *Intercultural Encounters with Japan: Communication, Contact, and Conflict*, Tokyo: Simul.
Ueyama Shunpei, Umehara Takeshi, and Yano Tōru. (1989) 'The Imperial Institution in Japanese History', *Japan Echo* XVI, 1: 46–52.
Ugaki Kazushige. (1968–71) *Ugaki Kazushige nikki* 1–3, Tokyo: Misuzu shobō.
Usui, Katsumi. (1983) 'The Politics of War, 1937–1941', in J.W. Morley (ed.) *The China*

Quagmire: Japan's Expansion on the Asian Continent 1937–1941, New York: Columbia University Press.

Vining, Elizabeth Gray. (1952) *Windows for the Crown Prince: Akihito of Japan*, 1st Tuttle edn 1989, Tokyo: Charles E. Tuttle.

—— (1960) *Return to Japan*, New York and Philadelphia: Lippincott.

Wakabayashi, Bob Tadashi. (1991) 'In Name Only: Imperial Sovereignty in Early Modern Japan', *Journal of Japanese Studies* 17, 1: 25–57.

Ward, Robert E. (1965) 'The Commission on the Constitution and Prospects for Constitutional Change in Japan', *Journal of Asian Studies* XXIV, 3: 401–29.

—— (1987) 'Presurrender Planning: Treatment of the Emperor and Constitutional Changes', in R.E. Ward and Sakamoto Yoshikazu (eds) *Democratizing Japan: The Allied Occupation*, Honolulu: University of Hawaii Press.

Watanabe, Akio. (1977) 'Japanese Public Opinion and Foreign Affairs', in R.A. Scalapino (ed.) *The Foreign Policy of Modern Japan*, Berkeley, Calif.: University of California Press.

Watanabe Osamu. (1987) *Nihonkoku kenpō 'kaisei' shi*, Tokyo: Nihon hyōronsha.

—— (1989) 'The Sociology of *jishuku* and *kichō*: The Death of the Shōwa *Tennō* as Reflection of the Structure of Contemporary Japanese Society', *Japan Forum* 1, 2: 275–89.

—— (1990) 'The Emperor as a "Symbol" in Postwar Japan', *Acta Asiatica* 59: 101–25.

Watanabe, Shōichi. (1991) 'The Emperor and the Militarists: Reexamining the Prewar Record', *Japan Echo* XVIII, 2: 73–9.

Webb, Herschel. (1968) *The Japanese Imperial Institution in the Tokugawa Period*, New York: Columbia University Press.

Welfield, John. (1988) *An Empire in Eclipse: Japan in the Postwar Alliance System*, London: Athlone.

Whitney, Courtney. (1956) *MacArthur: His Rendezvous with History*, 1977 reprint, Westport, Connecticut: Greenwood.

Williams, Peter and Wallace, David. (1989) *Unit 731: The Japanese Army's Secret of Secrets*, London: Hodder and Stoughton.

Wilson, Bryan R. (1976) 'Aspects of Secularization in the West', *Japanese Journal of Religious Studies* 3, 4: 259–76.

Wilson, George M. (1969) *Radical Nationalist in Japan: Kita Ikki 1883–1937*, Cambridge, Mass: Harvard University Press.

Wilson, Sandra. (1989) 'Popular Japanese Responses to the Manchurian Incident, 1931–1933', unpublished PhD thesis, University of Oxford.

Windsor, HRH The Duke of. (1951) *A King's Story*, London: Cassell.

Yamamoto, Shichihei. (1976) 'The Living God and His War Responsibility', *Japan Echo* III, 1: 64–78.

—— (1989) *Shōwa tennō no kenkyū: sono jitsuzō o saguru*, Tokyo: Shōdensha.

Yamauchi Toshihiro. (1976) 'Tennō to guntai: sengo kenpōshi ni okeru mondai', *Hōritsu jihō* 48, 4: 104–14.

Yamazaki, Masakazu and Kōsaka, Masataka. (1989) 'The Shōwa Emperor and His Era', *Japan Echo* XVI, 2: 15–21.

Yanaga, Chitoshi. (1956) *Japanese People and Politics*, 1964 edn, New York: John Wiley.

Yasuda, Hiroshi. (1990) 'The Modern Emperor System as It Took Shape Before and After the Sino-Japanese War of 1894–5', *Acta Asiatica* 59: 38–58.

Yoshida, Shigeru. (1962). *The Yoshida Memoirs*, Cambridge, Mass: Riverside.

Yuri Shizuo and Higashi Kunihiko (eds) (1974) *Tennō goroku*, Tokyo: Kōdansha.

Index